'Man is born free, and everywhere he is in chains. One man thinks himself the master of others, but remains more of a slave than they are.'

Jean-Jacques Rousseau, *The Social Contract*, 1762

'Everything is awesome . . .
It's awesome to win and it's awesome to lose.'

The Lego Movie, 2014

JACQUES PERETTI

DONE

The Secret Deals that are Changing our World

HODDER &
STOUGHTON

First published in Great Britain in 2017 by Hodder & Stoughton
An Hachette UK company

Choose a paperback publication date if applicable

1

Copyright © Jacques Peretti 2017

The right of Jacques Peretti to be identified as the Author of the Work has been
asserted by him in accordance with the Copyright, Designs and Patents Act 1988.

A CIP catalogue record for this title is available from the British Library

Hardback ISBN 9781473646391
Trade paperback ISBN 9781473646407
EBook ISBN 9781473646414

Typeset in Plantin Light by Hewer Text UK Ltd, Edinburgh
Printed and bound in Great Britain by Clays Ltd, St Ives plc

Hodder & Stoughton policy is to use papers that are natural, renewable
and recyclable products and made from wood grown in sustainable
forests. The logging and manufacturing processes are expected to
conform to the environmental regulations of the country of origin.

Hodder & Stoughton Ltd
Carmelite House
50 Victoria Embankment
London EC4Y 0DZ

www.hodder.co.uk

For Esme and Theo

CONTENTS

INTRODUCTION

What if the way we understand the world is wrong? What if it is not politicians and world events that have fundamentally transformed our everyday lives but business deals? Deals made in secret: high up in boardrooms, on a golf course, or over a drink in a bar.

These deals changed everything: money; work; why we buy what we buy. They changed our attitude to wealth and inequality, even how we define illness. These deals taught us to embrace financial risk and a world of perpetual upgrade. They changed the power balance between business and government; and rewrote the facts on what even constitutes truth.

These deals often had far-reaching consequences the protagonists did not foresee: triggering the Arab Spring and fourth wave Jihadism by 'shorting' the price of wheat on Wall Street. Harnessing the science of food to fatten the planet and then using the business opportunity created to thin the human race down.

These deals changed our collective mindset, rebooting society to think in a different way about how we live. And each sprang from a single brilliant idea with a profound psychological insight at its core. Planting the seed of doubt in something we buy to 'engineer dissatisfaction'; transforming medicine from the treatment of illness to the medication of modern life itself. Turning tax from a duty to an avoidance industry. Selling freedom through technology but automating human behaviour at the very moment automation transforms life on earth.

These deals did not happen by chance. They were hard-edged business decisions made by people who reconfigured our lives with a plan, and at their heart was one simple conceit: invent a problem and then sell the solution.

CHAPTER ONE
CASH: WHO IS KILLING IT AND WHY

In 2014, we tipped into a new world. It happened without fanfare, a mention on TV, a spike on Wall Street, it did not even trend on Twitter. But for the first time in history, card and contactless payments overtook cash transactions.

By 2025, even drug dealers will not take cash. South Korea plans to have no cash at all by 2020.[1] In Sweden, the European country going cashless first, buskers use contactless machines. A new app, BuSK, lets Londoners do the same thing. In Holland, a coat developed for the homeless allows people to give money by swiping a card on their sleeve.[2]

Physical money in your hand – a system of payment that began 600 years before the birth of Christ – is coming to an end. Apple's CEO Tim Cook says the next generation 'will not even know what money was.'

Coins first began circulating on three continents in the sixth century BC. A technological innovation every bit as far-reaching as the iPhone. Small metal discs were exchanged for a desired trade. Coins were a physical embodiment of trust, a simple way of doing something astoundingly complex: creating an agreed value between two strangers. Vikings and textile manufacturers in Southern India could cut a deal over a shipment of silk. Cash created 'globalisation' two thousand years before it became a term of abuse on a placard.

By the 1860s, there were over eight thousand separate currencies in operation in the US alone. Different banks, railroads and retailers all had their own form of money: bonds, exchange systems and numerous forms of credit. The National Bank Act of 1863 tried to end this fragmented chaos and unify the United States under one currency: the dollar.[3]

With the end of cash, the world of eight thousand currencies is returning. Mobile money, bitcoin, digital vouchers, Apple Pay, iTunes, exchangeable shop credits, everything from overseas currency transfers to billion-dollar deals with the digital handshake of block chain. All of it is money.

But the death of cash is not simply part of the natural evolution of payment: making it ever more seamless and consumer-friendly. The death of cash is the result of a plan – to cede control of money away from the banks and even governments, and place it instead in the hands of the new players: tech companies.

And this plan was hatched as the result of an experiment proving something blindingly obvious to anyone who has ever used cash, but is also an observable neurological process: paying causes actual pain.

THE DEAL AND THE EXPERIMENT

When we pay with cash, neural pathways light up like a Christmas tree. This is the flinch moment we experience when our hands are forced to part with money. In that instant, the brain is telling the hand not to let go. We are torn between wanting to buy an object we desire and avoiding the neural pain, and this creates the flinch.

Having cash in your hand is not, as we might assume, a licence to spend irresponsibly. In fact, cash does the opposite: it stops us spending. So in creating a payment system that eradicates cash, we remove the neural pain – the flinch moment – and open the brain to limitless spending. Which is exactly what two men decided to do in 1998.

Max Levchin and Peter Thiel, two strangers, met in an empty lecture hall at Stanford University. The meeting was not by chance. 'I basically went there,' says Levchin, 'to see this guy Peter Thiel, who was giving a free lecture about currency markets. I figured it would be a filled auditorium, but actually it turned out to be a lecture with six people. So it was fairly easy to make contact afterwards ... I came up and said: "Hi, I'm this guy Max. I've been in Silicon Valley for the last five days and I'm going to start a new company and how are you doing?" '[4]

Levchin was a wild, directionless ball of energy. He had run a few start-ups that had 'sort of blown up in catastrophic ways where people started the company and it was sort of like marrying the first person one met at the slot machine in Las Vegas. You might hit the jackpot but chances were things would just blow up.'

Thiel was different. Now one of the overlords of Silicon Valley and part of President Trump's inner sanctum, Thiel is reported to inject the blood of eighteen-year-old girls to keep himself looking young (he doesn't). In 1998 he was already legendary in Silicon Valley for a different reason. Thiel believed he was the future, even though he did not know how. Levchin wanted to do a deal with him, because Thiel was one of the few people on the planet that shared his limitless ambition, and with whom he could get a meeting.

Thiel grew up in South Africa and was sent to a strict boarding school where pupils were struck for the pettiest transgression of the rules. As a teenager, Thiel had already identified himself as a libertarian with a hatred for what he considered to be mindless conformity.

In 1998, when Thiel met Levchin, he was clear on one thing: he wanted to change the world. Thiel is a follower of the mimetic theory of French philosopher René Girard, and the idea that imitation destroys genuine innovation. Only by stepping outside the mimetic prison of trying to be like other people do you truly succeed. Be yourself, however strange that might appear to anyone else.

When the sub-prime crash began in 2007, Thiel told the *Washington Post*, we had put too much trust as a society in science and technology and been let down. But in mimetic terms, our confidence was misplaced. The technocratic elite had told us to believe in ever-increasing wealth creation, when the truth was that only those in Silicon Valley were going to own the future. We should have seen all of it for ourselves long before it happened. To this degree, the crash was our own fault.

When Levchin approached Thiel in that empty lecture theatre in 1998, Thiel had the mimetic mindset to take over the world, but did not have the vehicle. A couple of venture capital failures under his belt, but with nothing promising on the horizon. No idea.

In 1998, the internet had just arrived. No one had figured out how to monetise it yet. The holy grail in Silicon Valley was finding a secure online payment system. Whoever created it would own the coming century. Something both Thiel and Levchin were keen on doing.

Levchin was an encryption genius, but it was Thiel who knew finance, and for Levchin to ensure his out-there ideas on encrypting an online payment system did not bomb like all the others, he needed Thiel. Which is why he turned up at that empty lecture. Thiel and Levchin only talked for minutes, but it was enough. They did a deal to start a business called Confinity.

'Max and I spent a lot of time brainstorming different ideas on different types of markets,' Thiel explains. 'We finally decided that we wanted to try something with encrypted money on Palm Pilots. We thought this was going to be the future of the world.'[5]

The truth was that for all their ambition, Thiel and Levchin were like all the thousands of other tech entrepreneurs standing in queues in various coffee houses across California: prospectors sifting through pans in the great internet gold rush. There was no reason they should succeed first. Except for one thing. In

Palm Pilot, they saw something no one else saw: a proto-iPhone, and one that could be used for buying and selling.

Three thousand miles away, an experiment was being carried out by a Serbian neuro-psychologist at MIT into what happens to the human brain when we pay in different ways. Drazen Prelec was fascinated by the irrational behaviour people demonstrate towards money: why do we buy lottery tickets and insurance at the same time? Because we do not have a consistent approach to spending. Instead, Prelec says, we accumulate random rules and ideas about money throughout our lives which then co-exist irrationally in our heads, such as buying the cheapest brands at the supermarket, but insisting on getting a cab home because we do not like the bus. Or using cheap cosmetics, but having a monthly spa massage.

Prelec wanted to know how that irrationality towards money manifests itself when we use cash and decided to measure the brain's response to paying with cash versus credit.

Prelec asked five hundred students on the MIT campus to make sealed bids for a silent auction for a sold-out basketball match. Half were asked to use cash; and half, cards. Prelec had an instinct that the credit-card bids would be higher, but the degree to which they were higher blew him away. The credit-card bids were on average twice as high as the bids made with cash. Some were six times higher. The cash bidders simply refused to part with their money, whereas the card bidders saw no limit on what they should spend.

Prelec was stunned. 'That's got to be crazy, right? It suggests the psychological cost of spending a dollar on a credit card is only fifty cents.' This is because credit cards give the pleasure of buying with none of the pain. 'The moral tax gets blurred. When you're consuming, you're not thinking about the payments, and when you're paying, you don't know what you're paying for.'

The psychological self-delusion that credit cards are a free lunch is so strong, Prelec said, it is the reason most debit cards carry a credit-card logo. 'The logo alone is a powerful inducement to spend. Consumers get excited just seeing the logo. It's like waving a hamburger in front of a hungry person.'[6]

So the appeal of credit cards is clear, but Prelec wanted to know why we had such a problem paying with cash. Is this resistance to spending cash hardwired? Prelec set up an MRI scan with the students who had bid in the silent auction with cash and what he found out next was to change the future course of money.

When we pay for something with cash, Prelec realised, a specific neural pathway lights up. Prelec had discovered the 'flinch moment', the nanosecond in which we feel measurable neural pain as the brain registers the hand parting with money. The moment we literally feel the loss.

Those bidding with cards in the experiment had felt no such pain. Only the pleasure of shopping. Prelec's discovery was to have far-reaching implications. Cash, he concluded, does not enable but actively hinders spending. By removing it, and making payment instantaneous, the brain has no time to register pain. We are released to spend without limit because it is simply too fast for the brain to catch up with the transaction.

Peter Thiel and Max Levchin were working on cracking the holy grail of Silicon Valley: an encrypted payment system. But Prelec had discovered the real holy grail: pain-free shopping for the consumer. Deliver that and you owned the internet.

STAGE LEFT: ENTER IRON MAN

In 2000, a year into Confinity, Levchin and Thiel met with an entrepreneur who understood the significance of Prelec's work on the neural pain of payment. Elon Musk. Musk, like Thiel, was a visionary open to the visions of others. Twenty years on, he is known as the man who will do whatever it takes to colonise Mars and save humanity from global warming with a planetary exodus. He is serious, too. Musk was the inspiration for Tony Stark in the *Iron Man* movies.

Like Thiel, Musk had grown up in South Africa, and like Thiel, Musk forged a fiercely ambitious and anti-authoritarian spirit from childhood trauma. In Musk's case, bullying at school was so bad, he was once hospitalised after being left unconscious from a beating.[7]

Back in 2000, Musk used the money he had made from his first venture, Zip2, to propose a merger with Thiel and Levchin's Confinity. He recognised their vision. If Confinity could crack secure encrypted payment, Musk said, they held the keys to the kingdom of limitless spending. But to sell this to the consumer as a way of removing neural pain – in other words, to turn it from a clever but small Silicon Valley tech-innovation that could be stolen by other clever, small Silicon Valley tech companies, into a globally recognised brand that would take over the world – they needed to do something very important. Promise the consumer that payment would be instantaneous: to 'one click away'.

Thiel brought in a money guy from Wall Street, Jack Selby. We met in their huge offices in San Francisco, right next door to George Lucas's offices. Thiel and Selby's office is decorated in mid-twentieth-century Scandinavian furniture and with rows of bookshelves filled with philosophy: Kirkegaard, Ayn Rand, Marx, and the collected works of Donald Trump. Jack swanned in looking like the title character in *The Great Gatsby* with slicked-back hair and smashed-up boating shoes, as if he had just parked his yacht (in fact, he had just parked his plane).

'You make it sound like it was all going to happen – a fait accompli,' says Jack, 'but these stories get made up. The truth was, it was touch and go we'd survive. It was tremendously risky. But Peter was brilliant, because he realised we needed to get into business before the whole dotcom bubble burst. When that popped, it cleared away the dead wood and Peter knew the guys left standing were going to be huge. We made sure we were those guys.'

They called their new company PayPal and 'one click away' was the promise. Four men now had the key that would unlock the internet. In 2002, only a year later, PayPal did a deal with eBay for $1.5 billion. The internet now had a market place with which to trade through PayPal, and PayPal was now accepted in over seventy per cent of all eBay auctions. The PayPal founders were now legendary in Silicon Valley. They became known as 'The PayPal Mafia' – Selby smiled his Gatsby smile when I mentioned it. 'Yeah, they called us that.'

Back at MIT, Drazen Prelec's research into the neural pain of cash should have served as a warning that we were about to enter a fathomless, glittering new world of untethered online spending. Instead, his work unwittingly signed the death warrant on cash. Cash, he says, is the one thing that firmly tethers us to spending within our means. 'You want to know how out of kilter we are with our spending?' he tells me when we meet. 'Try using only cash for one week. Buy everything with it. Pay your mortgage with it. Look at a thousand dollars as a mountain of cash. You will never treat money the same way again.'[8]

GIVING THE PUBLIC CREDIT IS 'LIKE GIVING SUGAR TO A DIABETIC'

Prelec was not the first to warn of the dangers of moving away from cash for the 'convenience' of credit. In the 1950s, credit cards moved out of the exclusive domain of business and began being marketed at the general public. They were sold as giving greater speed and efficiency to a transaction than cash. Their true appeal lay in giving the illusion of wealth, magically conjuring whatever you desired – a new sofa, fur coat, car – but without a genie and a puff of smoke, merely the wave of a signature.

In early ads for American Express, a card was taken coolly from the pocket of a suave businessman and flashed impressively like VIP ID to a breathless air stewardess. Credit cards turned failing middle managers into James Bond. Here was something too good to be true, and it was.

Concerns were soon raised at the highest levels of government. President Johnson's Special Assistant for Consumer Affairs, Betty Furness, believed the aspirational dream the credit card offered was a mirage. In 1967, she said pushing credit cards on a general public of 'compulsive debtors' was as responsible as 'giving sugar to diabetics'.

But were the public 'compulsive debtors'? The great myth of the masses and especially the poor is that they cannot manage money or budget and therefore demand new technologies that 'help' make precarious lives more 'manageable'.

The truth is the opposite. The poor have a tighter rein on money than anyone else. With each new payment innovation – from credit cards in the 1950s to digital and mobile money now – technologies arrive doing the complete opposite of what they claim. Instead of 'helping' the masses 'manage money', they make them even more indebted.

In 2016, the average American family owed $16,061 on credit cards.[9] Seventy per cent of Americans own at least one card, but fifty per cent have two and ten per cent more than three, with the average American family carrying $40,000 of debt. Debt in Britain is at the same level, and is increasing. In the last quarter of 2016, the average British family accrued more debt in the last three years than in any other period in history.

When the economy boomed in the 1950s, debt was encouraged, but tethered to paying it back. In the mid-1980s, credit cards replaced hire-purchase, and by the 1990s they were given to anyone who could sign their own name (dog owners could even get credit cards in their pet's name, because no one bothered to check to whom the card was going). Any notion that debt should be paid off was gone. Instead, debt became a way of life.

Each time credit has become easier and faster, we have normalised ever higher levels of debt. And every time the economy goes into recession (the early 1980s, the early 1990s, post-2007) credit cards take on a new role – enabling people to survive.

Credit cards are now a tool for subsistence: paying for heating, food shopping and the monthly mortgage. Debt is also the *modus operandi* for governments claiming 'growth' by factoring credit-fuelled consumer spending into GDP. Debt provides a politically expedient role, window-dressing a stagnating economy by faking a healthy balance sheet.[10]

ENTER EBAY: TURNING THE WEB INTO A MACHINE FOR SELLING

When PayPal did the deal with eBay in 2002, the aim was quite simple: to define what the internet was for. Up until that point, Web 1.0 had been a static page forum for the circulation of ideas within academia, the government and the military. By transforming into Web 2.0, the internet became a living thing, fed, cultivated and grown by every human on earth with a connection.

Beneath the grand promises that this new living internet would deliver 'empowerment', 'decentralisation', 'connectivity', even a new kind of 'democracy', was the hard-nosed reality: PayPal would turn Web 2.0 into a giant machine for selling.

When the deal was done with eBay, the first true behemoth of Web 2.0, the internet clicked. On a beach in Honolulu, eBay's reclusive founder Pierre Omidyar now whiles away his time funding the *Honolulu Civil Beat*, an online investigative journal. In 1998, aged thirty-one, Omidyar set up eBay. The apocryphal story is that it was a speculative punt trading Pez dispensers. The truth is that he knew exactly what he was doing.

With eBay, Omidyar consciously recreated the bustling market place in which coins were first traded two thousand years ago. A space in which everything is up for barter and value is infinitely fluid and market-driven.

Now every tech platform is a marketplace: Google is a marketplace for information, Uber for cabs, Airbnb for space, Deliveroo for food. But the first of these big digital souks was eBay. An empty space to be filled with the detritus of Planet Earth: shoes, furniture, concert tickets, vacuum cleaners, holidays, sex, old cameras, spare human organs, an unwanted husband.

eBay is capitalism in its purest form: one giant peer-to-peer trade in which the buyer, not the seller, controls the market and value is determined entirely by what someone is willing to pay. $1,209 for a Dorito shaped like the Pope's hat (bought by the same buyer as a grilled-cheese sandwich with the face of the Virgin Mary); Kurt Cobain's chair; Britney Spears's chewing gum; $55,000 for a ghost in a jar; ad space on someone's forehead, and perhaps most poignantly, the meaning of life, which was worth just $3.26.

Entire countries are signed up. Sixty per cent of all Australia's online shoppers use eBay, but Australia is also the prime eBay trader with Jan Mayan, a tiny Norwegian island in the Arctic Circle with a population of eighteen, who bought twenty-six items in 2014 from Australian eBay sellers – just over one Australian export item per person.[11]

eBay offered something that cash did not: the addictive thrill of the online auction. The endorphin rush of gambling. In comparison, cash was boring. Online shopping exploded in the early 2000s at the same time as online gambling, and both shared the binge quality of an addiction without constraints that could now be indulged in privately behind closed curtains.

Online shopping opened up, according to social anthropologist Benjamin Barber, a 'candy shop of instant gratification'. It re-infantilised the adult consumer, turning us back into children. 'When a child says, "I want that! And I want it now!" there's an adult there to say no, but when an adult demands the same shopping online, they can have whatever they want.'[12] The neural pain we experience parting with cash is gone and there is nothing to stop us shopping without boundaries. The parent figure is removed.

YOU ARE THE NEW CURRENCY

If I hand you a ten-pound note or a dollar bill, no one is making money from that transaction. It is cash from one hand to another. But if I make the payment digitally, someone has to facilitate that payment. The space between you and me becomes the place where money can be made.

This is the space the big tech giants – Facebook, Apple, Google, Amazon and Microsoft – all want to own, and it is a race to own money itself, and thus redefine what it is. Which is to make you the currency.

The value in that space is not even the charge for the transaction. This service is now given away free. It is the data on you that can be mined. Data is the hidden price tag in any transaction we make. It is a price we are willing to pay, because we are not handing over our cash. What we hand over instead is every last detail of our lives: from the euphoric or mournful playlist chosen to suit our mood to a preference for Chinese over Indian food, whether you are straight, gay or Mormon, surf or knit, have Attention Deficit Disorder, go on holiday to the Caribbean or Canvey Island.

In 2016, data was used to hone the profiles of potential swing voters in both the Brexit referendum and the US presidential election, and it proved decisive. In 2017, the UK's privacy watchdog launched an investigation into how personal data is affecting political campaigns. The company that supplied the Leave campaign, Cambridge Analytica, targeted voter intention in a sharper way than was ever possible before. Without it, any political campaign – especially one run on tight margins – is sunk.

Critics describe such data mining by businesses as a privacy issue, but the public are less alarmed. As the *Harvard Business Review* pointed out in 2015: 'Our research shows that consumers are aware that they're under surveillance . . . (but) consumers appreciate that data sharing can lead to products and services that makes their lives easier and more entertaining, educate them, and save them money.'[13] We simply do not care that we are handing it over. We are more concerned when data mining strays into the realm of our health, which is the space the tech giants are coincidentally most interested in.

In 2007 came the moment of crystallisation: year zero for this new world. The banking system began to crash and the iPhone was launched. Subprime set explosives beneath the banks that had controlled the ebb and flow of money for centuries and were now about to implode like derelict tower blocks.

These financial institutions had ridden the epic cycles of boom and bust for over a century: through the Wall Street Crash, Glass-Stiegel and regulation, Reagan and deregulation, the 1990s recession, the longest bull market in history, and the hidden time bomb of subprime. They were momentarily vulnerable and someone else was poised to move in: the tech giants.

These giants call themselves 'tech' companies, but tech is a stepping stone – they want to become the new banks. And with the implosion of the old banks came their chance to take the first step.

In 2008, the iPhone propelled shopping off the laptop and onto the phone – the first stage in moving money away from the old institutions and shifting power to the tech companies. First, they would own shopping, then money management and financial services, and finally they would become the new banks. But first base was shopping and for this, they had a new weapon: the app.

Initially, Steve Jobs did not get it. It took a venture capitalist called John Dooer and the activities of a group of 'jail-break' hackers breaching the defences of the phone to turn Jobs on to third-party apps and what they could truly do for the potential of the iPhone.

In just days following the launch of the iPhone, these jail-breakers developed a refined copy-and-paste system. One that far outstripped Apple's. Jay Freeman, the Godfather of jail-breaking, created Cydia – an app marketplace where phones could be jail-broken and freed up to use powerful software to customise outside the rigid control of Apple.

Apple could not believe it and needed to act fast. Within weeks of the iPhone's launch, Apple decided to create the App Store to claw back control. It was the best thing Apple did from a business point of view, yet it was prompted not by the company's own programmers, but a bunch of hackers.

I arrange to meet Jay on a park bench in San Francisco. A tall man with shoulder-length hair, in a wide-brimmed hat and a leather coat, appears from behind the trees and strides purposefully over. Jay is sanguine about his achievement: that he inadvertently handed Apple a model for turning the iPhone into the world's most successful platform for selling.

'Sometimes I wish I hadn't done what I did, because if I hadn't, who knows what else Apple would have invented? On one level it opened things up, but also closed things down.' Did Apple ever offer you a job? 'They reached out to me, though I wasn't aware they were. I kind of turned them down, which you shouldn't do. Other hackers went to work for them: classic poacher turned gamekeeper.'

All of this happened behind the scenes. When Steve Jobs announced the launch of the App Store, Apple was a platform for third-party apps: a platform for selling, and with the potential to not just transform payment systems but ultimately replace banks.

Third-party apps justified the Apple boss's claim that once in a while a technological advance comes along that 'changes everything'. They proved pivotal in propelling the iPhone from merely attaining phenomenal success to becoming the defining invention of our time.

Apple was first to plant their flag on a new moon: the space in the middle of a transaction where everything now happened. If you prised this space open, you would walk out onto an infinite plain of information – the data on one specific purchase connected by digital threads to millions of other purchases made by you, your family and everyone you know. And beyond these dead purchases, the living purchases yet to be made as the result of algorithmic suggestion: the things you, your family and everyone you know – and don't even know, but should know – will buy in thirty seconds' time.

The race was on to own this space, and to give an example of how fiercely this space was fought over, here is what happened when Apple did the deal with Chase over Apple Pay in 2014.

From its inception, the project was top secret. One insider described it as 'code name frenzy': card companies had code names for Apple and Apple for the card companies. At Visa, the code name was another consumer electronics company, chosen to avert attention from employees who were not involved.

In the summer of 2013, Apple approached each of the five major banks – the old keepers of money – to be involved in the project, without revealing the other banks involved. JPMorgan, the largest card issuer in the US, set up a war room in a windowless conference room in San Francisco. Only about 100 of the 300 JPMorgan employees working on the project knew that it was even a partnership with Apple.

On 9 September, JPMorgan Chase's chief financial officer, Marianne Lake, took to the stage in New York and waited for a signal. Two thousand miles away, Apple's chief executive, Tim Cook, stepped on to the stage in California and nodded to his assistant. Apple and JPMorgan believed timing was everything, to catch their competitors and the markets off guard, and create theatre.

At 11.35 a.m., Tim Cook dropped the bomb: Apple was launching a payment system you would not pay for, but to which every store and online shopping business on earth would subscribe. A new currency called 'Apple Pay'. In New York, one of Lake's deputies took a green apple out of her bag and put it on the table. It was the signal to Marianne Lake that the moment was right. She nodded to her aide.

'So,' she said, 'we are very excited.'[14]

In London, I met with one of the key players in the deal and asked him how they pulled it off. 'By getting all the ships to cross over the horizon at the same moment. It was very difficult.' I told him about the apple-on-the-desk story and he smiled. 'Huh. I didn't know that.' No one told him.

This was not 'disruption'. This was an earthquake, shaking the businesses that had run money for a century to the core. Mastercard's vice president, James Anderson, said the Chase Apple Pay deal did not 'respect and honour the payment networks'.

What he meant was that Apple Pay did not respect and honour the revenue stream of the big banks and credit-card companies. Apple and Chase had parked their tanks in the middle of the prime real estate of America's oldest financial institutions.

More importantly, Apple was going to give away its service for free. The space in the middle of a transaction where the money was, was no longer where the money was. Apple was stealing a march on its competitors by deliberately vacating it. Why? Because Apple saw value simply in facilitating a transaction to become a major money player. But to Apple's competitors, like Google and Facebook, the value of this space was not just about becoming a player but about a new type of money that wasn't money at all: data. The new currency.

AFRICA, NOT SILICON VALLEY, IS WHERE IT IS TRULY AT

In December 2016, Facebook CEO Mark Zuckerberg wanted in on this new world of data as money. His jet touched down in Kenya. Zuckerberg, like Apple, knew that information, not charging to facilitate a transaction, was the future. But also that the plains of central Africa, not Silicon Valley or Wall Street, might hold the key to winning.

In 2007, M-Pesa, a mobile money system allowing Kenyans to transfer money directly from one phone to another, was launched across the country. Not through an app or a complex encrypted payment system, but by text.

M-Pesa was a revolutionary exercise in the democratisation of money, using an entire nation as the laboratory. It not only cut out transfer fees, but made banks – as well as cash – extinct. It did not require an iPhone or a bank account, all it required was a twenty-year-old Nokia.

Within a year of its launch, M-Pesa had seventeen million users in Kenya. Forty per cent of the population. By 2010, more people used M-Pesa than had a bank account. It proved that Kenyans did not need one.

I visited Twiga Foods, the same banana-storage depot outside Nairobi that Zuckerberg visited months earlier. Twiga have used M-Pesa to become one of the fastest-growing companies in Kenya and Zuckerberg wanted to find out how. He met with Edna Kwinga, head of HR, and Kikonde Mwatwela, the COO.

'We didn't even know we were meeting Zuckerberg until ten minutes before he came in,' Edna told me. 'We were told it was the regional head of Facebook, and then in walks Mark Zuckerberg.' What did he want to know? 'He was very interested in how we'd used M-Pesa to grow. He was very nice. He'd been in West Africa the previous day and was off to South Africa in the evening.'

Mwatwela is under no illusions that the big tech companies are muscling in on M-Pesa's innovation and sensing an amazing opportunity. 'Silicon Valley often looks up to the top of the pyramid to see where money can be made, but Zuckerberg is incredibly clever. He's facing the other way and seeing that it's at the bottom of the economic pyramid that far more money is to be made.' Hoovering up the poor of the world and sticking them on Facebook in the process.

Twiga pay everyone through M-Pesa. On a banana plantation

near Mount Kenya, farmers pay their employees not with cash, but through their mobile. People who do not have a mobile get a lesson from the boss into how to use one. Did he foresee a time when he wouldn't use cash? I asked him. 'What? We don't use cash now. No one does. It's heavy and difficult to transport, it's unsafe, you can be robbed, you can be extorted. That is gone. I might use cash to buy a tea.'

M-Pesa has allowed Kenya to leap-frog the standard twentieth-century stages of development: infrastructure and banks. Once you needed a bank account to get a business. Not anymore. M-Pesa loans money and so it is making banks irrelevant, too.[15] M-Pesa has genuinely disrupted money, and has done it with the most basic technology available.

But Zuckerberg can take it to the next level with Facebook, opening up the poor half of the planet to a money revolution. And if it has worked in Kenya, it could work across the world.

M-Pesa offers the gateway to digital consumerism. Selling money transfers, payday loans, credit, food, cars and holidays, even alcohol and online gambling.

But these money transfers using text garner as much information about someone as their online shopping footprint. In 2016, a group of Kenyan police officers were arrested for making huge M-Pesa money transfers. They were not using bitcoin as drug cartels do, or banks to launder cash, they were using text. Zuckerberg realised that M-Pesa offered micro-data surveillance on transactions in much the same way Facebook can, but it could also potentially access billions of people that Facebook cannot.

When digital money arrived in 2000, the likeliest scenario seemed to be the cementing of global inequality. The wealthy half of the planet would use digital and mobile money, while the poor would continue with cash. In fact, M-Pesa proved the complete opposite. M-Pesa both empowered the poor and netted them. Exactly as debt did.

IS CASH AS IRRELEVANT AS WE ARE TOLD?

The subtext – and in many cases the text – of the drive to kill cash is the eradication of the black economy. Kenneth Rogoff, former chief economist at the IMF, says the global end of cash is both an inevitability, and a good thing.

We met in his office at Harvard and Ken showed me his extraordinary mountain range of a graph detailing the boom and bust cycles of Western capitalism for the last two hundred years. The tax revenue generated, coupled with the devastation of the black economy – an economy fuelled by cash – would make a cashless world the greatest leap forward in fiscal management since the end of fixed exchange-rates. It would also provide, he said, a far more effective policing of illegal immigrants than building walls or banning entry to the country at passport control. But something perplexing is going on, said Ken. He demonstrated with his hands, crossing in mid-air. 'As governments attempt to decrease the availability of cash and phase it out, there has never been more cash in circulation. People just keep using it, and it's not apparent who or for what.' To governments wanting to kill cash, it has become Hydra. A multi-headed gorgon: they chop off one head and it simply grows another.[16]

The black economy – the cash or 'shadow' economy – is really a euphemism for the livelihoods of the poor. Freakanomics economists Ceyhun Elgin and Oguz Oztunali, using a dataset for 161 countries between 1950 and 2009, estimated the shadow economy to account for over twenty-two per cent of the world's GDP.[17]

Nearly a quarter of the planet's entire wealth is cash in hand. Cash provides an essential mechanism of survival for billions of people across the planet. Criminals use the shadow economy, but so does someone cleaning an office, working on a building site or keeping a business afloat waiting to be paid. For those on the cusp of paying tax, cash can be the difference between surviving and going under. And if they pay tax, they are finished.

Scooping up the poor quarter of the globe that use the shadow economy, by forcing them to use digital money instead of cash because tax has so far failed to net them, is a strategy that governments are embracing around the world, especially with their failure to collect revenue at the other end of the wealth spectrum: from corporations and the super-rich.

Aren't you simply seeking to use cash as a Trojan Horse to collect revenue from the poorest because you can't collect it from the richest? I asked Rogoff. He shrugged. 'Cash isn't going to disappear as quickly as anyone might want it to, and I'm not saying it should. It serves a purpose for sure.'

In 2016, the Indian government suddenly and unexpectedly withdrew 500 and 1,000 rupee notes (the rough equivalent of a $7 and $15 note) from circulation. Their explicit aim was to cut the legs away from the huge Indian shadow economy. The results were disastrous.

Cash shortages lasted for weeks: twenty-five people collapsed and died after queueing for hours outside banks. The legitimate economy suffered a stock market crash, there was an agricultural crisis and road haulage stopped. The black economy, the intended target, remained untouched.

WHEN DRUGS MONEY BAILED OUT THE BANKS

India is still a significant cash economy, but Western economies rely on cash, too, and especially when there is a crisis. In August 2007, one of the world's largest multinationals, the French bank BNP Paribas, did something unprecedented in their history. They terminated withdrawals from three hedge funds citing 'a complete evaporation of liquidity'. The major banks of the US, Europe, Asia and South America followed suit. In a matter of hours, an entire banking system built on liquidity – one bank being able to borrow from another bank based on the cash in the system – ground to a halt. No one was prepared to lend to anyone else, and capitalism was about to stop. It was like that scene in *Reservoir Dogs* when everyone draws a gun and stares at each other, waiting for someone to make the first move.

But there was one place the banks could still borrow from. An entire global network flush with cash running in parallel to the world's banks: the drug cartels. Antonio Maria Costa was head of the UN Office on Drugs and Crime. A year after the crash, he says evidence began to emerge that as liquidity seized up in the legitimate banking system, the banks turned to the cash available in the drugs economy to keep the Western banking system afloat.

'Organised crime was the only liquid investment capital available to some banks on the brink of collapse,' he explains. Cash had stopped flowing, but drugs money would save us. It may have been earned from heroin and cocaine deals carried out on street corners from Los Angeles to Reykjavik, but this was money the banks now needed to stay alive.

So Western banking effectively laundered drugs money to keep the cash flowing. In the days following the crash, as governments bailed out the banks and liquidity came back into the system, normal service was resumed. But for a crucial period of time, the hours when capitalism teetered on the brink of collapse, you could only draw cash from a cashpoint machine because the world banking system was being propped up with the help of drug cartel money.[18]

The IMF estimate that large US and European banks lost more than $1 trillion on toxic assets and from bad loans between January 2007 and September 2009, and more than two hundred mortgage lenders went bankrupt. Profits to gangs from the drugs trade in the same period are estimated to have been worth $352 billion, according to the UN. These drug cartels had traditionally kept proceeds in cash or moved them offshore to hide them from the authorities, so moving the money discreetly back above radar – giving it to the banks to reboot their liquidity – was not a problem.

Costa says the evidence that this drug money flowed into banks came directly from bank officials working in Britain, Switzerland, Italy and the US, and he claims, 'That was the moment when the system was basically paralysed.' We may view what happened as immoral but if we use a bank as I, and I assume you do, we are also complicit. Drugs money pumped into the system allowed us to keep paying our mortgages.

However, it is what happened next, according to Costa, that was most disturbing. 'The progressive liquidisation to the system and the progressive improvement by some banks of their share values has meant that the problem of illegal money has become much less serious than it was.'

Banks became far more willing to turn a blind eye to laundering criminal money post-2008, because banks recognised that they owed crime. The quid pro quo of banking and criminality has a long history – moving money discreetly offshore and aiding criminals in investing in legitimate businesses to launder money – so when banks needed to borrow some cash from the drug cartels, they were more than happy to oblige.

BLOCK CHAIN – THE NUCLEAR KEY

In April 2014, the SSL encryption protocol providing watertight security for millions of online transactions carried out every second, and used by millions of businesses across the globe, was hacked. SSL was generally regarded by security experts to be the most secure payment system yet devised.

So how does it work? SSL is a new generation of 'block chain' payment. Block chain was originally developed as a way of allowing huge corporations to do billion-dollar deals securely. It now works for everyday transactions carried out by you and me, and is based on the principle of the nuclear key.

In a nuclear submarine, with missile capability to destroy an entire continent, control does not lie with one person but with a number of individuals, each of whom has a separate key. These keys need to be inserted in the control panel in the right order and at the right time for the missile to go off. The crew do not know who has the keys, and thus there is theoretically no way of overriding the system.

With a financial transaction carried out using block chain, computers take the role of crew members. Each algorithm is primed to play its role inserting a password at the correct moment. No one party can override the system. It is an inter-locking process with layer upon layer of security. It appears impregnable. Block chain is so trusted that the Pentagon are researching the use of it to encrypt nuclear weapons.[19]

Yet in 2014, SSL was hacked. Millions of people all over the world were told to change their passwords – the first nuclear key. After millions of passwords were changed, Walmart in America and the Chinese restaurant chain PF Chang both reported a further security breach. The very act of changing passwords had made the system easier, not more difficult to hack.

In 2015, a year later, the entire Talk Talk mobile network went down, because a teenager in a bedroom in Northern Ireland figured out the company's key passwords. The hack destroyed Talk Talk's credibility, resulting in thousands of customers leav-ing and the stock value of the company collapsing. When PayPal launched itself as a secure online payment, the deal seemed done on security. But twenty years on, the inherent fragility of this security is now a given.

When coins were first created two thousand years ago, their value was dependent on mutual trust between the two parties involved in the transaction: the buyer and seller. Today, in killing cash, trust is one way. We have no choice but to put our faith in the tech companies, and hold no cards of our own. Yet the belief we are supposed to have that they can securely hold on to our money is seeping. Forty per cent of bank fraud now goes unin-vestigated, because banks simply write it off.

Police have neither the resources nor the expertise to deal with fraud; the number-one crime to get away with. Lax security checks, and an ocean of easily accessible current accounts with ever faster payment systems, allow fraudsters to move money nanoseconds after a fraud has been committed. This is the truth of online security.

Yet a parallel can also be drawn with terrorism: for every large-scale event you hear about, there are hundreds of thwarted attempts that you do not. On this basis, the battle with fraud could be argued as well fought; the write-off, simply the unavoidable collateral.

THE EMPTY BANK VAULT

In Sweden, where cash is set to disappear in the next five years, a debate rages over the dangers of embracing its extinction without first pausing to think about it. A debate no other country is openly having.

In 2016, cash made up less than two per cent of all payments in Sweden. Cards are the main payment method: an average of 207 swipes per year. Three times more than any other European country. Mobile phone apps, primarily Swish, developed by the country's four biggest banks, are fast taking over from cards: the final nail in the coffin of Swedish cash.

Nine hundred of Sweden's 1,600 banks do not even keep cash on hand, or take cash deposits. In April 2013, a bank robber found this out the hard way.

At 10.32 a.m. on a Monday morning, CCTV footage picked up what police described as 'a single culprit, male, entering a bank in Östermalmstorg, central Stockholm, with a gun-like object.'

After demanding the staff open the safe, a woman behind a screen informed the robber that the bank held no cash. The vaults were empty. CCTV footage captures the moment the robber exits the bank less than two minutes after going in, penniless.

In 2012, there were only twenty-one bank robberies in Sweden. Half that reported in 2011, and the lowest level ever recorded.

Yet as physical bank robberies become all but extinct, online fraud in Sweden is at a record high.

Bjorn Eriksson, former president of Interpol, now runs Cash Uprising – a pressure group lobbying to keep cash flowing to stop fraud. The end of cash will, Eriksson says, marginalise the poor and hand over economic power to the new tech giants, who cannot and do not know what to do about fraud.

However bad the banks have been with fraud, Eriksson declares, they will prove to be paragons of vigilance next to the tech giants. Eriksson is no anti-capitalist protestor. He ran the biggest anti-fraud police force in Europe.

The cash divide is generational. The older generation trust cash and the young trust digital money. 'Cash-free' businesses like coffee shops across Sweden are run by young entrepreneurs who use a sole trader app called iZettle.

The watershed for this divide between the young and the old in Sweden is the banking crash of 2008. The old remember a time before the crash when the banks could be relied upon. The young believe the banking crisis fatally holed the banks beneath the water. Instead, they put their faith in the new tech giants, who wish to replace the banks.

In 2007, with the invention of the iPhone, a device was created for the passing of trust from the banks to these tech giants. They were now the new custodians of money. But are they any more secure than the banks? Critics of digital money like Bjorn Eriksson say a digital crash is inevitable and will be far worse than the last.

The risks managed by banks in 2007 were spread bet, but one breached block chain is enough to wipe digital money off the face of the earth with the single press of a button. We could live without a Lehman Brothers, but we cannot live without Google and Facebook, because they are the infrastructure.

Beyond the technological deficiencies of a secure payment system that was never secure to begin with, a crash is made far more likely by the sheer amount of money being created by fractional reserve banking. The key element fuelling economic growth is consumer spending. But this spending boom depends on consumer prices staying low. When the price bubble eventually bursts – as commodity prices go up and inflation follows – the whole house of cards comes crashing down.

THE CONTAGION

We are now about to embark on walking the high wire of an entirely digital capitalism, with another crash potentially encrypted in the system. The glitch. The ostensible reason is greater speed and efficiency for the consumer, but the truth is the eradication of the black economy and the control of money in the hands of five tech companies.

A decade ago, as the digital revolution got under way, a mountain was drilled through in order to produce a high-speed internet connection that increased the speed of transactions on Wall Street by one thousandth of a second. This extra thousandth of a second translates to a billion extra dollars transacting through Wall Street every hour. But as speed becomes the God of new money, the dangers of an entirely digital economy being wiped out because a rogue algorithm decides to sell instead of buy, or a cyber attack is launched, becomes ever more likely.

In May 2017, an unprecedented 'ransomware' attack was launched simultaneously across the globe on the same day. A cyberattack like none ever seen before. The Wannacry malware aimed at extracting ransoms from its victims and wreaked havoc on four continents at the same moment. Operations were cancelled as the NHS in Britain became paralysed. FedEx and Telefonica in Spain watched powerless as their operating system crashed. The ransomware spread like wildfire across Asia, the US, South America, Europe and Russia. 150 countries were affected. And it was only down to a 28-year old called Darien Huss inadvertently activating a 'kill switch' hardcoded into the malware by registering a nonsensical domain name that the whole thing stopped.

Because the ransoms involved were relatively small, various culprits were fingered: North Korea? Russia (attacking itself as well as everyone else)? Islamic fundamentalists: the cyber-Caliphate? A darkweb crime syndicate avenging the closing of the Silk Road?

The day before the attack, I was in the research lab of a major credit card company being shown amazing new prototypes for payment systems such as hand and body swipe and augmented reality shopping. I asked about cyber crime. This is all great, I said, but couldn't the whole system go down with a single attack? 'Oh, don't worry,' I was told. 'We're ahead of the game.' They were winning the fight with cyber crime and malware, they said, because they were trialling new defences on the criminals themselves. The Catch Me If You Can approach.

It's a battle and both sides are arming up fast, but as the events of 12th May 2017 showed, the cyberattacks are getting bigger and potentially more catastrophic each time.

I went for a sandwich to Pret A Manger the other day. The card machines had mysteriously stopped working and they were taking only cash. Staff politely asked customers to take money out from the ATM machine next door, but no one did. Because it took a minute out of their day. It took too long.

Instead, people preferred to queue for the card readers to come back online. Staff said it could take up to half an hour – but people preferred to wait, because they had habituated to a new way of paying.

My Pret experience perfectly demonstrated the irrational behaviour we demonstrate to paying that Drazen Prelec discovered at MIT. A few days after supermarket chain Asda made customers wait up to an hour to pay, and that sixty-minute delay cost the company £10 million.

When the system crashed, cash was the speedy and logical thing to use. But we consider cash to be dirty. Visa have carried out research on how much bacteria is carried on a bank note.

Contactless payment companies are demonising cash by drilling into our fears that cash is dirty.

The psychological contagion cash carries is fear of poverty, and this is the true success of the digital revolution – to make us believe cash is synonymous with social inferiority, and using it, even coming into contact with it, could mean contracting the contagion of failure. One of the reasons young Swedes prefer digital money to cash is that they believe, as Visa researched, that cash teems with germs. To the socially aspirational, digital equals clean, and clean equals success.

Cash is over, but we should seriously question why, and who truly benefits from its demise. In 2017, police discovered $20 million hidden under a mattress inside a wooden frame bed in Massachusetts.

A Brazilian man called Cleber Rene Rizerio Rocha was charged with laundering money to Brazil via Hong Kong on behalf of a defunct internet phone company. Rocha's defence was that, in the scheme of things, the amount he was laundering was tiny compared to the billions being laundered by banks online. Cash was small fry. It was a nice argument, but did not stop him being convicted.

In 1989, something similar happened in Britain. Comedian Ken Dodd was charged with tax evasion after his bank account was discovered empty, but £336,000 was found in cash, stashed in suitcases in his attic and under his bed. When asked by the judge, 'What does a hundred thousand pounds in a suitcase feel like?' Dodd replied, 'The notes are very light, m'lord.'

Dodd was acquitted, but had only gone on trial because it was assumed that if he was stashing cash under his bed, he must be doing something criminal. That is because cash is inherently criminal. It is guilty of being cash, and for that it will never be forgiven.

When it finally disappears, the question of whether it was a good idea to get rid of it will be academic. Cash will be gone, and all the result of a meeting in an empty lecture hall between two men who wanted to erase the pain of payment, and succeeded.

CHAPTER TWO
RISK: HOW CHAOS
CAME TO WALL STREET

SHORTING AND THE ARAB SPRING

On 16 December 2010, a twenty-six-year-old Tunisian street vendor called Mohamed Bouazizi did something he knew was risky. He borrowed money. Bouazizi needed to buy fruit and vegetables to sell at market the following day. As a result of an astronomic rise in food prices, brought about by a single decision made thousands of miles away, Bouazizi, like every other street trader across North Africa, had no choice.

Bouazizi woke early the following day. He was saving for an Isuzu pick-up truck to move his produce, but did not yet have enough. He was at his usual spot at Sidi Bouzid market by 8 a.m., but by 10.30 a.m., according to eyewitness accounts, local police began harassing him to move on, ostensibly because he did not have a vendor's permit.[1]

An argument ensued over money. Officials had extorted bribes from Mohamed in the past, but this time he refused. As he stood his ground, a forty-five-year-old municipal officer called Faida Hamdi slapped him in the face. She then spat at Bouazizi and confiscated his electronic weighing scales. Two unnamed men with Hamdi then overturned Bouazizi's cart into the alleyway.

In court, months later, Hamdi denied all charges.[2] Not in dispute is the fact that as Bouazizi tried to recover his overturned cart, officials kicked and punched him. His goods were then confiscated. He now had no means of making a living.

Bouazizi – a quiet man who did bookkeeping and accounts for other traders – was enraged. He and his uncle attempted to retrieve the cart from the municipal office. He asked to see the governor – Hamdi's superior – but was ignored.

Bouazizi then left and bought a large container of paint thinner. On the pavement outside the governor of Sidi Bouzid's office, he poured the paint thinner over himself. Onlookers gathered and took out their phones. Bouazizi is alleged to have shouted, 'How do you expect me to make a living?'[3] He then set fire to himself with a match and a revolution began.

Forty-two years earlier, a Czech student called Jan Palach set himself alight in Wenceslas Square, Prague, in protest at the Soviet invasion of Czechoslovakia. A month after Palach burned himself alive, another student, Jan Zajic did the same thing in exactly the same spot. Seven more followed, burning themselves to death to keep the protest alive.

Days after Bouazizi set light to himself, a one-thousand-strong funeral procession was forbidden by the Tunisian government from passing the place where he died, for fear of inspiring copycat acts. But it was too late. The Arab Spring has begun. The crowd chanted, 'Farewell, Mohamed, we will avenge you,' and on social media, people were mobilising.

The Arab Spring is often described as a 'Twitter Revolution'. but there were only two hundred active Twitter accounts in Tunisia on the day Bouazizi committed suicide. There were, however, two million Facebook accounts, and it was the handful of Twitter posts shared with these millions of Facebook users across North Africa that fuelled the uprising. One image in particular went viral; not of Bouazizi, but a woman in a hijab holding her BlackBerry aloft to film the growing mob. The fact that Bouazizi's act could be communicated was as important as the act itself.

The Arab Spring erupted in days over the whole of North Africa, toppling governments like dominoes: first the Tunisian government of Ben Ali, then Mubarak in Egypt and Gaddafi in Libya, then Seleh in Yemen. In Syria, Assad was challenged by pro-democracy rebels, erupting into a complex civil war that drew in Russia, the US and Europe.

In a strange twist of fate, Faida Hamdi, who first confiscated Bouazizi's goods and later said she blamed herself for the Arab Spring was herself arrested and imprisoned for 'civil offences'. She was made a scapegoat for the government and had become another victim of unfolding events.

The political vacuum created across North Africa was filled by Islamic State, who unlike their predecessor al-Qaeda saw territory gain in the crumbling regimes as an opportunity to create a continent-wide Caliphate. A borderless Islamic State from the Atlantic to the Red Sea, wrapped in a black flag. When IS rolled into town, the first thing they did to win hearts and minds was to bring down the price of wheat.

Mohamed Bouazizi's death sparked the most dramatic reconfiguration of the Middle East since the Sykes-Picot Agreement of 1916 carved up the map of North Africa to create French, British and Russian 'spheres of influence'. Sykes-Picot enshrined religious conflict by promising home-lands to both Jews and Arabs in exchange for support in the First World War.

A century on, the Middle East is reshaped by a humiliated street vendor pushed over the edge by a sudden rise in food prices. Sykes-Picot fuelled religious fundamentalism and in 2010, the ramping of wheat prices fuelled the rise of Islamic State and fourth wave Jihadism.

The Arab Spring was portrayed in the West as a spontaneous outpouring of anger to bring freedom and democracy. But that was not how it started. The Arab Spring was the direct result of a decision by four big food companies to begin gambling with the value of wheat on the international markets.[4]

Bouazizi set fire to himself because a chain of events in Sidi Bouzid market led him to a place where he could not make a living, and this desperation was the result of the most basic foodstuff on earth becoming financialised. Global wheat was now a chip in a casino thrown on the roulette table. If the bet went wrong, millions of people starved.

AS SIMPLE AS ABCD

ADM, Bunge, Cargill and Louis Dreyfus are the biggest food companies on earth, known by their initials, ABCD. They collectively control ninety per cent of the world's wheat. In essence, ABCD feed the planet and decide how much the world should pay to be fed.[5] In the early 1970s, President Nixon tried to win the Cold War by suggesting the food giants hike corn prices to Soviet Russia and starve communism into submission. They refused and Nixon backed down.[6] That is how powerful they are.

SOAS Professor Jane Harrigan has extensively researched the control these companies exert on food prices and their influence on the Arab Spring.[7] In doing so, she made a startling discovery. Sub-Saharan Africa is the most 'food insecure' region on earth: the gap between what is needed to feed the population and how much is imported to fill that gap is greater than anywhere else on the planet. Fifty per cent of food is imported and thirty-five per cent is wheat. In short, the entire region lives on bread and if the price changes even slightly, people starve.

But in 2005, the food giants ABCD faced a crisis of their own. Because harvests are unpredictable, pricing cereals is notoriously volatile and in 2005 profits were down. So ABCD made a fateful decision: they decided to start betting against their own crops on the international markets. If a crop went bad, they actually made money. If it did not, and they bet the wrong way, they simply raised prices. It was a win–win. They had shorted the world's wheat.

In sub-Saharan Africa, this was devastating. In Egypt, bread is known as *aish* meaning 'life'. In Yemen, there are over twenty different types of bread. As Rami Zurayk, professor of agricultural and food sciences at the American University of Beirut points out,[8] 'the fertile crescent, stretching from the Egyptian Nile to the mouth of the Tigris and the Euphrates, is where agriculture began, where wheat, lentils, chickpeas, sheep and goats and olives were first cultivated.'

In spite of the fertility of the region, it is also one of the poorest on earth. Forty per cent of Egyptians and Yemenis live in poverty. Why? The richness of the soil should on paper make it one of most self-sustaining regions. Since the 1980s, when the IMF and World Bank introduced policies that reduced farming subsidies and encouraged the export of fruit to the West, rather than investment in local grain production, the region became increasingly dependent on the imported wheat of US food giants ABCD.[9] And as a result of wildly fluctuating prices, life for millions of people barely able to afford a loaf of bread began to be lived on a knife edge.

In 2006–7, there was a bumper harvest, which would logically mean a price drop, but ABCD did the opposite. They hiked the price of cereal across the planet. In Africa and the Middle East, where a tiny price rise has catastrophic consequences, a food crisis ignited across the continent.

There have always been 'bread riots', but this was different. 'The first protests of the Arab Spring in Tunisia were quickly dismissed as another bout of bread riots,' Zurayk says. 'Arab regimes responded by making adjustments to food prices and offering more subsidies. Increasing the subsidy slightly relieves the popular pressure, but also increases the profit margins for importers and manufacturers. But this time round, truckloads of flour did not do the trick.'

In 2010, weeks before Bouazizi set himself alight, President Obama went to war with ABCD. Under pressure from the World Health Organisation, UNICEF, British Prime Minister Gordon Brown and French President Nicolas Sarkozy, Obama attempted to pass legislation curtailing a food conglomerate's ability to short on grain prices in the poorest part of the world. Obama called the behaviour of ABCD 'immoral' and politically destabilising. He failed.

The price of wheat went through the roof across sub-Saharan Africa, including Bouazizi's market in Tunisia, the Arab Spring erupted and Islamic State's 'fourth wave' Jihadism rolled across border after border. In ancient Rome, the poet Juvenal described *panem et circenses* ('bread and circuses') as a strategy politicians use to buy the contrition of the masses. As Islamic State marched forward, they understood the importance of 'bread and circuses' to winning over the people they advanced on. A lesson the West had failed to learn.

ABCD were playing a risky game, and the people who lost that game were those that did not even know they were playing: the people of North Africa. They could now be 'liberated' from the colonial West, and the black-flagged advance of the Caliphate had leverage with the people they 'liberated' when it came to food prices.

As North African states collapsed, refugee ships began sailing across the Mediterranean sparking a crisis on mainland Europe. This in turn fuelled fears of a migrant invasion which in turn propelled the rise of anti-immigration parties across Europe. And all because some food companies thought they could win a bet on Wall Street.

At the heart of the food companies' gamble was the idea that risk was the way to do business. And risk as an all-encompassing business philosophy was sold to Wall Street by one man.

I INVENTED THE BOMB. I DIDN'T DROP IT.

In New York, overlooking Central Park, is an anonymous apartment block. On the fiftieth floor, Robert Dall is being moved from his bedroom to the chintz living area by a nurse. Dall uses an oxygen canister to move around the flat, but when I arrive, he greets me with a strong slap on the back.[10] Back in the 1980s, Robert Dall was the man who changed the world by teaching it to embrace risk, and in so doing, inventing the mechanics for shorting. In *Liar's Poker*, Michael Lewis says that Dall shaped the world to come because 'he began to think thoughts years into the future.'

Robert Dall's light-bulb moment was 'securitisation'. It was a conceptual shift in the very idea of trading. Instead of trading with physical assets and their value now, Dall said you should be able to trade in what something would be worth in the future, but secure it against something that existed now, like a mortgage policy.

Dall was the man who turned capitalism into gambling, and risking trillions of dollars on the roll of a dice in the casino of the trading floor. Dall inadvertently placed the first bricks on the road that would lead to subprime, ABCD shorting wheat, and the Arab Spring.

At Solomon Brothers, Dall loomed over the trading floor, a giant in a pin-striped suit, who by his own admission 'worked hard, partied hard, did everything hard'. He was 'a down-and-dirty brawler. But I was coasting for a while there in Wall Street.' Till something changed. Dall discovered Black and Scholes. Two Harvard economists with a formula that could magic money from thin air.

Fischer Black and Myron Scholes were the Copernicus of stocks and shares. In the early 1970s, they took economic wisdom and turned it on its head. Everything you know about the way the market works, they said, is wrong. To risk everything is not bad but good. Do not avoid risk, embrace it. They encapsulated risk in a single equation, known as the Black-Scholes formula:

$$\frac{\partial V}{\partial t} + \frac{1}{2} \sigma^2 S^2 \frac{\partial^2 V}{\partial S^2} + rS \frac{\partial V}{\partial S} - rV = 0$$

This equation was to become the basis for options and derivatives, today worth $1 quadrillion. Ten times the value of all goods

produced on earth. ABCD took a risk with wheat prices in North
Africa in 2010, because Robert Dall read Black and Scholes in
the late 1970s and then taught Wall Street how to put risk into
practice in the 1980s.

One of the reasons for the huge impact of their formula on the
markets was the fact that they had recently been given a breathtaking real-world lesson in how Black-Scholes could work;
a master-class in casino capitalism carried out – with neat
circularity – in the desert of North Africa.

On 3 October 1973, an Arab coalition of states led by Egypt,
Syria and Iraq invaded Israel on the holy day of Yom Kippur.
OPEC, the oil producers of the Middle East, used the moment
to hike the price of oil overnight. It was a massive gamble, entirely
dependent on the US dithering over what to do about the invasion of Israel.

OPEC were playing high-stakes poker. With the eyes of the
world on Arab tanks rolling through the desert, the price of oil
smashed through the roof and more to the point, stayed there.

The Yom Kippur War had been spotted as a business opportunity and OPEC correctly identified this disruption in global
politics as the moment to strike. Instead of going for moderate
price increases, they audaciously pushed it to the very limit –
and then over. In 1973, the Shah of Iran told the *New York Times*,
'Of course the world price of oil is going to rise ... certainly!
And how! Let's say ten times more.'

The OPEC price hike was Black-Scholes in action. The riski-
est gamble imaginable, and it paid off. The received wisdom on
business decisions was that they were finely calibrated judg-
ments based on minimising risk, not maximising it. OPEC's
gamble was the opposite. They had put everything on black –
risked big – and won.

It was a wake-up call for Wall Street and Western governments.
The OPEC oil crisis demonstrated perfectly the Black-and-
Scholes view that the coming world was volatile, not control-
lable, and business needed to harness this volatility, like a skilled

sailor harnessing a storm. And risk did not only make you money, if you did not risk big, you would not survive in the new cut-throat business climate. From now on, a company that stopped taking risks was like a shark that stopped swimming. It was dead in the water.

The Black-Scholes formula spread like wildfire through Wall Street. They were hailed as economic prophets, heirs to Adam Smith and David Ricardo. But one man in particular took their equation and turned it into banking reality – Robert Dall.

Dall homed in on one target: the mortgage. By taking a safe asset like a mortgage and using a complex series of 'financial instruments' to turn it into a risky 'liquid asset', that house could now be traded as a 'security'. An ironic name, because there was nothing secure about it.

Wall Street was no longer trading real things, but promises 'securitised' or underwritten by real things owned by real people. 'Securitisation' was Dall's creation, but it was really Black and Scholes on the trading floor. You were Jesus and they were God, I told Dall. And you were doing God's work on earth. He rasped in agreement, laughing.[11]

By the early 1980s, Dall would walk into a downtown restaurant and brokers would come up to him and shake his hand or buy him bottles of champagne. 'I'd turned them into multimillionaires. Of course they thanked me!'

Securitisation dropped like a bomb onto the financial markets. If you could securitise a house, why not a bank? Or a supermarket chain or global corporation? Why not securitise a whole country? In 2000, the European Union shoehorned Greece into the Eurozone, taking a risk on the balance sheet of an entire nation that had flagged how risky it was as an asset. In doing so, the European Central Bank was risking the entire stability of Europe.

What the world did not know was that Goldman Sachs had been tasked with massaging Greece's accounts in order to make them 'eligible' for entry into the Eurozone.[12] An entire country became liquid on the promise of a better credit rating sometime in the future. Goldman Sachs warned that it was risky, too, but we were now in a post-Black and Scholes world. Risk was good.

I wondered what Robert Dall thought when he woke on the morning of 9 October 2007 and heard that the entire banking system of the West had collapsed, built largely on a system of risk that he had conjured.

His nurse fusses about him. He rearranges himself in his penthouse apartment, and takes a brief hit from his oxygen mask. 'I always knew it would go too far. That they'd push it too far.' But don't you have to take some blame? You created this thing. Dall thinks about the possibility that he might be the man that lit the fuse that nearly brought down the entire banking system. 'I was like Robert Oppenheimer,' he answers. 'I invented the atomic bomb, but I didn't drop it.'

In 2010, that bomb dropped on North Africa, as food prices exploded for no apparent reason on the people on the ground. The decision of ABCD to short wheat prices had the same catastrophic consequences as dropping a bomb. More people have been displaced from the region in the seven years that followed the Arab Spring than during the whole of the Second World War. The geo-political impact – the rise of ISIS, the Syrian civil war and the displacement of millions of people across Africa and into Europe – is ongoing. But to the food giants, a simple decision to short wheat prices was a risk worth taking.

HOW AIDS INSPIRED SUBPRIME

In 2007, the Jenga pyramid of subprime mortgage bundles built on Black-Scholes risk-taking was pushed to the edge. But years before this financial cataclysm unfolded, Wall Street had already been given a tantalising glimpse of the Jacuzzis of cash to be made from bundling risky loans, not in the housing market, but with AIDS patients.

In 1982, as Robert Dall's securitisation revolution was cours-
ing down Wall Street, a health insurer down on his luck was
sitting on his porch in Florida reading his local paper. Tucked
inside was a story that piqued his interest – about gay men dying
of a mysterious disease in San Francisco.

Peter Lombardi ran a small Florida-based health insurance
company called MBC. And in 1982, things were not looking
good. But when he read this story, he had an idea. One that
would light a separate fuse from securitisation, but lead all the
way to the same powder keg of subprime.

Lombardi discovered that gay men dying of AIDS could not
access their life insurance when they needed it. While they were
still alive. This was money that could buy them better health
care, pay off a mortgage for a partner, or they could blow on a
holiday. Money that would massively improve the remainder of
their life, but they were not able to get their hands on.

So Lombardi had a deal to put to them. I will give you the
money. Well, not give you the money. I will loan you the money
you need now. And in exchange, I will collect on your life insurance when you die. You win now, I win later. Lombardi came up
with a name for his weird new loan: he called it a 'viatical'. He
had created the death futures market.[13]

It was a genius idea. The insurance policies of a few men dying
of AIDS amounted to little in themselves, but when thousands
were bundled together into a viatical, suddenly you were looking
at hundreds of millions of dollars. Money that could be used as
leverage to make far bigger loans and deals. Which is exactly
what Lombardi did. Without knowing it, the first handful of gay
men dying of AIDS that Lombardi signed up were going to
make him a major player on Wall Street.

But viaticals depended on one crucial element to work: the
men dying quickly. The quicker they died, the quicker he
collected and paid back whomever he had borrowed from. The
only reason Lombardi could loan all this money in the first place
was because he himself had borrowed it at extortionately high

interest rates. It was a pass-the-parcel of debt, just as subprime would be.

If these men died fast, he collected promptly, and could pay back his loan and pocket the difference. The quicker they died, the more money he made. Lombardi's viatical pyramid was colossally risky, but Lombardi could handle it. What could go wrong?

In 1985, it did. An AIDS drug was discovered. Clinical trials on an HIV inhibitor called AZT began at Duke University, led by a Burroughs-Wellcome virologist, Marty St Clair.

To the rest of the world, from the millions of HIV-positive people in sub-Saharan Africa to the men in San Francisco and their families, it was a miracle. But to Peter Lombardi and his business partners at MBC, brothers Joel and Steven Steinger, it was a disaster. MBC were loaning out hundreds of millions of dollars to people who were now going to renege on their end of the deal by living.

The money started slowing down and Lombardi got frantic. MBC were no longer collecting the life insurances fast enough to pay their creditors. They had forked out over $100 million to more than 28,000 people with terminal AIDS, but now it was no longer terminal, they needed a new strategy: they needed terminally ill people with other diseases.

Lombardi and his associates widened their net, seeking out ill people with other terminal diseases. People who had an immediate need for cash up front, as Lombardi now did.

By the early 1990s, AIDS had dried up, but MBC had found new, deep wells into which to drop their bucket. Between 1994 and 2004, the company raised £1.2 billion from 30,000 new 'investors' across the globe.

They were back on track, but then disaster struck again. The IRS came calling. In 2003, the Securities Exchange Commission swooped, accusing MBC of the largest health fraud in US history.[14]

Lombardi was bullish in his defence. His behaviour could have been interpreted as a public service to people who could not access money any other way – a kind of cash Dallas Buyers Club. But the court did not see it that way. The 'MBC 3' were imprisoned for twenty years each.[15]

Lombardi's story, and the story of the thousands of people he signed to his extraordinary Ponzi scheme, would be a curious historical footnote, were it not for what happened next.

The gay men whom Lombardi had been targeting were high-risk customers – they were people that no one would lend to, but when their insurance policies were bundled together, they were worth a fortune.

In 2004, the year Lombardi went to jail, viaticals got a surprise resurrection as Lehman Brothers, ACC Capital Holdings, Merrill Lynch, Wells Fargo, Countrywide Financial, HSBC, Loan Star, JPMorgan Chase and the twenty-five other biggest lenders in America looked at new models of bundling risky loans.

Imagine. Just imagine, if you could bundle a viatical for the home-owning market, and call it a 'subprime mortgage'? Robert Dall had embedded risk in the psyche of Wall Street, but thanks to Lombardi, Wall Street was about to take it to the next level with subprime, risking the entire global economy.

Just as OPEC had bet everything on black and won, the banks bet it all on red and lost. Wall Street failed in – or should I say learnt a lesson from – the banking crash and in 2016, subprime was back. Wells Fargo, Bank of America and the very same banks responsible for the first crash began again offering mortgages with less than a three-per-cent down payment. All you needed to do was 'state income' without any proof of that stated income whatsoever.[16]

Wells Fargo had a new deal with the consumer. If you had no savings, you could be eligible for a lower interest rate. All you needed to do was sign up to a government-sponsored 'personal finance class'. A tutorial on debt so you could get into more. Bank of America had a special low rate that could only be accessed if you could prove to them your income was below the national average.[17]

In 2016, the biggest economy on earth got in on risk. Chinese banks began using complex financial instruments to disguise risky loans as 'investments'. Chinese lenders began using shadow banking – shifting loans off the balance sheet through partnerships with non-bank institutions such as trust companies and securities brokerages – to disguise the fact they were now in the game of risking everything, like everyone else.[18]

China's central bank governor, Zhou Xiaochuan, warned in 2016 that the world should not underestimate the levels of toxic debt being created in China. It mattered, Xiaochaun said, because China was underwriting the world's debt. China was the economy that the US turned to when it sold $700 billion of bonds to bail itself out in 2008.[19] China had effectively granted a giant overdraft extension.

A back-of-the-envelope calculation in 2016 by Dallas-based short seller Kyle Bass, of Hayman Capital Management, estimated Chinese debt at $10 trillion,[20] dwarfing anything even Western banks managed. If this toxic debt went belly up, who would bail them out? The Bank of Tomorrow, otherwise known as more debt.

Yuan Yang and Gabriel Wildau of the *Financial Times* have investigated how difficult Chinese debt is to penetrate and quantify. Lenders use 'assets that are in effect loans but structured to appear as holdings of investment products issued by a third party. Such financial alchemy allows banks to evade regulations designed to limit risk.'

In June 2016, regulations designed to curb banking risk were blamed for encouraging greater risk-taking. The Basel Committee on Banking Supervision were criticised by lenders for proposing safety regulations on banks aimed at making it harder for banks to cheat the rules.[21] These new measures might encourage banks to lend more, not less, to their weakest lenders.

Like the Sorcerer's Apprentice, who destroys the enchanted broomstick by chopping it with an axe, only to discover the pieces rising up into hundreds more broomsticks, any attempt to curb debt simply multiplies the debt infinitesimally.

Risk is at the heart of the banking system, but we too have become encouraged to be risk takers. In the 1980s and 1990s, as securitisation drew in Wall Street, the 'shareholding democracy' attracted the high street, with ordinary people encouraged to see themselves as players on the stock market.

Prudent, hard-working savers trotted off to financial advisers offering schemes that prised their savings from them. Of course, the financial adviser would say, there is always a little risk involved – but you have to risk a little, sir or madam, to win. If savers wanted any convincing, all they had to do was look at their bank balance – low interest rates wiping out any attempt at sensible, incremental wealth accumulation.

We have now normalised risk to such an extent that it is synonymous with the financial system. It is the system. But the biggest risk of all is the sheer amount of debt that has been sucked up by every household in the Western world. This ever-burgeoning debt is the iceberg beneath the surface of our lives, accruing more heft by the hour.

CHINATOWN

Risk is seen as a daredevil high-wire act played out by clever traders, but the only people actually taking risks are real people with real houses and jobs, who lose everything when the markets gambling on our behalf get it wrong.

In accepting risk as good, we have accepted the gravest risk of all: the extinction of the planet. According to Maria-Helena Semedo of the FAO, the UN Food and Agriculture Organisation, the world has only sixty harvests left in it.[22]

Intensive farming has leached the soil, which is fast turning the planet into a global dust bowl. We are putting ourselves out of business as a species by 2080, when the food stops growing.

The UN estimate that to keep up with global food demand, six million new hectares of farmland will be needed every year.

We currently lose twelve million hectares a year through soil degradation. In 2014, scientists analysed the sediment at the bottom of a French lake, undisturbed since the eleventh century.[23] By measuring the nitrate quality of the sediment, they concluded that as a result of the intensification of farming over the last century, the rate of soil erosion had increased sixty-fold.

In other words, we are over (unless vertical farming takes off with a newly invented soil substitute). But on the bright side, the end of humanity is an unprecedented chance to make money, offering investment opportunities unlike any other in history.

Elon Musk's Space X program plans to have two super-rich space tourists orbiting the moon by 2019, but Musk's long-term plan is planetary exit and life on a new biosphere: the *WALL-E* escape ship for real, a giant shopping mall floating in space inhabited by the wealthiest 0.01 per cent.

As the sixty harvests begin running out, the trading endgame begins. And the new shorting gold rush is not even depleting food, but the planet's most basic resource: water.

'It is intuitively appealing to talk about water as a traded asset,' says Deane Dray, a Citigroup analyst heading up their global water-sector research.[24]

Oil, wheat and gold are all traded on the futures market but, Dray says, 'if you look at projections over the next twenty-five years, you'll see that global water supply and demand imbalances are on track to get worse. The majority of the world population is living in water-scarce and water-stressed regions of the world.'

Water is disappearing and as it does, its value as a commodity escalates. Researchers at Aarhus University in Denmark estimate that the world shortfall in water need will be forty per cent by 2030.

Shortages of water due to global warming and increased demand to produce energy, are turning it into a political weapon. In the Middle East, the Euphrates river has been a focus of resource conflict between Turkey and Syria. In 2014, Turkey turned off the supply, affecting the lives of millions of people in Syria and Iraq.[25]

We are now entering a *Chinatown* scenario. In 1975, Robert Towne's script for the Roman Polanski movie about the control of the water supply to a drought-ravaged Los Angeles, and the nexus of corruption it creates between business and government officials, won an Oscar. But we are now embarking on an era in which a thousand similar storylines are created across the globe. Wherever supply dwindles to a trickle, the shortage will be engineered to hike prices.

In 2015, Los Angeles got a taste of *Chinatown* for real. An investigation by the San Bernardino *Desert Sun* discovered Evian owner Nestlé had been allowed to siphon water from some of California's driest areas on permits that expired nearly thirty years ago, in order to produce premium crystalline products like Arrow Head and Crystal Geyser, sold across the world.

In March 2015, protestors at Nestlé Waters North America's bottling plant in Sacramento forced a one-day closure. They brandished plastic Evian bottles as batons and even made plastic pitchforks out of them.[26] The US is the world's second biggest consumer of bottled water behind China. Nestlé, like Coca Cola and Pepsi, have cut deals with isolated rural communities, taking a percentage of the local water supply, but with the incentive of keeping municipal local rates lower for local residents, so they will agree.

As water runs out, global companies are able to buy up the supply through such locally negotiated deals, just as oil companies bought up land rights in the twentieth century. I met a lawyer a couple of years ago, whose job consisted of flying round the world and persuading indigenous peoples to sign away their land rights to the global oil company for whom she worked.

This job is now being carried out by water companies, and the deals that are cut over the heads of communities by municipal governments in North Africa, Australia, South America, China and India, will mean local people suddenly find themselves without access to the water that comes from their own village.

In 2006, Coca Cola were accused of 'drinking India dry' by opening a bottling plant in Rajasthan that left local farmers unable to irrigate their fields.

But in Australia, where water shortage is historically acute, a solution has been attempted. The Murray-Darling Basin provides the life blood of New South Wales – the two rivers stretching thousands of miles and providing water, not only for millions of people in cities such as Canberra and Murray Bridge, but for the hundreds of farms that lie adjacent to the rivers, and rely upon this water to survive.

By the mid-1990s, seventy-seven per cent of the Murray's average annual flow was being consumed by humans. The resulting reduced flow, combined with silting and increased run-off from saline soils churned up by farming, were killing the river. So in 1995, the state and federal government capped extraction, meaning that if you wanted to use more, you had to pay. Rhondda Dickson, chief executive of the project, explains that 'one of the most significant reforms we have made in Australia is to separate water property rights from land rights and cap water use, so water can be traded on the market.'

Australia had done something seemingly impossible: squared the circle of need and price. A water user could sell their allocation of water for a year or hold on to it. Supply and demand, and transparent. But it did not solve the bigger picture – water is drying up across the planet as demand for water explodes. In 1992, governments from across the globe convened in Ireland to produce the 'Dublin Principles' on water: recognising it as an economic good. But little has happened to produce a coordinated strategy for the global crisis.

The *Desert Sun* investigation in California unearthed what happens at micro-level: government oversight of water falls between the cracks of under-resourced agencies like the Forest

Service and local community groups. Nestlé's pumping operation at Strawberry Creek in the San Bernardino National Forest, sixty miles east of Los Angeles, took advantage of the fact that the site had been unlicensed since 1987.[27]

Companies can exploit the fact that water is a natural phenomenon – a 'common pool resource'. Rights are often in conflict, and therefore can be negotiated their way. Water is easy pickings.

When they do, the money to be made is phenomenal. The average price of water piped into a home is approximately $1.50 per 1,000 litres. At $3 to $4 for bottled water, that is a price increase of 280,000 per cent.[28] But you do not have to drink bottled water to feel the price hike from the commoditisation of the water shortage. Ratings agency Finch polled seventy-eight per cent of the forty-six retail water utilities in California in 2015 and estimated a coming price rise in piped water to the home of up to thirty-one per cent.[29]

The trouble with water is that it is very heavy and difficult to transport, like oil. According to Professor John Reilly, co-director of the Joint Program on the science and policy of global change at the MIT Center for Energy and Environmental Policy Research,[30] 'In terms of large-scale international trading of water, we already have bottled water moving around. I think it is more likely we will see desalinisation and other sorts of things – such as water reclaimed, cleaning up and recycling of water – before we see large scale trading of massive amounts of water.'

The result of shortages of water in drier parts of the world, which also happen to be the poorest, will be to move production of food to the richer, wetter parts. Rather than carry the water elsewhere, acute shortages of water will be the catalyst for widening global inequality. Not only will the poorest in the driest places pay the highest premium for useable or drinkable water, they will suffer the most from highly volatile jumps in food price – food imported because there was no water to grow food where they lived.

The money to be made is not in water's transportation but in betting on price – on the water futures market. On risk. Michael Burry, the one-eyed visionary trader who shorted subprime and was made famous by *The Big Short*, moved swiftly on from betting on a mortgage crash to trading on the price of global water. A man always ahead of his time.

BETTING ON THE END OF THE WORLD

This is the dawning of the Anthropocene age – a new epoch in which humanity decides the fate of the planet. It began in the 1950s with the dispersal of radioactive elements from nuclear tests such as Mururoa Atoll and marked the end of the Holocene, twelve thousand years of stable climate since the last Ice Age.[31]

The Anthropocene age is marked not only by global warming, but deforestation, pollution and the toxification of our planet, the mass extinction of species, and the manipulation of the ones we choose to keep – the battery-bred chicken is now the world's most common bird,[32] even though in evolutionary terms, it should not be.

The Anthropocene age cements the fact we are bigger than God, but even now, we cannot let go of risk, because risk is what propelled us here.

Professor Chris Rapley, a climate scientist at University College London, believes we should drop our addiction to economic risk when it comes to saving the planet: 'The Anthropocene marks a new period in which our collective activities dominate the planetary machinery. Since the planet is our life-support system – we are essentially the crew of a largish spaceship – interference with its functioning at this level and on this scale is highly significant. If you or I were crew on a smaller spacecraft, it would be unthinkable to interfere with the systems that provide us with air, water, fodder and climate control. But the shift into the Anthropocene tells us that we are playing with fire.'[33]

We are doing so because we have a planet constructed, and now spiralling to destruction, on an economic model of risk. But the risks that need to be taken now should be in saving us, not destroying the planet further. The tipping point will come when business discovers there is more money to be made from saving the planet than killing it, or using the futures market to bet on its imminent demise.

In 2015, Toyota produced a hydrogen-powered car that produces water as a by-product from the exhaust. But in 1946, more than sixty years ago, scientist Vincent Schaefer first discovered cloud seeding – the artificial creation of clouds using basic chemical agents. No one has yet decided to put an Evian or Coke logo on the side of a cloud, but when they do, then perhaps we will decide it is an idea worth pursuing.

Instead of following the Black-Scholes formula, we should be utilising $2H_2 + O_2 = 2H_2O + Energy$. The formula for the creation of water. It is actually pretty simple.

CHAPTER THREE
TAX: WHY EVERYWHERE WANTS TO BE THE CAYMAN ISLANDS

On 2 January 2012, a cash machine at the Blockbuster video store in the Fallowfield Shopping Centre, in Manchester, was robbed. The thieves had spent six months digging a 100-foot-long tunnel under the car park, even fitting it with lighting and roof supports. Once they had dug the tunnel, the gang needed to cut through fifteen inches of reinforced concrete to reach the cash machine, which held £20,000 on a normal business day. But this was not a normal business day. It was 2nd January and there was only £6,000 in it.

The gang of four had worked seven days a week for six months to dig a tunnel to rob a cash machine no one was using. By my calculations, they had earned £8.33 a day for their labours.

There are far easier ways to make money. You could instead become a global corporation and stick your profits in an offshore tax haven. According to the last two American presidents, Obama and Trump, this is one of the greatest ongoing crimes perpetrated on the taxpayer.

Yet it is a crime that governments are keen to enable. The twenty-first-century race to become the nation on earth offering the most advantageous tax breaks has replaced the twentieth-century race to become the most productive manufacturing economy.

In 2017, Theresa May suggested that by turning itself into a tax haven, Britain could forge a post-Brexit identity. In the US, Donald Trump wants to do the same to attract US businesses back. If you wanted proof that growth was over as a governmental goal, you need look no further than the frantic scramble to own the low-tax crown.

Yet politicians also claim to deplore tax avoidance. In *Casablanca*, when Captain Renault is confronted by gambling in Rick's Bar, he is affronted. 'I am shocked, shocked to find that gambling is going on here!' he says, as the croupier hands him his winnings under the table. 'Oh, thank you very much.' Then he turns to the other tables. 'Everybody out!'

This is how politicians behave when they talk about tax avoidance. But how tax itself went from a duty to pay to a duty to avoid is a comical one. In truth, a ubiquitous business strategy that politicians claim to deplore was hatched and most enthusiastically promoted by government itself.

The lesson to be learnt by the hapless cash-machine robbers digging beneath Fallowfield Shopping Centre is this: save your energy and make sure the next crime you commit is legal. So how did it happen? How was business schooled into thinking that tax avoidance was not simply a justifiable tactic, but an entrepreneurial imperative?

No one knows how much corporations have hidden offshore. A 2012 study based on data from the IMF put it at between $21 trillion and $31 trillion. Not million or billion. Trillion.

The top ten private banks, including UBS, Credit Suisse and Goldman Sachs, moved an estimated $6.2 trillion to tax havens in 2010 alone.[1] This figure quadrupled between 2011 and 2015, so at the very time that banks came under the spotlight for enabling tax avoidance they went industrial with it.

The US Senate Homeland Security sub-committee claimed one bank, HSBC, was alone responsible for 'failing to monitor' £38 trillion going offshore. They turned a blind eye, just like Captain Renault.

It is not just Google, Facebook and Amazon who reroute their profits. Everyone from Burger King to Sainsbury's and Manchester United do it, too. Even bus companies. Passing through a labyrinthine system of subsidiaries around the globe before ending up in the Cayman Islands or Bermuda or Luxembourg or London or Delaware. (Appropriately nicknamed 'the small wonder', Delaware has over five thousand global companies 'registered'. More than the Cayman Islands. Prior to becoming a tax haven, Delaware's main earner was poultry and soy beans.)

HOW WE BENEFIT AND HOW WE DON'T

Tax avoidance is integral to the way the world does business. It is perfectly legal, yet has real-world consequences. An estimated $700 billion has left Russia since the 1990s, $305 billion from Saudi Arabia, another $300 billion from Nigeria. The money taken out of developing countries could have wiped out their entire debt at a stroke. In the UK, much is made of the fact that one in three benefit claims is fraudulent, costing £1.3 billion a year. The tax gap created by tax avoidance is thirty-five times greater than benefit fraud.[2]

This smooth-functioning system, oiled by an army of lawyers and accountants, is not merely taking advantage of the increasingly borderless, frictionless global economy, it rewrote the rules to make it legitimate in the first place.

It would not matter if it didn't impact directly on ordinary tax payers, but it does. Every adult in Britain and America picks up the tab left by corporations, paying higher tax bills as a result of big companies not paying theirs. Tax avoidance is anti-capitalist: by squeezing small and medium-sized companies trying to grow, in order to make up the shortfall, governments cut off new business at the knees.

Yet the companies avoiding tax feel maligned by a world that does not understand what they do in terms of contributing to the economy, and are positively bullish about defending their use of tax havens – or 'financial centres' as they have rebranded themselves.

When I was invited to speak at an offshore tax event in Geneva in 2016, the hedge fund managers and representatives of corporations attending seemed genuinely baffled that the world sees them as villains. The consumer, they argue, gets a cheaper Amazon package, or packet of tomatoes from the supermarket, only because they avoid the full tax whack, and we benefit from that.

They have a point. The consumer is an inadvertent beneficiary of tax havens. But only a bit. If I weighed up a cheaper book from Amazon against the billions in lost tax revenue to fund the NHS or the education of children, the money lost to key services, or reinvestment in basic infrastructure of the state, I think I might be inclined to add 2p to the price of my book.

HOW TAX AVOIDANCE BECAME LEGITIMATE AND PAYING IT BECAME FOR 'LITTLE PEOPLE'

So how did tax avoidance become the mechanism by which the modern globalised world does business? Who rebranded it as business savvy and turned tax from something you had to pay, into – in billionaire Leona Helmsley's immortal words – something paid only by 'little people'?

Once upon a time, dodging tax was actually wrong. In 1975, Baron Alfred Ernest Marples, who had served as Postmaster General in the Conservative government, overseeing some of the biggest changes to British life – the opening of the first section of the M1 motorway, the introduction of premium bonds and the postcode system – did something very strange.

He boarded a night ferry, hours before the end of the tax year. According to a *Daily Mirror* account from the time, he had with him only 'his belongings crammed into tea chests, leaving the floors of his home in Belgravia littered with discarded clothes and possessions. He claimed he had been asked to pay nearly thirty years' overdue tax. The Treasury froze his assets in Britain for the next ten years. By then most of them were safely in Monaco and Liechtenstein.'[3]

Lord Marples was portrayed as a classic upper-class rogue – a cad who had skipped the country. He had defrauded the nation, but his night-time escape was also seen as a very British two fingers to the establishment, and magnificently sneaky. And at the very moment Marples was boarding the night ferry, two accountants in London were setting about changing the British mindset on tax avoidance – from criminality to clever accountancy.

JOHN LENNON: PATIENT ZERO

Their story begins in London. It is 1969 and John Lennon is at a drinks party in Mayfair. He is introduced to two men in suits called Roy Tucker and Ian Plummer. They stand out, because everyone else is a rock star or a groupie, but these men have a very enticing proposition for Lennon.

Tucker and Plummer had worked for the big accountancy firm Arthur Andersen, but now wanted to go it alone and believed that they had a new way to attract business: be creative with the accounts and magic a tax bill to zero. When the Labour government under Harold Wilson began taxing the rich at an unprecedented ninety per cent, they saw their chance.[4]

The fact they targeted John Lennon at the drinks party was not a coincidence. When taxes rose, the Beatles were livid. George Harrison wrote the song 'Taxman', even name-checking Harold Wilson fleecing hard-working, international rock stars:

> *Let me tell you how it will be*
> *There's one for you, nineteen for me*
> *'Cause I'm the taxman, yeah, I'm the taxman.*

Should five per cent appear too small
Be thankful I don't take it all
'Cause I'm the taxman, yeah, I'm the taxman.[5]

Tucker and Plummer saw pound signs when they began chatting to Lennon. They were in the process of creating a 'bank' called Rossminster in discreet Mayfair offices. But this one was very different from the banks used by 'little people'. This bank would have a discreet entrance with a small gold nameplate. They would deal only with super-rich clients. If Lennon came on board, they could potentially get Roger Moore, Led Zeppelin, maybe Mick Jagger and Bryan Ferry. And in return, they promised Lennon a tax bill of £0.00. In fact, they said, the Inland Revenue will be paying you money.

Lennon signed up and Rossminster had its first big-name client. Two men were going to change the British attitude to tax, but first they had to content themselves with merely creating the first orchestrated tax dodge of the 1970s.[6] Tucker and Plummer found all kinds of cunning places to spirit away large sums of money for their clients: charitable donations or shell companies with no evident business or board directors. Fellow Beatle George Harrison ploughed his royalties into the failing British film industry – a guaranteed money mineshaft – producing some great films like *Scum* and *Withnail & I* in the process.

Then Tucker and Plummer made their first mistake. They started getting cocky. As their fame in super-rich circles spread, their cavalier behaviour towards the Inland Revenue started to become a form of taunting. One morning in 1974, HMRC got its revenge. Twenty police officers and seventy-eight tax inspectors swooped on their offices.

Tucker and Plummer were shut down, but not before having set the template for a whole new tax specialism: creative accountancy. Instead of breaking the law by outright evasion of tax, you sailed to the very edge of criminality, twisting the rules to within an inch of prison, thus avoiding it. Thanks to Rossminster, that is what you pay a creative accountant to do.

Tucker and Plummer were prosecuted, not because they had broken the law, but because of what they represented: a wilful exploitation of the loopholes of the system. In this respect, they were a precursor of insider trading in the City in the 1980s. If Lord Marples had hung around, rather than sneaking off to Monaco, Tucker and Plummer could probably have got his bill down to zero.

Their message was profoundly subversive to a post-war society predicated on 'doing your bit'. They upended the duty of wealth creators from paying their way in society to doing their utmost to avoid it. Rules, they said, were no longer there to be followed, but broken. When they were arrested, Tucker and Plummer may have been over as accountants, but they had changed the morality of Britain.

TURNING A MOSQUITO-RIDDEN SANDBAR INTO A TRILLION-POUND ISLAND

All tax avoidance needed now was to go legit. And for that, the British government was on hand. In the late 1960s, the British Empire was being dismantled, and the colonies were faced with a choice. Some, like Jamaica, went fully independent. But for others, Whitehall had another plan.

In 1969, a civil servant called John Cumber was called into the Foreign Office. He was shown a map of the Caribbean and a circle was drawn round a small mosquito-ridden sandbar called the Cayman Islands. Pack your bags, he was told, because next week you are going to be the Governor.

So-called 'treasure islands' such as Switzerland and Monaco had long provided the rich with tax-haven status, but now the British government saw an opportunity to muscle in on the act with an actual physical island, surrounded by sea. Why, they surmised, could not ex-colonies like Cayman be retooled for the same purpose? Remain under British sovereignty, guaranteeing political stability, but acting independently, so they can write their own rules.

The reason Cayman could rewrite the rules was down to two little words: common law. Economist Jan Fichtner has analysed the importance of common law to Cayman's success as a tax haven in a 2016 report for the University of Amsterdam:[7]

> The key difference between common law and civil law is that common law only stipulates what is prohibited, whereas civil law, as practiced in Japan, Germany or France, identifies what is permitted. The consequence is that new financial innovations such as hedge funds or CDO's (collateralized debt obligations) can be set up easily, because strict regulation is only put in place with conspicuous misconduct or strong pressure from powerful foreign actors – governments.

In other words, they can do what they like, until someone stops them. And no one, least of all the British government, wanted to do that. Until Cayman was retooled as a tax haven, places such as Switzerland and Monaco were exceptions to the global financial system. Not the model for how it should work. But one man in Whitehall saw Cayman as a way of making tax havens the norm: the place where all business is conducted.

George Bolton was a director of the Bank of England and on 28 February 1958, he noticed something very weird going on. The Midland Bank were handling a transfer of $800,000 on the trading floor that had not been flagged. These were not dollars at all, they were eurodollars, normally used to keep large sums of US money secure outside the States by holding it in trustworthy banks across the world.

Trades with eurodollars were always traceable, above-board and relatively small. This transfer was different. It was huge. So big that it looked like laundered money. Except it appeared it was being laundered in broad daylight through one of Britain's biggest banks. When George Bolton saw the Midland Bank deposit, he had a choice: do something or turn a blind eye. He turned a blind eye.[8]

In that moment, Bolton saw a whole new potential for eurodollars: as a parallel trading system in its own right, not simply a way of safeguarding assets. This could be a way of doing deals between companies and moving huge amounts of cash around the globe free of government and currency controls. Why be a criminal doing it illegally, when you could do it legally? The key was for these transactions to happen 'offshore'. Eurodollars were an offshore market before offshore banking even existed.

The plan for making offshore real – a physical place, not just a concept – was to create a wheel.[9] At the centre was London, where legitimate deals could be carried out. But the spokes would extend far out to offshore havens thousands of miles away, where deals of a shadier nature could be transacted, and dirty money laundered. No one would be scrutinising these deals too much. London could turn a blind eye.

Civil servant John Cumber arrived on Cayman in 1969 and became the island's first Governor. It was sparsely populated: only fishermen, their families, the Cayman crocodiles that give the islands their name, and the mosquito-ridden swamps. A huge programme was undertaken to spray the lagoons with insecticide and prepare the island for a new purpose. Tax avoidance.

However, Cayman's first clients were not big business as the British government hoped, but drug dealers. The idea of offshore coincided with the Labour and Democrat governments in London and Washington suddenly ramping up corporation tax, and refusing to allow companies to exile their profits abroad by maintaining restrictions on capital flow. Cayman was hamstrung.

But there was business: from Miami and Cuba, Colombia and El Salvador. Cessna planes would fly over the beaches dropping suitcases of cash to be deposited and laundered on behalf of the emerging drug barons of central America, flush with cocaine money and with nowhere to put it. In years to come, Pablo

Escobar would become one of Cayman's most loyal customers.

Then there was a further stroke of luck for Cayman. The Bahamas, their neighbour and one of Cayman's leading offshore rivals, descended suddenly into political turmoil, becoming independent in 1973. The Bahamas' accountants fled *en masse* to Cayman, bringing their business with them.

The Bahamas had benefitted hugely from the collapse of the Bretton Woods agreement in 1971, a system of monetary management signed up to by the world's biggest economies. Bretton Woods lasted forty years, strictly controlling exchange rates and capital movements. But now it was gone, controls disappeared overnight. Currency was suddenly free to flow across the globe unscrutinised, exactly as George Bolton had imagined it would in the 1950s. And now all the accountants had moved from the Bahamas to Cayman, it was Cayman that would benefit from this big bang.

Cayman was all set to open its doors to the world's corporations. Yet in spite of the gonzo accountancy of Tucker and Plummer in the late 1960s, tax avoidance was still not widely accepted as best practice by the public, let alone government policy. That was all about to change.

In 1979, there was a revolution, and it was led by the two most powerful leaders of the free world: Mrs Thatcher and Ronald Reagan. They did not trust government with money, least of all with taxpayers' money, and both wanted to break the regulatory shackles that tied big business down. Markets, not government, should henceforth decide what was best for the economy, and at the heart of this revolution was low tax.

For forty collectivist years, taxation was seen as necessary. The price paid by citizens and business to have a functioning civil society. We would all do our bit by paying for roads, hospitals and battleships. But if business was freed from this burden, it was now argued, we would all benefit in the long run. Lower taxes would mean greater productivity and profit margins, and the economic benefits to business would 'trickle down' to the rest of us.

Capitalism was about to change course. After forty years of broad agreement on the need for taxation, it was now perceived as a stone around the neck of big business, and one man was to provide the evidence, with a single stroke of a pen.

THE DOODLE ON A NAPKIN

Arthur Laffer was an economist from the Kennedy era who had fallen out of favour. He had long argued that low (or no) taxes would create a 'rising tide that lifts all boats'. In 1980, he had lunch with two smart young senators working for Reagan: Donald Rumsfeld and Dick Cheney.

About halfway through lunch, Laffer got out a pen and began drawing a curve on his napkin. This doodle became known in economics as the 'Laffer Curve'. It was a moment that would change the course of the Western world and the Laffer Curve became sacred to the revolutionaries of low tax: the Turin Shroud of neo-liberalism.

Using the curve on the napkin, Laffer showed Rumsfeld and Cheney that the lower you taxed, the higher the long-term growth of the economy. Taxes created a vicious cycle for business, he asserted, and lowering them did the opposite: it created a virtuous cycle in which growth and incremental reductions in tax worked in tandem, for the benefit of government, business and the public. Everyone was a winner.

Rumsfeld and Cheney were impressed and they did a deal. Laffer became Reagan's in-house economist and his low-tax doctrine became government policy. Tax havens were no longer a shady offshore secret, but a shining beacon of what could be done cleverly with money. A duty to be part of, not a crime to be covered up.

More than thirty years later, I meet Arthur Laffer in a bar a block away from the restaurant where he met Cheney and Rumsfeld. He arrives beaming from ear to ear, talking so fast and bouncing around with such manic energy, he could easily have become a talk-show host had he not become an economist. I can see why Rumsfeld and Cheney were impressed.

Laffer is tremendous company and we get on like a house on fire, drinking away pretty much as he must have done in that restaurant forty years ago. Laffer relishes criticism of his theory. He defends the economics with a theatrical wave of his arm. At one point, he gets out a napkin and starts drawing his curve. I interrupt him. 'That's great Arthur, but what I want to know is, how you got away with it?'

'What do you mean, how I got away with it? Because it's true!'

'But it isn't. As a result of the low-tax doctrine, didn't business move offshore? Manufacturing collapsed in the US, and half the American population became disenfranchised.'

'No! No! This is so wrong! So wrong! We were proved right! Rich people are different from other people. The rich are the one group of people where if you lower their tax rate, you get more revenue. Taxing the rich would make society poorer. If you tax rich people and give the money to the poor, you're going to get lots and lots of poor people and no rich people. The dream is always to make the poor rich, not the rich poor.'

Laffer believes in his curve, and made everyone in government believe it, too. And it certainly worked for big business, just not for everyone else. Tax havens are available only to companies that can afford the entrance fee, not start-up businesses or sole traders, and this means they contort markets rather than allow the market to work properly. Laffer argues the opposite.[10]

On both sides of the Atlantic, the reinvention of tax avoidance as entrepreneurial initiative meant government gave business a tacit nod and wink to ignore the rules the rest of us follow. When the Conservative chancellor Nigel Lawson was asked in the 1980s why his government were so keen on dropping corporation tax to next to nothing, he said that big corporations would no longer have a reason to avoid tax. Why would anyone bother, he said, when they did not pay anything anyway? It did not occur to him that government generosity can be pushed well beyond zero.

We have been programmed to think that low tax promotes enterprise. It does, when businesses are small and need to get off the ground. When global corporations scour the globe looking for the most 'tax efficient' place to register themselves, rerouting their money through numerous shell companies, then low tax has nothing to do with enterprise. In fact, it destroys entrepreneurialism by forcing small, growing businesses to shoulder the bill the corporations have dodged.

By the mid-1980s, the low-tax orthodoxy was so hegemonic, the idea of raising taxes was seen as far-left madness. The fact that German and Swedish right-of-centre governments kept taxes high to create corporate responsibility was conveniently ignored by those seeking to brand tax as a socialist dogma rather than a neo-liberal one. By maintaining reasonable levels of corporation tax for native companies such as BMW and Siemens (happy, by the way, to pay them), these countries also held on to their manufacturing base. Something Britain and the US destroyed by offshoring tax and jobs.

The US car industry collapsed, creating a rust belt from the very areas that had turned America into the number-one superpower. In Britain, the story was the same. Workers in traditional industries were deemed 'uncompetitive'. The reality was that the carpet under their feet had been ripped away and sent offshore. When Nissan opened a factory in Britain's North-East, workers were suddenly 'competitive' because they were cheap.

As financial services, not manufacturing, became the future, a huge creative accountancy industry sprouted in London servicing the tax-avoidance juggernaut, with a revolving door between the HMRC and the big accountancy firms. Richard Brooks was a senior tax inspector for the Inland Revenue, who became a whistle-blower after witnessing what he believes was the cosy relationship developing between tax inspectors and corporations.

'I saw people basically demoted or ignored for doing their job, which is collecting tax. But you were promoted for fostering relationships with the corporations and advising them on tax-efficient strategies.'[11]

Brooks thinks a two-tier system emerged at that time in the Inland Revenue. On the ground, stretched tax inspectors were struggling to do their best to chase tax evaders. But above these overworked inspectors at the coalface of avoidance, there was a cadre of senior officials who lunched and socialised with the big-time accountancy firms representing companies like Google and Facebook.

This upper echelon of the HMRC, Brooks believes, were fatally compromised by this association. They were 'in awe' of the very companies they should have been investigating, and were keener to impress than investigate. Not least, because they had an eye on their next job. Even if an individual had wanted to go after a big tax scalp, the culture prohibited it.[12]

Going easy on these big companies meant a shortfall in tax revenue and this shortfall could only be made up by coming down hard on small and medium-sized businesses. Easier targets, who pay up fast when a little brown envelope lands on the mat.

The revolving door between tax inspectors and the big four accountancy firms meant the rules on tax were now being written by people who six months later would be working for an accountancy firm, looking after a big corporate account and advising them on how to get around the very rules that they had written.

When the Cayman Islands Monetary Authority (CIMA) was created in 1997 to police wrongdoings and investigate the criminal behaviour of accountants and lawyers, it was not Whitehall or the Bank of England who drafted the limits of its powers, but Maples and Calder, the biggest law firm on Cayman. They wrote the rules on how to police themselves.[13]

Is it any surprise that the island's global clients, Google, Facebook, Starbucks and Amazon are being asked to decide for themselves what tax they should be paying? No one else is going to. Ever since John Cumber was called into the Foreign Office and shown a circle on a map, the Cayman Islands waited twenty years to become useful to big business. But when they did, they became indispensable.

SHADOWS BENEATH THE WATER

When I arrive on Grand Cayman, it is very different from the island John Cumber landed on half a century ago. Today, the place feels like an affluent suburb of Florida. Low-rise buildings run along the main road that provides the island's spine: white sandy beaches and turquoise ocean on either side. Mega-cruise ships from Miami arrive daily, dispatching thousands of tourists who buy T-shirts and conch shells with 'I Love Cayman' written on them, before re-boarding their ship for a cocktail.

To look at the place, you would not think it was a hub of global finance. There are no gleaming glass towers, like London or Wall Street, but that is the point. Wealth here is hidden. Cayman has capital assets of a trillion dollars, well over 1,500 times Cayman's domestic economy. This single five-mile bar of sand in the ocean has more external assets than Japan, Canada or Italy. It is the number-one legal domicile of choice for the hedge fund industry (sixty per cent of the world's hedge fund managers operate from this one stretch of sand). It is also the number-one destination for asset-backed securities and collateralised debt obligations across the globe.[14]

In other words, Cayman holds all the profits, and all the debt, too, housed in anonymous low-rise banks and offices staffed by casually dressed accountants in Bermuda shorts and flip-flops, who avoid driving showy Ferraris in favour of a Toyota Prius. The thousands of corporations that are registered in Cayman – everyone from IKEA to HSBC, Starbucks to Vodafone, Pepsi to Disney – have no visible presence. Nothing.

I know, because the first thing I did was to look. There is, however, one building tucked away at the end of the beach in which more than twenty thousand companies are registered. In

2008, President Obama singled out Ugland House as 'either the biggest building in the world or the biggest tax scam in the world.'

There are no big gates or security guards. It is all hidden in plain sight. I walk up to the glass doors to have a look inside. A relaxed doorman eventually saunters out to see who I am. 'I wonder if I could have a look inside?'

I am politely told to leave the property, but not before looking though the darkened windows. A lot of desks, but not a single person from those twenty thousand companies sitting at any of them. Cayman euphemistically calls itself a 'financial centre', but this really means it is a giant deposit box with palm trees. A place to hold on to unimaginable sums of money, away from the prying eyes of the world.

It is very strange they have even let me in. After decades of secrecy, including a law forbidding journalists from even asking questions, let alone investigating anything, suddenly they want to open up and show they have nothing to hide. Why? The answer is simple, and it is all to do with business.

Because the race is now on between Western governments to offer the lowest corporation tax, Cayman faces fierce competition. Everyone is vying for attention by offering ever cleverer and more complex financial 'arrangements'. And looking even remotely shady to these global companies no longer cuts it. Cayman is looking to stay ahead of the game by opening up and showing the world it is legit. In effect, laundering its own name.

Cayman comes in at number five on the financial secrecy index of least transparent tax havens.[15] Secrecy that takes the form of opaque financial structures enabling scams like Enron and Parmalat to happen.

Yet Cayman is only number five. That is less secretive than Switzerland (number one) or Singapore (number two). By stealing a march on their competitors by opening up, Cayman hopes to win their business. In 2009, the IMF said the greatest danger to Cayman's future as a tax haven was not governmental interference or even outside investigation, but 'reputational risk' – continuing to look dirty.

But if you ask Caymanians why they think their islands have such a bad reputation, it is not industrial tax avoidance or Pablo Escobar that is mentioned, but a 1993 movie starring Tom Cruise. I thought this was a joke until I had to stop counting how many times people kept mentioning it.

The Firm tells the story of a sharp attorney working for a law firm who comes to realise his bosses are laundering money for the mafia through guess where. *The Firm* cemented a reputation that Caymanians say was unfair to begin with. Now they want to clean the slate. Hence my invite. Unfortunately, the week does not start well on the PR front. Google are caught siphoning eighty per cent of their profits through tax havens. Apple admit to moving $74 billion offshore, paying two per cent tax. I decide it is best to cough and not mention these headlines.

I am dutifully introduced to the island's Governor, a polite woman in a pink hat who lives in a big colonial house, with whom I have tea. I am introduced to the elected Premier, a polite if brusque man who clearly wishes he was not talking to me, and to various prominent business people, including John Cumber's grandson, who are all unfailingly charming. The message is clear: we are an open book, confident in the knowledge I will not find anything.

The place is a cross between a Caribbean island and Britain in the 1950s. I am given free rein to wander about asking anyone anything I want, as long as it is not about the corporations registering their profits here. I find out from a police officer that stealing a coconut from a neighbour's garden can result in a prison sentence. He doesn't explain why he is not downtown arresting the accountants responsible for laundering over a hundred million dollars for FIFA officials, and it seems rude to ask.

Once a year, the islanders put on ceremonial garb for the

annual Queen's birthday parade, involving a brass band and prize giving. It is like being in a country fête in Somerset. Accountants turn out to the Governor's garden party, where they eat cucumber sandwiches in a heat of 100 degrees.

I ask one of the accountants at the garden party about the FIFA revelations and he smiles. 'It's a bit old school, isn't it?' He is right. Nowadays, Cayman is simply the way business is done, and there is no need to go the criminal route, when the legal options for hiding money are so infinite. Yet criminality still takes place, and the world shrugs its shoulders.[16]

In the noughties, US, Dutch and British companies took advantage of Cayman because their governments enabled them to use it as a direct investment conduit, but now Brazil and China do the same. In 2000, accountancy firm PricewaterhouseCoopers devised a legal 'innovation' for Chinese corporations to list publicly abroad, so getting access to foreign capital and circumventing China's restrictions on foreign investments. It is called a VIE (Variable Interest Entity), a variation on the holding company. And their number-one target was the US.

In 2014, Chinese e-commerce giant Alibaba raised a record $25 billion with its initial public offering (IPO) in the US, using PricewaterhouseCoopers' holding company innovation. The ICIJ (International Consortium of Investigative Journalists) have revealed that certain wealthy relatives of China's Communist Party elite also use VIEs to create shell companies in tax havens.[17]

Cayman is known to the world for tax avoidance, but its real function lies many layers beneath clever accountancy. And it is a big one. Cayman's biggest secret is that it provides the mechanism for foreign companies to buy up US companies and industrial infrastructure, without appearing to be foreign. And the magic euphemism is 'portfolio investment'.

In 2015, Cayman reported 'portfolio investment' assets to the IMF of $61 billion. Jan Fichtner at the University of Amsterdam drilled into the figures and put the real assets at $2,574 billion

– forty-two times greater than reported. This huge discrepancy is down to one thing: reported assets exclude hedge funds. Derived liabilities (the real figures) do not. Hedge funds are at the absolute heart of below-the-radar Cayman (which explains why sixty per cent of the world's hedge funds operate here).

And their primary role is to buy up America, without America realising. On the face of it, the true 'nationality' of any portfolio investment is impossible to establish, because investment instruments cross-multiply jurisdictions, sometimes over dozens of countries. The only way to understand how they actually work is to look at two basic numbers: the money going in, and the money coming out.

This is called 'inward' and 'outward' investment and the biggest discrepancy in these figures on Cayman is with Japan: in 2015, $51 billion in, and $558 billion out. But mysteriously, less than a tenth of the Japanese portfolio investment of over half a trillion dollars went back to Japan.

Why? Because it was used in the US to make below-the-radar deals. Hong Kong and Japanese investors use Cayman as a conduit for portfolio investment into the huge American equity market. Cayman acts as a giant hedge, protecting Japanese investors buying into the US from being found out.

But these portfolio investments are also being used to hoover up opportunities in emerging markets, and politically sensitive China. Cayman is a hub for the buying and selling of the globe. Cayman 'intersects', Fichtner says, 'the nexus between Pax Americana, the Anglo alliance and Greater China sub-network.' Five countries alone are responsible for ninety per cent of Cayman's portfolio investment: the USA ($1,206 billion), Japan ($558 billion), Hong Kong ($343 billion), the UK ($91 billion) and Luxembourg ($83 billion). But don't be fooled by the numbers. The companies that appear to operate through these countries do not. These jurisdictions are merely convenient temporary vehicles, like Cayman, till a better offer comes along.

And post-Brexit, post-Trump, two have come along. Britain

has given up making anything. The former Chancellor of the Exchequer, George Osborne, said in February 2017 that the economy per se is clearly 'no longer a priority' for the government. By this, he means that low tax has become the sole plank of economic survival in a post-Brexit world. Once we were a manufacturing economy. Then we became a service economy. Now we are a tax haven.

In the US, Trump faces two ways. Historically low interest rates provide a once-in-a-generation opportunity to rebuild the infrastructure of America *à la* Roosevelt's New Deal. But the temptation to provide the lowest taxes on earth to corporations in Trump's America and out-Cayman the Cayman Islands might prove too tempting to resist. Meanwhile the infrastructure of America is indeed being rebuilt. Just by the Chinese.

In 2016, two thousand jobs were created by Fuyao Glass in Moraine, Ohio. Eight years earlier, on 23 December 2008, the last General Motors truck rolled off the production line at GM's factory in Moraine. The very same factory now being resurrected by Fuyao Glass. When that last truck rolled out two days before Christmas, Moraine seemed finished as a town. The closure of the GM plant symbolised the end of American manufacturing. The rust belt was not simply a term for the death of the heartland of America, but shorthand for the end of the US as a global superpower.

Yet eight years on, the jobs are back. Moraine is heartland Trump-country, yet those very same voters applaud the return of jobs through the Chinese glass giant. And there is no contradiction in their minds in holding both positions.

If Cayman becomes the instrument by which Chinese and Japanese companies are able to buy up America by stealth, but return manufacturing jobs in the process, then a simplistic moral position on the role of tax havens and the 'patriotism' of job creation becomes more difficult to sustain.

Railing against offshore is like railing at the ocean. It is there, and there is no changing it. Beneath that blue ocean, dark shapes move – the corporations waiting to come in. What started as a relatively simple mechanism for tax avoidance on a sand bar has mutated into an impossibly complex financial mechanism, with the moral complexities to go with it.

Offshore is how the world works, and this total global system operates beyond the control of any one government.

'How does Cayman benefit the British public?' I asked the Governor of Cayman on my final day there. 'I'm sorry, I don't . . . ,' she was lost for words. 'I'm going to have to think . . .' The Governor consulted with her press officer, struggling to find the right answer. It had clearly never occurred to her that such a childishly simple question would ever be asked.

It was a tough one to answer. How does Cayman in any way benefit Britain, taking billions of pounds in tax revenue out of the pocket of government and thus contributing directly to the under-resourcing of basic services.

I have an answer, even if she didn't. Cayman has shown us the way forward. If you reduce income tax to nothing you need to tax everything else. A packet of fish fingers costs £5. A monthly rent for a corrugated shack is more than a three-storey house in central London.[18] What you save on direct tax, you pay in indirect taxes. The only people who can afford these massively hiked indirect taxes are the wealthiest, for whom the cost of daily living is irrelevant. For everyone else, life is harder, so greater inequality is the price.

I asked the Governor one more question. 'Could Cayman be shut down?' She looked shocked. 'What do you mean?' Could the British government shut you down? 'Good God, no. Cayman is an independent state.'

I put the same question to the Premier. 'Ultimate sovereignty,' he told me, 'lies in London, with the British government.'

So, no one is responsible. Cayman operates in a very convenient no-man's-land, outside the remit of anyone. It is truly offshore in the way the entire banking system is offshore: operating somewhere out there in the middle of the sea, where dark shapes swim beneath the surface.

CHAPTER FOUR
WEALTH: INEQUALITY AS A BUSINESS OPPORTUNITY

Take a golf buggy that can carry eight people. Then put the eight wealthiest people on earth on that buggy. You would have Mexican telecoms mogul Carlos Slim (worth $50 billion) riding up front. Next to him, Bill Gates ($75 billion). On the middle seats, Zara founder Amancio Ortega ($67 billion), Warren Buffet ($60.8 billion) and Jeff Bezos of Amazon ($45.2 billion). A row back, Facebook's Mark Zuckerberg ($44.6 billion) and Oracle's Larry Ellison ($43.6 billion), with Michael Bloomberg (a mere $40 billion) in the bucket seat at the back.

These eight people now own the equivalent of fifty per cent of the planet's wealth with a combined worth of $426 billion. Eight people with as much money as 3.75 billion people, who also happen to be the poorest fifty per cent of the earth's population.[1]

This polarisation of global wealth has become human global warming. A seismic, irreversible process, widening and deepening like a tectonic fissure. Should we care? Absolute global poverty is reducing and, as the Institute of Economic Affairs argues, the widening gap is the price you pay for the planet as a whole getting richer.[2] Whether you think it matters or not, the fact is that widening inequality is happening and to paraphrase Arnold Schwarzenegger, it doesn't give a damn whether you believe in it or not.[3]

But in March 2006, long before inequality was on the radar or viewed as a disaster, a group of analysts saw the whole thing coming and did something quite mind-blowing: they decided to treat coming global inequality as a business opportunity to be exploited, and widened.

These men were going to figure out how to make money from the greatest divergence in history and in so doing, turbocharge inequality and make it a self-fulfilling prophecy. If the chasm between rich and poor was a seismic widening problem, that meant it was also a gift-horse like no other. Before 'the 99% and the 1%' became a slogan on the banners at Occupy, they had already coined the term in a boardroom.

THE HOURGLASS

Tobias Levkovitch is a very smart man. He meets me in his vast office overlooking the Hudson River on the forty-ninth floor of the world's fourth-largest bank, Citigroup, where he also happens to run 'Global Strategy'. He tells me about a book he loves: *The Leviathan* by Thomas Hobbes. A political treatise based on the premise that human beings will do whatever they can get away with, unless strong rules prevent them from doing it.

When not reading seventeenth-century political philosophy, Tobias likes to think about the world deeply, differently and a lot. And in 2006, Tobias held in his pocket a photograph of the future which, if he chose to share it with his clients, was going to make them a lot of money. A very large amount indeed.

Tobias is one of the most important bankers on earth: he is responsible for identifying the plate-tectonic shifts in the way the global economy is moving, and advising Citigroup and Wall Street to invest not merely millions or billions, but trillions of dollars in whatever he thinks is going to happen next.

In 2006, Tobias spotted something big. Three Citigroup colleagues – Ajay Kapur, Niall Macleod and Narendra Singh –

had written an internal equity strategy report entitled 'Revisiting Plutonomy: The Rich Are Getting Richer'.[4] In it they argued that global wealth was polarising, not merely a little or a lot, but in an unfathomable way that would eclipse anything seen in history.

'We talk about the one per cent, but to get technical, we're actually talking the zero-point-one per cent,' Tobias tells me. 'We've always had the haves and have-nots, but now we would have the haves, the have-nots and the have-yachts.'

Tobias predicted – to the incredulity of his colleagues – that by 2015, then a decade away, the one hundred richest people would own the same as half the world's population. It is actually eight: the guys sitting on the golf buggy.

Tobias dropped his bombshell in 2006 in the very boardroom where I meet him,[5] before a sea of stony-faced men and women in business suits. These people represented the biggest companies on earth: oil, steel, construction and hedge fund giants; food and chemical multinationals; supermarkets; aviation constructors; pharmaceutical companies and car manufacturers; mobile and internet providers on every continent.

'The coming decade will be marked by polarisation and social unrest,' Tobias said. 'A direct consequence of growing economic inequality.' The clients coughed and looked down at their notepads. 'Many will be worried by this. We at the bank worry less.'

I wondered why Tobias said that: 'We at the bank worry less.'

'You can't sit there and say, this doesn't meet everyone's social happiness criteria. I have to deliver results or they're going to take their money and give it to someone else. It's not cynical. It's practical. That is our job. We are supposed to make them money.'

Tobias predicted correctly at that meeting that inequality between different countries in the coming years would lessen as inequality within each country grew, and this was where he gave his corporate clients a chillingly simple analogy: an hourglass.

Every country will come over time, he said, to look like an hourglass. At the top, the super-rich global elite, to whom you will be able to sell Lear Jets and Bentleys. At the bottom, the global poor, to whom there will be unimaginable new opportunities to sell poverty products: payday loans, zero-hour contracts, high-interest credit. As stress increases for the poor, gambling and alcohol will once again become boom industries. Pound shops and discounting will become huge, as people fail to make ends meet.

It was a breathtaking vision, but I was intrigued by the hourglass. What was the deal with the tapered bit in the middle? 'Oh, that's the middle class. They will be squeezed out of existence. They will cease to have any purchasing power, and thus be over as an investment opportunity,' Tobias told me cheerily.

In fact, the middle class would be subsumed into the lumpen poor. They would sink into the lower globe of the hourglass, but continue to live for a period of time beyond their means, desperately clinging on to the tropes of being middle class (such as foreign holidays or a new car). Delusions of status.

To put it in context, an average Lamborghini costs £180,000 – the same price as the average British house. If you were one of Citigroup's clients faced with a dissolving middle class, would you flog a Lamborghini to the one per cent, who see £180,000 as loose change, or become a mega-landlord owning ten thousand slum properties? Both, but you would not bother with the middle class.

In Tobias's long-term view, the bottom orb of the hourglass would come to represent one giant, new global class: all of us, including the dissolved middle class. What we now know as the ninety-nine per cent, living one payday away from broke. The so-called 'precariat'.

As Tobias painted this brave new world to Citigroup's clients, he noticed something in the room. Total silence. 'You could have heard a pin drop.' At first Tobias thought this might simply be shock at the apocalyptic future he was predicting. 'It must be true if Citigroup are saying it, right?' But then he realised it was something else. There was an expression of awe on their faces as it began to dawn just how much money there was to be made.

In the two years between the Citigroup presentation and the 2008 crash, the companies in the room diversified their portfolios exactly as Citigroup advised, focusing on businesses at both ends of the hourglass: high-end luxury for the rich and poverty products for the poor.

But it was only when the crash happened that things really took off for Citigroup's clients. Tobias's prediction had come true faster than anyone could have dreamt.

THE *HUNGER GAMES* FOR REAL

The people on my golf buggy all think inequality is terrible. They say so all the time, as do the heads of the IMF, the World Bank, the Bank of England, the Fed and every other financial institution that spent the last twenty years putting in place the mechanisms that allowed inequality to open up like a chasm.

In 2015, I interviewed French economist Thomas Piketty, the author of *Capital in the Twenty-First Century*, who believes that selling to the rich and poor spheres of the hourglass is merely a by-product of inequality; the underlying process that drives its perpetuation is wealth extraction from the poorest to the wealthiest.

This, Piketty argues, is uniquely dangerous for society as a whole, because it tests society's reason for existing. It pushes the contract of shared rules to the edge, which is when society begins to break down. So, what can be done? Piketty shrugged his shoulders. 'Perhaps retool the IMF, so it has transnational jurisdiction to prevent multinationals escaping their legal obligations.' A kind of International Task Force like *Thunderbirds*, able to swoop on unsuspecting corporations and slapping them with a fine for tax avoidance. In short, as likely as wooden puppets saving the world.

Inequality is here to stay and we now live daily and acceptingly with its extremes. In London, it is possible to get a facial in a Knightsbridge beauty salon with a throwaway liquid gold mask and a caviar massage. A top-of-the-hourglass product. Treatments cost up to £30,000. Some clients come three or four times a month. The staff who apply the gold mask and caviar massage are sometimes on, or just above, the minimum wage. If they need a payday loan to make ends meet, they are using a poverty product from the bottom of the hourglass.

In Newham, East London, a group of single mums living in secure housing were evicted by the council in 2015 in order to make way for luxury flats.[6] When they went to see the mayor, they were told, 'If you can't afford to live in Newham, you can't afford to live in Newham. What do you want me to do about it?'[7] They refused to leave and the police were called, yet the officers themselves baulked at the idea of forcibly removing women and children who had committed no crime. In the stand-off, the single mums began squatting in a disused community centre.

Less than a stone's throw from the centre, luxury glass-fronted flats have risen up, standing largely empty because they were bought off-plan by foreign investors to tie up huge amounts of surplus capital. These investors do not even see them as flats, but 'security boxes'. The mums watched these empty mausoleums of wealth being constructed as the power and water were cut from their own properties, forcing them out. They could see right into the luxury flats from their squatted building, but from the luxury flats you see only sweeping panoramic views across London, in which the grittiness of the unfolding poverty below is just part of the brutalist, urban picaresque.

This cohabitation of the two orbs of the hourglass is nothing new. In 1845, Frederick Engels wrote about Victorian Manchester in his *Condition of the Working Class in England*: 'The members of the money aristocracy can take the shortest road through the middle of laboring districts . . . without ever seeing they are in the midst of grimy misery.'[8] In Mike Davis's *Planet of Slums*, the eradication of the poor from view is catalogued across the globe – from slum clearances in Lagos to the displacement of 1.5

million people in Shanghai to make way for a reskinned city of glittering wealth.[9]

Extreme divergence is happening everywhere fast, but in London, it is acutely visible. If London were a separate country, it would be the seventh richest in the world. Yet twenty-eight per cent of Londoners live officially in poverty, and two-thirds are 'just managing' to survive. There have been £80 billion in austerity cuts since the 2008 crash – by neat coincidence, the same amount given to bankers in bonuses.[10]

For most people in Britain, wages have stagnated for ten years and remain at pre-crash levels. The average family earn £429 a week, as they did in 2006. But for the richest thousand people, their pay has more than doubled over the same period: from £200 billion to £500 billion.[11]

As the world's super-rich poured into London post the 2008 banking crisis to take advantage of 'quantitative easing' (money printed to save the banks, ninety-five per cent of which actually went directly to the bubble of the one-per-cent richest),[12] the fear for London was that it would become 'socially cleansed' of the poor.

London would become two cities. A mega-sprawl like Mexico City, Cape Town, Shanghai, Lagos, Los Angeles, or Capitol in *The Hunger Games*: an inner sanctum populated by the super-rich, living a gilded life of darkly lit exclusive restaurants, weekends in Monaco on the superyacht, skiing in Gstaad, shopping in Dubai for $100,000 handbags, and perpetual private-jet ('PJ') transit. This roped-off state of 'Richistan'[13] floats above and beyond the masses like a fluffy champagne cloud, but is uniformly identifiable as the same place, with the same brands and schedule, wherever you are on the planet.

And the other half of the city is an outer sprawl of the massed poor, bussed in to service these new masters. People living one payday away from destitution and so stressed by this precariousness, they die ten years before the rich. The *Hunger Games* analogy is serious. In 2014, a report into global inequality part-funded by NASA's Goddard Center concluded that a 'Hunger Games scenario of inequality is likely on current trends by 2030'.[14]

One can already see social cleansing in operation in every crevice of London. I live in the centre, and my local mini-super-market is a microcosm of inequality. Seventy-five per cent of the customers are fast-rising career people from Europe and the US in their mid-twenties and early thirties working for big corporations such as Google, banks in the City, or digital companies clustered round 'Silicon Roundabout'. They come into the mini-mart wearing hoodies and tracksuit bottoms after a run, buy some milk or quinoa salad, and leave.

There are eight staff members, who work twelve-hour shifts, employed on zero-hour contracts. They are similar in age to the customers, but their lives are very different. Three of them live at least a ninety-minute journey from the minimart. One lives in Essex; another in Luton – thirty miles away. They cannot afford to rent in central London, but cannot afford to give up their job either. They travel so far to and from work that they earn barely anything.

Yet my minimart is actually an aberration. In 2015, Hannah Aldridge and Tom MacInnes of the New Policy Institute analysed population movement in London in the wake of cuts to housing benefit and discovered something unexpected.[15]

The *Hunger Games* two-city scenario understates what is happening. The reality is a single city in which the rich and poor coexist in the same space, but are invisible to each other. The poor do not aggravate the rich, but defer to them – in public spaces and wherever they intersect (like my minimart). The poor have become transparent and instead of interacting, the rich power-blank any awkward situation. It is *The Hunger Games* with workers from the districts moving like ghosts amongst the rich.

So why aren't the poor moving out, if they cannot afford to live in London? Moving means destroying everything. Key to surviving on a low income with highly precarious work is a social network of friends and family upon whom you can rely, allowing you to juggle these precarious jobs. This cannot easily be recreated elsewhere. Neither can cobbled-together childcare, hard-won school places, nor the cluster of casual, local low-paid jobs that together make up a barely survivable income. The 'working poor' cannot afford to leave.

While better-paid people in offices hot desk, the working poor 'hot bed'. This means sharing one room and sleeping in shifts in the same bed. A childcare worker whom I met shift-slept in the same bed with another woman working nights. They each had their own sheets, and took eight-hour shifts. Childcare worker: 10 p.m. – 6 a.m.; Woman Working Nights: 6 a.m. – 2 p.m. The maths would suggest they under-utilised the potential of the bed by failing to monetise between 2 p.m. and 10 p.m. Perhaps there was a third woman they didn't tell me about.

The staff at my minimart staff are atypical. They moved out. The majority of the working poor living in London have to cut back on food and heating to meet the rent. They are trapped, holding on to a rising balloon of costs, but unable to move for fear it will be worse elsewhere. And they are growing exponentially in numbers in the centre of London, at the very moment they cannot afford to live there. As Aldridge and MacInnes conclude, the poor are being absorbed to service an insatiable machine of wealth, and it is a symbiotic relationship.

Notice how freely and unashamedly I use the words 'rich' and 'poor'. Thirty years ago, both were derogatory terms. No one worries about that anymore. Becoming rich is not shaming. It is not a term of abuse as it once was on the left. It is now a universal aspiration. And with rising household debt and low wages, the fear that poverty could tap you on the shoulder at any moment is real.

As absolute global wealth rises (very poor countries becoming slightly less poor and thus categorised as richer), widening inequality within each country is exploding, and the two are intertwined.

In *The Great Convergence*, Richard Baldwin at Harvard argues that a combination of free-flowing information technology and low globalised labour costs is making countries more equal: poorer countries growing as the richer ones stagnate, until eventually we are all the same. Between 1820 and 1990, the share of the world's income going to wealthy countries soared from twenty per cent to almost seventy per cent. But in the last twenty-five years, that share has fallen back dramatically to where it was in 1900.[16]

Countries across the world, regardless of their starting-gun wealth, are all in a race to become the same: Malawi, Spain, the United States, the UK, Uzbekistan. We are all morphing inexorably into the same kind of country with the same basic social stratification, defined by yawning divergence. We are all becoming equally unequal.

WHO STOLE THE PARACHUTE?

In 2008, the banks crashed. But the bail-out went to an unexpected place. Quantitative Easing (QE) – the printing of money by government – designed to keep mortgages paid and small businesses afloat, vanished. So what happened? I ask Tobias Levkovitch. 'Ninety-five per cent of quantitative easing, sold as bailing out the whole economy, went to the top of the hourglass.' Straight to the super-rich and the banks – the very people who had created the need for a bail-out pocketed the bail-out.

QE enabled the one per cent to be able to invest in the poverty products from the hourglass that would widen inequality still further, and the single thing that tied all these poverty products together – extended loans on cars, furniture, holidays, property, and bridging-loans to cover heating and food bills – was debt.

'Debt is really the key to the whole thing,' according to LSE economist David Graeber. 'The finance industry and the debt industry are really the same thing. To a large extent, "finance" really just means "other people's debts". They're simply trading our debts with each other.'[17]

The pre-crash diversification of Citigroup's companies into brands that could exploit the hourglass fuelled inequality. QE took it into orbit. And QE was the very thing sold to us as the solution. The crash affected the one per cent profoundly, just as it did everyone else. They became profoundly richer.

Economist Anatole Kaletsky of the Institute for New Economic Thinking says QE was a fork in the road, and puts forward an alternate reality.[18] Had QE not gone to the banks but to everyone else in the form of a one-off payment, every household in Britain and the US would have received a cheque on their mat for £25,000 ($30,600). This money would have been spent on holidays, fridges and cars, rebooting consumerism and a Keynesian boom. But it did not happen – instead QE went to the top of the hourglass and fuelled inequality.

Cash-bombing the crisis was never on the cards, even though it was endorsed by economists across the political spectrum from neo-liberal thinkers such as Deidre McClosky to Keynesians like Kaletsky. Giving cash directly to people was deemed outrageous. No one would believe it was a sensible idea, even if it was. There was however a politically expedient solution everyone would get: more debt, which – David Graeber argues – was the plan all along.[19]

'Our indebtedness, our addiction and entrapment by debt, fuelled London and New York as finance centres in the wake of the crash. It was at the heart of the recovery of finance, and our debt was the engine. So what you see after the crash are some fairly intentional government policies which are designed to guarantee most people are in debt.' Household debt in Britain now stands at a record £350 billion.

Tobias Levkovitch's hourglass prediction back in 2005 is now a reality. But global inequality is about to go up several notches. Tobias admits even he could not have predicted some of the opportunities created at either end of the hourglass: pure Canadian oxygen pumped into super-rich apartments in Shanghai, or a debt collector in Newcastle who will extend your payment deadline in exchange for information on neighbours committing benefit fraud.

Citigroup's report was a prophetic document that turned the prophecy of inequality into reality. No one outside that boardroom on the forty-ninth floor of Citigroup knew it was coming, but the deals it enabled were going to change the lives of millions of people walking the streets below.

WHY THE MIDDLE CLASS MATTER

One of the research papers mentioned in the footnotes of the Citigroup report was by a then unknown post-graduate student at the London School of Economics called Thomas Piketty, who was writing a dissertation on inequality – the dissertation that ten years later became *Capital in the Twenty-First Century*.

I asked Piketty, now the world's most celebrated economist, about the hourglass and the part of it that is fast tapering to extinction – the middle class.[20] Why does it matter that the middle class will cease to exist?

'The middle class is very important for the economy because they have been the means by which it's been possible to develop mass consumption and mass investment in construction.' The opportunity to become middle class in the 1950s and 1960s was what drove greater equality and distributed wealth evenly throughout society, reaching a high watermark in 1976. The year, according to opinion polls, when Britain was happiest.

'But the middle class has begun to shrink in the last twenty years,' Piketty says. 'And this is a major threat to democracies if it continues shrinking in the coming decades.'

Piketty thinks the death of the middle class will leave society as a whole with no way back. Between 1945 and 1978, wealth was more evenly distributed throughout society than at any other time in history. A thirty-year aberration of equality sandwiched between two periods of huge inequality: the 1930s and now.

And the reason for this was that the middle class had the means to own private property. Starting in the 1930s, interrupted by the war, but then vastly expanding in the 1950s, as a huge building programme by successive Labour and Conservative governments enabled millions of people to buy their own homes for the first time. It was the dream my immigrant grandfather followed as he moved out of the poverty of Kentish Town to the clean air and neatly trimmed hedges of suburbia.

Yet since 1996, that dream has dissolved as home ownership reversed. Widening inequality has coincided with the stagnation of wages and the consequent end of access by the young to the property ladder. If my grandparents aged twenty-five were looking to buy now, they would be stuck in the slums, lucky to even cobble a monthly rent together.

'Are we going to continue in the direction of a shrinking middle class?' Piketty asks. 'It's difficult to know how far this will go. What we know for sure is that in recent years, what we've observed in Britain and other countries is that the wealth of the top wealth holders – billionaires – is rising much faster than average wealth and much faster than the size of the economy. You can see that if this continues for several decades more, the share going to the middle class will decline.'

In years to come, renting – not ownership – will become the norm. The family that rents is £561,000 worse off over its lifetime than one that buys (it is £1.36 million worse off in London). In 2013, rents were going up five times faster than salaries.[21]

And this will be make it virtually impossible to reverse inequality, because the middle class (and those aspiring to become middle class) will have lost their primary means of wealth accumulation. The reason there will be no going back for us as a society is because the hourglass will be structurally entrenched.

'How unequal will we become?' Piketty asks. 'On these trends, it looks pretty frightening.' But if you disenfranchise the middle class, you are also dealing with a highly combustible force. A contented middle class do nothing, but if they are either scared for their future security or growing greedy on a rising economic tide, they will drive revolution.

In Russia in 1917, an impatient and newly emboldened bourgeoisie drove the provisional government that replaced the Tsar, which in turn was overthrown by the Bolsheviks. In Paris in 1968, middle-class intellectuals and organised labour nearly toppled President Charles de Gaulle (but famously didn't). In both cases, a disgruntled if ambivalent middle class was at the heart of the mobilisation.

Nick Hanuer lives in Seattle and was one of the first investors in Amazon. He is now worth $6 billion, and sees the hollowing of the middle class in the new hourglass model of society as a threat to capitalism. 'Capitalism, the greatest economic system ever created, does need some inequality, just like plants do need some water to grow. But in precisely the same way that too much water kills plants, too much inequality kills capitalism by drowning the middle class.'

Hanuer stands in a modest office with a spectacular view of Puget Sound, watching sailing boats darting across the water. 'In the middle ages, inequality was not a problem. You grew up expecting the world to be unequal. He's a peasant. He's a king. That's how it works. But when you live in a modern capitalist culture that encourages everyone to have more and to believe you can have it, then equality becomes a much bigger problem. You can't have what other people have and this is the cause of discontent. Capitalism has bred resentment, and the equality of opportunity it promised hasn't happened.'[22]

Hanuer has a personal stake. He is worried that when this happens, the massed ranks at the bottom of the hourglass will be coming for him. 'Are the pitchforks coming? Maybe not tomorrow, but for sure they will come. You show me a highly unequal society and I will show you either a revolution or a one-party state.'

NO ONE WOULD REMEMBER THE GOOD SAMARITAN IF HE'D ONLY HAD GOOD INTENTIONS. HE HAD MONEY AS WELL.

In 2007 the Ministry of Defence was worried, and asked Rear Admiral Chris Parry to write a ninety-page report on what a military response should be to mass civil disobedience.[23] The MoD had identified growing inequality as the fuel that would light the fire. In 2011, it came true as Britain's major cities erupted in the worst rioting since the 1980s. The MoD had gazed into a crystal ball and been right, just as Citibank had been.

I met Rear Admiral Parry in Haringey, North London, where some of the fiercest rioting took place, and asked him what his report had predicted. 'That this was waiting to happen. When enough people say "I don't have a stake in society", they will bust out. They'll reject capitalism and the market, and take action into their own hands.' Parry and the MoD's findings were not welcome in Whitehall, who were not interested in army people talking like angst-ridden social workers. The army were ignored, and only called upon by government when the riots actually started.

The deal Tobias Levkovitch did with Citigroup's corporate clients in 2006 may have fuelled the inequality the MoD report predicted would ignite civil disobedience. Citigroup did not create it. But the chasm of inequality we face today has a founding stone, and 6 January 1980 at 12 p.m. was when it was laid, in a two-minute section of a forty-six-minute interview.

A deal had been just struck between Margaret Thatcher and the British electorate, and they were about to find out what this deal meant. The newly elected Prime Minister sat down for her first ever interview as premier with *Weekend World* presenter Brian Walden,[24] the sharpest political journalist of his time and as it would turn out, the most prophetic.

Mrs Thatcher's government were convinced that the solution to the recession they faced was to lower taxes dramatically for the richest one per cent. A strategy that depended for its success on wealth trickling down to the rest of society – as Arthur Laffer had predicted with his curve drawn on a napkin. But at what price? Walden asked:

Walden: Is the price, Prime Minister, for our economic recovery and prosperity greater inequality in this country?

Thatcher: You will get a more thriving society when people can rise to the limits of their talents, and out of the wealth they create, we shall all be better off.

Walden: So you think a more unequal society is actually better for Britain?

Thatcher: A more opportunity society (sic) that enables you to earn more.

Walden: But that does mean more inequality?

Thatcher: Yes, indeed. If talent and opportunity are unequally distributed, then allowing people to exercise their talent will mean more inequality, but it means you drag up the poor people. No one would remember the Good Samaritan if he'd only had good intentions. He had money as well.

This was the moment when twenty-first-century inequality was conceptualised and the fragmentation of our society became not a by-product, but integral to the plan. Mrs Thatcher was the most visionary prime minister Britain has ever had – her vision was so precise, stark and eviscerating, it was like a beam of light.

So did trickle-down, the theory Arthur Laffer sold to governments on both sides of the Atlantic, actually work? If anyone knows, Nick Hanuer should, one of the billionaires who directly benefited from the policies ushered in by Mrs Thatcher's Good Samaritan speech.

'Trickle-down economics is as old as civilisation. We used to call it Divine Right. It's simply the idea that I matter, and you don't. That what I do is indispensable and what you do is extra.

That's how we keep you in line. The great problem we face in the US and UK is we have formed our economic policy on essentially the idea of Reagan-Thatcherism. That if you make rich people richer, everyone will be better off. It's just not true, it's not how the economy works.'[25]

'Use me as an example. I earn approximately a thousand times more a year than the median wage in the US. But I don't buy a thousand times as much stuff. I own three or four pairs of jeans, a couple of pairs of shoes. I have a big, beautiful house, but I don't have a thousand houses. So no matter how much money I have, I cannot sustain a national economy. Only a robust middle class can do that.'

At Cambridge University, economist Ha-Joon Chang has carried out an extensive comparative study of global inequality. We meet in the library where John Maynard Keynes first lectured on his *General Theory* and William Phillips constructed his famous 'water machine' to show students how money flows through the economy, using pumps, pistons and coloured water.

'In theory, trickle-down is not a stupid idea. But in reality, it has not been borne out. In country after country like the US and UK, investment as a share of national income has fallen. Economic growth has fallen. So where's the proof? The idea that if you give the richest more money, they'll create more jobs and more income for everyone else? It hasn't happened.'[26]

Inequality is bookended by Mrs Thatcher's Samaritan speech at one end and Tobias Levkovitch at Citibank, who put his ear to the ground, heard the earth cracking in half, and told his clients to buy.

Perhaps the pitchforks are not coming for Nick Hanuer and his fellow billionaires quite yet. They may never. But the millennial cohort coming of working age now are the hollowed middle class with a loss of entitlement. They are utopian cynics, working hard and reaping none of the rewards, and as a result are potentially the most combustible force in a generation. Plus they have Facebook to organise on.

The Ministry of Defence predicted this in their 2007 report: 'The middle classes could become a revolutionary class, taking the role envisaged for the proletariat by Marx.' Inequality would mean the middle class would 'unite, using access to knowledge, resources and skill to shape (outcomes) in their own transnational class interest.'[27]

A global precariat conjured by inequality would, according to the MoD, have fathomless potential power. Loss of entitlement + Facebook = X, whatever X turns out to be. As Edmund Burke said in 1777, 'those who have much to hope and nothing to lose will always be more dangerous'[28] than the dispossessed, who were at the bottom of the hourglass to start with. The tapered bit in the middle has the potential to shatter the whole thing.

CHAPTER FIVE
FOOD: OWNING FAT AND THIN

When you walk around a supermarket, what do you see? Walls of highly calorific, intensely processed food, tweaked by chemicals for maximum 'mouth feel' and 'repeat appeal' (food scientist speak for addictiveness). This is what most people eat. Pure science on a plate. The food, in short, that is making us fat.

And next to this? Row upon row of low-fat, light, lean, diet, zero, low-carb, low-cal, sugar-free, 'healthy' options, marketed to the very people made fat by the previous aisle and now desperate to lose weight.

What you see in a supermarket is the entire 360 degrees of obesity in a single glance. The whole panorama of fattening you up and slimming you down, owned by companies that have analysed every angle and money-making opportunity. They have made society fatter – we have not changed metabolism as a race – but they are now also making money from the obesity epidemic.

There is a deep, symbiotic relationship between dieting and obesity. Weight Watchers was bought in 1978 by Heinz, who in turn sold the company in 1999 to investment firm Artal for $735 million. SlimFast was bought in 2000 by Unilever, which owns Ben & Jerry's and Wall's sausages. Jenny Craig was bought by Swiss multinational Nestlé, which also sells chocolate and ice cream. In 2011, Nestlé was listed in the *Fortune* Global 500 as the world's most profitable company.

The story of how fat and thin became intertwined for the purpose of making money is a strange and remarkable one, marked by fierce battles between rivals, bizarre experiments, skewed data and dirty tactics; and in the middle of it all, scientists and businessmen who set out to alter the nature of what we eat. In the process, making deals that changed the shape of the human race.

INVENTING OBESITY AS AN INSURANCE SCAM

Long before we even had a real obesity epidemic, the idea of a weight problem was conjured from thin air. In 1945, a statistician called Louis Dublin at Metropolitan Life Headquarters in New York was on his lunch break. He was down on his numbers and needed to impress his bosses. Dublin began looking at the health premiums being paid by Met Life's customers and realised that it was hugely influenced by their weight. Then he had an idea.

By lowering the threshold weight at which policy holders would move from the 'overweight' to the more health-critical 'obese' category, Dublin discovered that you could create tens of thousands more customers. And tens of thousands of 'normal' people could now be re-categorised as 'overweight'.

These newly 'obese' and 'overweight' customers would pay a higher insurance premium, because the health risks associated with their weight would be deemed greater. Dublin needed a scientific metric by which to make this happen, so he invented BMI (or 'Body Mass Index'). A combination of weight and height. It seemed far more scientific than anything before, but it confused muscle density and fat. According to his BMI reading, Usain Bolt, the world's fastest man, is obese.

Overnight, half the American population were redefined as either overweight or obese and would now have to pay higher premiums. 'It wasn't based on any kind of scientific evidence at all,' according to Joel Guerin, an investigative journalist who has analysed Louis Dublin's methodology. 'Dublin essentially looked at his data and just arbitrarily decided that he would take the desirable weight for people who were aged twenty-five and apply it to everyone.'

Forty years before a real obesity epidemic existed, Dublin had invented one in his lunch hour. Met Life did a deal with grocery stores, doctors' surgeries and supermarkets across America, which began installing weighing machines with the Met Life logo on them. Concerned housewives and businessmen visited their doctors and were assured that, yes, the new BMI calculations did indeed show they were now a danger to themselves. There was a ticking time bomb inside Americans: fat, and it had to be dealt with immediately. Newspapers reported a nationwide fat panic. People with an especially high BMI were told they were at imminent risk of a heart attack or stroke. But help was at hand.

In 1960, the *New York Times* reported on a strange phenomenon sweeping America. Mothers were mixing up their baby's formula milk to drink themselves. They had discovered that a liquid diet made them lose weight. Chemical giant Mead Johnson & Co. spotted a gap in the market and launched Metrecal, the first powdered diet drink.

Johnson's head of marketing, C. Joseph Genster, had come up with the name by blending 'metre' and 'calorie'. Genster then did a deal with celebrity TV dietician Sylvia Schur to front Metrecal.

Like BMI, Metrecal sounded scientific, but it also needed scientific credibility with the public, gained by attaching a trusted name such as Sylvia Schur. But this infant diet industry already had some genuine science under its belt that it was less keen to share with the public.

THE MINNESOTA STARVATION
EXPERIMENTS

Six feet beneath the centre circle of the Minnesota Golden Gophers Football Stadium is a network of underground cells and tunnels. In 1944, as Europe was being gripped by malnutrition, the US government wanted to find out what would happen if America was faced with the same kind of chronic food shortage. They decided to test what occurred to the human body when it was starved.

The esteemed nutritionist Dr Ancel Keys was tasked with experimenting on thirty-six conscientious objectors to monitor the effects of being systematically deprived of food.

During the Second World War, Keys had been responsible for creating the K-ration for soldiers: a highly calorific boost bar and in effect, the first energy snack. In the 1960s, he gained international fame promoting the 'Mediterranean diet'. He appeared on the cover of *Time* magazine and was hailed as the new guru of nutrition. But in 1944, he was working in secret for the US government.

Over a year, Keys kept his human guinea pigs in the underground cells beneath the Minnesota Stadium, limiting their calorie intake to 1,500 a day. Three hundred calories more than the average woman on a diet in the US consumes today. They were given a relentless exercise regime, dropped into tanks of cold water, and forced to stare at food to see how they would respond.

The men quite simply went mad. In their diaries, they obsessed about food, fantasising about meals they would have when it was over. When allowed onto the grass pitch above the cells, some began trying to eat the grass; one of them bit a scientist; another chopped off three of his own fingers with an axe.

But Keys was most amazed by what happened when he began feeding them again. They began getting fat, and fast. Not just regaining their original weight in a matter of weeks, but surpassing their original weight and continuing to gain. Dieting, he realised, made them fat and had altered their metabolism, giving them a propensity to be fat where none had existed before.

Dr Traci Mann works for NASA at the University of Minnesota, studying the physiological effects of dieting on the body, only a stone's throw from where Keys carried out his starvation tests. 'The more and more I look at Keys's findings, the more remarkable I find them.' Keys had provided irrefutable evidence that diets do not work, Mann says. But he had also found that we steadily gain pounds each time we go through the yo-yo cycle of dieting, incrementally becoming fatter over time. Because we do not see this incremental gain, we keep coming back to diets as a quick-fix solution.

This science should have spelt the end of the diet industry before it even started. Instead, it provided the perfect business model. Before the war, diets had existed as fads, but never as a coordinated, multibillion-dollar business. Keys changed all that, giving the diet industry the science it needed to know that there was a returnable business here.

If you buy a car and it does not work, Mann says, you take it back to the dealer and get a new one, but if a diet fails, you tell yourself it is your fault and keep going back. It is the bullet-proof product.

Diets were a licence to print money. When Sylvia Schur did a deal with Johnson to front Metrecal in 1960, Keys was the science underpinning Mead Johnson's amazing new cure for obesity. Diets do not work, which is the very reason that makes them work as a business.

I JUST HAD THOSE TWO WORDS: 'SLIM' AND 'FAST'

Metrecal evolved into something huge, created by New Jersey chemist, Danny Abrahams. Danny grew up above the pharmacy his dad owned and the antiseptic smell is one of his earliest memories. Danny became a chemist himself. Then one morning, everything changed. He woke bolt upright with two words in his head: 'slim' and 'fast'. Those two words were to end up earning Danny $6 billion when he did a deal to sell SlimFast to Unilever.

I meet Danny at his William Randolph Hearst-style castle residence in Florida, where he has a huge superyacht parked on the lagoon – 'I always wanted a boat when I was a kid, now I've got one.'

How did Danny come up with SlimFast? 'I just had those two words. No product. But I figured anything called SlimFast is going to sell.' Abrahams experimented at the development stage with Metrecal-type drinks, but they always wound up tasting chalky and medicinal. So instead he went down the milkshake route. Something all-American that should taste like an indulgence, but minus the calories. Slimming as if by magic.

Danny is now in his eighties, but looks fighting fit, taking me to his gym where he works out in front of me to show how much he can still bench press. He then theatrically takes out a SlimFast milkshake from the fridge and swigs it. 'Damn. Tastes as fine today as the day I came up with it.'

I put it to Danny that not only he, but the entire diet industry has made a fortune essentially peddling a lie. A miracle cure in a bottle. 'No, no, no,' he says, waving me away with his arm. 'Jack. Let me ask you a question. Who's in charge of you, Jack? Huh? You are. No one else. If people blame other factors for failing to lose weight, they're looking in the wrong place. Get on the scales, go to the gym, it's up to you, no one else.'

As I drive away, Danny waves goodbye and shouts: 'Remember Jack, you're in charge of you.'

Is this true when it comes to dieting? Are you 'in charge of you'? The diet industry was created as a conscious business decision to take advantage of a health panic that – at the time – was not real. But now obesity is a real health crisis, the diet industry cannot solve it. And it is not as if people trying to lose weight lack motivation: a few succeed, while the vast majority fail and keep failing. Over ninety-five per cent of dieters are returning dieters. Are these people simply weak-willed, or is something else going on?

Kelly Brownell is Dean of the Sanford School of Public Policy at Duke University, and one of the world's leading epidemiologists in the field of obesity. I put Danny's point to Brownell. 'Of course we are in charge of ourselves, but when it comes to losing weight, it's not quite that simple.' Dieting is like playing poker. We are all handed a different set of genetic cards at birth. If you are starting with a weak hand, you are going to find it harder. The heavier you are when you begin dieting, the weaker you make your hand.

It is what we all know. Some people find it easy, others hard. But when you diet and you are already obese, your weak genetic hand is amplified exponentially. It becomes almost impossible.

There's something else, says Brownell. The body has its own thermostat. Once we go over a certain weight, our thermostat is reprogrammed. To lose weight once we have crossed this tipping point is doubly difficult, because the body's thermostat is fighting even harder against the diet.

The body thinks it is starving and wants to reset itself back to the new, heavier thermostat weight. So the truism that 'in every fat woman there is a thin woman trying to get out' is the exact opposite of the biological truth. In every newly thin woman, there is a fat woman fighting to make herself fat again.

For a planet becoming obese at unprecedented speed, conventional diet products are not the solution. But the message of self-empowerment – you can do it, as Danny Abraham shouted to me – is key to the insulation of the diet industry from criticism. If your diet fails, try again, because you did not try hard enough first time.

SOMETIMES WE WOULD ASK OURSELVES THAT QUESTION: HOW ON EARTH DO WE GET AWAY WITH IT?

In New York, I arrange to meet Richard Samba, the finance director of Weight Watchers. Samba is a jovial man in his sixties with a touch of the Donald Trump about him – luxuriant hair and a relaxed swagger as he wanders over to shake my hand. From 1968, when he joined the company, to 1983 when he left, Samba transformed Weight Watchers from an $8 million a year franchise operation to a $300 million a year global brand.

Weight Watchers was begun around a New Jersey kitchen table in 1963 by Jean Nieditch, a housewife who had lost weight by following some simple commonsense advice she had seen on a poster pinned to the wall of a local clinic run by the New York Health Department: cut out carbs, exercise a bit, and form a support group to keep motivated.

Nieditch started her own support group and quickly became such a polished, inspirational speaker that local entrepreneur Jim Chambers saw business potential in charging to see Jean's motivational talks. Nieditch and Chambers did a deal to go into business together. Jean would do the talking and be the front woman, Chambers would take care of the money.

Chambers had a brilliant idea to exploit Jean's talents nationally: franchise out her inspirational message to thousands of other Jeans across America and charge these franchisee speakers for the privilege. Sign them and the dieters to the brand, and call that brand Weight Watchers.

By the time Richard Samba came on board, the company was America's number-one weight-loss brand, offering not a stark diet, but an entire 'lifestyle' change. What Samba called a 'lifelong commitment' to Weight Watchers, meaning a lifelong commitment to yo-yo dieting.

But how could a multibillion dollar business, now the number-one diet brand in China and India as well as the US and Europe, be constructed on 'lifelong commitment' to statistical failure, as Ancel Keys discovered all those years ago in Minnesota?

Samba smiled and shook his head incredulously. 'Well, you know. Sometimes we would ask ourselves that same question. How on earth do we get away with it?' Richard says they would see mothers bring their daughters, who would in turn bring their daughters when they became mums. Mothers who had spent a lifetime on yo-yo diets would be passing Weight Watchers on generation to generation, like a hereditary disease.

Weight Watchers point to their longevity as proof of their success, but the facts tell a different story. After five years on Weight Watchers, according to the Oxford University statistical research unit, less than sixteen per cent of participants reach their goal weight. That leaves eighty-four per cent who have failed. And yet they still come back for more. Why? 'Of course they come back,' Samba says. 'Because the eighty-four per cent: that's where your business comes from.'

Ancel Keys was right. Diets fail, but for the diet industry this simple fact was all that was needed to turn it into a multibillion dollar business. And the returning customers are that business. When Weight Watchers came to Britain in 1967, Bernice Weston, the UK head of operations told the BBC: 'When it comes to eating, the problem with fat people is they are very stupid.' The diet industry, as Richard Samba says, could not believe their luck.

HOW FOOD BECAME TOBACCO

In the 1940s, Louis Dublin redefined half of America as fat, fifty years before it was. But now obesity is real, there is a new game for the food industry. Denial.

In the 1960s and 1970s, the tobacco industry spent millions of dollars refuting the emerging scientific evidence that smoking caused lung cancer, and now the food industry seeks to do the same with obesity. The difference between cigarettes and food is that you don't need cigarettes to live. Food is not a lifestyle choice but a necessity: we need to eat.

Proving this causal link all hinges on 'satiety': the feeling of fullness. If the science stacks that the food industry did not simply alter the metabolism of the body by creating highly calorific processed food, but did so knowingly in order to short-circuit satiety, then we are in a new ballgame.

Culpability for obesity will move from the individual who ate too much and could not control themselves to the companies that took advantage of that individual's metabolic predisposition – the cards they were dealt – leading them to get fat. Blame will lie squarely at the door of the food industry. According to Kelly Brownell at Duke, the resulting class actions across the globe would make the tobacco industry payouts to thousands of lung-cancer victims seem tiny by comparison. This would be millions of people.

The United Nations have classified obesity as the fastest growing threat to world health in the twenty-first century. In the UK, sixty per cent of us are overweight. In the US, it is seventy-five per cent. Ethiopia, stricken with famine in the 1980s, now faces an obesity crisis. This self-inflicted disease strikes the poor and rich alike: in the United Emirates, the richest five per cent are the fattest. In Brazil and China, obesity has risen in tandem with the growing affluence of the middle class. To eat at McDonalds is an expensive luxury only the metropolitan elite can afford.

The creation of the diet industry was the result of a specific business decision to provide a solution to a health problem long before it actually existed. But once the real epidemic did exist, new opportunities were created for the companies that had made it happen.

THE FIRST OBESE MAN

Up a rickety staircase at the Newarke Houses Museum[1] in Leicester, England, hangs a portrait of Daniel Lambert,[2] painted in 1806. Lambert weighed 53 stone (335 kilograms) and was considered a medical mystery. Too heavy to work, Lambert came up with an ingenious idea: he would charge people a shilling to see him. Lambert was Britain's first documented obese man and made a fortune displaying his body across the country. His portrait shows him at the end of his life: affluent and respected. A celebrated son of Leicester.

Two hundred years on, specially designed vehicles called 'bariatric ambulances' pick up a dozen Daniel Lamberts round his home town of Leicester every week. Fifty-three stone is nothing special for these ambulance crews, it is at the lower end of the weight spectrum with only the 80-stone patient worthy of mention when a shift finishes.

The specially designed ambulance carries an array of bariatric gizmos including a 'spatula' to help with people who have fallen out of bed or, on one occasion for the crew I visited, an obese man jammed between the two walls in his hallway whom they prised free by using the spatula.

As well as the ambulance, there is a convoy of support vehicles including a winch to lift patients onto a reinforced stretcher. In extreme cases, the cost of removing a patient to hospital can be over £100,000. One 62-stone teenager in Britain had to have her home partially demolished to take her to hospital.

But the morbidly obese are not where the heartland of the obesity crisis lies. On average in the UK we are all – every man, woman and child – three stone heavier than we were in the mid-1960s.[3] We have not noticed it happening, but this glacial shift has been mapped by bigger car seats, swimming cubicles, XL trousers dropped to L (L dropped to M). An elasticated nation with an ever-expanding sense of normality.

Why are we so fat? We have not become greedier as a race. We are not, contrary to popular wisdom, less active. A longitudinal study by Professor Terry Wilkin at Plymouth Hospital measured children's physical activity over twelve years and found it the same as fifty years ago. But something has changed: the sheer amount of sugar in our food.

Just as science in the 1940s proved diets do not work, so science in the 1970s began to examine the effect an unprecedented increase in sugar consumption would have on obesity. Unlike the first science, which provided the basis for the diet industry, the science on sugar was ignored.

FOOD - FAT = FOOD + SUGAR = OBESITY

In 1971, Richard Nixon was facing re-election. The Vietnam war was threatening his popularity at home, but equally as big an issue with voters was the soaring cost of food. People demonstrated outside supermarkets with placards. If Nixon was to survive, he needed food prices to go down and that required getting a very powerful lobby on board – the farmers. Nixon appointed Earl Butz, an academic from the farming heartland of Indiana, to broker a compromise. Butz had a radical plan that would transform the food we eat, and ultimately, the shape of the human race.

Butz pushed farmers to farm on a new industrial scale, and one crop in particular: corn. US cattle were fattened by immense increases in production. Burgers got bigger. Fries fried in corn oil became fattier. Corn was now the engine for a massive surge in the quantities of cheaper food being supplied to American supermarkets: everything from cereal to biscuits and flour, as well as myriad new uses for corn. As a result of Butz's free-market reforms, US farmers went almost overnight from smallholders to multimillionaire businessmen with a global market.[4]

Nixon could have used the export of wheat as a Cold War weapon, starving the Soviet Union of corn. But instead, the farmers and the big food producers protected their lucrative export market in the communist bloc. They, not the President of the United States, held the power.

By the mid-1970s, there was a surplus of corn. Butz flew to Japan to look into a strange new scientific innovation: HFCS (high fructose corn syrup), an intensely sweet, gloppy syrup produced from the waste of corn processing, that was also incredibly cheap. HFCS had been discovered in the 1950s, but it was only in the 1970s that a process had been found to harness it for mass production.

HFCS was soon pumped into every conceivable food: pizzas, coleslaw, even meat. It provided that 'just baked' sheen on bread and cakes, made everything sweeter and extended shelf-life from days to years. A silent revolution in the amount of sugar that was going into our bodies began to take place.

In Britain, too, the plate of food on a family table became a scientific experiment – each processed milligram tweaked and sweetened for maximum palatability. The public was oblivious to the changes taking place to the foodstuffs they were putting in their mouths.

But it was one product above all that HFCS was to profoundly alter, which in turn would create obesity: soft drinks.

Hank Cardello is a tall man with a hesitant manner, who greets me with a business-like handshake in a diner in downtown Manhattan. In 1984, Hank was head of global marketing at Coca Cola, which was about to make a momentous decision: to do a deal that would swap sugar for HFCS. As market leader, Coke's decision to endorse corn syrup sent an unequivocal message to the rest of the industry, which quickly followed suit. It was the Papal puff of white smoke that they needed.

At the time, Hank says, there appeared to be 'no downside'. HFCS was two-thirds the price of sugar, and even the huge potential risk of messing with the taste (a slight metallic tang in their first test batches) was a risk worth taking when you looked at the margin. What could go wrong? In 1984, Hank says, 'obesity wasn't even on the radar.'

But another health issue was: heart disease. And since the mid-70s, a fierce debate had raged behind the closed doors of the medical profession over what was causing it. Professor John Yudkin, a researcher at UCL in London, blamed sugar. But there was someone else keen to pin the blame on fat: Ancel Keys, the man behind the Minnesota starvation experiment.

In their fractious arguments, both in public and private, Yudkin began to become isolated. Keys was an internationally renowned nutritionist, a titan in his field, and Yudkin was an outsider with an unorthodox and unpopular view within academia: sugar is not only harmful, but potentially lethal.

Endocrinologist Robert Lustig at San Francisco Hospital believes there was a concerted campaign to discredit Yudkin, because his ideas threatened the bottom line of the sugar industry. Keys did research that aligned far more closely with the direction the food industry was intending to take in the future: to demonise fat and exonerate sugar of blame for heart disease.

Yudkin's colleague at the time, Dr Richard Bruckdorfer at UCL, remembers that 'there was a huge lobby from the industry, particularly from the sugar industry, and Yudkin complained bitterly that they were subverting some of his ideas.' Lustig puts it more simply. Yudkin was 'thrown under the bus'.

Yudkin's ideas were published in a book, *Pure, White and Deadly*.[5] It was a bestseller and became a key text for the growing health-food movement of the 1970s, but it was rubbished in academic circles and by Yudkin's peers.

Yudkin eventually became a pariah: ostracised and forgotten. But according to Lustig, Yudkin had predicted the future by identifying the potential dangers of sugar, not just in relation to heart disease, but in an obesity epidemic. He was silenced, according to Lustig, because too many people had too much at stake for him to be heard.

Ancel Keys, who had spearheaded the fight against Yudkin, was the same Ancel Keys who thirty years earlier had starved conscientious objectors under the Minnesota Stadium and discovered that dieting makes you fat. Keys not only lent his medical credentials to the food industry's defence of sugar, much of his research was funded by the food industry. He was a stakeholder.

And there was more at stake than simply protecting sugar as a commodity. Something new was brewing: an opportunity. The public was starting to get fat and keen to embrace a new product to fight the very obesity epidemic Yudkin had predicted. The food industry had the answer. A product in their research labs ready to fly onto the shelves: a brand-new concept in food called 'low fat'.

THE RATS GET FAT

Low-fat products were an industry dream: a new type of food forged in the panic around heart disease that could now be rolled out to deal with the coming catastrophe of obesity. But there was a problem. 'When you take the fat out of a recipe,' endocrinologist Dr Lustig says, 'food tastes like cardboard, and you need to replace it with something – that something being sugar.'

Overnight, miraculous new products arrived on the shelves that seemed too good to be true. Low-fat yoghurts, spreads, even desserts like Black Forest Gateau. One low-cal biscuit, the oddly named *Ayds*, launched with disastrous timing as the AIDS epidemic unfolded, tasted far sweeter than its full-fat counter-part. And there was a reason: all these magical have-your-cake-and-eat-it foods had had the fat stripped out and replaced with sugar.

Nutritional wisdom in the 1980s became beholden to what food historian Gary Taubs calls 'the low-fat dogma', with sales of this incredible wonder-food rocketing across the globe.

And as low-fat took grip, so too did obesity, rolling like a glacier over the Western world. By the mid-1980s, doctors were being visited by patients who were getting fatter than any patients they had ever seen before. Neither the doctors nor the patients knew why. The food industry began stressing that individuals must be responsible for their own calorie consumption, but even those who exercised and ate low-fat products were gaining weight. Everyone was getting fat and nothing seemed to work.

In 1966, the proportion of people with a BMI of over 30 (classified as obese) was only 1.2 per cent for men and 1.8 per cent for women. By 1989 the figures had risen to 10.6 per cent for men and 14 per cent for women. And no one was joining the dots between the huge increase in sugar consumption and this explosion in obesity.

There was something else going on. The more sugar we ate, the more we wanted and the hungrier we became in the process. Sugar appeared to be a new kind of addiction.

A professor at New York University, Anthony Sclafani, began to investigate. Sclafani was particularly interested in the connection between appetite and weight gain, and began to notice something very strange about his lab rats. When they ate rat food, they put on weight normally. But when they were given processed food from a supermarket – sugared cereal or snacks – they ballooned in a matter of days. Their appetite for sugary foods was insatiable: they carried on eating and could not stop themselves, long after their bodies were physically full.

Sclafani had identified a paradox of obesity: the more you eat, the hungrier you get. Over time, the more sugar in a diet, the more malnourished the body becomes as it is slowly starved of essential nutrients, pushed out by an insatiable desire for sugar. In short, we cannot get enough.

This, Sclafani believed, was unlike any nutritional attack the human body had faced before: a three-pronged assault on the metabolism that alters our metabolism in the process. Sclafani observed his lab rats not only gorging on sugar, but on low-fat products, too. And if he put them on a diet, they got fatter when the diet stopped, exactly as Ancel Keys had observed with conscientious objectors in those cells beneath the Minnesota Football Stadium.

The obese, Sclafani concluded, cross a line of no return. They reprogramme their body thermostat to make weight loss a near-insurmountable challenge. It is like playing poker with that genetic hand of cards, and finding you have a two of clubs.

THE MONICA LEWINSKY BLOW JOB

At San Francisco Hospital, on the same wards that treated the first AIDS patients in the early 1980s, Professor Jean-Marc Schwarz is now trying to understand what is going on inside an obese body. Schwarz studies the precise way in which the major organs metabolise sugar and calls the momentum it builds in the body 'a tsunami'.

The effect this has on our primary organs is only now being understood. Around the liver, it coalesces as fat, leading to type-2 diabetes. Sugar may even coat semen and result in obese men becoming less fertile. But the organ of most interest is the gut. According to Schwarz, the gut is a highly complex nervous system – the body's 'second brain' – and this second brain becomes conditioned to wanting more sugar, sending messages back to the first brain that are impossible to fight.

There is growing scientific evidence that fructose can also trigger processes that lead to liver toxicity and a host of other chronic diseases. Men who drink sweetened beverages most often are twenty per cent more likely to have a heart attack than those who drink the least. Schwarz says this assault on the body is so comprehensive, it's analogous to an attack on the nervous system.

So, if the food industry was responsible, how did they get away with it? What the World Health Organisation has called the most serious health global crisis of the twenty-first century? In San Francisco, I meet David Kessler, the former head of the US government's most powerful food agency, the FDA, and the person responsible for introducing warnings on cigarette packets in the early 1990s.

How was Kessler able to introduce warnings on cigarette packets and not on food packaging? Kessler sips his tea. 'Because at that point the science couldn't be refuted any more on the link between cigarettes and cancer, but more importantly, we were pushing at an open door. The tobacco industry had given up on the US and Europe. Their new markets were in China, India and South America, that's where the business lies. So they let it happen.'

Kessler believes the same will happen with the food industry when (and if) the science on culpability in the obesity epidemic becomes impossible to refute. The difference is that the tobacco industry is relatively weak compared to the food industry, which is tied into a complex matrix of other interests: drugs, chemicals, dieting products, and tobacco itself. The panoply of satellite industries that make money from obesity means the food industry's relationship to obesity is a net-profit one.

As one Kay Street lobbyist in Washington put it to me, the food industry is up there with oil and weapons in terms of access to the White House. 'When you can get the President of the United States on the phone in five minutes, then you don't need people like me to lobby.' The food industry has real power.

A joke, she said, that did the rounds in Washington in the late 1990s to illustrate the access of the food industry went something like this: How do you interrupt President Clinton when he's getting a blow job from Monica Lewinsky? Tell him Monsanto are on the line.

The reason the food industry is so powerful is simple. Food is an essential that has become a vice. And sugar has turned food into a vice by creating an unbreakable link between gut and brain. It is as addictive as cigarettes or alcohol. But unlike cigarettes and alcohol, the temptation cues are every ten yards, unregulated and unrelenting: vending machines; coffee shops;

fast food outlets; supermarkets, cinemas, even gyms, libraries, supermarkets, swimming pools, train stations. Everywhere.

'Sugar is hedonic,' Kessler says. 'Eating it is highly pleasurable. It gives you this momentary bliss. It takes over your brain.' And it has taken over our brain at the very moment that a 360-degree, obese-genic environment has been handed to us on a plate.

THE SODA SHARK ATTACK

Dr Tony Goldstone is not interested in generalities about what happens to the brain. At Hammersmith Hospital in London, he is concerned with mapping out the specific parts of the brain and neurological pathways stimulated by sugar.

In so doing, he may have discovered a smoking gun. According to Goldstone, when you become obese, a hormone called leptin ceases to work properly. Normally, leptin is produced by the body to tell you that you are full. However, in obese people, it becomes severely depleted, and a high intake of sugar is a key reason. When the leptin does not work, your body simply doesn't realise you should stop eating, just as Sclafani's lab rats could not stop gorging on sweet snacks.

Leptin raises a big question: did the food industry knowingly create foods that were addictive and inhibited leptin? Kessler, back in San Francisco, is cautious in his response: 'Did they understand the neuroscience? No. But they learned experientially what worked.' Lustig agrees. 'Has a food industry whistle-blower come forward yet? No. Does one exist? I haven't met them.'

If it is subsequently proved the food industry did knowingly inhibit leptin – and there is science behind the fact you still feel hungry after eating a Mars Bar or a Big Mac – then those tobacco lawsuits will be sure to follow, and sink the industry that keeps us fed.

Kelly Brownell at Yale University believes it will happen and we are only a couple of years away from the first successful lawsuit. On current obesity figures, half the planet would be able to sue the food industry for engineering the body's response to leptin in order to make us eat more. It is one thing to mess with the constituents of food, quite another to mess with the body.

The food industry's defence has always been, as was the tobacco industry's, that the science is not there. Susan Neely, president of the American Beverage Association, is a perky, smiling woman in a neat, coordinated trouser suit, who arrives for our interview in the ABA's New York office and briskly settles down as if to watch a movie. 'Very warm in here, don't you think?'

The ABA are a lobby group funded by the soft-drinks industry, and Neely's job is to routinely defend Pepsi, Coke, 7-Up and the dozens of brands signed to ABA from charges that they caused and continue to cause obesity.

'There's a lot of work to try to establish causality,' Neely says, 'and I don't know that I've seen any study that does that.' Does she think soft drinks contribute in even the smallest way to the obesity epidemic? Susan smiles at me. 'I think that when you swim in the sea, doesn't mean you are going to get bitten by a shark. Because you drink a soft drink, doesn't mean you are going to become obese.'

It is a weird answer, but also strangely apt. Neely knows that the science can be fought and if proof is ever established, they will fight it, just as they fought attempts to introduce a sugar tax by Mayor Bloomberg in New York, by the Obama administration, and by Chief Medical Officer Professor Sally Davies in the UK in 2015.

The food industry can tough it out and even if it eventually loses, the defeat would be no great loss anyway. Just like cigarettes, Europe and America are small fry compared to the rest of the planet: a sustainable hit when the world is waiting to be conquered.

PROGRESS

It is dawn on the Amazon and the mist rises off still water. On a bend in the river, a ship sails into view covered in huge, painted hoardings for chocolate bars and milkshakes. It makes several short bursts on its horn and people emerge from the forest.

The *Nestlé Até Você a Bordo* ('Nestlé Takes You Onboard') boat is described on Nestlé's website as a 'floating supermarket'. Its mission is to sail up the Amazon stopping at remote villages and encampments, reaching a potential 800,000 low-income tribal people. The crew of the Nestlé ship hand out free 'starter packs' of ice cream, baby milk, milkshakes and chocolate bars to people who have never seen or eaten processed food before.

In Brazil, the collapse of the traditional Amazon diet and rise in obesity has coincided with the adoption of highly calorific, Western processed food. At the same time, urbanised middle-class Brazilians are adopting the 'Amazon diet' to lose weight and be healthy. This is twenty-first-century progress, just as it has been in India: urbanisation and rising obesity running in tandem. Is the arrival of highly processed, calorific food a new form of colonialism, or is the real discrimination denying people across the world the same opportunities that the West has had to get fat?

In San Juan Chamula, Mexico, the country with the fourth-highest consumption of Coke in the world, the walls of the town's church are studded in coke bottles – coke has been deified since its introduction to Chamula in the 1960s. It is both worshipped as a God and reviled as a health risk. In Mexico, as in Brazil, India and China, all working rapidly through the gears of economic change, obesity is the corollary. China is not only the world's fastest growing economy, it is now Weight Watchers' biggest market.

Is obesity the inevitable price of growth? France has one of the lowest rates of obesity in the Western world and has maintained its indigenous food culture – it has held on to home-cooked food and a sense of pride in its national cuisine, just as urbanised Brazilians are trying to do. But France also went through industrialisation 150 years ago and so it does not equate economic growth and social mobility with more convenient, scientifically produced food. Processed food was not around then, and that is why the nation is not fat now. It never got the chance. Brazil, India, China and Mexico had the misfortune to modernise when they could equate the two.

THE CURE

In spite of a seemingly obvious correlation between growing economic prosperity and obesity, scientific causality between food manipulation and a fatter population has eluded the medical profession. Why? The reason has little to do with science and more to do with the fact that the same scientists conducting research into the food industry's role in creating obesity are also funded by the food industry.

With so little money set aside for independent research, and what little there is being cut, the food industry has become a vital source of income. This means not only are they slow to establish causality, the very same science going into combating obesity is being used to hone the products that are making us obese. Many of the scientists I spoke to are wary about going on the record, because they fear their funding by the food industry will be taken away if they speak out.

So how did the two become so inextricably intertwined?

Let me sketch two alternative scenarios. This is the first: in the late 1970s, food companies made tasty new food. People started to get fat. By the 1990s, the medical costs related to obesity were ballooning. Government, health experts and, surprisingly, the food industry were brought in to consult on what was to be done. They agreed that the blame lay not with them but us, the consumer. We needed to take responsibility, go on a diet and exercise. But the plan did not work. In the twenty-first century, people are getting fatter than ever.

OK, here is scenario two. Food companies made tasty new food. People started to get fat. By the 1990s, food companies and, more to the point, the pharmaceutical industry looked at the escalating obesity crisis and realised there was a huge amount of money to be made. A multibillion-pound cash cow encompassing not only low-fat foods, but diet drugs, home fitness, fad diets, crash diets, diet and recipe apps, with newly thin celebs promising an 'all new you' in just three weeks.

Seen purely in terms of profit, the biggest market was not the clinically obese (those people with a BMI of 30-plus). It was the billions of ordinary people worldwide who are a little overweight, and do not consider their weight to be a significant health problem. To make money from them, these millions of people needed to start seeing their weight as a problem.

To make it happen, the science needed to say they were at risk. And it all hinged on one deal on one day. On 3 June 1997, the World Health Organisation (WHO) convened an expert consultation in Geneva, which formed the basis for a report that defined obesity not merely as a coming social catastrophe, but an 'epidemic'.

The word 'epidemic' is crucial when it comes to making money out of obesity, because once it is an epidemic, it is a medical catastrophe. And if it is medical, someone can supply a 'cure'.

The author of the report was one of the world's leading obesity experts, Professor Philip James,[6] who as a doctor in the 1980s had been one of the first in the world to spot obesity on the rise. In 1995, James set up a body called the International Obesity Task Force (IOTF), which reported on rising obesity levels across the globe and on health policy proposals for how the problem could be addressed.

It is widely accepted that James first put obesity on the radar, and thus it was appropriate that the IOTF should draft the WHO report of the late 1990s that would define global obesity. The report painted an apocalyptic picture of obesity going off the scale around the world.

The devil was in the detail – and the detail lay in where you drew the line between 'normal' and 'overweight'. Several colleagues questioned the group's decision to lower the cut-off point for being 'overweight' – from a BMI of 27 to 25. Overnight, millions of people across the planet would shift from the 'normal' to the 'overweight' category. Just as they had done when Louis Dublin first lowered the cut-off point in the 1940s.

Professor Judith Stern, vice president of the American Obesity Association, was critical and suspicious. 'There are certain risks associated with being obese. But in the twenty-five to twenty-seven area, it's low-risk. When you get over twenty-seven, the risk becomes higher. So why would you take a whole category and make this category related to risk, when it isn't?'

Why indeed. Why were millions of people previously considered 'normal' now overweight? And why were they considered in as much danger as those who are genuinely obese?

At his London apartment, I asked Dr James where the science for moving the cut-off to BMI 25 had come from. 'The death rates went up in America at twenty-five and they went up in Britain at twenty-five and it all fits the idea that BMI twenty-five is the reasonable pragmatic cut-off point across the world. So, we changed global policy on obesity.'

James had once again redefined who was fat and who was not. A decision that would affect the health outcomes of billions of people. It was a decision that directly influenced our global understanding of obesity and what could be done about it. And it was all based, as James told me, on 'prewar data provided by Metropolitan Life', the very data Louis Dublin had concocted in the 1940s.

Who stood to gain from the WHO report? I asked James where the funding for his report came from. 'Oh, that's very important. The people who funded the IOTF were drugs companies.' And how much were you paid? 'They used to give me cheques for about two hundred thousand a time. And I think I had a million or more.' And did they ever ask him to push any specific agenda? 'Not at all.'

James says he was not influenced by the drugs companies that funded his work, but there is no doubt that, overnight, his report reclassified millions of people as overweight and massively expanded the customer base for the pharmaceutical industry, looking to exploit the weight-loss market. The people who 'used to give me cheques'.

Back in the 1940s, Louis Dublin had created an obesity epidemic on paper when there wasn't one, and fifty years on Philip James had used the same data to expand the parameters of a real obesity epidemic.

His critics called it alarmist in order to benefit drugs companies, but James rightly points out that he needed the muscle of drugs companies to press home the urgency of the unfolding obesity crisis. But clearly these companies were not in it for altruism. If the WHO classified obesity as an 'epidemic', the drugs industry were in a position to supply the 'cure'. It needed to be globally critical to justify their involvement.

SPEAK TO THE MEDIA AGAIN AND SOME VERY BAD THINGS WILL START HAPPENING

The problem was that the cure was not easily at hand. Since the 1950s, the drugs industry's answer to weight loss had been amphetamines, prescribed to millions of housewives who wanted to lose pounds. In the 1970s, they were banned for being highly addictive and for contributing to heart attacks and strokes.

But now drugs were once more on the agenda as a 'cure' and the potential cash-in was huge. The drugs industry focused on one specific area: appetite suppressants called fenfluramines. After trials in Europe, the US drugs giant Wyeth developed Redux,[7] which was approved by the Food and Drug

Administration (FDA) in spite of evidence of women developing pulmonary hypertension while taking them.

Dr Frank Rich, a cardiologist in Chicago, began seeing patients who had taken Redux and started to develop what he felt were alarming symptoms. When a woman in Oklahoma City collapsed and died, Rich decided to go public, contacting the US news show *Today*.

We meet in Rich's Chicago home and he tells me what happened next. 'That was filmed in the morning and when I went to my office, within an hour I got a phone call from someone claiming to be a senior executive at Wyeth who saw the *Today* piece and was very upset. He warned me against ever speaking to the media again about his drug, and said if I did, some very bad things would start happening, and hung up the phone.'

The Wyeth executive concerned has denied Rich's version of events. But once legal liability cases began, evidence emerged from internal documents that Wyeth knew of far more cases of pulmonary hypertension than had been declared either to the FDA or to patients. Redux was taken off the market and Wyeth set aside $21.1 billion for compensation. The company has always denied responsibility.

But with Wyeth out of the game, obesity was now an open door for other drugs companies. 'Oh, let us be very clear,' Rich says. 'If you have a drug that drops your weight and doesn't do you any other harm in terms of side effects, that is a multibillion megabuck drug.'

IT'S A WAR, AND WE NEED TO WIN IT

I am standing on the floor of the planet Krypton with a marble atrium stretching high up into the heavens and glass shards hanging futuristically down to reception. A receptionist with a headset nods curtly and tells me Gustav is ready to see me. Gustav Ando is a director at IHS Healthcare Group, and one of the pharmaceutical industry's leading experts on drugs and obesity. His offices in central London are pretty damn impressive but – as Ando tells me – little of the money that went into creating this billion-pound empire came from obesity.

I want to know if the drugs industry's funding of the people who defined obesity as an epidemic had been worth it. How important was the WHO decision in making the industry money? 'It really turned a lot of heads. Defining it as an epidemic has been hugely important in changing the market perception.' Because the drugs companies could now provide 'the magic bullet'.

The race was on to manufacture this magic bullet. British giant GlaxoSmithKline (GSK) found its antidepressant Wellbutrin had a handy side effect – it made people lose weight. Blair Hamrick was a sales rep for the company in the US tasked with getting doctors to prescribe the drug for weight loss as well as depression, a move that would considerably widen its market and profitability. In the trade, this is called 'off-labelling'.

'If a doctor writes a prescription, that's his prerogative, but for me to go in and sell it off-label, for weight loss, is inappropriate,' says Hamrick. 'It's more than inappropriate – it's illegal; people's lives are at stake.'

GSK spent millions persuading doctors to prescribe Wellbutrin as a diet drug, but when Hamrick and others blew the whistle on conduct relating to Wellbutrin and two other drugs, the company was prosecuted in the US and agreed to a fine of $3 billion, the largest healthcare fraud settlement in US history.

Drugs companies have attempted to make a magic bullet and capitalise on obesity, but have failed spectacularly. Ando says 'the magic bullet' would be great if it existed. 'I haven't seen one yet.'

A cure would also mean no more customers. Simply medicating and managing the obesity crisis is far more lucrative than fixing it. Type 2 diabetes is a by-product of obesity and also one of the pharmaceutical industry's golden geese, continuing to lay for as long as there is an obesity epidemic.

And the drugs industry is not the only one benefiting from managing the health crisis. By creating diet lines for the huge grey zone of the concerned and slightly overweight, not just the clinically obese, the food industry, too, has an ever-refilling pot of gold.

There now exist two clear and separate markets. Those who go on endless diets, losing and then regaining the weight, and providing a constant revenue stream for the food, pharmaceutical and diet industries throughout their adult lives. And the genuinely obese, who are being cut adrift from society, having been failed by health initiative after health initiative by government.

As Dr Kelly Brownell points out, the analogy with smoking and lung cancer also goes deeper than you think.

'There's a very clear tobacco industry playbook, and if you put it next to what the food companies are doing now, it looks pretty similar. Distort the science, say that your products aren't causing harm when you know they are.'

But the solution to obesity could follow the cigarette trajectory, too. It was, Brownell says, only after a combination of heavy taxation on price, heavy legislation (banning smoking in public places), and a long propaganda campaign (warnings on packets; an effective, sustained anti-smoking advertising campaign; and most crucially, education in schools) was brought to bear on a resistant tobacco industry, that smoking became a pariah.

There was a generational shift in attitude and, Brownell says, it is only this kind of seismic shift that will do the same with obesity. The great unmentionable with health experts across the globe is that, as with lung cancer, a generation were cut adrift and allowed to die before this shift took place. In public, governments pledge health drive after drive to combat obesity, but in reality, they know it is futile.

It is ironic, that analogy with smoking. Because deep in the archive at San Francisco University is a confidential memo written by an executive at the tobacco giant Philip Morris in the late

1990s, just as the WHO was defining obesity as a coming epidemic, advising one of the food giants on strategies to employ when it started being criticised for creating obesity.

Titled 'Lessons Learnt from the Tobacco Wars', it makes fascinating reading. The memo explained that in the same way as consumers now blamed cigarette companies for lung cancer, so they would end up blaming food companies for obesity, unless a panoply of defensive strategies were put into action. The plan was to follow the same playbook: deny the science, discredit the critics, go on the offensive, do not give an inch. If the plan was followed, valuable time could be bought.

It's a war, the memo said, and we need to win it. There was a good reason why the food industry bought into dieting – it was nothing personal, it was simply business.

CHAPTER SIX
DRUGS: THE MEDICATION OF MODERN LIFE

At 10.15 a.m. on 14 October 2008, I was in a meeting in London when something very odd began to happen. The floor began heaving beneath me. The walls started approaching me, then receding. I felt as if I was on a ship in a storm.

I went to the bathroom and splashed my face with water. The droplets in my hands wobbled. My reflection in the mirror was warping. Then my fingers began to tingle. The tingling moved through my hand, up my arm and into my shoulder. By the time I was on my way to hospital, I felt as if a giant hand had come down from the sky and was crushing my body into a tiny corner of the ambulance.

I was having a stroke, but I was lucky. I could speak and I knew who I was. In the hospital beds around mine were seemingly fit and healthy men aged between twenty-five and forty. A refuse collector, who did the equivalent of a mini-marathon every day; a city trader, who went to the gym three times a week; a barman, who did salsa in his spare time; a criminal informer, visited by two policemen who brought grapes; and me.

We had all suffered strokes, years before any of us imagined you should decently have one. Why? Stress? Everyone has stress, but not everyone has a stroke. I had lost some feeling, but it returned in minutes. I was not blind or struggling to stand, as some of the other patients were. 'When we had strokes,' the guy in the bed next to me said, 'we were hit by a hammer, but you ducked.'

I left hospital with a carrier bag of drugs.

I went home and looked at the drugs. There were bottles and bottles of them. They were a chalky terracotta colour and all had one word on them: Simvastatin. I popped one in my mouth.

THE GREY ZONE

The United States has 320 million people. According to the US government's National Center for Health Statistics, roughly half of all adults go to their bathroom cupboard every morning and take a drug like the ones I had just been given.[1] This is a way of life and our dependency on this way of life is escalating fast. In 2000, only eight per cent of adults took five or more prescription drugs, but in less than twenty years, that has more than doubled.

We are the most medicated society in history and on current trends by 2050, every American adult could be swallowing a prescription drug. To avoid one will seem freakish, even irresponsible.

We do not magically have more illnesses than we did fifty years ago. Since 2000, we have become older and fatter as a society, but increased use of prescription drugs vastly outstrips these needs. Pills are taken by all socio-economic groups: wealthier, non-Hispanic white Americans take roughly twice as many prescription drugs as poorer Mexican Americans, even though – if need was dictated primarily by wealth – the opposite should be true. Epidemiologists call it the 'Hispanic Paradox'.[2]

The drugs industry's backbone is built on the so-called 'Big 3 Ds': depression, diabetes and dementia. But the fastest-growing drug on earth is statins, used to lower cholesterol. The drug I was given when I left hospital.

Statins are the key to understanding how we all became

hooked on medication. When I had my stroke, I entered the grey
zone between the sunny uplands of health and the deep valley of
the unwell. This grey zone is where the pharmaceutical industry's business lies.

In widening this grey zone to its fullest extent, the pharmaceutical industry maximised the potential of illness and stum-
bled upon a revelation. Instead of treating existing illness, they
would medicate modern life itself. They would reinvent illness
by labelling the nebulous anxieties and neuroses of modern life
as medical syndromes. And so – in fact – we do magically have
more illnesses than we had fifty years ago.

By having a stroke, I put myself in the lower foothills of the
grey zone in which drugs are taken as a 'sensible preventative
measure'. But millions of people across the globe who take
Simvastatin have not even had a stroke. So why are they being
prescribed statins?

A few days after being discharged, I asked the consultant who
had been looking after me that question. 'Do you want the official line or what I think?' Both. 'OK. The official line is that even
if your chance of another stroke is around 0.05 per cent, you
should take statins for the rest of your life.'

So what about everyone else?

'About a decade ago, drugs companies came along and were
given *carte blanche* to hand out statins to doctors not only for
strokes, but for everything. So we now prescribe them like sweets
to anyone over forty as a preventative measure. It is sold to the
patient like putting de-icer in your car or de-furring your kettle.

'But we don't know who they work on,' he continued. 'It could
be less than five per cent with ninety-five per cent popping them
pointlessly. But there's one thing for sure. There's a winner here
and that's the drugs industry.'

I am not an anti-pharma person. Quite the opposite. I get
angry with people who take a knee-jerk view that everything the
pharmaceutical industry does is bad. Prescription drugs kept my
grandparents alive. Drugs have kept my dad's high blood

pressure at bay for forty years. The pharmaceutical business has prolonged life and alleviated pain on a daily basis for billions of people.

But here I was doubting that I needed to take a pill that I was assured would keep me alive. What was my problem? My problem was that I wasn't the only one in the new grey zone between health and illness. Everyone is.

A STICK OF WRIGLEY'S GUM

How was the grey zone created? The answer lies with the decision of one man. The vision of a beleaguered CEO of a multinational drugs company, who – in trying to save his business from collapse – quite simply changed the definition of illness, from something you get to who you are. He was to shift illness from an aberration to a state of normality and his aim was simple: to make patients of everyone.

In 1980, Henry Gadsen, the CEO of Merck Pharmaceuticals, was interviewed by *Fortune* magazine.[3] The six pharma-giants were in trouble for the first time in their 150-year history. The post-war boom in prescription drugs, reaching its apex in the 1960s with Valium, was now under threat. The patents they had relied upon to turn them from nineteenth-century corner shops into twentieth-century multinational conglomerates were about to go generic. And these patents were hitting the wall at the same time.

To get an idea of how this disaster can also be viewed as a colossal opportunity, here is what the drugs company Actavis UK did in March 2016. Two investors called John Beighton and Guy Clark made a presentation in a wood-panelled boardroom at the Waldorf Hotel, London, to fellow investors. Actavis were successfully selling a hydrocortisone tablet to the NHS, but it was about to lose its patent and go 'off-brand'; no longer subject to price regulation and producible by any drugs company as a 'generic'.

The clue to Beighton and Clark's ingenious solution lay in the first consequence: no longer subject to price control. Some drugs that go generic can be easily reproduced by competitors but, they said, if we develop niche medicines with complex processing, we limit this post-patent competition and can maximise the true profit potential of the drug. We replace the patent with an exclusive license. Generic is the complete opposite of what will happen.

But here was the clever bit. With the end of price regulation, the end of the patent becomes an opportunity to ramp the price to an astronomical level. Beighton and Clark proposed a deal between Actavis and the NHS on hydrocortisone, raising the price of a 10-milligram pack of tablets from 70p to £88. A 20-milligram pack was ramped up in price by 9,500 per cent.[4]

In 1980, Henry Gadsen's solution to the patent cliff was different, and even bolder in its conceptualisation. 'The problem we have had is limiting the potential of drugs to sick people,' he told *Fortune* magazine. 'We could be more like Wrigley's Gum . . . it has long been my dream to make drugs for healthy people. To sell to everyone.'[5]

Gadsen's solution was genius. He wanted to turn preventative drugs into a stick of gum. Popped in the mouth every morning without thinking about it. Gadsen wanted the healthy to begin taking drugs and keep taking them for the rest of their lives as a preventative measure. It was a breathtaking vision for expanding the client base: from fifteen per cent of the population who are actually ill to one hundred per cent of the population who might one day get ill. It did not matter how small the risk was, it could be medicated. And for everyone else, a raft of new or obscure syndromes or illnesses could be diagnosed. Gadsen's plan was to make patients of us all.

In order to make his dream come true, drugs companies needed to strike out boldly from their comfort zone by inventing or rediscovering an entirely new slate of illnesses. Drugs companies would no longer be in the game of merely curing illness, but conjuring it.

MODERN LIFE MAKES YOU ILL

They had a surprising fellow traveller. In 1960, psychiatrist R.D. Laing published *The Divided Self: An Existential Study in Sanity and Madness*.[6] The book became a counter-cultural bible. It was carried by hippies, beatnik poets and anti-war protestors mobilising on university campuses in America and Europe, quoting Laing's dictum that insanity is a 'perfectly rational response to an insane world'.

Laing's fame spread quickly. He became the figurehead of the 'anti-psychiatry' movement, advocating the end of mental-health labelling. Laing viewed madness as a construct. In a society, he said, that promotes war in Vietnam and the shooting of college students on campus, the mentally ill can hardly be considered any more mentally disturbed than society itself. In fact, labelling dissenting voices as 'mad' was a way of silencing them.

Post-Vietnam and Watergate, the Shakespearean idea of the mad as the only people who see the truth became a key tenet of the anti-authoritarian left, articulated by dystopian sci-fi writer Philip K. Dick, who summed up insanity as 'an appropriate response to reality'.[7]

But R.D. Laing took this idea further by giving it medical credence. Laing said that imprisoning the mentally ill in psychiatric institutions and force-feeding them pacifying drugs was political oppression. The inmates were political prisoners. By contrast, taking mind-expanding drugs like LSD could help the public see through the charade of modern life.

Laing was taken very seriously. He appeared on earnest TV discussion programmes and was hailed a genius at universities across America. Laing argued that our entire understanding of illness in modern society was flawed. It was not you who were ill, capitalist society had made the public ill, forcing us to conform to degrading rituals such as consumerism and office work. If you sought to break out, you were labelled mad. But it was not you who were insane, it was the system.

Laing's 'LSD Marxism' was everywhere, but with Vietnam ending, Watergate receding in the memory, and the collapse of counter-culture and the rise of New Right ideas in the mid-1970s, he was suddenly out of fashion. His ideas disappeared as quickly as they had appeared.

But then something extraordinary happened. In 1980, Gadsen did his interview with *Fortune*. America was now in thrall to yuppies, Wall Street and power lunches. But the drugs industry looked at Laing's discredited theories and saw something no one else had picked up on before.

If, as Laing said, it was not you who were ill but capitalism that had made you ill, this was useful to them. Illness could be created by your job, your home, your friends and your children. By your anxieties around cleanliness, or your neighbourhood. By sex, eating, your pets, crowds, shopping, big spaces, small spaces, quiet places, loud places, your partner, your car, sunlight, too much dark, or your phobia of everything from grass lawns to clowns at children's parties. And these illnesses could take the form of sweats, palpitations, irrational fear, dizziness, nausea, compulsive behaviour, even the simple fact that your leg was restless when you watched television. All of this could be redefined as 'illness'.

R.D. Laing, the high priest of anti-capitalism, had inadvertently come to the rescue of the drugs industry. Modern life could be shown to make you ill, but unlike Laing, the drugs industry had prescription drugs to fix it. And the key to getting these drugs to market was to get them passed by the US Government's highest regulatory body, the FDA.

The problem was that the FDA required evidence. And this meant tapping into university departments. In the early 1980s, these departments were in trouble. President Reagan had recently been elected with a promise to slash public spending, and first in line for cuts were left-leaning university departments. The same ones teaching R.D. Laing.

But the very factor that made these university departments so unattractive to the Reagan administration was the same thing making them so useful to the drugs industry. To get FDA approval, the pharmaceutical industry needed these departments to provide credible academic research for these syndromes. They needed a plan.

University departments were historically independent of outside funding. Their independence was intended to protect the American public from 'evidence' being supplied to sell ineffective, even potentially harmful drugs to the American public. The precise outcome now sought by the drugs companies. But there was a way around the problem.

Senator Bob Dole was not merely a friend of President Reagan and a respected Washington player, he was also on the board of Verner Lipvert Bernhard, a Manhattan law firm on a retainer to drugs company Pfizer. Dole was to sponsor a bill – the Bayh-Dole Act of 1980 – which would open up university departments for the first time in history to direct funding from drugs companies. If it was passed, the bill would have ramifications for every man, woman and child in America.[8]

As drafting began, a race was on to sign up academics to give the bill some heavy-hitting credence. Professor John Abramson at Harvard, one of the world's leading experts on primary care, was approached and refused. 'The American public will look back upon this moment in fifty years' time as the moment government abandoned them to the pharmaceutical industry,' he said.[9]

It is now fifty years on. The bill was passed after Abramson, who initially opposed it, was told he would find it very difficult to get funding if he stood in the bill's way.[10] The act was passed in 1980, and the world was about to become ill from all sorts of disorders it had never heard of before.

Peter Rost is a former drug-marketing executive at Pharmacia.

Rost says that the safeguards against untested drugs being blocked by the FDA were circumvented by this new 'partnership' of drugs companies and university departments. A ping-pong game was created: a drug would be passed to the university, who would cook selective research, then test it on behalf of the drugs company with their 'independent' hat on, and give a heads-up on any possible FDA problems.[11]

The holy grail was to create a brand-new condition that the American public did not even know it had. Vince Parry was an executive at Roche and described the process of discovering these new ailments as a careful process of cherry-picking.[12]

Parry's job was something wondrous to behold: 'to foster the creation of medical disorders, little-known conditions created afresh, and forgotten disorders reheated.' Could students living on pizza with the curtains drawn be said to be suffering from low Vitamin D and thus at imminent risk of rickets, or 'Seasonal Affective Disorder'? Parry likened it to being a fashion designer, bringing back long-forgotten illnesses and attaching a drug.

Lo and behold, a raft of syndromes arrived that no one had previously known about, popularised and broadened in their definition to cover huge new swathes of everyday life affecting millions of people. If any conditions had existed before, they would have been rarely diagnosed. Not anymore. Now they were a household name: Attention Deficit Disorder, ME, bi-polar, OCD, HRD, PTSD, IBS, Metabolic Syndrome, PDD or Pre-Menstrual Disorder, SAD (Social Anxiety Disorder and Seasonal Affective Disorder). On top of these acronyms were a host of oblique phobias and addictions ranging from fear of shiny surfaces to the anxiety created by missing out on a bargain at the sales.

The important thing for the drugs industry was that any hazy or nebulous feeling or anxiety could now become a cast-iron medical condition authenticated by university research. The task was not to create something entirely spurious. Many conditions had been around for decades and had genuine sufferers, for whom a diagnosis and medication could be valuable. But the business opportunity was in popularising and broadening the diagnosis to millions of other people for whom it had been hard to make a cast-iron diagnosis, but was no longer. They were now patients. The millions of people in the grey zone.

There was an upside. For core sufferers of irritable bowel or an obsessive-compulsive disorder, a genuine problem was recognised and believed. They were no longer isolated, they could form support groups and gain confidence from other sufferers. This diagnosis turned people's lives around. But it was not these genuine sufferers that were the huge exploitable market – it was the millions of people on the edge of a diagnosis who could now have a drug prescribed that roped them definitively into being labelled with something. It was the grey hinterland where the money lay.

NOOTROPICS AND THE TECHNOSAPIEN: LIVING TO 150

This grey zone is where adult Britain and America now sits. The sweet spot for not only pharmaceutical companies, but a new industry created by Henry Gadsen's stick of gum: 'wellness'. A trillion-dollar behemoth incorporating everything from preventive medication to fitness and vitamin supplements. From wearable tracking technology to clean eating, super foods, and the panoply of alternative therapies and diets we use to armour ourselves against modern life and the potential illnesses it brings. And that is just the beginning. Coming online are bespoke genetic editing programs that will 'edit out' hereditary disease, and edit in desirable attributes, like high cheekbones or intelligence.

The wellness industry is predicated on prevention not cure, and prevention is an amazing product to sell because it is impossible to test its efficacy. Who knows if it works or it doesn't? If nothing happens to you, then it worked. If you get ill, then something else is to blame. What matters is that you sign up to the ideology of wellness in the first place.

So who benefits from you looking after your health? You do, when it works. But the underlying truth of wellness is that those who want to look after their health, will; and those who ought to, do not. As a health strategy for everyone, 'wellness' does not work because it simply preaches to the converted.

In May 2014, Gallup published a Rand Corporation study on wellness programmes offered in US workplaces. More than eighty-five per cent of US companies employing more than one thousand people offer some form of wellness programme, but only sixty per cent of staff are even aware the programme exists. And of that, just forty per cent use it. Only twenty-four per cent of employees participated,[13] corresponding roughly with about twenty per cent of the US population who exercise to a recommended weekly minimum, but do it off their own back.[14]

The unpalatable truth for governments and companies running health programmes for their employees (not least because they improve the bottom line of attendance and productivity) is that most of us are immune to calls to exercise more, even if help is handed on a plate.

The hope that wellness will create a 'contagion effect' – spreading amongst employees as they crunch and plank their way to health – is less likely than a 'preach effect', people resisting wellness because they feel they are being told what to do.

A gulf is emerging between the well and unwell, with the twenty per cent who practise wellness pulling away from the eighty per cent who do not. In Britain and America, a growing 'Quantified Self' (QS) or 'life-logging' movement is gaining momentum. People who record and 'quantify' every activity and input in their life. This is not simply about 'wellness', but creating the ultimate 'optimised' you.[15]

They meticulously count every single calorie they consume and burn. Record the amount of caffeine in their body, the level of toxins in their food, stress levels, how much they work, sleep, the quality of the air they breathe, how often they have sex and for how long, even the chemical make-up of their urine and faeces. The goal of the quantified individual is to create a machine of their body – an 'optimal self' – functioning at maximum efficiency at all times.

Aligned to QS is the nootropic or smart drug movement – people taking drugs to enhance their cognitive ability and productivity.[16] This is not drug-taking to get high, but to focus. Students have long used amphetamines to work round the clock, but nootropics hone this to targeting areas of the brain for specific tasks: Adderall to improve working memory, methylphenidate to improve mental performance, or eugeroics like modafinil to short-circuit sleep deprivation. Nootropics are taken up most enthusiastically by millennials as a tool to get an edge at work. It has been estimated that as much as one in four students at British universities use smart drugs.

I am on a roof in San Francisco, overlooking the city. A man with a headband connecting his brain-waves to the internet is meditating. 'Alexa!' he commands his robot assistant, a small, black tube. 'Play my soothing rain soundtrack.' If Eric Matzner meditates competitively enough, birdsong will spontaneously burst forth from Alexa and he will move on to his next task.

Downstairs, in his extraordinary steam-punk, techno-Victorian house, Eric does a three-minute rapid workout in his state-of-the-art, chrome-and-leather gym. He jumps up and speeds over to a deck of screens and begins typing furiously at the keypad while standing on a rubber platform. I ask Eric what he is doing. 'I'm racing other cars by seeing how many words a minute I can type.' Eric's fingers are a blur. His accuracy is pretty extraordinary, too. He can type about eight times faster than normal human beings. It is like watching a person on fast-forward. Eric is an evangelist for nootropics and two in particular: noopept, a memory aid developed in the 1960s in Russia, and phenylpiracetum, which cosmonauts used to boost stamina.

Eric takes between seventy and eighty supplements every

morning, grabbing them in handfuls and gulping them with water ('water is good'). He has them arrayed in glass jars and they range from the shell-casing of silk worms to deep-sea algae, dried and reconstituted as a bright-green gunk. Eric takes a potion out of a silver sachet and asks me to sniff it. It is one of the foulest things I have ever smelt. He drinks it in one gulp. Nootropics were inspired by Romanian scientist Corneliu Giurgia. Like Giurgia, he sees no reason why he should not live to 150 and use nootropics to do it. He plans to have communication with 'once-dead' scientific geniuses when they are cryogenically resurrected.

Eric is deadly serious. 'If somebody invented a drug that improved the brains of the world's ten million scientists by one per cent, it would be like creating ten thousand new scientists.' Eric is fantastically engaging company, though his nootropic habit has the unfortunate side-effect of making him talk faster than any other human being I have ever met. For long periods of time, he is talking so fast, I have absolutely no idea what he's saying.

Eric sells his cognitive enhancers as Nootroo – a silver pill and a gold one, like the pills in *The Matrix*. His main competitor is Nootrobox, who have backing from Silicon Valley. Their founders tell me digital was the old frontier and 'the body is the new platform'. Twenty years ago, tech was an end in itself, but now the optimised self is the huge, untapped market; technology and data simply the tools for making the post-human technosapien happen.

These movements are the extreme version of what we all do now. Using wearable technology like fitbit or jawbone to monitor and improve our body's performance. For those who are already healthy, this is simply data confirmation of what we already know: that we are OK and exercise enough.

But for those who are unfit, it masks another agenda: policing of the body not for health purposes, but to label the unwell as a prelude to withdrawing health support. The same data you record and amass through wearable technology can be used by insurance companies or the NHS to deny or cancel a healthcare plan or benefit claim. Data ostensibly collected on your behalf then becomes a weapon used against you.

If your phone says you have not climbed enough stairs today, or your watch says that you did not work hard enough in the gym, this data turns into irrefutable fact. In 2013, Boots the Chemists introduced breathalysing for smokers and rewarding the clean with nicotine patches. The NHS plan to do the same with the obese, using data tracking on diet and exercise to offer or withdraw healthcare.

But is telling someone who is fat and does not exercise that – *drum roll* – the data confirms they are fat and do not exercise benefiting them? Once someone has been definitively labelled as failing, more data only reinforces that label.

In 2016, Admiral Insurance began scrolling through the Facebook posts of first-time drivers to assess the risk they posed to other drivers.[17] This was based not on their driving, but how many pictures they posted of themselves drunk at parties. Facebook subsequently blocked Admiral from using their information to price car insurance. But if companies are making policy decisions culled from some blurry photos that magically become 'data', what will health companies do with 'data' mined from how many times you ate at McDonalds last month?

Data drives far more than individual health, it underpins the 'MedTech' revolution and the idea that responsibility for health in a post-NHS future will lie firmly with the individual. This is fine for those on the sunny uplands of good health who also happen to practise wellness. But for the chronically unwell, who also chronically fail to practise wellness, failure to hit your health targets will be a self-fulfilling prophecy. When the NHS door closes, the only option left will be a private healthcare provider charging a far higher premium.

More than twenty-eight million Americans have no medical insurance,[18] creating a cost per capita of $6,223. The sixty-four million British citizens currently covered by the NHS have a per capita cost of £2,008. Half that of the US. But this could be about to change radically. The lesson of the demise of Obamacare and the difficulty in finding its replacement has been the crushing confluence of extreme need and inability to pay. The very people who need healthcare most cannot afford it at all, and will not take out insurance for that reason.

In Britain, the NHS still operates as a comprehensive health provider, but is moving rapidly to a new model in which access could depend primarily on your data. Doctors' surgeries heave with patients allocated ten-minute slots and allowed to discuss only one health problem per visit. In a system stretched to its limits, data steps into the breach to make a decision for you. Beneath the glowing surface of the prevention industry lies the hard reality of ending comprehensive healthcare and where this will really take us.

I CAN'T PRESCRIBE A BETTER HUSBAND

Dr Marie Williams is a GP in Blackpool, Britain's most medicated city for depression. 'I can't prescribe a drug for a better job or a better husband or better housing. There is a direct correlation between poverty and bad health and yet dealing with the underlying causes is not my job. It's beyond my remit.' Does Dr Williams believe she is enabling poverty rather than treating depression when she prescribes pills? 'Wow, that's an immensely complex question. But short answer, yes.'

I spend a couple of days meeting some of the people whom Dr Williams sees. John (not his real name) is twenty-four and has tried to commit suicide a number of times. He never goes through with it, because he can always envision himself alive at the end and 'I don't want to feel the rope cutting into my neck.' When he is in an 'episode', he needs anti-depressants to help him out of the hole. But sometimes they take weeks to kick in and in the meantime, he is dependent on talking therapy.

I meet a number of people like John in Blackpool with clinical depression and suicidal tendencies. They all say the same thing: talking therapy – maintaining an ongoing connection with an empathetic individual – is what keeps them going, not anti-depressants. Talking therapy costs the NHS a fraction of the ever-escalating cost of anti-depressants and, according to Steve – a psychiatric counsellor I meet who works in the North West – is the only long-term solution for the patients that will bring them back into the functioning world. Certainly not anti-depressants.

John agrees, and says that anti-depressants are viewed in Blackpool like illegal drugs, 'but just don't make you feel as good.' They're traded with street drugs and simply provide another option for getting out of it, often in combination with temazepam or heroin.

Part of the self-fulfilling prophecy of an over-medicated society is that once it has been created, we demand the medication. Dr Williams says she has patients who come in because their pet has died and they demand anti-depressants. They are sad, she says, not depressed, and feeling sad is part of being human. But because unhappiness is not part of the brochure for modern life, we demand medication to obliterate it. 'People have an expectation that happiness should be a perpetual state of normality. It isn't, but we've created an unrealistic expectation that it should be,' and so drugs are there to make it happen.

Vince Parry worked for Eli Lilly in the States, where the anti-depressant Prozac was originally developed as a slimming drug. It was going nowhere as an aid for losing weight and then someone at the company had a light-bulb moment.[19] Loren Mosher, a psychiatrist at Princeton, believed the plan was to take Prozac out of slimming and put it in the depression market. Prozac was about to boot up the happiness industry.

The problem with launching a new anti-depressant was the crowded field. So, for Prozac to stand out and make a splash, it needed a USP (Unique Selling Point), and Eli Lilly had come up with one: make depression aspirational. Prozac would take the shame and stigma out of depression and make taking a drug a positive lifestyle choice.

The problem with depression, says Mosher, was that it was depressing. If Eli Lilly could make users pleased to brag about using Prozac, spreading its virtues by word of mouth, then they would have a major hit on their hands. Prozac was to become the first anti-depressant drug you became happy to say you were on. And it worked. Prozac is worth $6 billion a year to Lilly.[20]

Happiness is a universal human desire, but the expectation that we need to be perpetually cheerful has, Dr Williams says, made us more depressed and increased a sense in patients that they do not measure up. The bar has been raised and anything under it cannot be tolerated when we have unrealistic expectations to feel flat-line happiness at all times, and demand medication to maintain it.

And for subtle or nuanced mood swings that do not fit this Soma state of emoji bliss, we have definitive syndromes and drugs to put you on the cloud. Prescription drugs become a normalising sedative for any state: manic euphoria, restlessness, boredom, depression, over-achievement and burn-out, poverty and anything in between. Drugs for coping with modern life, as Henry Gadsen had dreamt of, and a pill to flatten and numb any sensation. And nowhere is this labelling and numbing with medication more widespread than with 'difficult' children, millions of whom are scooped into being diagnosed with ADHD.

More than six million American children, eleven per cent aged four to seventeen, have been diagnosed with ADHD (Attention Deficit Hyperactive Disorder). The figure has doubled in a decade, and increases incrementally year on year.[21] And look at that age range again: four to seventeen. Four-year-olds are not the youngest children diagnosed. Two- and three-year-olds are regularly prescribed Adderall and Yvanse for ADHD, and there is no lower limit to when a child can be diagnosed as a problem, placed on drugs, and normalised for the purposes of fitting in at school and at home.

Just as anti-depressants enable the underlying economic structure of poverty to be maintained, so Ritalin and Adderall medicate 'problem' children, sustaining the architecture of the modern atomised family.

By parking drugged-out five-year-olds in front of an iPad or Xbox, parents stretched by long hours with multiple jobs, low income, and the stressful demands of home life have this pressurised structure enabled by drugs – both for themselves and their children.

In San Bernardino, I sit in on a therapy session between a psychiatrist and a nine-year-old diagnosed with ADHD. He was first diagnosed when he was five, though the therapist sees kids as young as three. The boy fidgets nervously throughout. When asked why he is here, he mumbles that he doesn't know. Asked how he feels, he wrings his hands furiously. I ask his parents why he is like this. 'He's medicated.' And do you think that benefits him? 'Definitely, he's far more focused at school.' How did he come to be diagnosed? 'We didn't think there was a problem, but when he started at school, the teacher said she thought he was ADHD, so he was diagnosed.' You didn't think there was a problem before? 'No.' How many kids in his class are like him? 'About thirty per cent are ADHD.'

Are the economic pressures on a modern family any greater than a hundred years ago? No. But the expectations are. Medication for ADHD kids provides a chemical child minder, a tool for keeping a class quiet, or enabling the over-stretched family unit to cope at home. In the wider context, drugs are an enabler for stress and low pay to continue to bear down on millions of families and be endured. Treating illness or promoting wellness does not come into it.

Parents often wonder if they are doing the right thing by giving their kids drugs, but they are given the drugs by doctors anyway. As one parent on an ADHD support chatroom said: 'Perhaps my child is just being a child.' The medical basis for ADHD is often questioned by the very people responsible for diagnosing it, and the journey this syndrome has taken from non-existence to cast-iron, bona fide condition illustrates the journey all syndromes take from invisibility to enabling modern life. A solution to a problem we never knew was a problem, till we were offered the solution.

DSM-III

The journey towards the medication of modern life took a decisive turn in the early 1970s. The psychiatric profession faced a reputational low. In the Soviet Union, psychiatry had been used to silence political dissidents by labelling them schizophrenic. Psychiatrists in the West began to examine the reliability of their profession's own diagnostic practices. What they were to discover and subsequently propose would change the way we define normality.

David Rosenhan, a social psychologist at Stanford, wanted to put psychiatry's diagnostic acumen to the test. While a student, Rosenhan had attended R.D. Laing's lectures at Stanford. It was at these lectures that Laing argued schizophrenia was 'theory not fact' and began to formulate his argument against the 'medical model of mental illness'. Laing was like a cult leader pronouncing before a rapt audience of devotees and Rosenhan was as enthralled as anyone else.

In 1973, to test the medical basis for a diagnosis of schizophrenia, Rosenhan recruited a number of pseudo-patients, screened to exclude anyone with a prior history of psychiatric disorder. Rosenhan instructed them to show up at a local mental-health facility and complain that they were hearing voices in their heads saying things like 'empty' and 'thud'. Otherwise, they were to behave normally.[22]

What happened amazed Rosenhan. All the pseudo-patients were immediately admitted as inpatients and diagnosed as psychotic. Their psychosis was labelled schizophrenia: a diagnosis based solely on the patients hearing the word 'thud'. Even other patients spotted the fact that they were fake pseudo-patients, but the doctors did not. When eventually sent home, having ceased to exhibit further signs of psychosis, many were discharged with the label 'schizophrenia in remission'. One was refused discharge, however, and had to be rescued by Rosenhan after several weeks in confinement.

Two years after Rosenhan's experiment, Ken Kesey's book *One Flew Over the Cuckoo's Nest* was released as a movie starring Jack Nicholson as a pseudo-patient refused discharge from a mental institution. The 'anti-psychiatry' of R.D. Laing and Rosenhan was now box-office: the anti-establishment message of anti-psychiatry meshing with America's widespread distrust of authority in the wake of Watergate. Politicians and psychiatrists were on a par in the minds of the public – equally distrusted and part of an institutional culture of lies.

Melvin Sabshin, medical director of the American Psychiatric Association, believed psychiatry needed to fight back. In 1977, he said that 'a vigorous effort to re-medicalise psychiatry should be strongly supported.' Sabshin declared a public relations war on psychiatry's critics.

To re-establish its reputation, the psychiatric profession was to co-opt Columbia University's Robert Spitzer to come up with a plan to devise 'reliable' scientific criteria for all psychological conditions. A rock-solid, diagnostic bible that would leave no psychological condition unmapped or undefined.[23] If someone came in off the street hearing a word 'thud' in their head, they would be able to put an exact label on that thud immediately. Spitzer was to set America down the road of labelling everyone as a sufferer of something.

In less than three years, mental illness shifted from a broad series of symptoms subjectively read, to a categorical disease. A psychiatric bible was produced called the DSM, or *Diagnostic and Statistical Manual of Mental Disorders*.

To create a definitive clinical diagnosis, the 'DSM-III' task force led by Robert Spitzer adopted a 'tick the boxes' approach to assigning symptoms and mental-condition labels. Find any six symptoms from a list of ten and *voilà*, you have before you a schizophrenic. Why six? As Spitzer later explained, six symptoms 'felt about right'.

This emphasis on symptoms benefited a number of interests. It helped silence the critics of psychiatry, who claimed that mental illnesses could not be defined in an objective way. It allowed clinicians to obtain reimbursement from insurers, and most crucially, it gave pharmaceutical companies specific mental illnesses for which they could now supply drugs.

Two more DSM bibles have been published since 1980, and each new edition comes with a raft of new mental conditions. The DSM tops the bestseller list and each edition is thicker than the last. Even its authors now argue that DSM has led to the widespread misdiagnosis of mental illness. Dr Allen Frances, who led the DSM-IV task force in 1994, later issued a *mea culpa*. He now confesses that the epidemic of new diagnoses of autism, ADHD and depression that followed the issuance of DSM-IV was largely 'iatrogenic' – the product of a series of well-intentioned mistakes on his part.[24]

We met in San Diego, where Frances now lives. He is a formidable character and shockingly forthright. 'There were reasons this all happened you know.' Was it wrong? 'Of course it was wrong. We were wrong. Everyone involved has regrets. You can't go through life not talking about things you did that you regret – that's why you're here talking to me. Can we put it right now? I don't know. We have medicated billions of people we shouldn't have, based on the flimsiest evidence.'

Allen believes many of the doctors involved in the pushing of DSM over-diagnosis and over-medication have the same regrets.

In 2013, DSM-V was published. 'Most of the changes made to the DSM-V,' Frances says, 'are based on limited data, the evidence is remarkably weak for changing anything. DSM-V opens up the possibility that millions and millions of people currently considered normal will be diagnosed as having a mental disorder and will receive medication and stigma that they don't need.'

DSM-III created clear, standardised, psychopathological categories. This provided the drugs companies with an incentive to launch randomised controlled trials to test newly developed drugs for the treatment of specific new DSM-III disorders.

DSM-III was great news for the pharmaceutical companies. For any medication to be approved by the FDA, a drug needs to be proven effective in the treatment of a specific disease. But thanks to the connections FDA panellists have with pharma companies, it can be.

DSM-III created a massive new market. In the years following the publication of the DSM-III, billions of dollars were allocated by government and pharmaceutical companies for psychophar-macological research. Throughout the 1980s, the federal research budget allocated to the US National Institute of Mental Health increased by eighty-four per cent to $484 million annually.[25]

The ever-widening definition of mental illness, and its enshrining as medical fact in each new edition of the DSM, meant that millions more Americans each year found themselves on drugs. But it was when the DSM extended its reach over children, via ADD and ADHD, that a bridge was crossed and a taboo broken. By ceasing to see children as children but instead as patients, and expressions of childhood not as part of being a child but symptoms of an illness, a paradigm shift occurred.

Drugs companies and psychiatrists did not do this in isolation. Whether modern life became more stressful or not, adults began to perceive their lives as more stressful, and this willingness to accept a diagnosis of psychiatric illness in children was because this diagnosis then formed a justification for tran-quilising them. We would not have to deal with the problems a child displayed at home or in school, especially if we conflated the problem with the child. By popping pills before work, we could survive the day, and in the evening, domestic life. By giving pills to kids, they were no longer a 'problem'. The medicalisation of modern life enabled modern life to function, and this was the brilliance of Gadsen's insight in 1980, when he first saw the future in a stick of gum.

AN ILLNESS NO ONE IS IMMUNE FROM

By 1987, seven years after Gadsen's interview in *Fortune*, his dream had not yet been realised. DSM was well on its way to hoovering up half the American population as mentally ill, but the drugs industry had yet to find a new illness that no one was immune from. That was all about to change, and this is where my stroke drugs make a grand entrance. A disease was discovered that was bigger than cancer, bigger than heart disease, and everyone would get. It was called 'risk'.

When the medical profession treats people who are actually ill, they are treating a tiny percentage of the population. By treating people at risk, the number of patients given drugs grows exponentially. If you can define risk at its widest possible parameter, the entire game is changed. We are all patients.

Risk worked wonders reinventing Wall Street, but applied to illness, it could reap rewards that even those who pioneered its adoption in medicine could scarcely believe were possible. Risk has become the key medical concept of the last twenty years. It does in many ways the exact opposite of what Spitzer and the DSM sought to do with mental illness, to make diagnosis cast-iron.

With risk, the opposite needs to happen. A clear, diagnosable illness needs to become a fuzzily defined risk of potential illness that you might get in the future. 'You have cancer, here are the drugs to deal with cancer,' becomes, 'Here are the twenty risks associated with cancer, and here are the twenty drugs that can be taken to deal with that risk.' Risk is the clincher in creating the medicated society. Because we are all ultimately at risk of getting something, and no one dare take the risk of not following the prognosis.

In 1987, risk found its vehicle. Merck launched Mevacor, a statin for cholesterol. Cholesterol had always been considered a factor in heart disease, but now it was to be made the main factor in heart disease and it was up to Merck – and Pfizer, with Lipitor – to make cholesterol the only game in town.

Here is how the magic happened. In 1995, thirteen million people in the US (five million in the UK) were said to be 'at risk' from high cholesterol. These figures were determined by the National Institute of Health, the leading independent health body in the US. Figures based on the level at which a cholesterol reading is considered high.

How did it happen? Raymond Moynihan and colleagues at *PLOS Medicine* undertook a cross-sectional study of widening risk and the ties between experts and drugs companies between 2000 and 2013. Of sixteen publications on fourteen common conditions, ten proposed changes widening definitions, and only one narrowing them. Among fourteen panels with disclosures, the average number of ties with the pharmaceutical industry was seventy-five per cent.[26]

We might imagine a panel like the NIH, or indeed the FDA, to be independent bodies. They are not. It is normal practice for a large number of panel members on an 'independent' panel to have direct ties to one or other of the six pharmaceutical giants. It is naïve to think this does not happen or is even at one level necessary. The pharma giants are developing drugs that need constant testing and re-evaluation; they are inevitably and appropriately in consultation with the people deciding whether this drug gets a licence. The question is whether this closeness means they cross a line.

Panel members are under immense pressure, and when they get together and make a decision that will prevent a multibillion dollar drug from gaining a licence, they are suddenly a problem. It is in the drugs industry's interest for that problem to not arise.

Following the decision of the NIH in 2001, the number of

Americans defined as being 'at risk' from high cholesterol trebled overnight from thirteen million to thirty-six million. In 2004, it went up again to forty million. In Britain, there was a correspondingly miraculous leap from fourteen million to twenty-seven million. This was not an incremental increase, this was an unprecedented leap. In the same period, those diagnosed with Attention Deficit Disorder went up by eight hundred per cent.

This was a staggering jump in numbers, but could the cholesterol spike be explained by something else, such as the explosion in obesity over the same period? Not really. The obese have high cholesterol to begin with. They are already factored into the original numbers.

The explanation is simple: millions of people previously on the safe side of the line were suddenly swept up and dumped in the red zone marked 'at risk'. This is known as 'net widening'. Roping patients with relatively minor symptoms into a far more serious condition. In this way, osteoporosis becomes an umbrella term for anyone with some kind of rheumatoid ache.

Another way of net widening is diagnosing someone as 'on the spectrum'. Depression can be widened to include anyone feeling a bit down – the sad patients that Dr Williams sees in Blackpool – who demand medication. 'Spectrum autism' encompasses anyone from the socially awkward, right through to those genuinely severely autistic. There is another term for 'spectrum autism'. It is called being male. In 2014, the *British Medical Journal* estimated that forty per cent of men are on the autism spectrum. That is widening the net in spectacular fashion to forty per cent of fifty-two per cent of the population.

Net widening is sold as progress; greater complexity of diagnosis must mean a better understanding of a condition. But it could equally be the exact opposite: a fuzzing of previously distinct medical terms to net more potential patients, meaning more people taking drugs.

Once these potential customers have become alarmed by

being told they are at risk from a disease, they can be further alarmed by the helpful information available about where those risks could lead. Peter Rost's job at Pfizer was to identify illnesses that could be 'astro-turfed': creating a fake grass-roots campaign, or groundswell of public opinion, quietly funded by a drugs company.

The Boomer coalition emerged from nowhere in 2004, a patient advocacy group highlighting the healthcare needs of fifty-something baby boomers. Henry 'The Fonz' Winkler and 'Wonder Woman' Lynda Carter fronted the campaign. But buried in their seemingly innocuous drive to get middle-aged people to do more star jumps to stay fit was a call to 'know your numbers' on cholesterol.

The Boomer campaign got worldwide coverage, thanks to a video of Henry Winkler doing press-ups in his leather jacket going viral. But in the small print of their 'Boomer Manifesto' was a demand for statins to be prescribed to everyone over forty. It turned out that Pfizer, the owners of cholesterol statin Lipitor, were behind the entire grass-roots campaign.[27]

Joe Dumit, associate professor of Anthropology and Science Technology at MIT, has made a study of net-widening practices which, he says, work in two ways: genuine well-established conditions like high cholesterol, or osteoporosis, are used to scoop up millions of people with far milder versions under a single banner.

But 'I wouldn't draw such a clean line between manufactured and real diseases.' And the ambiguity is what makes it work for business. In the 1990s, Gulf War veterans seeking a meeting in Washington to discuss the appalling cluster of symptoms they were experiencing on their return from battle (nausea, depression, violent and suicidal thoughts) met a wall of silence. Gulf War Syndrome was something both the Army and the White House hoped would go away.

But when they got the backing of drugs companies, the character of the debate changed. Gulf War Syndrome became conflated with the controversial socio-medical condition of 'Post-Traumatic Stress Disorder', or PTSD, a condition for which experts were still debating the medical basis. 'When Zoloft was approved in 1999 for PTSD, almost every article that came out about PTSD now more or less no longer questioned the existence of the disease, but instead talked about the treatment.'[28]

By attaching Gulf War Syndrome to Post-Traumatic Stress Disorder, Bayer could wheel out Zoloft as the solution. PTSD was now accepted as a condition and not simply for ex-soldiers waking in the middle of the night shaking with fear, but for a child who had fallen off a slide, or an old lady bitten by a dog. PTSD had been net-widened to include anyone, and trauma could be widened infinitely to mean anything nasty that might have happened to you.

I WILL SURVIVE AND IF I DON'T IT IS MY FAULT

We now medicalise every aspect of our lives, every last crevice. Each neurosis, anxiety, twitch or strange uncomfortable feeling we get while walking round a shopping centre or stuck in traffic, washing the dishes or telling off our children. All can be given a label, smoothed out and dulled, allowing us to float serenely through the day on a cloud of medication. Gadsen was more visionary than even he realised.

When he was interviewed by *Fortune* in 1980, you would have been hard pushed in New York to find more than a sprinkling of cranky health-food shops run by sallow people in home-knit jumpers, selling some dusty bottles of vitamins.

Today, the 'wellness' industry is worth $300 billion. Supplements, vitamins, superfoods, yoga, cranial realignment, mindfulness, serotonin therapy, colonic irrigation, detox your gut, liver, intestine, or simply retreat and reboot your entire being (for $500 a time) in a bleached-granite health spa with a single, strategic orchid on a huge, marble reception altar. Greeted by someone dressed in a lab coat, as if boarding your own private medical jet.

Gadsen made wellness not solely insulation from future illness, but an elitist identity. Wellness is really code for successful and wealthy. A marker of how seriously we take competing in the world. The fact that we have monetised our bodies and treat them as a commodity with a market value to be measured against other buff bodies, is a measure of how far the neo-liberal notion of the market has spread into everyday life. Gym clothes are now worn tight rather than baggy, as they were twenty years ago – as a display of your physical stock value, with its transferable value at work: proof you work hard in the gym becoming implied proof you will work tirelessly in the office.

Wellness is an identity for the successful and illness has become an identity for the poor. Just as the late 1960s and early 1970s saw an explosion in identity politics for the politically marginalised and disenfranchised – the Gay Liberation Front, the Black Panthers, feminist movements across the world, separatist nationalist groups from the Basques to the Palestinians – so identity politics became co-opted by those with medical conditions.

Just as the drugs industry piggy-backed on R.D. Laing's 'antipsychiatry', now it piggy-backed on far-left politics, specifically the 'identity politics' of empowering the disempowered. One of the key selling-points of syndromes is to give the sufferer a label. As the disempowered gained empowerment by labelling themselves as 'gay', 'black' or 'feminist', so those suffering from a medical condition could now label themselves as 'bi-polar', 'clinically depressed' or 'cancer survivor'.

Positive thinking is deemed essential to surviving a disease such as cancer. But the subtext of empowerment is that it shifts responsibility subtly away from the healthcare provider to the patient. The onus is on you: if you survive cancer, then you did it yourself through courage and force of will. If you fail, you did not try hard enough.

'Positive thinking' is the mantra of our times. By dramatising disease as a battle between the hero (the patient) and the invader (the illness), we have inadvertently turned health into the ultimate platform for self-determination. A battle with ourselves: our strong self-willed half versus the weak disease-ridden half. A fight for our own bodies. The real message of positive thinking is that only the most determined and focused survive, as in business. But this is medically false. You survived cancer because you did, and the drugs played a major role. But 'positive thinking' suggests that self-agency is the key, and everything else is background. A moral subtext described by writer and breast-cancer survivor Barbara Ehrenreich as 'smile or die'.[29]

Applied to the NHS, positive thinking and the self-policed body will ultimately be the battering ram for dismantlement. You do not need care if you work hard, and if you did not work hard, you don't deserve care. By obsessively monitoring cholesterol, calorie intake, steps taken, visits to the gym, the drive of the new self-help philosophy is to create a steel trap of irrefutable data that will decide precisely what you get when that need for help arises.

For those that failed to work hard enough, there will always be drugs. But there is a sting in the tail. Take statins. Statins make the pharmaceutical industry $35 billion. Dr Navid Malik, a pharmaceutical analyst at Matrix Partners, has analysed their effectiveness, just as my consultant did when I had a stroke: 'Statins are very high margin, so if a statin generates around twenty per cent of a company's sales, it's likely to contribute thirty per cent of its profits.'

But do they work?

'Statins have been the fairytale story in the industry,' says Malik. 'But heart disease is still the number-one killer in the Western world, so one could argue how much value for money have we really got out of their use?' The miracle catch-all drug, the fastest-growing prescribed drug on earth, does not even touch the number-one killer.

TWO SPECIES

Professor Julian Savulescu looks out of the window across the immaculately manicured lawn of the Oxford college where he lectures, smoothing his pink shirt.

'I've been accused of being a Nazi.' (He's not a Nazi, he is a quietly spoken Antipodean academic.) 'Some of my colleagues are more out there.' (One – a Swedish geneticist called Anders Sandberg – believes human beings will be able to develop wings as a cosmetic genetic addendum, should they wish to do so.)

Savulescu is one of the world's evangelists for 'gene editing' – a bespoke advance on genetic engineering that allows certain genes, such as those for inherited disease, to be isolated and edited out at the embryo stage. It is made possible by an extremely precise technique developed in 2012 called CRISPR-Cas9, allowing the genome to be sliced and the offending gene removed. More controversial still, certain attributes (better cheekbones, intelligence, physical strength) could be 'edited in'. It is a chance, Savulescu says, to perfect humanity.

In April 2015, Francis Collins, director of the US National Institute of Health, said that CRISPR-Cas9 is a profound danger to humanity. It is, he says, quite simply 'a line that should not be crossed.'

'There is already proof that you can gene edit monkeys to be more hard-working,' says Savulescu. 'Do we want this in humans? Do we want to be able to isolate Downs Syndrome or autism and edit them out? These are questions for society, but the technology is there.'

But isn't that eugenics? 'It is eugenics, but so was what went before. The human animal is not some finely balanced masterpiece of divine creation. It is the result of natural selection under particular environmental pressures. Humans exhibit some two hundred and fifty genetic disorders, only twenty to twenty-five per cent of embryos are fit enough to develop into a baby, and six per cent of newborns exhibit a major birth defect. DNA manipulation allows us to correct genetic aberrations ... it allows us to liberate ourselves from the biological constraints of evolution and move toward a state of self-designed evolution.'

To deny the power humans now have to supersede nature, with all nature's inherent cruelties and aberrations, would be, Savulescu says, a perverse error. Nazism, Savulescu has said, gave eugenics a bad name. Gene editing makes it possible for human beings to perfect themselves by eradicating everything unwanted: from serious hereditary disease such as Huntingdons, to small cosmetic tweaks for characteristics we dislike.

Blonde blue-eyed babies? Why not? Savulescu says the decision of whether to perfect your child will be yours – it will not be Nazism, but consumer choice. These moral decisions will to some degree be no different from today: if you wish to go ahead with or terminate a foetus with probable Down's Syndrome, that choice is given to you now with the CVS test.

According to Savalescu, the brave new world of gene editing is already here. It is an arms race and the West is losing it. China is experimenting on an 'industrial scale' with embryos, because it does not have its hands tied by the ethical constraints of the 'Judeo-Christian tradition'. What does losing this genetic arms race mean? 'Will China be able to make themselves a physically superior master race? Not just yet but why ultimately not? They see no qualms about winning and how they win.'

THE WOMAN WHO STOPPED AGEING

Elizabeth Parrish is genetically modified. The world's first GM person. With injections, she has lengthened her telomeres, the ends of her DNA strands. Telomeres protect the genetic material held in DNA from damage caused by ageing. By changing her telomeres, Parrish has effectively stopped ageing.

We meet in London and I spent an overly long amount of time

staring rudely at Liz's face. Parrish only had this gene editing done a couple of years ago so it's hard to see physical evidence of it working yet. Liz is running constant tests and thinks her genectic age could be ten years younger than her actual age, putting her biologically in her mid-forties but genetically at thirty-five. 'But that isn't the goal, the goal is to reverse ageing till it stops at the peak age, which is around twenty-five.' It won't be like Benjamin Button. She won't end up a baby.

How much does this cost? 'It's prohibitively expensive at the moment.' Over a million pounds. So the rich, if they choose to do what Liz has done, will be perma-young whilst everyone else ages as they always have. Isn't it wrong to use technology in this way? 'The goal is not beauty treatment for the rich but to eradicate diseases associated with ageing.' Liz isn't doing this for fun, she's CEO of BioVia, a Seattle-based biotech company and the plan is to use herself as a human guinea pig to show the world what can be achieved. At a price.

'You know,' she says, 'it's pretty silly to see human beings as the polar opposite of technology. Human DNA is just a code sequence that runs as a program throughout your life. You are a machine running to the program and nature too is technology. So why can't we utilize that technology to enhance ourselves if we can? I see a squid swimming in the sea and I think there's a beautiful piece of technology. Some people might want to have the technology available to animals. Amazing eyesight like a bird has or to glow like a jellyfish, and soon we will be able to.'

THE GAME WE'RE ALL PLAYING

In East London, I'm at a five-a-side football match with a fantastically intense man called Eddie Perello, who is one of the few people in this brave new world talking any sense. Perello is founder of DeskGen, who don't just analyse the direction gene editing is taking humanity but seek to establish some ground rules. Eddie has asked to meet at a football match because he wants to explain where CRISPR gene editing could go.

'If you look at these players,' he says, the rain pelting down, 'What do you see?' 'Ten men playing football?' 'Right, with comparable DNA. Imagine if one wanted to be a better footballer than the rest and could use gene editing, would he do it?' 'For sure.' 'And the rest, once they found out why he was a better footballer?' 'They'd follow suit.'

An arms race would ensue. A different arms race from the one between nations. An arms race between people and one without end. Because the players would all be genetically enhanced, they'd effectively be back to square one on a level playing field.

Gene editing could lead not just to an arms race to get ever stronger and fitter but to all manner of unexpected genetic side effects: some beneficial, some not. 'That same edit to improve football skill could thirty years down the line in old age strengthen bones, which would slow osteoporosis, so it would have an unintended knock-on effect.' Intervention to improve athletic performance would over time become a medical intervention.

To tinker with your genetic code is to throw a huge rock in a delicate genetic pool and create myriad unexpected ripple effects. Gene editing is precise, Perello says, but not so precise as not to potentially interfere and produce random ripples that amplify over time.

'Compare what happened with global warming. Humanity came to the table too late and even then, cannot agree on what to do. Gene editing has the potential to be every bit as far-reaching for the fate of humankind and what's needed is to get to the table now and agree an international code of conduct that we all sign up to.'

Intervening at DNA level with serious medical conditions such as cancer, MS, heart disease or Huntington's, isolating and snipping the gene is not the issue: that's a no-brainer. It's lengthening lifespan and genetic enhancement – the arms race – that needs the code of conduct.

But if we were to look at global warming as a prelude to gene editing, then the future for a coordinated governmental strategy does not look encouraging. 'Governments,' Perello says, 'are so, so far behind the curve. How can they even begin to conceive what's being done in laboratories, be up with the latest developments in a field that's constantly moving?' They haven't a clue, nor a way of getting up to speed, let alone staying there.

The consequence of gene editing will be two separate species. Those practising gene editing will be able to take themselves to the next level of perfection – to a genetic state of superiority: stronger, fitter, better-looking and even glowing in the dark at cocktail parties.

The poor will continue as humans: subsisting as mere mortals with the same illnesses, facial features and tendencies to grow fat, old and as frail as their ancestors. They'll be two teams playing football but one team will be the Human A Team and the other the Human B Team. 20th-century economic inequality will have become 21st-century biological inequality: the wealthy will just have a different genetic make-up from everyone else. A better species of human, and it all began with a stick of gum.

CHAPTER SEVEN
WORK: FROM WHAT WE DO TO WHO WE ARE

This is what twelve per cent of the population are going to do tonight: wake up and check their email. In the morning, fifty-one per cent of us are going to spend more time checking email than eating breakfast. Seventy per cent will check email on an hourly basis throughout the day, ten per cent every ten minutes.[1]

The line between work and personal time has gone, and the way we work has become a way of life. Eighty-one per cent of us check work email at weekends, fifty-nine per cent on holiday. One in ten parents at sports day are checking work email as their kid runs a race. People at funerals are tap-tap-tapping into their phone as the coffin passes. Work has taken over our lives, but those checking email at a funeral are not a freakish, work-obsessed few. Given a chance to work – anywhere, any time – we will.

In 2015, researchers James Roberts and Meredith David at Baylor University Business School analysed the phone behaviour of 453 Americans and identified 'phubbing', or phone-snubbing, as a form of powerplay in a relationship. Checking work email is the clincher.[2] Snubbing your partner by scrolling through your work email, you display disdain and superiority and destroy any chance of romantic connection.

But on a first date, checking your work email performs a useful biological function, putting down a social marker that you are in demand and successful. Work has enmeshed itself into the mating process.

At night, the technology we use to monitor work really comes into its own. The blue glow that phones emit wreaks havoc with melanin, the sleep hormone, tricking our brains into thinking it is day. Consistent lack of sleep leads to higher blood pressure, increased risk of heart disease and diabetes, anxiety, depression, even a drop in fertility.

The average person now spends more time on their phone and laptop than asleep: 8 hours 21 minutes versus 8 hours 41 minutes on media devices. Eighty per cent of thirteen-to-fifteen-year-olds use screens in bed and this generational normalisation of glowing screens on our pillow is changing the nature of rest.[3]

Scrolling through a phone and checking mail in bed creates 'active' shallow sleep by reactivating the working memory. Technology puts the brain in a state of borderline anxiety, prepped to wake at any moment. This means we never truly switch off when asleep. Three quarters of all adults are now failing to get adequate rest at night so we are exhausted when we wake.

Putting work first is sacrosanct, yet we hate ourselves for it. In the movie *Elf*, James Caan plays a workaholic father on Christmas Eve given the choice between looking for his missing son and staying late at work to go through a PowerPoint presentation. 'If you walk out that door,' his boss shouts, 'you're finished.' James Caan chooses to look for his son and leaves. It is an empowerment fantasy everyone wants to believe – choosing life over work – but the truth is that no one contradicts the boss for fear they will be finished.

In times of extreme stress, work provides an all-consuming diversion from emotional trauma. We turn to what we know, which now increasingly means burying ourselves in work rather than the emotional support of our families. How did this come to be? How did work embed itself so completely in our lives, and where is it taking us as a species?

THE INVENTION OF EFFICIENCY

In 1888, a jeweller in Aubern, New York, called Willard Le Grand Bundy invented a clock. The Bundy Clock did not simply tell the time, it allowed employees to punch in the exact time they 'clocked' in and out.

Unlike previous versions of punch cards and time clocks, the Bundy Clock had individual keys for each employee, so no one could cheat the system by getting one person to mass-punch a bunch of cards. For the first time, a fail-safe machine for policing the hours of the workforce had been created and its introduction was thanks to one man: Frederick Winslow Taylor, the man you can thank for waking yourself up at 3 a.m. to check your email.

In 1878, a decade before the invention of the Bundy punch-in clock, Fred Winslow Taylor, a Harvard law student with failing eyesight and from a wealthy family, ditched the law and became a machinist at the Midvale Steelworks, New England. Thanks to his eagerness for promotion (and his family connections to the owners), Taylor rose quickly from machinist to middle manager. Then, one day, Taylor approached his bosses with a plan.[4]

I've noticed, he told them, that my colleagues are not working as hard as they might. In order to maximise efficiency, Taylor suggested a 'scientific evaluation' of their work rates with a view to identifying the slackers. They did a deal.

Over the next six months, Taylor was a blur of activity, racing around the plant with a clipboard, frantically making notes and using a stopwatch to measure the productivity of the workers. The Midvale management were impressed with Taylor's findings: he supplied 'time studies' (later to become 'time and motion studies'), optimal lifting and resting periods calculated for the shifting of pig iron, and a 'science of shoveling'. Taylor had a forensically detailed breakdown of every task of the labour force; even an optimal time for toilet breaks. There was only one problem.

He had made the whole lot up. Taylor had worked late into the night falsifying charts and inventing data to give 'scientific' credence to his findings. Findings he knew in advance he was going to make.[5]

Taylor is now widely credited with inventing 'scientific management'. But at the Midvale Steelworks, he had already applied the first rule of management consultancy: tell the client what they want to hear. Midvale had previously identified a number of inefficiencies. After months of 'scientific' evaluation, Taylor miraculously came to the same conclusion.

Taylor's real talent lay in using 'science' to justify a plan already being implemented. But this was crucially important: by claiming the conclusions reached were scientific, the management had 'evidence' that could not be argued with by disgruntled workers. Management could blame the expert, who could in turn point to the science. In this way, decisions appeared to cease being made by humans at all, and were instead made by an objective, God-like arbiter called data.

Following his triumph at the Midvale Steelworks, Taylor was hailed a genius and became the world's first management guru, thanks largely to his cultivation in circles of power by Boston lawyer Louis Brandeis. Taylor wrote a book, *The Principles of Scientific Management*,[6] which became a bestseller. In 1911, Taylor toured America to packed houses explaining his science of efficiency and how it would change the world.

The public lapped it up eagerly, because science appeared to be able to solve anything. In 1886, Charles Darwin used science to explain evolution. Freud had used science as a way of deciphering the subconscious mind. Management guru Peter Drucker said Taylor was a titan in the same league. 'The first man in history who did not take work for granted, but looked at it and studied it.' Drucker saw Freud, Darwin and Taylor as the foundation of the modern world: decoders of the scientific formula for all human behaviour.[7] American industry was soon queuing at Taylor's door: coal, banking and the railroads all sought his expertise. Taylor became a multi-millionaire and one of America's richest men (a billionaire in today's terms).

Not once did anyone think to check that anything he said was true, and so in 1913, he was invited to brief government on how to implement his ideas for the benefit of America. When President Theodore Roosevelt said in his address to the first Conference of Governors at the White House that 'the conservation of our natural resources is only preliminary to the larger question of national efficiency', he was channelling pure Taylor.[8]

A consultancy deal with government would have cemented his place at the heart of power and pocketed Taylor a fortune. But in 1915, Taylor died suddenly in the middle of the night. He never got to see his grand 'science of management' take over the world. But that is what it did: lighting a touch paper that has you burnt out after a long day at the office, still checking your email at 3 a.m.

THE ABERRATION OF A JOB FOR LIFE

We give our all to work, day and night, but we baulk at the idea that we are merely cogs in a super-efficient machine, as Taylor wanted. We crave freedom and autonomy, a sense of self-worth, not to be moving human parts of a production line.

In actual fact, Taylor did not want workers to feel worthless. He believed efficiency would lead to a greater sense of contentment. By working to the best of our abilities, we would be valued by our boss. This value would bring job stability. Efficiency would become a virtuous circle.

In the 1880s, employment was as precarious as it is today. Taylor believed greater productivity by the workforce would create equilibrium for company and employee alike. Efficiency would buy security.

But viewing this quid-pro-quo trade-off in the first half of the twenty-first century, it is tempting to ask what went wrong. We have never worked harder and with less security. We are as vulnerable to laying off as the Midvale steel workers, threatened not only by cheaper labour, but the automation revolution. Taylor made us work harder, but we were cheated. The security he promised never happened.

Not quite. For a while, it did. For a thirty-year period between 1950 and 1980 there was an aberration called a job for life. So how did this historical anomaly of workplace stability come into being and who took it away again, bringing us back full circle to an age of uncertainty?

Take three generations of my family. My grandfather was a Corsican immigrant, who came to London in the 1930s looking for casual work. He played the cello and so began performing in café orchestras. Employed by a different café every night, my grandfather was paid cash in hand, but did not know from one night to the next if he had a job the following day. His life, and thus the life of his family, was balanced on a knife edge.

In the 1950s, everything changed. My dad, who had grown up with perpetual financial uncertainty, got a full-time job. He had the same state employer, the Greater London Council, for thirty years. Unlike his father, my dad got a guaranteed pay-cheque at the end of the month. He did not need to go out and hawk for coins with a cello. He got up every day, shaved and went to work. A career structure was mapped out before him, with even a pension at the end of it.

But this security was a management construct, as the scientific efficiency of Taylor had been. In the 1950s, Peter Drucker, an Austrian sociologist (the one who had seen Winslow Taylor as an intellectual titan on a par with Freud and Darwin), moved to the US and reinvented himself as a management consultant.

Drucker wanted to change the mentality of the huge corporation. He believed a new kind of boss was needed. In the nineteenth century, sociologist Max Weber had modelled a vision of the corporation on the Prussian army: disciplined and hierarchical, with a CEO behaving like a general.[9]

After the Second World War, Drucker believed productivity

would be better harnessed by a kinder, paternalistic boss. A
father-figure who would be looking after your long-term career
interests and with whom you would play golf on Saturdays to
gain advantage over your colleagues.

This was the world of work into which my dad stepped in the
late 1950s. But this 'caring company' masked an equally tough
drive for targets. Drucker advocated a new 'science' of the workplace – one in which the manager was still God, but psychological coercion rather than the stick of efficiency was used to get
results.

Using Drucker's theories on psychological coercion, corporations like IBM would write to the wives of male employees,
saying that Stanley would not be getting his bonus this year
because Stanley had not worked hard enough: no bonus, no new
fur coat for you – this was the pre-feminist world of *I Love Lucy*,
satirised most acutely in the late-1960s comedy *Bewitched*, in
which Samantha and her neurotic husband's entire lives revolved
around what the boss thought of their new curtains. In this suffo-
cating, controlled environment, Drucker wanted wives to
become agents of the company. Drucker reasoned that the
husband was far more likely to do what his wife said than what
his boss demanded.

This paternalistic company was not so nurturing after all. It
was a total system: an all-seeing eye, determining not only what
happened at work, but using the family to push work, too. The
company had seeped its way into the fabric of domestic life,
keeping up the pressure when Stanley's wife poured him a drink
at the end of the day and questioned why she had got that critical
letter from his boss.

But then something happened that blew the world of Drucker
away and brought efficiency into sharp focus. In 1973, the
OPEC oil crisis plunged the world into global recession and
suddenly companies were seeking profit not from finding new
business, but by making internal cuts. The post-war boom, which
had delivered a historical blip of stability and prosperity for

millions, was over. The world of precariousness that my grand-dad had lived in was about to make a dramatic return, swallow-ing up my dad's job and defining the working world into which I would step.

The catalyst was swift. One morning in 1979, my dad arrived at work. A group of men he had never seen before, wearing what he described as 'Willoughby suits', had taken over a floor and were walking around each department with note-pads, asking people what they did. Three months later, the redundancies began.

These Willoughby-suited men were 'management consult-ants' and were about to streamline the working world with a new 'science' of efficiency, every bit as persuasive as Winslow Taylor's. Their gurus were two men, Tom Peters and Robert Waterman, two rising stars at the world's most elusive and powerful agency: McKinsey.

In 1979, the day my dad went into the office and saw these men with note-pads, what he did not know was that they were following a brand-new business model developed by Peters and Waterman.

It was called the 7S Framework, and it was a remarkable piece of work. Peters and Waterman said the successful business of the future would not be a rigid, hierarchical management pyramid, but resemble a complex molecule.[10]

The molecular business would have 'seven interlocking elements, all of which need to be in perfect alignment', like stars on a horoscope. These key elements all began with an S: 'strat-egy, skills, structure, systems, style, staff, and the nucleus, super-ordinate goals (or shared values)'. The boss would 'walk around' – micro-managing and generally nosing about. In fact, this would be called MBWA ('Management by Walking Around').[11]

This soft-carpeted panopticon was nothing new – Drucker's corporation micro-monitored the employee – but Peters and Waterman's approach was about changing the employee's mind-set. The new world, they said, was turbulent and either you were super-productive or you were out (McKinsey's dictum to its own employees is 'up or out'). Nothing short of total obedience to the company was required if you were to survive, but this obedience must be self-willed. Work would become your cult, and the staff would be devotees worshipping the company like a religion.

THE CULT

For inspiration, McKinsey looked to Japan, where employees knelt on the floor of the canteen each morning and prayed that Hyundai or Toshiba be more profitable. The Japanese cult of work was extreme: employees regularly died at their desk through exhaustion. It was so commonplace, the Japanese even have a word for it: *karoshi*. Outside Tokyo is a 'suicide forest', where stressed workers go to hang themselves. There are helpful instructions left at the foot of trees by previous visitors to the forest.

In the late 1970s, Japan was an economic miracle and the world was keen to learn its lessons. Peters and Waterman were as in awe as everyone else, and keen to apply its formula for success. They knew the Japanese work cult would not translate to the West, but wondered how you could create a self-willed version of devotion to the company.

The problem was that employees in the West had an entirely different mindset to the Japanese. The Western sense of self-worth had been shaped not by subsuming one's identity into the company or the nation, but by Locke, Descartes and the Enlightenment. Individualism is as deeply embedded in the Western psyche, as dutiful collectivism is in Japan. Jeffersonian freedoms are written into the US constitution. In short, Western workers would not buy a cult.

But Peters and Waterman had a plan. Instead of selling a cult, they would sell devotion to work as freedom. As 'creative' and 'fulfilling'. If the employee felt fulfilled by their job, they would be more likely to sign up to the company as a devoted follower of the company ethos. The cult would happen without anyone trying.

The first thing to do was get rid of the idea of work as a nine-to-five drudge. Work needed to become 'rewarding'. The goal of work would cease to be waiting for five o'clock to come around so you could go home, and would instead be the completion of the task, and that happened when it happened. Stay all night, but get it done.

People in the office needed to stop seeing themselves as wage slaves and start acting as autonomous, self-motivated mini-bosses. They needed to become freelance in their heads. The people around them would not simply be colleagues, they would have a schizophrenic new identity: friend and rival. A friend in the canteen, but a rival for promotion. Work should become an all-consuming concern, and you should be on your game at all times. Confide in colleagues as you would family (but not too much), and by putting emotional investment in work, you will work harder.

Here is an extract from an anonymous employment website written by a recruitment coordinator, who worked for Airbnb in Dublin:[12] 'The hours we had to work were beyond ridiculous and excessive. Having any kind of family or personal life is very difficult outside of work. A lot of the time it feels like a lot of very young people just running around not knowing what they are doing, pretending to be important with their meetings and high-fives. This company also wastes an enormous amount of money on . . . excessive alcohol for employee happy hours, sweets, cakes. You'd rather have (all) that going into your paycheck. There are people who have very weird job titles, and it is not really clear what they do . . . Their recruitment process is so intense . . . one of the things they interview you on is "core values", which have to match that of the company. Be warm and welcoming and a team player . . . selling hospitality. Well, most of the people I worked with were the exact opposite of this! I felt like I was working in the movie *Mean Girls* every day.'

In the mid-1970s, people stopped referring to each other in

the office by their formal last name and began using first names. 'Good morning, Mr Johnson' became 'Hi, Pete'. The aim of this new management approach was to create a 'fun' faux-home environment. It began with coffee machines, then moved on to in-house leisure facilities such as gyms; organising team-build-ing away-days, and mass nights out with colleagues to cinemas and restaurants. Tear down walls and make it open-plan, and create comfy, communal seating areas instead of hard, regi-mented rows of desks. By blurring the boundary between home and work, making the environment pleasurable, you would want to stay longer and give your all to work.

Today, most successful big brands have a cult of loyalty. I am at 'Fruit Towers', the headquarters of Europe's largest smoothie producer, Innocent. They have fake grass instead of a carpet and rows of park benches where desks would normally be. Every Monday morning, they hold a giant motivational meeting where the employee of the month is awarded the 'Lord or Lady of the Sash': a ribbon is worn and they stand before their colleagues, who bow down in mock obeisance. An idea the founders got from *Bill And Ted's Excellent Adventure*. In the courtyard, delivery vans covered in fake grass drive out with the first smoothies of the week. The staff gather and blow bubbles and cheer as each van leaves. It feels more like a movie premiere than Monday morning in an office.

I speak to the founder of the company, Douglas, and Dan who's been working at Innocent for eighteen years. It is laudable that they make work fun and energising but haven't they merely taken the cult and put ironic comedy quotations round it? 'If people enjoy themselves at work, that's not a crime. It means they're more productive so of course we get something out of it,' Douglas says.

Dan thinks the ceremonies such as bowing, a 'banana phone' the public can ring, Lego walls, table football, bunting hanging from the ceiling and a red phone box – the 'we're all having great fun!' and incessant 'everything is awesomeness' of the place might not suit everyone, but it masks the serious intent of the business. They also have a giant switch on the wall which tells you to go home if it's late, and a sign reminding you which direction home is. 'We don't want people checking their email at 3am. That's not cool and means they've lost sight of the work–life balance. Keeping that in equilibrium is key for us.'

Peters and Waterman realised that turning work into a loyalty cult was alien to the Western workplace, but it need not be. People needed to lose their inhibitions, they said. Give themselves totally to their work, and work would repay them by fulfilling deep emotional needs. Innocent have been shrewd in taking elements of the cult of work but not others. For other companies, devotion is total and work has replaced family.

At the Barbican complex in London, I was waiting to go into the cinema recently when I heard screams and shouts of exaltation coming from one of the large conference halls adjacent, rented out for corporate events. I sneaked a peep round the door. A major high-street coffee brand was hosting its annual employee-of-the-year event. Baristas from across Britain had come to London to 'share' for one day what it means to them to be making soya cinnamon pumpkin lattes for £7.50 an hour.

I watched in awe as men and women in the same identical purple uniform bounded up to the stage and took to the mike stand. 'Hi, I'm Mario from Italy.' (Applause.) 'I just wanted to say I have been working with my team for two years now, and you guys are my life!' (Whoops and hollers.) 'Hi, I'm Veronica!' (Hi, Veronica!) 'Give yourselves a round of applause, because I love you guys!' (More cheers and applause. Veronica leaves stage, emotional.)

The deity they all worshipped hung above them: a giant coffee-cup logo, brimming with exultant froth. If the door had not been slightly ajar, I would never have even heard this ceremony was going on: a devotional church gathering complete with clapping and singing, but with a giant coffee cup where a cross could be.

It is thanks to Peters and Waterman that people like this give themselves mind, body and soul to their employer. And the bigger the brand, the bigger the cult of loyalty, and secrecy. A food industry analyst I spoke to said that whenever he attends industry conventions, one group stand aloof from everyone else – 'the McDonalds guys' – as if they know something no one else does.

In San Francisco, locals often see the 'Google Bus' on a night out. Google employees from the 'campus' at Mountain View, Palo Alto, are driven into the city and eat at restaurants or go to the cinema *en masse* (agreed days before in a round of emails). Google employees believe in Google not as just any other company, but the only company that matters, and you cannot fake that belief. There's a difference between wearing a sash on a Monday morning at Innocent and fostering a sense of world historic cult destiny as Google does.

Ask anyone with a serious stake in rising up the corporate ladder at any of these companies how critical they are of the company, and they will wince. Disdain and non-conformity are *verboten*. Criticism can be a useful tool of self-promotion however – companies with a cult identity 'welcome' criticism from followers, because constant 're-evaluation of goals and aims' is part of today's corporate lingua franca. Just make sure the criticism is 'constructive'.

THE IMMIGRANT FLIP-FLOP

Peters and Waterman remade work as a cult and a family with a pay-cheque at the end of the month. Big companies like Google, who now rival small nation states in power, gain unwavering loyalty from their 'citizens'. The vast majority of the coffee recruits I chanced upon at the quasi-religious rally were from South America and Eastern Europe. Thousands of miles from home, often with no support structure in a big city like London, work is genuinely a new family. They do not see themselves in a dead-end job, but lucky to be part of their coffee-chain family, and the family ties them in.

In 2016, Costa Coffee twice gave a pay rise to their workers above the national living wage of £7.20 an hour. Costa, like their high-street rivals Pret A Manger and Caffè Nero, use a high percentage of foreign workers, many of whom cannot afford the exorbitant rental costs. As a result, they have introduced loan schemes to help shore up housing rent for their staff. The company becomes a benefactor, one you cannot afford to turn your back on and for whom you are eternally grateful. In many ways, this directly replicates the Victorian philanthropy of employers like Lever Brothers, who built villages for their employees such as Port Sunlight (named after the cleaning brand they made).

Pret also offer free food at work and fifty-per-cent discount on eating there when not. When you work at Pret, the recruitment literature says, 'you'll be joining the Pret family where we have fun and look after each other.'

The British service industry boom of the 2000s was powered by immigrant labour, primarily from the new EU members of Eastern Europe: Poland, Romania and the Czech Republic.

In 2003, as Europe waited to see what the effect of EU enlargement would be, an economist called Christian Dustmann at UCL was phoned up by the Home Office. Would he write a report predicting the likely immigration figures to Britain?[13] Dustmann pulled together a crack team of economists, including a researcher who would go on to become Chancellor Merkel's chief economic advisor.

Their prediction was cautious. They believed that in all likelihood the net numbers (once emigration and immigration had been set against each other) would be a couple of hundred thousand.

As Dustmann explains to me: 'You have to remember that in 2003, the British economy was booming. You couldn't get a plumber or electrician, and here were skilled people from Poland or Romania coming in with skills.' These workers were not seen as a problem, but an asset. As the Blair Government nailed its colours to the service economy, immigration from the EU was seen as necessary to power this service boom.

The underlying assumption was that British workers did not have the right attitude. They were diffident, did not work hard nor smile enough. Immigrants would do jobs no one else wanted to do, were prepared to smile twenty times a minute serving coffee and would sign up to the cult of the surrogate family at work, because they were hundreds or thousands of miles from home.

In the late 1960s, with full employment and a fast-growing economy under a modernising Labour government, immigration from the West Indies and the Indian subcontinent powered a similar service boom – on public transport and in the retail sector – and so it happened again forty years later under Blair, in coffee shops, on building sites and in pre-school nurseries and cleaning companies, with workers from the new EU countries.

But there was a problem, Dustmann says. The plan was predicated on Germany and the other established EU states taking the same kind of numbers as Britain. Dustmann and his colleagues had a get-out clause covering this eventuality: a small section of page fifty-seven of their report. It was the report's 'get out of jail' card.

Did anyone in government read your report when it came out? 'I don't know.' But what happened next? 'I wasn't prepared for what happened next.'

The numbers coming in far exceeded the report's predictions. Dustmann and his colleagues were attacked in the media and by MPs in Parliament. One called their report the most inaccurate economic forecast in history, out by thirty thousand per cent.

Germany had reneged on its part of the deal, just as page fifty-seven predicted. Did Dustmann know that the Home Secretary, David Blunkett, and the government already suspected Germany was not going to open up its borders in the same way, but carried on with an open-door policy for Britain anyway? 'I didn't know that. But why wouldn't they? Net immigration benefits the economy as a whole, those are the facts.'

I asked David Blunkett, with the grand backdrop of the House of Lords, if he knew Germany would not open its doors? Blunkett is remarkably candid about what happened. It was not only Dustmann who got it wrong. The government did, too. Blunkett had long warned of the dangers of opening up, but it was an unpopular and politically incorrect position; the political climate was boom and expansion, not recession and anti-immigration.

And as the economy flipped from boom to bust after 2008, Eastern European immigrants stopped looking like a good idea but a problem to the poorest paid, the very poorest of whom – Dustmann says – were adversely affected by immigration from the EU. The immutable fact of immigration benefiting the economy as a whole stopped mattering, when placed against the specific fact of the lowest ten per cent losing out. Britain was on a course for Brexit.

Britain was now taking itself out of Europe. Anti-immigration now powered Brexit as immigration had once fuelled the service revolution: an economic positive had become a political negative. Now every job in Britain is a service job. The police have rebranded themselves from a 'force' to a 'service' and are sent on courses to learn how to arrest people politely. Debt collectors have stopped being enforcers and become a 'service' for people whose doors they are about to kick in. They even host annual 'debt collector of the year' awards.

Both the police and debt collectors have been at the sharp end of austerity in Britain since 2008 and it is no surprise they have become adjuncts of service culture. In order to do their jobs, they have had to turn into social workers by another name, dealing with the most vulnerable and needy in a moment of crisis. The police bear the brunt of cuts to social services and are now making decisions about extreme situations of need that once fell outside their remit. And as one debt collector in Newcastle told me, 'If I'm not sympathetic to someone's situation, we can't make an agreement, and no one gets what they want.' Service is really just the most efficient way of doing business when times get tough.

HUMANYZE

I am in Boston outside an office building waiting to be buzzed in. In the lobby, I meet Greg and Tony. I already notice something strange about them: they are both wearing small white boxes dangling from their necks emitting an intermittent flashing light.

What is that? 'Oh, that's my socio-metric badge,' Greg says brightly. Every employee in the company wears one from the moment they arrive at work till the moment they go home.

These are the offices of Humanyze, with the most advanced form of workplace surveillance anywhere on the planet. Humanyze are taking micro-tracking of the employee to the next level by amassing and then analysing every single second of their day. It is Winslow Taylor's dream of total monitored efficiency of the worker come true over a century after he proposed it.

The small white boxes around Greg and Tony's necks collect data on everything: who they talk to and for how long, whether these meetings are formal or informal 'collisions'. How long they spend walking as opposed to sitting, on the phone or online, collaborating with colleagues in meetings or in isolation in a glass box. Going to the toilet is a 'privacy issue', so the 'socio-metric badge' cannot monitor the data on what they do in there.

The badge can also detect subtle dynamics between colleagues. It registers speech patterns and assesses how dominant or passive you are. Who in a group is controlling the agenda. In short, it creates a total digital data map of your workplace character and every second of your productivity, or lack of it, throughout the working day.

Humanyze is reported to have contracts with Deloitte and Barclays, and is in dialogue with the NHS. Greg and Tony show me what happens once they have collected all this data on their employees. I sit in a glass room with a huge screen. On the screen, various molecular structures appear and begin morphing into each other.

What's going on? 'These are algorithms that have crunched down on the group dynamic of the team. So, what you are seeing is the group interactions and channels of communication, and how well they work.' In March, the team were stoked because their San Francisco colleagues were in town, so there was a great deal of high energy 'symbiosis' between the two offices of Humanyze. But then something goes wrong in April. The molecular structures suddenly drag apart – they are no longer fizzing excitedly.

Greg and Tony frown. There is a single orange blob connecting two rather forlorn-looking groups of molecules. What has happened? What is the orange blob? 'That's a bottle-neck,' Greg says. 'We know who it is,' Tony adds.

The extraordinary thing about the socio-metric boxes is that because of privacy, the data is farmed anonymously. The management cannot know to whom specific data connects, but by looking at the patterns, they can work it out. They do not need to know who it is, because it is obvious.

Who is the orange blob, Greg? 'We know.' So who is it? 'It's someone in management.' Management? 'Yes. Bottle-necks are often someone in management.' Someone who thinks they are doing a good job by rushing around and controlling everything. But they are not. They're doing the opposite.

The data, Greg says, throws up unexpected patterns in productivity: who is and isn't pulling their weight, or doing their job properly. But this is not, he hastens to add, 'Big Brother surveillance of the office'. The aim is to create 'personal dashboards'.

Employees themselves access their 'personal dashboard' data to see how they can improve. This makes Humanyze the realisation, not of the crude work panopticon, but the Peters and Waterman managerial dream of the self-motivated worker, self-policing their own productivity through a personal data 'dashboard' and driving on to be ever better. The voice in the head to work harder that became a box round your neck.

In November 1979, as management consultants were making an audit of my dad's workplace, Peters and Waterman were preparing a presentation of their 7S molecular system with a series of seven hundred slides to the German technology company Siemens, in Munich.

Word of Peters and Waterman's new theory of work spread fast. Pepsi's chief, Andy Pearson, and his co-executives at Pepsi Global HQ, Purchase, New York, asked to meet Peters and Waterman, to see how 7S could transform their empire.

The distilled seven-point-version of the Siemens and Pepsi presentation became a book called *In Search of Excellence: Lessons from America's Best Run Companies*. Far from being a calamity, global recession was an opportunity to reprogramme the workforce. The post-war boom had created complacent employees with an over-inflated sense of their own value. That value was now gone.

By pitting them against one another for their own jobs in an 'internal market', employees would learn to become competitive. It was corporate Darwinism. No one would work for anyone but themselves anymore. We would all henceforth be freelance.

The Japanese, who had inspired Peters and Waterman, had been working as hard as humanly possible for decades, yet that did not stop their economy going deep into recession, just as Peters and Waterman were extolling Japan as an economic model to follow. The book was a publishing sensation and the biggest-selling business title ever written.

In 1988, a film brought their philosophy to the big screen. In *Working Girl*, Melanie Griffith played Tess McGill, a receptionist whose brilliant business ideas got stolen by her conniving boss Katherine Parker, played by Sigourney Weaver. On Tess's first day in the office, she took her most prized belongings out of a box and placed them on her desk. At the top was a copy of *In Search of Excellence*. It was her bible for survival, and all the audience needed to know: nothing would stop this character. She was a winner.

When, thirty years on, anyone gets sacked on *The Apprentice* and utters the words 'Thank you for the opportunity, Lord Sugar,' they have Peters and Waterman to thank for instilling them with unshakable positivity.

Peters and Waterman based *In Search of Excellence* on 'scientific analysis of the world's sixty-two top companies'. The 7S chart was a distillation of everything they had culled from months of meticulous study of the management structures of each of these companies, made in conjunction with their colleagues at McKinsey. But in 2002, on the twentieth anniversary of its publication, Tom Peters had a confession to make.

They had made it all up. In reality, Peters and Waterman had winged it. In *Fast Company* magazine, Tom Peters explained what really happened in a series of 'confessions':[14]

> Okay, I confess: We faked the data . . . we felt that we had to come up with some quantitative measures of performance. Was our process fundamentally sound? Absolutely! Start by using common sense, by trusting your instincts, and by soliciting the views of 'strange' (that is, nonconventional) people. You can always worry about proving the facts later.

Tom feels he was misrepresented by the Fast Company article. And it's easy, having met him, to see how it happened. Tom is a born contrarian, and falls over himself to blow away the orthodoxies that stand in his way.

In the 1970s, he needed to use the language of scientific management to get his radical ideas through the gates of big business. So that's exactly what he did. And twenty years later, he had the guts to admit it was just a necessary strategy. Like all visionaries, Peters marshalled his own facts to his greater truth.

I meet Tom Peters in a plush Boston hotel that used to be a prison. It is a fitting place to talk about work, I say to Tom as we exchange pleasantries. On the surface, the place is all folded napkins, cool, darkly lit bars, and a coffee costing thirty dollars.

But this masks the architecture: a brutal panopticon for seeing anything, anywhere, at any moment.

'You know who the greatest management consultant of all time was?' Tom asks me with a glint in his eye. No idea. 'Ulysses Grant.' Before Grant became President of the United States, he was a general in the US cavalry. Grant's genius, says Tom, was to face his defeated enemy on the battlefield of the civil war. 'You know what Grant did? He rode a mile down the line of defeated soldiers doffing his hat the whole way. You know what that is? That's great management.'

Why did Tom undermine the research data for the 7S system – the greatest reform of work in the last forty years? 'Everything needs great packaging, right? That's what the 7S was: great packaging.' People want something to believe in. They want a system? 'People want to be told that other people know what they're doing. But the underlying principle was right: individuals need to take control of their own destiny. Read between the lines and that's what the book was saying.'

What do you have to say to all those people who put their trust in the corporate work environment and then found themselves shafted. People who are not able to determine their destiny?

'*Bon chance*. Because you'll need it.'

THE VALLEY OF DEATH

Like all revolutionaries, Tom Peters and Robert Waterman believed in themselves. They did not make history, they read its runes and simply worked out that 'if you want to be a part of the way it's going to be, read this book.' They were a living embodiment of how to act if you were going to make it in the new world.

In a post-OPEC 1970s world of profound uncertainty, in which the old rules no longer appeared to apply to anything, consultants stepped into the breach because, as Tom told me, people want to be told that other people know what they are doing. Government and economists no longer seemed to have the confidence in their own expertise to govern or determine the direction of the economy, and in the vacuum created, a huge business opportunity emerged. For people who talked the talk and appeared to know.

John Bennett was a management consultant in the 2010s for one of the so-called 'Big Four': Deloittes, KPMG, PWC, and McKinsey. His specialism was advising on healthcare decisions that would affect millions of people.

'Every time you go into a client, you are looking to find new problems to expand the job. It's like being a car mechanic who looks under the bonnet of your car, sucks in their teeth and says it is much worse than you think. We call this strategy "land and expand".'

Bennett says that key to this management strategy is the initial rolling out of a piece of diagnostic work: a 'template'. This template is a 'foot in the door', often given away for free. The money comes in 'landing and expanding' the job once you are in.[15]

David Craig is an intense man with horn-rimmed spectacles and a stick, which he uses to point at huge words in CAPS during his power-presentation. He meets me in a huge darkened board-room near Whitehall, where the only light comes from the overhead projector. The first words that appear on the white board say VALLEY OF DEATH.

David worked for thirty years as a consultant selling millions of pounds of contracts to the private and public sectors. He explains to me how he landed and expanded business. 'You need to give the client a big shock. Something along the lines of: "It's worse, far worse than you imagined." You are sending them into what we call the Valley of Death. "Only by correcting this immediately is there any hope of turning this around."'

What happens after the Valley of Death? 'Then you provide the sunny uplands of salvation in the shape of an IT project worth fifty million.' Like the pharmaceutical industry, the serious money is not in a cure, but in medicating an ongoing critical condition. Bennett calls it the 'fostering of a partnership'. 'You are looking to create a long-term dependency culture on your firm.' Creating a permanent crisis situation in which government or the business cannot do without them.

In Wales, PricewaterhouseCoopers came up with an ingenious new kind of 'partnership' called a 'risk and reward contract' designed to make money from austerity cuts. This is how it works. Instead of doing a deal that is potentially embarrassing politically by paying consultants up front to make cuts, you hide the pay-cheque. Consultants receive a percentage on all cuts made that they have suggested. In other words, the more cuts made to public services, the more they stand to earn.

Post-2008, when unprecedented austerity cuts were made to the public sector, the use of outside management consultants, stepping in to save central and local government from the Valley of Death, doubled – not only at the front line, but in administering the cuts. They became indispensable to the life support which, as David Craig points out, is exactly where they want to be.

THE SLAVE ARMY OF BOSSES

We are all our own boss now. And in this new globalised, de-unionised world, whether you are a boss picking bananas on a plantation in Kenya, a boss driving a cab in Oslo, a boss delivering a pizza in Newham or a boss writing a book in Hackney, we are all part of a giant amorphous freelance class known as the precariat.

We are as precarious as my grandad was, but our mindset is different. My grandad always imagined that one day he would get to play full-time in an orchestra. We know this will never happen so instead we live a paradox: boss of our own destiny, living hand to mouth. We are the boss and a slave simultaneously.

In 2016, Dr Rachael Orr at Oxfam carried out a study into the work attitudes of fourteen-to-eighteen-year-olds and noticed a consistent lowering of expectations for the future.[16] This plummeting of expectation has accelerated year on year in the 2010s, to the point where they now expect nothing from the future and are grateful for anything.

Dr Orr honed in on those at the very lowest rung of the zero-hours ladder in the US poultry industry. In Texas, poultry workers on eight-hour shifts wear adult diapers because they are not allowed to go to the toilet. Dr Orr interviewed one worker, who was told by his supervisor that safety was not an issue in the factory because 'your life is less valuable than the chicken's.' It was not only the conditions, but the fact that workers raised little issue with them, that exemplified the powerlessness of the globalised low paid.

These workers are powerless and have no leverage. This is no surprise. What about the middle class? Do they still have bargaining power? The middle class, Dr Orr noted, have swapped real-term wage increases for 'fulfilment'. The pay-off for low pay and precarious work is to imagine our work makes us whole as a person. Economic think tank the Resolution Foundation estimate that we are all in real terms no better off than we were twenty years ago, but middle-class professionals console themselves that what they do is self-determined. They have control, which is exactly what the poultry worker does not have.

The middle-class professional has dignity at work. But as wages go down, so too does that sense of self-worth. And as this army of slave bosses grows into an ocean of cheap available labour, so comes the biggest opportunity to transform work since Peters and Waterman invented the new cult of self-determination forty years ago. Now, for the first time, is the chance to create a planet of slave bosses.

THE CHAMPS-ÉLYSÉES EPIPHANY

It was a freezing night in January 2008, and two Americans were standing on the Champs-Élysées in Paris trying to hail a cab. Snow was falling thick and fast, and the traffic was rapidly grinding to a halt. They had less than an hour to make their flight to New York. As the Champs-Élysées gridlocked, horns beeping, a single, distant yellow light flickered – the one free cab on the whole of the Champs-Élysées, trapped in traffic more than five hundred yards away. They were never going to make it.

Then one of them, a thirty-four-year-old UCLA dropout called Travis Kalanick, had a eureka moment. 'Imagine,' he said to his colleague Garrett Camp, 'if every car you see became a cab?' Not one flickering light, but hundreds of flickering yellow lights, all offering a ride to the airport. What if every single person you saw in front of you became a cab driver?

Kalanick had invented Uber. He had not merely created a new cab service. He had transformed work by reconceptualising the slave boss. In 2008, the world was crashing and rising simultaneously, like two tectonic plates in a disaster movie. The subprime crash had plunged the world economy into unprecedented debt, at the same time as the iPhone and mobile devices were 'freeing' the world to work in a brand-new way. One plate rose up, as the other sank into magma.

With wages and growth gridlocked like the traffic on the Champs-Élysées, Uber did not merely 'disrupt' the economy, it reinvented the future. We were now all our own bosses with a mobile device, all striving to be corporations of one.

At the same moment Kalanick was inventing Uber, two roommates in San Francisco called Brian Chesky and Joe Gabbia were struggling to pay the rent on their loft apartment. They had only two bedrooms, which they slept in, so renting out another room was not an option. Then Chesky had an idea. 'Why don't we turn the living room into a bed and breakfast?' They advertised their 'Airbed & Breakfast' on a website for an upcoming design conference in the city, and had three takers instantly. Airbnb was born.

Like Uber, Airbnb was a conceptual shift in what constitutes value. Uber redefined labour value, Airbnb told you to reassess the space you stand in, asking a profound question: what is the true value of any physical space and how can that true value be extracted? Why can't a home be a hotel and vice versa? Everything in the new world could be fluid, endlessly redefining its role and extractable worth.

In 2016, less than eight years after Chesky and Gabbia pumped up an air bed in their living room and invented Airbnb, it was worth $30 billion. Uber was worth $70 billion. But the potential value of both far exceeds that.

Uber's seed-funding allowed it to launch in San Francisco, but within a year, they had signed deals with Google Ventures, Toyota and China's largest search engine, Baidu. Airbnb had an equally meteoric rise, buying out foreign competitors such as German rival Accoleo, and opening offices from Moscow to Sao Paolo within twenty-four months.

This incredible global expansion has been with cabs and flats. The real revolution begins when it is applied to every type of work.

Airbnb did with four walls what Uber did with four wheels, but they are now asking a bigger question of human beings: where is the extractable value in everything you do? Where is the slack in your life that can be monetised? Both business models dare us to find anything that cannot be turned into a commodity for sale.

A tsunami-wave of work apps already do the same – not with your car or your flat, but your time. Take the spare fifteen minutes you have at lunch. TaskRabbit matches free labour with local demand for dog walkers, pizza delivery, or someone to stand in a queue for the new iPhone. You can be back at your desk by two, before your boss even realises. But you are the boss, so what does it matter?

Who is anyone's boss? Your boss in the office is only your boss from nine to five. Say you need someone to pick up your dry-cleaning tonight. You sign in to a people-per-hour website and your boss, trying to earn some extra money on the side, picks it up. Then you are his or her boss for an hour. There is no boss any more – just the army of slave bosses and segments of time in which all our job titles change constantly. Only one thing is certain in this new world – you are the boss of you, because we are all corporations of one.

THE LIMB (B) WORKER

The last two paragraphs are, of course, a promotional lie. 'Micro-jobbing' and the 'gig economy' are Silicon Valley-sounding buzzwords that mask a very different truth. Making everyone an infinitely 'flexible' boss slave means making everyone infinitely exploitable.

We are entering a new age that is redefining every worker, every job, and what a union is too. And the people fighting the new battle to claw back rights and dignity for the lowest paid will be looked upon in fifty years' time as the 21st-century equivalent of Annie Besant and the striking 'match girls'. Women who in 1888, at the Bryant and May factory in Bow, East London, refused to put up with appalling working conditions, igniting trade unionism for the invisible low-paid below the skilled working class.

Megan does two four-hour shifts a day for Deliveroo. She has no idea if she'll be hired, she gets £7.50 an hour when she is, but burns so much energy cycling frantically across London to deliver food to people, she spends practically half her salary on chocolate and energy bars to simply keep her working. That means that after eight hours – after doing the equivalent of a marathon each day – she's lucky to have £50.

'In the winter, it's so cold you can't feel your feet. Last year I tried to take some days off because I was so knackered and was tagged by Deliveroo as 'inactive' meaning I was not going to be offered work. It means you can't take a day off. There's no one to talk to, no human at the other end to treat you like a human being. My life is at their mercy and I am a slave to algorithms.'

Last year, Megan got to meet the boss of Deliveroo. Did you tell him how bad it was? 'Are you joking? And lose my job? You can't complain and I don't think they want to hear it. He genuinely believes the people who work for him love it.'

Meg believes the system is very clever. It depends on young temporary workers who'll move on, so no one hangs around long enough to complain or cause trouble. There's never going to be an employee problem as there's always someone new to do the job.

But now the low-paid workers are fighting back. In 2016, Maggie Dewhurst, a courier cyclist for CitySprint, another gig economy firm, won her case against the company at an employment tribunal. It ruled that she could justifiably be called a worker, not a self-employed contractor, and therefore eligible to rights and protection such as holiday and minimum wage. In the same year, two drivers for Uber won a similar case, the tribunal ruling that the company exerted too much control over them to legitimately call them self-employed.

In defining the 'gig economy' the tribunal had stressed its exploitative downside to workers rather than the entrepreneurial 'freedom' or 'flexibility' it gave. Megan tells me that there is now a twilight-zone legal term to define her and the millions of people who will soon be working in the grey netherworld between employee and self-employed: a 'Limb (B) Worker'.

Under section 230(3)(b) of the Employment Rights Act 1996 and section 83(2)(a) of the Equality Act of 2010, a Limb (B) worker is defined as 'someone who undertakes to do or perform personally any work or services for another party to the contract whose status is not by virtue of the contract that of a client or customer of any profession or business undertaking carried on by the individual'.

You're not an employee or self-employed, you're Limb (B): a limbo worker floating between rights and no rights. But rights like sick pay – as one Uber driver tells me, 'you pay for yourself anyway'. So what is the company surrendering?

'It's really a genius idea,' an Uber driver tells me on a ride. 'They own nothing except the app – nothing. I buy the car, pay for everything: if I don't work, I lose money. And they take twenty per cent on everything I earn. Who's the fool?'

In 2017, Uber's founder Travis Kalanick took another Uber ride. Not on the Champs-Élysées, but wedged on the back seat in San Francisco between two women, playing distractedly with his phone and shoulder-shimmying to Daft Punk on the car radio. As the ride came to an end, the driver suddenly confronted Kalanick.[17] 'I'm bankrupt because of you,' Fawzi Kamel said. 'Bullshit,' Kalanick replied. 'You're raising the standards and you're dropping the prices,' Kamel continued. 'People are not trusting you any more. I lost $97,000 because of you. You keep changing everything.'

Kamel's problem lay with the fact that drivers for Uber Black are required to drive recent models of select premium cars, earning a higher rate, but competing with Uber's cheaper UberX rides. Kamel would have bought or leased a car on the basis of projected income to cover it, only to have Uber slash fares and increase commission.

Kalanick fiddled with his phone as Kamel explained his situation and then Kalanick delivered the killer punch line: 'Some people don't like to take responsibility for their own shit. They blame everything in their life on somebody else.' Then he got out and wished Kamel 'good luck'. And there, in that cab, you have the two competing visions of new capitalism: to be a slave or a slave boss.

The 'sharing' or gig economy – a planet of slave bosses – is the biggest transformation in our working lives since the Industrial Revolution. In 1998, a decade before Travis Kalanick stood on the Champs-Élysées trying to hail a cab, he dropped out of UCLA to create a peer-to-peer file-sharing service like MP3 music site Napster.

It was called Scour and like Napster, Scour was destroyed by the music industry. Metallica and Dr Dre sued Napster's Shawn Fanning for infringing copyright, forcing it out of business. Kalanick found himself facing a lawsuit from the American motion picture industry, the Recording Association of America and the Music Publishers Association. Scour was toast.

The idea of peer-to-peer seemed killed forever. Napster and Scour had tried to pickpocket the most powerful entertainment companies on earth. But they had created the germ of a new idea – one that Kalanick would resurrect eight years later when he found himself standing on a Paris pavement in the snow. Peer-to-peer with a difference. Instead of sharing music, share employees.

With peer-to-peer, peers are both suppliers and consumers at the same time. There is no one-way client-server. It is a collaborative system with peers contributing by dropping in and out. In the utopian sales bumph of the sharing economy, none of us has one job anymore, because we all do thirty jobs or three hundred jobs, whenever we feel like it. The only constant is that we are our own boss.

Optimists for the sharing economy refer to this free-market equality as 'dotcommunism'. In theory, dotcommunism undermines anyone setting themselves up as an authoritarian boss, because it empowers the individual to choose where and how to work. Infinite demands for different services mean work will become infinitely diverse and varied. We can stick it to any one evil employer, because they have no monopoly on employment. It destroys hierarchical structures by replicating the egalitarianism of social networking.

Here is the less optimistic view. Take Fawzi Kamel in his Uber cab. In theory, he has the opportunity to go and work for anyone, as Kalanick implies. But in reality, he is tied in to Uber, because Uber have a virtual monopoly on cabs in San Francisco. He could always make himself slave boss of another low-paid job, but he has invested in the cab and needs to pay it back. He is trapped.

Freelance or hyper-flexible, so-called 'contingent' work is growing at an exponential rate – from thirty-four per cent of the US workforce in 2017 to over fifty per cent by 2020. That is a sixteen-per-cent increase in people becoming their own slave boss in only three years. When people migrated in the

Industrial Revolution from countryside to city, it took twenty years. This is potentially more for-reaching and its happening five times faster.

The word 'contingent' is interesting: it means that you are employed 'contingent' on there being anything for you do. The new 'sharing economy' may offer new 'opportunities', but the number of people offering their services massively outstrips the demand. And with technology threatening to make billions of people redundant globally, we will all be slave bosses at the exact moment we have nothing to do.

PayPal founder and tech billionaire Elon Musk has suggested a solution – a 'universal basic wage'. We could essentially be paid to do nothing if automation delivers economic prosperity. Robots could be taxed on their labour and pay income tax, as humans currently do. The resulting revenue would then be used to pay us, and we could be paid to shop, as consumerism will continue to be the primary engine of growth. Shopping will be our paid job. Plus robots have not learnt how to shop, yet.

Robots would need to be taxed at a level humans never were. The average hourly wage has pretty much the same purchasing power it had in 1979. The $4.03 an hour rate of January 1973 has the same purchasing power as $22.41 today. And for this stagnation, we live a life where we never stop working, and never stop worrying that we are not working hard enough. But this is not accidental. It was a plan, and the irony is that it was sold to us as freedom to be our own boss.

In ten years' time, a staff job like my father's will be rare and highly prized. Everyone else will be CEO of their own business enterprise, whether they are Warren Buffet or the person cleaning out the bins under his desk.

THE CHEAP GOODS EQUATION

The global equation of low wages and zero growth depends on a third factor for its equilibrium: cheap goods. If things stay cheap, you do not have to be paid more wages. Take the package I have on my desk. It is a pen with cartridges bought online for £2. Less than the price of a coffee from Starbucks. It has been transported from India to London and cost more to process the transaction – £5.50 – than the object is worth.

This new age of flexible next-to-no-pay working is built on two founding stones: cheap goods made for next to nothing in the global sweatshop of slave bosses, where someone somewhere is being paid even less than you. To maintain full employment on low wages here, goods from elsewhere need to stay cheap, and get cheaper, to plummet in tandem with falling wages. Soon a child in a sweatshop in Singapore will have to pay me to take their T-shirt.

Glancing up from my computer, I see a package that arrived this morning from China. It contains a single item – a phone cable – that cost 99p. My books sit on a shelf that cost £24 from IKEA. There are books on that shelf that cost twice the price of the whole shelf. I am wearing a T-shirt that cost, shockingly, £2. The coffee mug I drink from cost £4. The beans that made the coffee cost more than the mug.

We are so accustomed to buying things cheaply that we cannot imagine it any other way, but we should. Because the price rise is coming, and we will not be able to afford it.

Cheap imports began with the entrepreneurial vision of one man looking for an opportunity from the Vietnam War. In 1967, shipping tycoon Malcolm McLean, the CEO of US container company Sea-Land Service Inc., did a deal with the US army, desperate to get supplies quickly over to Indochina. Sea-Land began transporting millions of tonnes of food, cigarettes and medical supplies in huge, oblong metal boxes over thousands of miles of sea. At a stroke, McLean had invented modern containerisation and by 1971, McLean's deal with the US army was worth $100 million a year.

There was only one problem, McLean's giant container ships were only earning money on their outward journey to Vietnam, returning empty to the East Coast of America. So McLean had a brilliant idea. Why not cut another deal, this time with Japan, the fastest-growing economy on earth.

Between 1960 and 1973, Japanese industrial output quadrupled. American consumers hankered for one product above all that remained prohibitively expensive, but one the Japanese could now supply cheaply: home technology.

Thanks to containerisation, the US was flooded overnight with hi-fis, radios and TVs. Once the preserve of the wealthy, technology was now 'Made in Japan' or 'Made in China' at a fraction of the price. These hi-tech luxuries were now affordable to anyone.

Cheap goods were a boon to consumers, but a disaster for Western industry. Imports coincided neatly with the collapse of manufacturing. Containerisation was the killer blow. Marc Levinson has calculated that 300 million containers are now crossing the world's oceans each year, twenty-six per cent of them coming from China alone.[18]

The downward price drive has continued relentlessly and we the consumer now expect it. TVs today cost three per cent of what they cost in 1980. Cameras are seventy-five-per-cent cheaper than they were in 2000, thanks to cameras on phones. Phones themselves are half the price they were in 2005. The first commercial mobile phone, the Motorola DynaTAC 8000X launched in 1983 cost $4,000. Technology, once the domain of the rich, is now owned by all of us as material recompense for stagnating wages.

But as wages are driven ever lower, can cheap goods keep getting cheaper with them? Not with the world's resources running out. Steve Howard, IKEA's global head of sustainability, says there is a problem. The coming global price hike.[19]

In the 1990s, before the internet took off, IKEA was offering a cunning template for how the internet would look if it was laid out like a store. Anyone who walks round IKEA knows how the lay-out ensnares: you follow a winding path that dictates your route but allows you to think you are diverting off to look at a bed, a toast rack, or some shelving. The lay-out of the store provides a hidden guiding hand, making you believe you have some choice in what you are looking at. It gives the illusion of freedom, just like Peters and Waterman's 7S work model.

Every item at IKEA is designed backwards, beginning with the space it will fill when flat on a shelf in the warehouse. It is also reverse engineered from the price backwards. The coffee mug has a fixed sale price of say £2 so all design decisions flow from there.

Eighty per cent of people who go to IKEA have in mind a single big purchase they are either buying that day or scoping out. But they get home with a sponge shaped like a strawberry, a rubber-duck wine stopper, scented candles and some Swedish biscuits.

What did all the things we did buy have in common? They were cheap. 'How long can we expect to push the margin, as the consumer demands cheaper and cheaper?' Steve Howard says. Price inflation will make an economic model built on low wages and stagnant growth simply unsustainable.

'At some point, prices will have to rise as resources get more expensive. This is the coming global price hike, and who's going to pay if it's not passed on to the shopper?' Steve says companies cannot pass it on because that will hit their customer base, so we have created an impossible conundrum.

At the moment, there is someone else picking up the tab: the person making the object at the other end. A woman in a Philippines sweatshop knocking out 100 jackets a day or the 200 million Chinese workers making smartphones using benzene, or using carcinogenic chemicals to extract gold, platinum or palladium from old laptops and phones.

Doubling the salary of a sweatshop worker would add less than 2% to the retail price but the companies that refuse to do this claim the consumer would not stand for it. Yet consumers are regularly polled on price and are willing to pay 15% more to know something has not been produced by someone on sweatshop wages.

At the moment, we think we have nothing in common with the people on the other side of the world making cheap goods for us, but very soon we will. We will all be the boss and with a small voice in our head – our inner boss – telling us to work harder. Or else.

CHAPTER EIGHT
UPGRADE: ENGINEERING DISSATISFACTION

Forty miles outside San Francisco is the town of Livermore. Halfway down the main street lined with cafés and antique shops is a fire station, and high up on the back wall, away from the gleaming vintage fire truck, polished daily by retired volunteers with bushy white moustaches, is the one thing of which the residents of Livermore are proudest. Making a low hum, flickering an eerie yellow glow, is a light bulb. But unlike any other light bulb on earth this one has not stopped working for 116 years.[1]

The Shelby Electrical Company made the Centennial Bulb in 1901. A hand-blown carbon filament emitting thirty watts, it now gives four watts like a child's night light, but here is the remarkable thing: it still works. Why? It is a mystery, and begs the question: why, if Livermore Fire Station has a light bulb still burning after well over a century, does the rest of the world have ones that break after six months?

In that dusty Shelby bulb is the secret of consumerism. It is the first step on the journey to how planned obsolescence was first concocted and the continuous upgrade created.[2] Today the upgrade is a way of life. We change our phones every eleven months; twenty-eight per cent of us change our sofa every three years;[3] our partner on average every two years nine months (for the twenty-eight per cent, a sofa lasts longer than a relationship).[4]

We belong to the global cult of what product designers call 'infinite new-ism' – a distrust of anything not just 'old', but 'old' meaning we upgraded it just a couple of weeks ago.

The upgrade has even transferred from objects to us. Perpetual self-improvement is an obsession in every sphere of life: perfecting the body in the gym, becoming ever more productive at work, a better colleague, partner, cook, lover, parent, carer, human. This relentless and all-encompassing self-improvement drive is upgrade culture. It did not magic from nowhere, it was engineered, and the Shelby light bulb is the first clue as to how it happened.

The second is 5,600 miles away. In 1989, as communism collapsed and crowds clambered over the Berlin Wall, a historian called Gunter Hess walked unnoticed into a building in East Berlin: the headquarters of the Osram Electrical Company.

Inside, Hess found overturned filing cabinets and papers strewn across the floor. Hess began sifting through the administrative detritus and then something caught his eye. Confidential minutes from a meeting in Geneva in 1932 between two of the most senior members of the Osram executive board and the five biggest electrical companies on earth. When two decades on, I met Gunter in a Berlin café and I asked him what was so special about these papers, Gunter opened his briefcase.

The five biggest light bulb manufacturers on earth were meeting in Geneva to make a policy decision that would change the course of history. They were to create a secret cartel, known as Phoebus, and with one aim: to put anyone out of business who created a light bulb that lasted more than six months.[5]

The papers prove something we all vaguely believe exists when our kettle mysteriously stops working six months after we buy it, but it turns out actually does exist: planned obsolescence.

The Phoebus cartel was founded by William Meinhardt of Osram and Anton Philips, the founder of Dutch electrical giant Philips Electrical. They wanted to systematise obsolescence, imposing a global policy on the lifespan of a light bulb and breaking any company that strayed from the cartel's dictum.

Hess showed me the signatories of Phoebus's inaugural meeting. They included America's biggest electrical company, General Electric, AE from Britain, Compagnie Des Lampes from France, GE Sociedad Anonyma of Brazil, China's biggest producer of electrical goods, General Edison, Lamparas Electricas from Mexico, and Tokyo Electric.

The minutes mapped out their plan in precise terms: shorten the life of every light bulb to six months. Should anyone not stick to the plan, a sliding scale of fines would be imposed, all paid in Swiss francs or German marks.

These five companies did not simply produce light bulbs. They provided the basic infrastructure of modern life: street lighting; copper wiring for phone lines; cabling for ships, bridges, train and tram lines. They made consumer durables such as refrigerators and ovens; provided the electrics for cars, homes and offices. And from 1932 onwards, it was all to be made to break.

Two thousand years of human ingenuity in manufacturing goods to last as long as possible was to stop. Henceforth, mass production would mean counter-intuitively reverse engineering an object from the moment it should break, backwards. Each object would have a different lifespan drawn up on a spreadsheet. Gunter Hess showed me the categories meticulously calibrated on a sliding scale of obsolescence, scrawled in boxes in spidery handwriting, each box stipulating lifespan. Crucially, the consumer was not to know a thing about it. The light bulb at Livermore Fire Station was the one that got away.

Was Phoebus doing anything wrong? In 1932, the free world balanced on a knife edge between economic depression and recovery. Hitler was poised to take power in Germany. The Phoebus plan to systematise planned obsolescence did not simply sell more light bulbs, but saved capitalism and therefore democracy when it was most perilously threatened. It kept people buying.

THE NEWEST NEW THING

Outside the Apple Store on Regent Street, London, there are two thousand people queueing for the new iPhone. They stand patiently, scrolling through the last iteration of the iPhone (in ten minutes' time, obsolete). The police overseeing the queue scroll through their phones, too. The line snakes around the building, down the next street and into an adjacent park.

Those nearest the front have been waiting nearly forty-eight hours. The man at the very front sits on a fishing chair with a roll-up mattress and plastic tarpaulin to keep off the rain. He has a small gas cooker with which he heats up soup. He began queueing on Saturday afternoon. It is now Monday morning.

'Do you mind telling me,' I ask him, 'what the new iPhone will do that your old phone doesn't?' He frowns, annoyed at the stupidity of the question. 'What do you mean?' 'Well, you've been queueing nearly forty-eight hours in the cold, so I'm just wondering what's so special about the new phone?'[6]

He sighs and leans forward. 'It's new.' And that is the point. It is four minutes to nine, and when the doors open and the whooping Apple employees in their blue T-shirts try to hold back the rushing human tide, my new friend will be the first person to own the very newest iPhone it is possible to own anywhere in the world, for a very short period of time. In two minutes, the first buyers will put it on eBay and then it will be old.

Obsolescence is built into newness – it is the flaw at the heart of everything we buy. Not far from the Livermore Fire Station and the oldest bulb in the world is a warehouse filled with brand-new tech-goods that have never even been used: phones, tablets, laptops, printers, microwave ovens, Sat Navs, headphones, drones, wearable technology to help you stave off your own obsolescence by becoming the optimum you. It is all still in its boxes, unopened, donated to a charity by companies that bought the products in bulk but then upgraded to another product before even opening them.

'Where's all this stuff bound for?' I ask the manager of the warehouse. To Baltimore, Bangladesh, anywhere that people want it. The trouble is, he admits, they don't want it, because out-of-date technology is as unappealing to the poorest half of the world as it is to the richest.[7]

In 2008 I visited Malawi, one of the poorest countries on earth. Remote villages without clean water or electricity still had villagers with an iPhone, because they already recognised the smartphone as an essential tool for modernisation. As William Wallis of the *Financial Times* put it in 2016, 'the mobile phone is to sub-Saharan Africa what the steam train was to nineteenth-century Europe: the mechanical workhorse driving social and economic transformation.'

Mark Essian, a Nigerian hotel entrepreneur, says the very lack of infrastructure in Africa works to its advantage as Africa upgrades itself wholesale as a continent. 'The future of technology for Africa is not in playing catch-up. But in looking at the things we lack and using those gaps as an opportunity to invent something we can use to leapfrog the rest of the world.'[8]

McKinsey estimate that half of sub-Sahara's billion people will have internet access by 2025: that is 360 million smartphones. There are already apps for herding cattle (i-Cow in Kenya); private security in Ghana (hei julor!); and an Uber-style service in Uganda connecting mobile washerwomen to people with dirty laundry (Yoza).[9] No one in Africa or Asia wants a ten-year-old Dell printer, and upgrade culture is grasped more voraciously in Africa and Asia than in the old developed world, because to upgrade is to be ahead of the game in two of the fastest-moving markets on the planet.

Tech companies are happy to oblige. Software updates like IoS render your phone or laptop redundant if you do not upgrade in step with the rest of the upgrading world. It is a train none of us can get off.

The Phoebus Cartel invented planned obsolescence and the rules companies would follow: the parameters for the upgrade diktat whether it be a light bulb or IoS software. But to become enthralled to the upgrade – to feel a psychological need to always want the newest new thing – required the failure of planned obsolescence, and a new idea to replace it. Obsolescence itself needed an upgrade.

ENGINEERING DISSATISFACTION

We think patronisingly of the 1950s as a naïve time when the public could still have the wool pulled over their eyes, but nothing was further from the truth. War had politicised and educated the public. As a result of working in factories and on production lines, people knew both how things were made and what they were worth. This meant they were now wise to being conned.

The 1951 Ealing Studios comedy *The Man in the White Suit* starred Alec Guinness as a scientist who accidentally invented a miraculous new material that would never wear out or go dirty. But instead of being hailed a genius, union leaders and industrialists ganged up to destroy his formula.

The Man in the White Suit was a satire about planned obsolescence and the complicity of industry and unions in perpetuating a con on the public. Its success revealed the depth of anger the public felt and the cynicism they showed towards those carrying out what appeared to be shady deals behind closed boardroom doors. Guinness's anti-hero wears a symbolic white suit standing for public integrity and honesty in a world of murky collusion.

But Roger MacDougall and Alexander MacKendrick's script is far from anti-capitalist. It pours scorn on both workers and bosses. This was a new kind of public disillusion: the disillusion of the consumer. Potentially far more dangerous than distrust of politicians, whom no one ever trusts. Disillusionment with consumerism threatened the growth of the economy at a critical moment, when Western governments needed the public to buy.

The year *The Man in the White Suit* was released, the Labour government was seeking re-election. They had delivered a welfare state in their first term, but failed to deliver a consumer boom. Winston Churchill sensed an opportunity to get back into office. 'What we need,' the Conservative manifesto stated, 'is abundance. The production of new wealth ... far more beneficial than class.'

Churchill was making a stab for a new demographic: 'consumers'. And consumers had a very political role to play in the resurrection of Britain. In 1951, the Korean War broke out. The world faced a seemingly stark choice between two competing brands: 'communism' and 'capitalism'.

For capitalism to win, Churchill and President Truman needed the consumer to do their duty and begin shopping for big-ticket purchases in Britain and America, powering a consumer boom and thus economic recovery. Consumerism was not merely shopping, it was an ideological weapon for fighting the Cold War.

Both communism and capitalism offered alternative nirvanas built on competing ideas of freedom: communism had tanks and the West had shoppers. Communism promised freedom from class and capitalism promised freedom to shop, but the difference was that capitalism could offer nirvana today, not the classless tomorrow in a never-never future.

This was a distinct advantage when it came to the battle for hearts and minds. Capitalism had tangible proof to workers that it worked: the things you had bought in your house. Communism had only a belief in tomorrow. In the struggle with communism, goods were evidence today and the act of buying them was your duty as a citizen.

But there was a problem. The duty of buying had something rotten at its core, and consumers had rumbled it. Planned obsolescence made a mockery of the ideology of consumerism and the duty of the consumer. Why should we do our duty if the whole thing was a con? If manufacturers wanted to reboot the credibility of consumerism in the minds of the consumer, they needed a new conjuring trick.

Alfred P. Sloan Jr was CEO of General Motors and had steered the company sensibly for thirty years. Though a proficient boss of GM, Sloan had for decades operated in the shadow of a colossus. A genius innovator of the car industry who even had his own -ism: Henry Ford of Ford Motors.

Ford's brilliance came with one simple revelation. In the 1880s and 1890s, meat packers in Chicago had become of great interest to him. They had figured out how to pull animal carcasses apart efficiently, piece by piece along a conveyor belt. In effect, they had created the first modern production line. What, Ford thought, if you reversed the process? Instead of using a production line to deconstruct a cow, use it to construct a car?

Henry Ford revolutionised mass production with the assembly line that built the Model T Ford in 1908. Sloan at GM became a passenger watching an automation revolution unfold. But in 1956, he stepped in and decided to change history himself. Sloan was about to reboot planned obsolescence, and he would do it by reprogramming how we think.

In 1954, at an advertising conference, Milwaukee industrial designer Brook Stevens had addressed delegates with what he believed was the greatest challenge facing post-war industry. 'Instilling in the buyer the desire to own something a little newer, a little better, a little sooner than necessary.'[10]

Sloan had a plan for how to make this happen. To resurrect the discredited doctrine of planned obsolescence, he would engineer a new mindset for the consumer. One in which we ourselves would choose to make a product obsolete.

The thing that would make a car unwanted was no longer what GM did mechanically to the vehicle to make it break, but the distaste the consumer projected on to it. The brain was to become the tool for obsolescence and Sloan described the whole process in two brilliantly chilling words: 'engineered dissatisfaction'.

In Sloan's autobiography, *My Years with General Motors*, he outlined the theory in more detail: 'The changes in the new model (of car) should be so novel and attractive as to create demand ... and a certain amount of dissatisfaction with past models as compared to the new one.'[11] Sloan was going to manufacture dissatisfaction in the consumer by inventing the rolling upgrade.

In San Francisco, I meet the man who was at the heart of Sloan's project, Tom Matano, who grew up in late 1940s Tokyo marvelling at American design such as the Parker pen, the Coke bottle and the GE refrigerator. The first chance he got, Matano headed to the States to become an apprentice designer at General Motors.[12]

One of Tom's first assignments was to work on the first car designed to 'engineer dissatisfaction': the 1956 Chevrolet Bel Air. It is a beautiful Spring day and Tom is driving me across the Golden Gate Bridge in an original model. 'You see the shine on the dashboard?' Tom points to the brilliant blue sheen reflecting the sky. 'That colour was derived from nail varnish. The car was to be an accessory, matching your new coat or handbag.'

The car came with a catalogue, too, showing you what the upgrade model would look like, available in just six months' time. The catalogue is key to understanding Sloan's thinking. At the very moment that you bought the Chevrolet, you were made instantly aware there was a better one coming, and so your new car was already obsolete. It was newly old and you felt automatic disappointment because you now wanted the new one.

How did Tom feel about working in this way? 'We were fashion designers, not car designers. The vehicle under the bonnet, no change. But we had to work on improving the add-ons: upholstery, tail-fins, bright new colours. These were the things that drove the sale.'

Alfred P. Sloan had up-ended everything. Reliability and performance were now irrelevant to selling a car, what mattered were cosmetic changes. But there was a sour taste to this sweet new purchase: it was already out of date, and you would need to upgrade soon. You had done your duty by buying the latest model, but it wasn't right. Your dissatisfaction had been successfully engineered.

Tom's apprenticeship at GM stood him in good stead. He went on to become head of design at Toyota. But as an apprentice coming into the car business, did he think he was duping the customer with the Chevrolet? 'Not really. It was a genius idea of Sloan's, to keep the car under the bonnet virtually the same and sell it as a new car. That is brilliant.'

What Sloan did was reboot obsolescence by turning it into a nagging kernel of doubt that the new thing we have just bought has the clock already ticking on it and is inherently faulty.

Yet there is a brief moment of pleasure to be had: the moment you hold a brand-new purchase in your hand and these doubts are banished. It is the moment my friend at the front of the Apple queue was hoping to feel briefly with his new iPhone. The newest new thing, with no taint of impending obsolescence.

THE DRUG AND THE LOOP: DECISION, REWARD, ENDORPHIN RUSH

Gabe Zickermann lives a stone's throw from the Golden Gate Bridge. A bear of a man, with a Zen-like bald head and talking at one thousand words to the minute, he seems too big for his tiny ultra-minimal, Asian fusion house, complete with contemplation zone and bamboo garden.

Zickermann is one of the chief prophets of the neuroscience of selling, studying exactly what ignites in our brains the very moment we buy something.[13]

He talks with an intense energy about what happens: 'The whole world is full of companies trying to sell you stuff, so how are they going to? The conscious brain thinks it is too smart to fall for a crude sales pitch. We know we are in an upgrade cycle so we have to make ourselves OK with this, and so we invent a new narrative with the product. Once upon a time, the narrative was brand loyalty over a lifetime to a cigarette brand or a washing powder, but now that loyalty is through the upgrade. It is what keeps us with the same brand of car or phone, because we now tell ourselves that we believe it is always improving.'

And this upgrade does not stop with the product. We think our lives should be pushing ever-forward, with a better job, house or partner. Upgrading in everything we do: a better holiday, body at the gym, dating on dating apps, clean eating our way to an upgraded health regime. Products fit this ever-improving narrative by upgrading as we do, and we in turn become an ever-upgradable product, on sale to other people. The human on a shelf, to be bought or left there.

Upgradable objects mark out the forward march of our lives. By surrounding ourselves with the latest and the newest, we tell ourselves we must be progressing with them. A kind of osmosis takes place between upgraded technology and our own sense of self-worth. We become as one.

Yet it is what happens at the very nanosecond of purchase that fascinates Zickermann, and has made him the Go-To guy for big companies seeking to get truly inside our heads. 'When we buy something new, our brain treats this decision as a reward. And a small endorphin rush is created, which we enjoy, because it's a high. A drug. So a loop is created between decision, reward, endorphin rush. And this loop becomes addictive.'

We glibly use the phrases 'retail therapy' and 'shopping addiction' as if we know what they mean, but these are crude terms for a complex neurological process that is real. It is not the object that we crave, but the endorphin rush that comes with purchasing something new. A rush that dissipates so quickly, it is gone before we have even received the confirmation email of purchase or left the shop. In order to get another hit, we buy again and the faster the better.

Sloane may have been rolling a new Chevrolet upgrade off the production line every six months, but today rolling obsolescence is a perpetual and unstoppable reality. A never-ending upgrade mindset. A non-stop nervy jangling in our heads that we cannot keep up. And with no purchase is this intense relationship of endorphin rush and the upgrade culture stronger than with the Apple iPhone.

ARE YOU GETTING IT?

It was 2007 and a tall man in a black polo neck walked out into a lecture theatre to complete silence. A giant silver Apple glowed in the darkness behind him. The man stopped and faced the audience. 'This is a day,' he said, 'I have been looking forward to. Every once in a while, a revolutionary product comes along that changes everything. One is very fortunate if you get to work on one of these in your career.'

There was not a sound in the auditorium. The man paused, looked around, and continued.

'In 1984, Apple introduced the Macintosh. It didn't just change Apple, it changed the whole computer industry. In 2001, we introduced the first iPod. It didn't just change the way we listen to music, it changed the entire music industry.' The audience began to clap.

'Well, today, we're introducing three revolutionary products.' He turned to the huge screen behind him and an icon appeared. 'The first is a widescreen iPod with touch controls.'

This was not any kind of 'icon' the audience were familiar with. It was not a Greek Orthodox painting of Christ, or a picture of Marlon Brando in *On the Waterfront* – it was a child-like cartoon of a white iPod against a bright-orange background. The applause began to intensify.

'The second is a revolutionary mobile phone.' A white telephone appeared magically in a green square. The crowd began to whoop and some of the audience got to their feet. 'And the third is a breakthrough internet communications device.' The place erupted.

'Three things. An iPod, a phone, and an internet communicator.' He repeated the words slowly and deliberately, over and over like a mantra. 'An iPod, a phone, and an internet communicator.' The icons began to spin round and round faster and faster, becoming one. 'Are you getting it? Are you getting it? These are not three separate devices. This is one device, and we are calling it iPhone.'[14]

Steve Jobs turned on his heel and the world was a different place. Hyperbole never normally matches reality, but in this case, Jobs had undersold his achievement. The iPhone was not to be part of the future, it was going to make it. As Jobs prepared his speech, the banks were collapsing in the biggest meltdown since the Wall Street Crash. The iPhone was to rise out of the dust to replace them – it had more computing power than Apollo 11, but its real power lay in what no one – not even Steve Jobs – could predict.

The iPhone was not going to become simply a digital tool for interacting with the physical world, it would remake the physical world to its own digital design. And all with an object the size of the compass that Christopher Columbus used to reach the new world of America 515 years before. Like Jobs, Columbus had dared to be first to a new world, the true scale of which he could scarcely begin to imagine.

THE FIVE-SIDED CIRCLE SQUARED

One of the designers Steve Jobs brought in to develop the iPhone was Dan Crow. We meet in his London offices at 'Silicon Roundabout' in Shoreditch. The iPhone was an extraordinary invention, but I wondered how indebted its upgrade iterations (the 5, 6, 7, 8 plus, etc.) had been to Alfred Sloan's theory of 'engineered dissatisfaction'. How conscious were they of a debt to perpetual upgrade when developing it?

Dan sips his water and replies. 'Apple had got better and better at iterating over many years, starting in the 1970s. Now partly that is driven by upgrade right? And that is interesting.

But the problem is that it's all driven by technology, and inevitably innovation with technology slows.'

Steve Jobs had spotted a problem with engineering dissatisfaction. At some point, even though you keep releasing iPhones with a 6,7,8,9 in front, the public are going to see through it. 'You can put in a sensor or better camera or make the phone gold or whatever, but you are inevitably going to see a natural plateauing of the product. There's a point where it gets about as good as its ever going to get.'

This inevitable slowing of innovation requires quitting ahead of the curve and inventing something new, which is why Apple did not stop with the Macintosh in the 1970s, they kept going. Jobs's genius was to create a giraffe, then throw the drawings away and create a rhino, then a lion and then a shark. He knew the public were never going to keep buying the giraffe, no matter how many times you resprayed it a different colour.

And colour, Dan Crow says, is the giveaway that something is over. When you get down to the colour changing on a product, you are scraping the upgrade barrel. Bright new colours are an unintended signal to the public that a product has done genuinely improving. It happened for the Chevrolet Bel Air and it hangs over the iPhone, which is why Apple are moving on, trying to invent the next elephant.

Steve Jobs learnt from Sloan and General Motors that you can only get away with the upgrade for so long. Ultimately you need the new species. The reason GM died was they never learnt that lesson and Jobs was determined that would never happen to Apple. That is what Jobs truly learnt from Alfred Sloan.

But before the iPhone, it seems Apple were guilty of some good, old-fashioned Phoebus Cartel-style planned obsolescence, just like everyone else.

In 2004, a student in New York called Casey Neistat called the Apple helpline with a problem. The jewel in Apple's crown at that time was the iPod, and Casey Neistat's iPod had mysteriously stopped working.

Casey phoned Apple Support, wanting to know how to change the battery. 'That iPod had cost 400 dollars. So when the battery died, I wanted to fix it. The Apple guy told me that it would cost 250 dollars plus postage to get a new one. Then he said, "At that price, you may as well go and get a new one."'

Casey was perplexed. 'How old is your iPod?' the Apple Support guy asked. 'Eighteen months,' Casey replied. 'Ah. OK. It's past its year.'

It seemed Apple's sales policy was to get Casey – and all iPod owners – to buy another iPod, for another $400. And so to spend potentially $400 on a new iPod every year.

The reason for this was that Apple faced a dilemma. Apple are more like Land Rover than Ford – they are a market leader and quite happy to keep a cap on market share if they can maintain their position as the number-one tech innovator. This matters more than sales, because without design excellence, there are no sales.

To make the iPod slim enough to work on your belt or in your pocket, the battery life had to be compromised. If the consumer wanted a longer-lasting iPod, that would mean a bulkier product. Design would be hamstrung by practicality and in Apple's world, that would mean the tail wagging the dog. Steve Jobs would not do it, which is why Casey's iPod died.

He was furious and began stencilling 'Apple's Dirty Secret: iPod's Unreplaceable Battery Lasts Only 18 Months' on the iPod ads of dancing silhouettes wearing headphones that adorned the streets of New York.

The accompanying video he made went viral on YouTube and was picked up by the *Washington Post, Rolling Stone,* Fox News and the BBC. In drawing attention to the iPod's battery life, Neistat kicked off a new grassroots anti-upgrade movement – 'iFixit' or 'downgrade' culture. Groups of tech volunteers, who tear apart new technology the moment it comes out in order to understand how it works, and do something most of us have long given up trying to do: fix it.

Carl Hebrau works in a small tech start-up in Silicon Valley, but instead of a uniform of chinos and button-down shirt, he and his colleagues at iFixit wear a proper uniform; the kind you would see in a car garage or depot: brown overalls with an iFixit logo on everyone's lapel. Hebrau and his co-workers are pulling apart every new upgraded piece of technology they can get their hands on to create something that most of us have not had with a fridge or TV for decades: an instruction manual.

He has written over two hundred such manuals and put them up for free on line, along with a YouTube video, so that people can work out how to fix things manufacturers believe we cannot be bothered to fix ourselves. If we can't be bothered, Carl says, how come people are flocking to his videos and manuals?

In dismantling the iPhone, Carl found something strange. A unique five-sided pentalobe screw for which there was no screwdriver.

In his workshop, I asked Carl why he thought they had done this. 'To keep the customer out. If you manage to get inside the phone, Apple use standard Philips screws, so clearly there's no aesthetic or practical reason for the five-sided screw on the outside, it's simply a kind of barbed wire to protect the phone from anyone trying to get in.' So Carl decided to make the only screwdriver in the world that can unscrew this five-sided screw, and now gives them away.

I wondered what the five-sided screw was all about and asked Apple for an interview. A smartly dressed man with glasses agreed to meet me in a giant glass office in central London. His name was Benedict Evans, a tech analyst and articulator of Apple's thinking.

'Do you think phones are really improving or are Apple just engineering dissatisfaction through upgrade?'

'We still see specific dramatic improvements. The products are built to last and Apple take great care to keep the customer happy.'

'But when I asked the man at the front of the queue for the

latest iPhone what those improvements were, he couldn't even tell me.'

'It's not the consumer's job to know something is better, or have an opinion on something they've haven't seen.'

People like the i-Fixit guys are a tiny percentage of the consumers who use Apple products. These products have to work for everyone, Benedict argued, and most people just want their phone to function. If something goes wrong, they generally take it to Apple rather than try to fix it themselves.

As for upgrade, he says, what is really so terrible about that?

'The argument (against upgrade) says we were a lot better off when we had much slower consumption and much slower lives. When eighty to ninety per cent of the population were peasants. The story of humanity's move away from peasantry is in part the story of consumption.'

Apple have changed the lives of billions of people with the iPhone and if the unintended consequence has been an obsession with upgrade as a society, that is not necessarily Apple's fault.

Throwing virtually new goods away is a consumer choice created by upgrade. We chase something better, yet are never able to attain it. This ever-receding shore is the perfect product. Apple merely invented a platform for this perfect product to be chased, we did the rest.

Benedict asks me if I have ever seen the Bill Murray plane sketch from *Saturday Night Live*? I haven't. Bill Murray plays a grumpy businessman on a plane, angrily complaining to the air stewardess that the ice in his whisky is not cold enough. He complains and complains, and his complaints get ever more tiresome.

Eventually the stewardess has enough. 'What you should be doing, sir,' the stewardess says, 'is marvelling at the fact you are travelling at one thousand, two hundred miles per hour, thirty thousand feet above the ground. Not worrying about the temperature of your ice.'

The iPhone is the plane and I am Bill Murray, complaining about the ice. Upgrade culture is bigger than the iPhone or criticisms of it. Upgrade culture subsumes everything and yet we know this mindset is a diminishing return. New products never really make us happy, and yet we don't care. We upgrade anyway. Why?

The upgrade is impervious to criticism because we were long ago conditioned to believe upgrade equalled technological progress, the most credible and unchallengeable kind of progress. It was a reprogrammed state of mind first conjured by the genius of Alfred P. Sloan. And this state of mind comes from somewhere far deeper than wanting something new, or even the endorphin hit from possessing the newest new thing. It comes from wanting to become a better person.

THE BIOLOGICAL UPGRADE: HUMAN 2.0

We are now for the first time in history able to upgrade ourselves. The Shanghai super-rich have begun to breathe different air from people on the street below. In Beijing, penthouse apartments overlooking the city are supplied pure mountain oxygen pumped from the Canadian Rocky Mountains by companies like Alberta-based Vitality Air, who sell canisters of 'the cleanest air on earth' for between $20 and $32 a canister. Each one lasts between 150 and 200 breaths. 'Our Chinese website keeps crashing,' Vitality Air's Chinese rep Harrison Wang says. 'When the air (outside) is bad, we see spikes in sales. The smog is definitely our best advertising.'[15]

According to its website, another pure-air supplier, Aethaer, is 'filtered organically by nature as it flows between the leaves of woodland trees, absorbs pristine water as it passes over babbling brooks and forest streams.' It is sold in a glass jar for £80 a jar and founder Leo De Watts says it needs to be savoured when inhaled, like a fine wine.[16]

If you step outside and need to breathe polluted air, you can use a smart air-quality monitor called a 'laser egg' for $79.

'People want to have an objective way of seeing air quality, and technology can help us control our environment,' according to Origins founder Jess Lam, who sell the laser egg.[17]

Shanghai is upgrading its air. It is simultaneously one of the most polluted cities and home to some of the richest people on earth. In London, another polluted hub for the global super-rich, every stop on the Jubilee Line travelling east from Westminster sees life expectancy drop by a year. Those living in Canning Town, eight stops away from Westminster, live eight years less. Seventy-two versus seventy-eight.

In the nineteenth century, the rich lived longer than the poor because they had better diet and social conditions, but now the gap is widening still further as a result of the biological upgrade opportunities coming the rich's way.

BCIs or 'Brain-Computer Interfaces' are implantable devices intended originally to help the disabled move lifeless limbs, but they could now be used to create robotic prosthetics for a more powerful you: a 'self-optimised' human, neither machine nor flesh, but a seamless amalgam of the two and perpetually upgradable. Limbs as the plastic surgery of the twenty-first century.

To bolster this self-optimised you, uploading memory and linking the brain directly to the internet will create infinite memory storage, and mean the rich never forget, as well as think faster. Human cyborgs versus plain old humans. 2.0 *vs* 1.0.

I am at a discreet white door in Harley Street, London. It is an exclusive health clinic called Viavi ('Health Managed – Life Optimised'). I am ushered into a white room with a white bed and white curtains. The only bright colours in the room are the blueberries and strawberries in a pristine porcelain bowl, brought to me on a tray.

I am here to meet Dr Sabine Donnai, one of the world's leading authorities on the potential of the human upgrade. Before setting up her own exclusive Harley Street business, she was the medical director at Nuffield and clinical director at BUPA, so I wondered why someone at such a senior position in the biggest private healthcare company in the UK would suddenly strike out alone. The reason was simple: she saw the future, and went for it.

'We are now, thanks to bio-tech advances, at a point where we can collect an infinite amount of data on you: what you eat and when, how it affects your body, your stress levels, your glucose levels, blood-pressure levels, your sleep patterns, how your body is coping every second of the day. But we can drill into these numbers in a micro-way never possible before – each set of data can itself further be broken down with a level of precision no one would have dreamt possible even five years ago. The point is not the amassing of this data, but what you do with it.'

To show me what Viavi do with it – a bespoke biometric mapping service costing £13,000 a year used by everyone from film stars to CEOs, politicians and premiership footballers – I had a go myself. Wearing an injected glucose monitor in my arm and uploading the data every five hours, a heart monitor blinking away measuring stress and heart rate for three days; spitting five times a day into different coloured serums to be analysed in a laboratory, urinating 'best morning urine' into test tubes and defecating into a space-age silver 'sleeve'.

The aim is to create the ultimate body MOT and use this data to become the 'optimum you'. Dr Donnai does not believe the super-rich clients she has actually seek to perfect themselves, but want to have a medical licence to live the way they want to live. With the data, they can find the 'weak links in the DNA chain, further weakened by lifestyle choices.' Their solution is a targeted strike on these weak links.

But the real opportunity lies not with the thousands of rich clients she has, but the potential millions she will have when she launches a cheaper high-street model of this service, rolling it out across Britain and Europe. Viavi will become the first high-street player to use state-of-the-art DNA editing called CRISPR. Boots Meets *Blade Runner*.

CRISPR has already identified the specific gene that causes cataracts and cystic fibrosis. It is being used to edit out potential hereditary disease and to perfect plants and animals for human consumption. Beijing-based BGI-Shenzhen, a Viavi of China, say they will be able to sequence your DNA for less than the price of an iPhone. Google's Deep Mind is racing to be first to unlock the genetic basis for intelligence.

George Church, a geneticist at Harvard, is working on developing tools that scramble the genetic code allowing us to engineer bacterium resistant to viral infection. He does not dismiss the possibility of changing human DNA to create a new kind of human that does not need to rely on powerful, enhanced robo-limbs, because it is biologically superior. A human 2.0.

I ask Dr Donnai if we should be scared by CRISPR and the future world dawning now, and fast. 'Not really. Twenty years ago, we were terrified by the thought of IVF babies. The scare stories were of genetic selection and super-babies, but the reality was millions of couples miraculously being able to simply have children they never thought they could have.'

Will the upgraded human be an upgrade for all as Donnai predicts, or the beginning of the creation of two species: Human 1.0 and its upgraded, faster, cleverer, stronger and richer relative?

Historian Yuval Harare thinks the latter. We meet in London and he is tremendously upbeat and high-octane as he tells me that the human as we know it will be over in a hundred years. 'Only the upgraded will matter.' It will in essence be inequality made flesh. Oxford bio-technician Anders Sandberg refers to this bifurcation of the human race into the upgraded and un-upgradable underclass as 'speciation'.[18] And what will begin as a medical divide created by income and access to DNA editing will after one generation become biological, irreversible and ordained. The upgrade will be passed on, just as genes are now.

When the Phoebus Cartel created planned obsolescence eighty years ago, six men sitting round a table in Geneva could not have imagined that the one thing ultimately made obsolete by the upgrade would be humanity itself.

CHAPTER NINE
POWER: THE FIRM WHO KNOW EVERYTHING

In 2014, I was in the Dorchester Hotel in London interviewing China's richest man, Wang Jianlin, chairman of the Dalian Wanda construction empire. Wang is worth $32 billion and was in London because he had $7 billion in loose change and was looking to spend it on something 'big'.

A parade of eager British business interests lined up to pitch Wang their 'unmissable' opportunity. Men and women in very expensive suits stood in the corridor with portfolios waiting to be summoned, including a film studio, a plan to build the world's tallest building in London, and a top Premiership football club.

How likely any of these deals were to happen depended entirely on how Wang was feeling today, such is the Caligulan whim of those that sit on the very, very top cloud of the super-rich stratosphere, unimaginably wealthier than the mere billionaires who sit on the lower clouds. His thumb might go up or down. Wang is one of the 0.000001 per cent richest people on earth. He is on the top cloud.

Wang remained unseen, like the Spectre boss in the Bond movie. He sat in a private darkened room with eight of his business associates and a translator (Wang told me later that he understood English perfectly well, but that it was useful sometimes to pretend not). People had been ushered in discreetly all day for their thirty-second pitch.

Minutes before I was summoned, two unassuming characters had been rumoured to be skulking in the corridor, pacing nervously. They were called David and Boris – one, it turned out, was the Prime Minister of Great Britain and the other was the Mayor of London (latterly the Foreign Secretary).

What struck me was not that they were supposedly meeting Wang, but they were waiting in line with everyone else. Once Wang would have gone to Downing Street, lucky to be granted an audience. Now they were lucky to see him, and had an allotted window like the rest of us.

Business, not government, now calls the shots. And business no longer has to even influence government, business *is* government. China claims on the tin to be communist, but it runs like the largest public limited company on earth, while a businessman is the president of the most powerful country on earth.

The job of government now is not to serve the people, no matter what politicians say, but to manage the economy as best it can on behalf of business. This is not a judgment, but a fact. Socialists rail against 'corporate capture', but the truth is that business believes politicians have done such a bad job managing the economy, they have had to step in. They don't even want to – it is just the deal.

The power relationship has been inverted. Seeing politicians meeting successful business people like Wang is like watching a simpering teenager meet a rock star. The politicians do not know what to do with themselves. It is embarrassing.

The corporations these business people run have become like elephants on the African plains, roaming imperiously across the globe in search of the best tax breaks and offshoring deals. These corporations operate above and beyond governments, who are too timid to challenge them, and have no tools at their disposal even if they wanted to do so.

Yet these companies also have more wealth to invest in a

country than the GDP of some of the nations in which they have a stake. Billionaires like Wang have the means to transform the lives of millions of people with a swish of his wand. Wang was being wooed in London with an 'opportunity' to plough his billions into affordable housing. What was in it for him? The chance to build the world's tallest building, outdoing the Burj Khalifa in Dubai. I still have not seen Wang's tower on the London skyline, so clearly the deal did not happen.

How and why did business people like Wang become more powerful than government? Who made the decisions that enabled it, and if business now writes the rules, could it actually do a better job of running the state? To answer these questions, you need to understand how and why government was first subsumed by business.

THE PRESIDENT WHO WARNED THE PEOPLE

On 17 January 1961, President Dwight Eisenhower made his farewell address to the American nation. Eisenhower was a military man to his core. A five-star general and Supreme Commander of the Allied Forces during the Second World War. In 1944, Eisenhower oversaw the planning for the Normandy landings. He went on to become the first Supreme Commander of NATO and then President of the United States. He was the most powerful man on earth, which is why his parting words to the American public on leaving office in 1961 were so extraordinary.

Instead of uttering banalities about leaving America a better place, Eisenhower chose to use his address to make a stark warning. Democracy, he said, was at risk from an insidious new force operating in the corridors of power. A threat he believed the public needed to know about.

'Three days from now,' he declaimed, 'after half a century in the service of our country, I shall lay down the responsibilities of office. This evening I come to you with a message of leave taking.'[1]

Eisenhower began by outlining the known threat: communism. But this danger, he said, had given rise to another one hidden from view: the muscle wielded in the corridors of Washington by the arms industry.

'In the councils of government,' warned Ike, 'we must guard against the acquisition of unwarranted influence, whether sought or unsought, by the military-industrial complex. We must never let the weight of this combination endanger our liberties or democratic processes. We should take nothing for granted. Only an alert and knowledgeable citizenry can compel the proper meshing of the huge industrial and military machinery with our peaceful methods and goals.'

It is still pretty much the most extraordinary thing an American president has ever told the public. A clear-eyed warning from a man at the centre of power: eye to eye from president to electorate. Subsequent interpretations of the speech have rightly pointed out that Eisenhower faced a particular set of circumstances when he made the 'military-industrial complex' speech. The Cold War was escalating. Fifty per cent of government spending and ten per cent of GDP was going on military expenditure each year, and the figure was rising.[2] The potential threat to democracy of military might looked real.

Ike was a staunch anti-communist, yet the idea of the 'military-industrial complex' taking over government was co-opted in the 1960s and 1970s by radical left-wing thinkers like Noam Chomsky as an explanation for the conspiratorial workings of capitalism.

Ike had given the American public a glimpse behind the curtain of power and told them the deal. And this reality check was very much at odds with the public's belief in democracy as transparent. It was the day the American public began to believe dark forces were at work behind the scenes. Their slide into mistrust of politicians began, and a politician had taken them there.

Before Eisenhower made his speech, the public believed the arms industry was defending democracy, not endangering it by using its power as leverage to extract greater profit and influence. Eisenhower inferred that these unseen forces were lobbying to control the levers of power. So who were the lobbyists and where did lobbying come from?

THE WILLARD HOTEL

In the 1870s, a gruff, portly man with a beard could be seen sitting in the lobby of the Willard Hotel, Washington, smoking cigars and drinking brandy. At sixteen, this middle-aged man had been nominated for the prestigious military academy at West Point. He had gone on to become a skilled horseman and decorated captain serving in the Mexican Civil War and at Fort Humboldt, eventually rising to Commanding General of the US Army.[3] But now he had a new job, which partly explained why he was sitting in the lobby of the Willard Hotel.

Ulysses S. Grant was the eighteenth president of the United States and in the afternoons he would go to the lobby of the Willard to get away from the politicians and bureaucrats on Capitol Hill. But there was no escape. They would sniff him out and confront him in the lobby to petition him and attempt to persuade him to support one piece of legislation or another. Grant had spent a lifetime in the brutal business of war, but did not take kindly to their tactics. He referred to them as 'those damned lobbyists' and the name stuck.

Is that true? The term 'lobbying' was already being used in 1850 to describe petitioners waiting to speak to legislators in the lobby of the New York State Capitol in Albany. Across the Atlantic in London, the same term described commoners waiting in the lobbies of the Palace of Westminster to speak to their member of Parliament.

Ever since the 1640s, following the English Civil War, this 'lobby' had been the accepted place to carry out confidential business with newly persuadable representatives of the people.[4]

For three hundred years, 'lobbying' worked to the mutual benefit of politicians and business. You scratch my back and I'll scratch yours. But in the 1960s, something changed. The power shifted and the lobbyists changed. Full employment, coupled with the rise of civil rights, brought two new powerful interest groups into the lobby – minority groups and organised labour. Consumer rights groups, environmentalists, gay rights, feminists, black rights, and the myriad new brokers of pressure-group politics came into the equation and were not simply an annoyance to the old brokers, they had muscle.

Politicians had a democratic duty to address (or be seen to be addressing) these groups. The lobby had been disrupted and these new players threatened to take the politician's ear away from business. Corporate interests felt muscled out of the corridors of power. Subversives and radicals were influencing the heart of government, pushing a reform agenda of special pleading. Voices in business began to become concerned. These new interest groups were not about getting a business deal through, or a piece of legislation amended, they wanted to change the nature of civil society. Something had to be done.

THE POWELL MEMORANDUM

On the 23 August 1971, one of America's most respected and prominent lawyers, Lewis Franklin Powell, sat down to write a memo to his friend Eugene B. Sydnor. 'The Powell Memorandum' was to become a pivotal moment in the fightback, a *cri de coeur* for the business establishment in retreat.[5]

'Business,' Powell said, 'has been the favourite whipping boy of politicians for many years. But the measure of how far this has gone is found in the anti-business views now being expressed by several candidates for President of the United States.[6]

'It is Marxist doctrine,' he continued, 'that the "capitalist" countries are controlled by big business. This doctrine, consistently a part of leftist propaganda all over the world, has a wide public following among Americans.

'Yet, as every business executive knows, few elements of American society today have as little influence in government as the American businessman, the corporation, or even the millions of corporate stockholders. If one doubts this, let him undertake the role of "lobbyist" for the business point of view before Congressional committees . . . one does not exaggerate to say that, in terms of political influence with respect to the course of legislation and government action, the American business executive is truly the "forgotten man".'

Business, Powell said, had been forced into retreat and persecuted by an array of liberal and outright Marxist enemies, who now had the ear of government. Powell outlined these enemies in more detail: 'television' and 'journalism'; the minority-interest groups of feminism, black and gay civil rights, who now constituted the lobby, and weak-minded judges in the Supreme Court, who had allowed these groups to contort the constitution to their own ends.

Then there were Marxist academics and student unions in universities, spreading an anti-American and anti-business agenda; union officials bent on thwarting productivity, who also had politicians in their pocket. Even the Chamber of Commerce, the business lobby in Washington, had proved 'impotent' in the face of this deluge of socialism.

'Current examples of the impotency of business, and the near contempt with which businessmen's views are held, are the stampedes by politicians to support almost any legislation related to "consumerism" (rights) or the "environment",' Powell said.

'Business must learn the lesson, long ago learned by labour and other self-interest groups. Political power is necessary, such power must be assiduously cultivated, and when necessary, it must be used aggressively and with determination.' He concluded, 'Business has shunned confrontation,' but there should now be 'no hesitation to attack.'

The fightback was about to begin and it needed to be dirty to take back control of government. Powell saw this as nothing short of a turning-point in history: the 'fight for freedom'.

Lee Drutman, author of *The Business of America is Lobbying* sees the Powell Memorandum as the touch-paper that lit a new political ideology: neo-liberalism.[7] In the 1960s, there had been 'a regulatory binge spurred on by a new wave of public interest groups. Large corporations had largely sat by idly, unsure of what to do.' This is what Franklin Powell meant by 'socialism': the invisible Lilliputian knots and threads of a thousand pieces of legislation designed to tie business down.

The Powell Memorandum was pinned up to a wall by a clutch of pro-business pressure groups that sprang up in small offices across Washington: the Heritage Foundation (funded by Coors beer), the American Legislative Council (ALEC), the Manhattan Institute and the Cato Institute. The Carthage Foundation was founded in 1964 by tycoon Richard Mellon Scaife to explicitly fund and make possible Powell's vision of pro-business anti-socialist government. The Carthage Foundation sought to roll back Keynesian interventionism and statist paternalism, which had begun with Roosevelt's New Deal, returning America to its rightful custodians: the industrialists.[8]

In Britain, the New Right think-tank the Centre for Policy Studies (CPS) was created. A rising star of British politics called Margaret Thatcher was its president. The CPS worked in tandem with the Institute of Economic Affairs (IEA) created by chicken-farming mogul Anthony Fisher in the 1950s. Fisher had picked up a copy of the *Reader's Digest* by chance one day and read an extract of Friedrich Hayek's *The Road to Serfdom*.[9] He was now a convert to neo-liberalism and wanted to make these ideas happen, just as the Carthage Foundation did in the States.

The Road to Serfdom became their bible and Fisher had a Road to Damascus experience reading it, deciding he would use his business fortune to fund a think-tank dedicated to rolling back the socialist state that Hayek believed would enslave us all.

In the 1970s, these groups dovetailed with the rise of the

supply-side economic revolution of Milton Friedman and the Chicago School. Together, they would become the foundation for an ideological revolution that would change the shape of the last third of the twentieth century, and mould the destiny of the twenty-first.

In his ten-part PBS series *Free to Choose* in 1980, Friedman outlined his grand vision: breaking the tyranny of government and freeing humankind through the sovereignty of markets. Friedman was indebted to the eighteenth-century Scots economist Adam Smith.

'Adam Smith's flash of genius,' Friedman said, 'was to see how prices that emerged in the market – the prices of goods, the wages of labour, the cost of transport – could coordinate the behaviour of millions of independent people, strangers to each other, without anybody telling them what to do. (Smith's) key idea was that self-interest could produce an orderly society benefitting everybody.'

An 'invisible hand' was at work. In *The Wealth of Nations*, Smith talked about 'the way in which individuals who intended only to produce their own interests would promote public welfare by an invisible hand that was no part of their intention.'[10]

It was a key flip from socialism and the state, which were synonymous in his mind. According to Friedman, socialism made people selfish in forcing them towards a collective good. But by simply allowing people to follow their own selfish interests, they would inadvertently create a collective good.

It is impossible to overstate the significance of the deal that was struck between business and ideology. Fisher (businessman) plus Hayek (intellectual) equalled a revolution postponed. But when Friedman (economist) plus Thatcher and Reagan (politicians) came together in 1980, history was jolted off one axis and onto the axis we are on today.

The last eighty years divide into two neat spaces: before and after this moment. Between 1945 and 1979, governments were the primary mover of history, with business attempting to influence them; and from 1979 onwards, it was the other way around.

In Klimov's cinematic masterpiece *Come and See,* about the German invasion of Belorussia, the last five minutes of the film involve twenty catastrophic years of history rewinding at speed before the viewer's eyes.[11] If history rewound at speed through Silicon Valley, the banking crash, deregulation, the fall of the Berlin Wall, and Milton Friedman first meeting President Reagan and Prime Minister Thatcher, it would suddenly freeze-frame in 1972, when Lewis Powell sat down at his heavy, leather-topped desk and began to pen a memo that kick-started the future.

Weeks after penning his memo, Powell became President Nixon's nomination for the Supreme Court. Eugene Sydnor, the head of the Chamber of Commerce to whom he had written the memo, began overhauling the Chamber from a relic of the past to an aggressive driving force for the business fightback.

Behind closed doors, a new secret lobbying organisation was formed, the Business Roundtable, with the leading CEOs of America's biggest firms. Their aim was to re-cultivate political influence in Washington and roll back the negative view of business on the campuses and workplaces of America. 'I think we all recognise,' Alcoa CEO John Harper told his fellow CEOs, 'that the time has come when we must stop talking about it . . . and do something.'

GET RID OF THE CIVIL SERVANTS

Their weapon was the lobbyist. And lobbying was to stop being a polite, discreet word in the ear and go industrial. Professional lobbyists were hired in their thousands and took over one street in Washington – K Street – a stone's throw from 'The Hill'.

Lobbyists badgered, cajoled, log-rolled, threatened and horse-traded their way round government. In London, they lined up down Victoria Street in glass office blocks and in anonymous

Georgian-fronted houses in St James's Square. Lobbyists did not skulk around hotel lobbies anymore. They were an industry in their own right.

The major K Street firms became feared and respected. They got labour law repealed, taxes lowered and most importantly, prepped the ground for public distrust of 'big government'. In less than a decade, lobbying went from a forgotten art to the way business was done.

By the early 1980s, Lee Drutman says, their success put them at a crossroads. 'Corporations could have declared victory and gone home. Instead they stuck around and kept at it. Many deepened their commitments to politics. After all, they now had lobbyists to help them see all that was at stake in Washington, and all the ways in which staying politically active could help their businesses.'[12]

Lobbying was about to make its greatest leap: from a reactive to a pro-active machine. Up until now, the lobbyist's job had been to stop government from meddling in business, and they had succeeded. Now lobbyists were to step over the threshold into government, pushing for legislative change, drafting legislation and pushing back the 'socialist' state. Business was about to become government.

Just one thing stood in the way: civil servants. For over a thousand years, civil servants had quietly burrowed away at the heart of government. Civil servants first rose to prominence in Imperial China. The idea of a civil service based on merit, not inherited entitlement, was revolutionary, with far-reaching effects on Chinese society. At a stroke, the Xiaolian system destroyed the idea of jobs passed down as heirlooms. Instead, candidates sat a fiercely competitive exam. Those who passed got the job.

In 2009, tiny 'cheat sheets' were discovered in Qingdao, Eastern China, and on the southern island of Hainan, dating back to the 1750s. These tiny booklets, printed on silk, were under two inches long and could fit inside a matchbox, but contained 140,000 characters to help cheat in the exams.[13] The cheat sheets are testament to the importance that was placed on passing these civil service exams, a gateway to social improvement.

In 1847, the British consul to China, Thomas Taylor Meadows, wrote a letter praising the meritocracy of the Chinese civil service exam: 'The long duration of the Chinese empire is solely and altogether owing to the good government which consists in the advancement of men of talent and merit only.'

The result of Meadows's letter was to open up the British civil service in the same way. Under the Northcote-Trevelyan reforms of 1854, exams were introduced. Meritocracy became the bedrock of the British and Indian civil service, the Prussian bureaucratic system and the modern US civil service, laid down by the Pendleton reform act.

Meritocracy became the driving force for a new middle class. In China, it drove urbanisation and the spread of education. Applied to Britain and Central Europe a thousand years later, it drove the growth of a middle class and undermined the political authority of an aristocracy already teetering on the edge of collapse. Meritocracy was a mechanism for change without revolution and a hand-picked civil service would deliver it.

However, by the 1960s and 1970s, the civil service was perceived as having become a force of inertia. A self-serving bureaucracy, as complacent as the aristocracy had once been. Civil servants became a caricature of dull, grey men in grey suits, pushing paper round a desk, hindering change by smothering it in administration.

In the 1970s, professional lobbyists had got business through the door in Washington and Whitehall, but now it was time to change the civil servants in the room. It was time for that consultancy buzzword – 'transformation' – and first up for transformation was the civil service.

THE FIRM

One company would make it happen: McKinsey, the world's most influential consultancy firm. McKinsey 'advise' ninety of the one hundred biggest companies on the *Fortune* list, and dozens of governments across the globe. New recruits are selected from Rhodes and Baker scholars at Oxford and Harvard, just as MI5 and the CIA once recruited spies.

When you start at McKinsey, you are given two analogies to make you understand better the kind of place you are working in. The first is the Jesuits. A specially chosen holy order closed off to outsiders, with a life-long loyalty to the order. Other management consultants do not even refer to McKinsey by name, they call it simply 'The Firm'. The second analogy is the bespoke Savile Row tailor; anonymous people working discreetly in the background of government about whom you know nothing, but who know everything about you.[14]

McKinsey is a 'consultancy' firm in the way Google is a search engine. Its true remit is power, just as Google's actual remit is the control and real-world application of all data. McKinsey ranks only seventh in size beside its global competitors: Boston Consulting Group, Bain, PricewaterhouseCoopers, and Deloitte. McKinsey is not about turnover, but power. It is more important than all the others put together: the indispensable secret cog in the machine of government that no one outside the corridors of Washington and Whitehall has even heard of.

In the late 1960s, politicians fired up by the desire for change saw obstructive civil servants as a problem, and McKinsey was there to help. The technocratic revolution – the 'white heat of technology' – had delivered confident new, smooth-talking experts, who looked far more dynamic than the old-fashioned civil servants.

They did not go to the Garrick Club for a long lunch, they talked the breathless modern management-speak of flip charts and graphs. They were efficient and they were outsiders. Tony

Benn, Energy Minister under Harold Wilson, distrusted the civil service to implement the kind of radical modernising reforms he sought, and began to bring in these new outside 'experts'.

In the 1970s, politicians began to use consultants more widely, and primarily McKinsey, which offered 'independent' strategy advice. 'Policy not politics' was the new mantra, and the civil service were seen as mired in the latter. McKinsey's sharp-suited soldiers on the ground, by contrast, had the aura of clever people in a rush to the next meeting, too busy for politics. Politicians were in awe of this confidence and McKinsey were to become the new quiet word in a politician's ear. They appeared to know something no one else did.

'The Firm' were instrumental in restructuring the entire staffing and running of the White House.[15] In Westminster, they were at the heart of the mammoth privatisation programme of the Conservatives in the 1980s. When the Conservatives shipped out and Tony Blair arrived in office, McKinsey stayed. Under New Labour in the late 1990s and early 2000s, McKinsey were integral to Blair's 'modernisation' of Britain, 'transforming the thinking' on health, education and in the key areas of government where they were now deemed to be indispensable. They asked politicians to think the unthinkable – there was nothing that could not be radically reformed. Nothing was sacred.

In 1997, McKinsey crystallised their revolution in just four words: 'The War for Talent'. Twenty years earlier, McKinsey had reconfigured the workplace with the '7S System' developed by McKinsey strategists Pascal, Peters and Waterman. The 'War for Talent' was the next stage of evolving the human in the workplace.

McKinsey's Ed Michaels, Helen Handfield-Jones and Beth Axelrod looked at seventy-seven flourishing US companies over a broad spread of industries, and made a surprising discovery. 'Talent' is in short supply. Only twenty-three per cent of the executives McKinsey polled believed that their companies attracted the best employees. Yet revenue for these firms had grown at twice the rate of GDP in the previous five years.

The fact that these companies were growing so fast in spite of employing the least talented people was seen by the McKinsey consultants as proof of their theory, rather than its contradiction. If they ran dry on their most precious commodity – good people – they were over, they said.[16]

The sub-text of McKinsey's declaration of a 'War for Talent' was a restatement of the need for employing McKinsey. In a booming economy, they said, do not be fooled by the numbers. Things will turn bad and when they do, you need the best people around you, not dead wood. You need us.

THE EMPEROR'S NEW SUIT

The immediate impact of the War for Talent was to justify an explosion in CEO pay, which jumped exponentially from double-digit multiples of the lowest employees' wage to seven hundred or eight hundred times that wage. I met Martin Sorrell, the founder of the world's biggest advertising agency, WPP, and worth an estimated £250 million. 'Do you know how much you're worth, Martin?' 'I couldn't really say.' 'Or how much you pay yourself?' 'I'm paid what the market decides I'm worth. That's the value we all have, Jacques.'[17]

The War for Talent was in reality merely a reheating of the 1950s McKinsey boss Arch Patton's tireless drive to promote higher corporate pay. At one point, Patton's own wages accounted for a tenth of the company's entire billings.

Talent was now king. It meant you could pay yourself whatever you wanted, because McKinsey had decreed that talent was the kryptonite of business. The 'talented' were immune from scrutiny and they ceased even pretending to play by the same rules as everyone else, because . . . they were talented.

In October 2000, at a sumptuous hotel ballroom in Palm Beach, Andrew Fastow, the chief financial officer of one of the world's fastest-growing companies, got up to speak to the company's finance committee. Houston-based oil company Enron was a success story like no other: the model for new aggressive, expansionist, go-getting business and the poster child for McKinsey's 'War for Talent'. Enron was the embodiment of the principle. To drive the company's further meteoric growth, Fastow said, we need 'partnership'.[18]

Enron's extraordinary growth in the energy-trading business had been built by one man, Jeff Skilling, who had previously been a McKinsey consultant for twenty-one years. And Enron, with Skilling at the helm, were now paying McKinsey $10 million a year for their 'advice'. This advice included over twenty reports by McKinsey, as well as McKinsey endorsing the accounting methods of Enron. The relationship was symbiotic. Richard Foster, a McKinsey partner, repaid the compliment by inter-viewing a senior Enron executive in his book, *Creative Destruction*. 'We hire very smart people,' the executive said proudly, 'and we pay them more than they think they're worth.' Pure 'War for Talent' thinking.

In October 2001, the fruits of the War for Talent were reaped. Enron collapsed in spectacular fashion: the most dramatic im-plosion of a single corporation in US business history.[19]

Enron had really taken McKinsey's War for Talent to heart: they had allowed flashy fast-talking executives with little or no expertise to rise quickly through the company, making deci-sions of huge import because they seemed like they knew what they were doing. Other executives pursued multi-million-dollar initiatives on a whim. No one knew what anyone else was doing. The place was utter chaos masquerading as a responsible busi-ness. But at the heart of this chaos was the principle that talent should be given its head. McKinsey's Richard Foster called it 'creative destruction'. In slavishly chasing the 'creative', Enron had brought about its own 'destruction'.

At the same time as McKinsey was devising the Enron strat-egy, it was also advising Wall Street banks, promoting the secu-ritisation of mortgage assets, and encouraging them to fund their balance sheets with debt. As financial journalist Ben Chu reported, 'driving down their equity safety buffers in order to juice profits (with) a practice that poisoned the global financial system and precipitated the 2008 credit meltdown.'[20]

The McKinsey boss himself was not immune from putting his hand in the pot. In 2012, company chief Raj Gupta was convicted for insider trading, passing on confidential information on corporations to a billionaire hedge-fund friend. Another McKinsey partner was also involved in the insider dealing ring.

Enron stung McKinsey. When Malcolm Gladwell wrote a piece in 2002 for the *New Yorker* – 'The Talent Myth' – unpicking the connections between McKinsey and Enron, McKinsey broke their code of silence and issued a rebuke. Something they never do.

In New York, I meet with Beth Axelrod, one of the McKinsey executives responsible for 'The War for Talent'. 'That article really hurt McKinsey,' she says. What about the collapse of Enron, did that not hurt McKinsey rather more? Arthur Anderson, the accountancy firm involved, went under in the aftermath, but McKinsey went from strength to strength. 'Some outrageous bad practice was going on at Enron, but that wasn't McKinsey's doing.' Would you not see your report, 'The War for Talent', as directly responsible for that same outrageous bad practice? Beth winces. 'No, I don't think you can connect them in the way you seem to be implying.'

McKinsey was bullet proof, and kept bouncing back. In 2012, Republican candidate Mitt Romney said that when he became president, McKinsey would be called in to 'fix' government. One of Mark Carney's first decisions on becoming Governor of the Bank of England in 2013 was to call in McKinsey to review the central bank's operations.

There is disagreement on whether McKinsey even do anything. Duff McDonald says they have undoubtedly streamlined government in some way, simply by virtue of having stuck around at the centre of power for so long, but Chu says there is not a 'single major technological or commercial development that McKinsey can claim even some passing credit for bringing into the world.'

If this was the case, it would be no mean feat for a company. To have remained at the heart of government since the 1920s and done precisely nothing. But perhaps they have simply followed the rule for success that Bob Hope followed when he was asked for his secret to show business: 'keep turning up'.

PFI AND THE PUBLIC SECTOR MEAT IN THE ROOM

So Enron collapsed, McKinsey's boss was found guilty of insider trading, and the seeds were sown for the financial crash, but McKinsey continued to move closer to the heart of government.

Britain and America's power-broking landscape was transformed unrecognisably by the War for Talent and key to this was allowing business to gain the whip-hand in its relationship with government. Put simply: they had the talent for dynamic change, politicians did not and knew they were useless, because they had been told so by consultants.

Three small letters came to symbolise this shift in power: 'PFI'. The 'private finance initiative' behind every major infrastructure project.

PFI put business in the driving seat when it came to making long-term investment decisions worth billions, sometimes trillions. In opposition, Labour had opposed PFI, but two months after taking office in 1997, Health Secretary Alan Milburn said, 'It is PFI or bust.'[21] George Monbiot in the *Guardian* made the observation that 'the free market has become a corporate welfare scheme.'[22]

Just as civil servants had been taught to lose confidence in their own ability to do their job, so now politicians underwent

an existential crisis of self-doubt. And as the public purse tightened, business could step in to save the day with PFI.[23] Allyson
Pollock has studied the use of PFI in the NHS as funding became
an issue under Labour, and has found that although funding
might seem an obvious rationale for explaining PFI, the one
used by politicians was poor management by the public sector
– by themselves.

The Chancellor of the Exchequer, Gordon Brown, 'declared
repeatedly that the public sector is bad at management, and that
only the private sector is efficient and can manage services
well.'[24] Funding was an issue, but the real issue was that business
would do a better job. A message broadcast by politicians with
McKinsey in the shadows.

The reason was simple. By repeating the narrative that business would do a better job with government money, that narrative became fact in the minds of everyone: the voter, business
and most importantly, government itself. The only people sceptical were the professionals in health, education or social services
who actually did the job. From that point on, PFI, out-sourcing,
and its endless upgraded permutations were simply logical
outcomes. And McKinsey was always there in the background,
whispering this narrative in the politician's ear. The new civil
service.

As the old civil service became hollowed out through rounds of
redundancies, McKinsey and other consultants watched them
depart Whitehall carrying thirty years of work in cardboard boxes.

Consultants were now the trusted ones and their role as the
new civil service was real, because they had become the only
continuity. They had outlasted the civil servants, and now they
would outlast the here-today, gone-tomorrow politicians. They
had made themselves indispensable to the working of government simply by turning up each day, like Bob Hope. But unlike
the civil service, or Bob Hope, they had an agenda.

THE COMPANY WITHIN A COMPANY

McKinsey are not the independent experts they appear. They wear two hats, advising government and simultaneously looking out for the business interests of their private clients, many of whom specialise in areas of government that McKinsey also happen to advise on.

In 2010, as the UK government embarked on the biggest healthcare reforms in the history of the NHS, McKinsey were at the heart of the drafting.[25] The plan was to have a collaborative open process involving doctors and health professionals as well as ministers, and of course, McKinsey.

Meetings took place not in Whitehall, but in McKinsey offices.[26] Dr Lawrence Buchmann represented doctors at the negotiations. I met him at his busy North London surgery between appointments. Dr Buchmann said he could not believe what happened when the talks began. 'Every time you went to a meeting, someone had written a report that appeared to be a *fait accompli*. Those of us who thought we were actually going to have a say in how this happened were continuously sidelined or told, "This is how it's going to be."'[27]

Buchmann soon came to realise that there was nothing open or transparent about the process, or what he believed would ultimately happen to the NHS. He says McKinsey were calling all the shots, and being paid millions to advise on cutting services. But that was not where the real money lay.

In 2016, the *Financial Times* investigated McKinsey and discovered that the company's partners run a private hedge fund for themselves. A company within a company, called MIO Partners. When advising on NHS reforms, McKinsey are in a position to suggest private outsourcing companies, often private med-tech companies that McKinsey have a direct stake in via MIO.[28]

Buchmann is in no doubt that the long-term objective of the NHS reforms is full privatisation, and that is not down to ideological belief, but the intersection of a crisis of funding and the continuous lobby from the sidelines to privatise and ease the crisis. It is attrition but we're getting there, said Buchmann. McKinsey could benefit directly through connections with private healthcare companies with which they have a relationship. But because MIO is a private company, the public have no way of finding out. The links cannot be made, because MIO is not transparent.

MIO Partners, the secret company within a company, allow McKinsey to be at the heart of the most lucrative and far-reaching reforms planned by the governments they 'advise' across the globe. But MIO and its role within McKinsey remains a mystery to anyone outside the inner sanctum of top partners. Even McKinsey employees do not know about its detailed workings.[29]

MIO Partners say they are fully regulated, delegate investment decisions to the division's management and have a 'rigorous policy to avoid conflicts of interest'.

Alan Leaman speaks for the whole consultancy industry. I met him in his giant glass box in London to find out what kind of controls are imposed on McKinsey by the industry when it comes to such a potential conflict of interest.

'Unfortunately,' Leaman tells me, 'you'd have to take that directly up with McKinsey. They aren't signed up to our code of conduct.' 'They don't follow your code of conduct? But you are the industry's watchdog. If you can't police them who does?' McKinsey are a law unto themselves.[30]

The key to McKinsey's hold over governments across the globe is their alumni, and the Jesuitical code of loyalty that comes from having worked for 'The Firm'. Sheryl Sandberg, COO of Facebook, is ex-McKinsey; so too are Tidjane Thiam, Chief Executive of Credit Suisse; Charlotte Hogg, the former COO at the Bank of England; and James Gorman, CEO of Morgan Stanley.

But it is with government appointments that the tie is strongest. Barack Obama's OMB director designate, Peter Orszag was ex-McKinsey; the Foreign Secretary under the Cameron coalition, William Hague, worked for McKinsey. Their alumni mop up the post of finance minister across the world: Corrado Passera in Italy, Lazar Krstic in Serbia, Eric Wiebes in Holland, Jayant Sinha in India and Toshimitsu Motegi in Japan.

McKinsey have even fostered a deep relationship with the Communist leadership of China. Walter Kiechel, author of *The Lords of Strategy*, has made an in-depth study of McKinsey working practices in emerging markets and says, 'The Firm's ability to insinuate itself into local elites drives its competitors slightly berserk with envy.'[31]

Shortly after the 1994 US presidential election, Republican whip Tom DeLay called prominent Washington lobbyists into his office. He had pulled the public records of the political contributions to the two main parties. He reminded them that the Republicans were now in charge and the lobbyists' donations had better start addressing the new reality 'or else'. According to Craig MacDonald's anti-corruption group Texans for Public Justice, the 'or else' was a threat to cut off access to the White House.[32]

Compare McKinsey's soft-power approach with this crass attempt to bully government. In 2007, the 'Honest Leadership and Open Government Act' was enacted by Congress to put a stop to the 'K Street Project', an explicit attempt by the GOP to pressure Washington lobbying firms to hire Republicans and to reward loyal GOP lobbyists with access to influential officials and committees.

Blatant cronyism is very much not the style of McKinsey, who have successfully made themselves part of the DNA of government. McKinsey operate rather like a consulting version of the Cayman Islands – a subtle and discreet mechanism by which corporations can call the shots without ever seeming to 'do' anything.

There is no gap between McKinsey and the governments they 'engage' with. They are one and the same with the revolving door on permanent spin. McKinsey have no need to persuade anyone of anything. They are McKinsey, and whatever they say is a given.

CHAPTER TEN
BUSINESS: WHY CORPORATIONS TOOK OVER

HITLER'S BANK MANAGER

In the 1930s, Herman Abs was a partner at private German bank Delbruck Schickler & Co. Delbruck Schickler managed a very special account, one that the bank took great pride in having secured and looked after so well: the bank account of the Nazi Party.

Hermann Abs was Hitler's bank manager, responsible for paying the Reich Chancellor's salary each month. As he wrote in his memoir: 'The Reich Chancellery in Berlin was (the) largest account, and it was through this account that Adolf Hitler received his salary as Chancellor of the Reich.'[1]

Abs had a personal connection to the Nazi Party, too. Abs was a friend of Martin Bormann, head of the Chancellery. In 1943, with the creation of the Nazi banking committee, Abs was able to assist Bormann in transferring capital, gold and stocks to Switzerland.[2]

But Abs was no card-carrying Nazi. He was above all a banker, maintaining an arm's length from Hitler while simultaneously doing everything – including assisting in the 'Aryanisation' of Jewish businesses – to protect himself should any criticism of disloyalty ever come his way. He was, according to Abs's biographer, Princeton historian Harold James, elusive. An enigma swathed in cigar smoke that no one, not even the Nazis, could read.

After the war, unlike the Nazi collaborators imprisoned or executed, Abs became Chairman of Germany's largest bank, Deutsche Bank. Abs oversaw the loans that rebuilt West Germany under President Adenauer. Like Werner Braun, the rocket scientist who invented the V2 bomb that obliterated large parts of London and was given safe passage to the US to work with NASA on the space programme in the 1960s, Abs was both too 'talented' and too clever to be connected to anything in the war that would mean he would be punished.

In 1958, as a powerful and respected business figure, now head of Germany's biggest bank, Abs stepped into history to make a bold proposal. The post-war world has been framed, he said, by a discussion of rights. There has even been the creation of a declaration of human rights, not least to prevent a repeat of the atrocities carried out by the Nazis. But what about, Abs said, the rights of business?[3]

Abs believed business had been marginalised after the war, coming second to the needs of the burgeoning government machine. But business, not government, should be ultimately sovereign over its own destiny. Abs proposed an international 'Magna Carta' for private investors, enshrining their sovereign rights over government.[4] In other words, corporations and banks should have the legal machinery to sue governments if they felt their inalienable right to make a profit was compromised.[5]

If a 'Magna Carta' for private investors was to be made real, it needed special international courts that could protect capital from the meddling of these politicians. Investment decisions were too big and too important to come under the legal jurisdiction of the country in which a company had invested. Governments, Abs inferred, should not be able to stop corporations going where they liked or doing what they wanted.

Abs had been key to the smooth running of the Nazi machine,

and in the smooth tarmacking of a new democratic Germany, was now instrumental in erasing any trace of this past. But his real legacy was in proposing a fundamental realignment of power in post-war Western democracies – away from government and into the hands of the emerging global corporations, which could now make government their servant.

'ISDS' – ONE WORLD UNDER A GAVEL

This court was to be called the Investor-State Dispute Settlement (ISDS) court and was set up by the World Bank in 1958 in New York. It was Abs's dream come true.

It was created to adjudicate over disputes between nation states and multinationals in a 'corporate court': one in London, another in Paris, two more in Hong Kong and The Hague. But the most important court was at the International Centre for the Settlement of Investment Disputes (ICSID) in the World Bank's J Building in Pennsylvania Avenue, Washington DC.

Forty years before terrorist suspects were interrogated on 'black sites' – physical spaces that do not exist on a map where the CIA decide the rules for torture – corporate black sites already existed for lawyers to interrogate governments.

In October 2014, *The Economist* explained how these corporate courts work: 'Foreign firms (have) a special right to apply to a secretive tribunal of highly paid corporate lawyers for compensation whenever a government passes a law to, say, discourage smoking, protect the environment or prevent a nuclear catastrophe ... through a process known as "investor-state dispute settlement" or ISDS.'[6]

As Claire Provost and Matt Kennard, research fellows at The Investigative Fund at The Nation Institute, discovered in their comprehensive 2015 analysis of the ISDS system, the courts were initially sold as a way of helping the developing world grow:[7]

'In the 1960s, the idea was taken up by the World Bank, which said that such a system could help the world's poorest countries attract foreign capital. "I am convinced," the World Bank president George Woods said at the time, "that those who adopt as national policy a welcome (environment) for international investment – and that means, to mince no words about it, giving foreign investors a fair opportunity to make attractive profits – will achieve their development objectives more rapidly than those who do not."[8] In short, suck it up.

The deal came in Tokyo in 1964 at the World Bank's annual meeting. Twenty-one countries – every Latin American nation plus Iraq and the Philippines – strongly opposed the motion. These countries interpreted the word 'development' as 'exploitation'. But their protests were ignored.

American legal academic Andreas Lowenfeld, who observed the process, said, 'I believe this (is) the first time that a major resolution of the World Bank had been pressed forward with so much opposition.' ISDS put all the cards in the hands of corporations who could strongarm the court, and had the lawyers to do it.

Emerging-world (then called 'third world') countries could not muster the same legal fire-power and were powerless to put up a credible fight in court. Since 2000, hundreds of companies have sued more than half the world's governments behind the closed doors of these courts, and won.

Vodafone took India to court for trying to make them pay tax. Vodafone won. US agribusiness giant Cargill/ADM sued Mexico for introducing a sugar tax on soft drinks to fight childhood obesity. Cargill/ADM won. Mexico was sued for daring to put a cap on the price of water, access to which is a basic human right under the UN charter. The manufacturer won and as a result, Coca Cola is now cheaper to drink than bottled water in Mexico.[9]

In 2006, Houston-based Occidental Petroleum sued Ecuador for hindering a huge mineral extraction programme, and won. Ecuador was forced to pay the equivalent of its entire health budget for one year.

It is not just the developing world that loses in the ISDS courts. Energy giant Vattenfall sued the German government for attempting to stop a coal-fired power station, widely opposed by the public. Vattenfell won.

Hermann Abs's 'Magna Carta' is now a reality. We live in a two-tier world: governments and corporations, the two tiers intersecting only where there is a dispute over tax, or when legislation does not go their way. Corporations operate horizontally across the planet, free to move at will, and governments are bounded vertically within the physical and legal constraints of national borders.

The effect of these grinding one-sided victories for corporations in the ISDS courts is the 'stick-flinch' effect. If corporations sue an entire country successfully, it makes other countries think twice before introducing policies with social or environmental benefits that will bring them into conflict with a corporation. Governments flinch before the stick has even been raised.

In Guatemala, Canadian mining giant Goldcorp faced huge public outcry, as well as a recommendation from the Inter-American Commission on Human Rights that a gold mine be shut down. The public demonstrated, demanding closure. The government opposed the mine, too, but let Goldcorp carry on because they knew they would lose down the line in an ISDS court.

The reason why the 1964 Tokyo agreement passed, in spite of huge opposition from poor countries, was because the rich Western powers never thought it would happen to them. But it has.

Forty years on from the Tokyo deal, any government can be sued. People from the rust belt of America to the sweatshops of South-East Asia understand what globalisation has meant for them. One world under the gavel of the corporate court.

PRESIDENT TRUMP *VS*
PRESIDENT ZUCKERBERG

ISDS was the mechanism that delivered the reality of globalisation and the capitulation of elected government. The business of politics now is between competing business leaders with two very different visions of the future: Globalisation Good *vs* Globalisation Bad.

On Thursday, 16 February 2017, a man posted a question on Facebook. 'Are we building the world we all want?' Facebook founder Mark Zuckerberg then outlined what he meant by globalisation. 'History is the story of how we've learned to come together. In times like these, the most important thing ... is develop the social infrastructure to give people the power to build a global community that works for all of us.'

His post was widely interpreted as an attack on President Trump.[10] Zuckerberg was quick to say he was not making a bid for the White House. Yet, 'I am reminded of President Lincoln's remarks during the American Civil War,' he concluded. '"We can succeed only by concert. It is not 'can any of us imagine better', but 'can we all do better?' The dogmas of the quiet past, are inadequate to the stormy present. The occasion is piled high with difficulty, and we must rise with the occasion. As our case is new, so we must think anew, act anew."'

Zuckerberg's State of the Union address on Facebook offered a utopian vision of an integrated global community meshed by shared progressive values, enabling change through a democratic platform with global reach called Facebook.

Here is the new political fault line. A straight-up face-off between President Trump, holding every political position from A to Z – a given strategy for success in business – and Team Silicon Valley, representing the relentless march of twenty-first-century globalisation, dressed as democracy.

This stand-off is simply the age-old divide of America: the liberal California/New York axis against the rest of the country, represented by Trump. In this regard, to see Trump, or even Zuckerberg, as anything fundamentally new is to buy their packaging.

However, when the so-called liberal 'elite' lost power in the past to the voters of middle America, no president began by declaring war openly on the infrastructure of government. Trump did so initially in 2017, because he said he believed in draining 'the swamp': the murky, impenetrable world of corporate influence, consultants, backroom deals and clandestine lobbying that Eisenhower first warned about in 1952. He wished to replace this with the open skulduggery of the deal and the brutal power struggle of the boardroom. The difference being: business will be banging on the table in the Oval Office, not skulking clandestinely in the corridor.

It never occurred to Trump that anyone would have a problem with this nuanced shift in seating arrangements – why would the world take issue with industrialists and CEOs directly making decisions about jobs, health and climate change, rather than lobbying to affect those decisions? It simply cuts out the person in the middle. Thirty years of hand-wringing about corporate capture became irrelevant in a moment with the ostentatious flick of President Trump's fountain pen.

DRAINING AND REFILLING 'THE SWAMP'

In his election campaign, candidate Trump was big on 'draining the swamp', but swamps have a nasty habit of refilling. During the last two UK general elections, the number of management consultants employed by government fell suddenly before the election, as they fell under scrutiny, only to increase again once a new government was re-elected and the spotlight moved on. After the 2010 election, the use of consultants in government more than doubled.[11]

As Tamasin Cave and Andy Rowell found in their investigation on the influence of lobbying in government, *A Quiet Word*:[12] 'The influence of lobbyists increases when it goes largely unnoticed by the public . . . they operate in the shadows deliberately.' Cave and Rowell identified ten strategies that lobbyists use to make it virtually impossible to drain the swamp of its dwellers.

First, they 'control the ground': dictate the parameters of the conversation on an issue they want to influence. Then they get the media and industry to sing from a 'common hymn sheet'. When accountancy giant KPMG's head of health Mark Britnell said in 2011 that the 'NHS will be shown no mercy and the best time to take advantage of this will be the next few years', lobby group NHS Partners Network moved quickly to get industry back on message with a 'common hymn sheet'.

Once this has been achieved, lobbyists 'engineer a following' – create a fake grass-roots movement; 'buy in credibility' – hire experts; or sponsor a think-tank – take an existing organisation and part-fund them, yet keep the relationship seemingly at arm's length. The neo-liberal Institute of Economic Affairs is part-funded by the tobacco industry, but remains an independent think-tank.

It is important for lobbyists, Cave and Rowell say, to 'consult with critics' when criticism arises, in order to appear to be listening. In this way, opposition can be 'neutralised'. When all of this groundwork has been done, the door is prised open to a politician's office, not forgetting that the door is revolving and the politician could be working for the same lobbyists in six months' time.[13] This 'log-rolling' means everyone involved has a vested interest in keeping the whole thing spinning.

When thousands of competing companies are all attempting to influence government using these tactics, government becomes a miasma of complex, seemingly contradictory interconnections. No one really knows who anyone else is working for, or what their real motives might be. To think the post-Trump world offered ideological complications and contradictions that did not exist before was simply to have not seen them before.

Trump, though shocking to elites schooled and embedded in the idea of there being rules, systems and ways of doing things, simply embodied a new stand-off. He was hand-to-hand combat while everyone else at least pretended to operate by the mechanics of executive, judiciary and legislature. Trump was no rules versus structure. Survival versus the law. In May 2017, his summary Apprentice-style dismissal of FBI chief James Comey, as the net tightened on Russian links to the 2016 presidential election, appeared to cross a line, but again this was to miss the point: with Trump, as in business, there was no line.

This brutal Nixonian approach to power was at odds with the murky waters of the swamp. To enter this world is to enter a soup of doublethink and triple bluff. Here is what happened when I tried. In 2012, researching the roots of the food industry's role in the global obesity epidemic, I was pointed by an esteemed academic, who advises government on health policy, to a secret deal being cut by a rival academic and a global food-industry giant. The gist of the accusation was that he had taken compromising funding in exchange for putting his name to a diet product the food company was developing.

'Why are you telling me this?' I asked the academic. 'I thought you ought to know,' she said. 'And who funds your research?' I asked. She named a rival food firm, developing a rival product.

Ten companies – Nestlé, PepsiCo, Coca-Cola, Unilever, Danone, General Mills, Kellogg's, Mars, Associated British Foods and Mondelēz – control nearly every large food and drinks brand on the planet.[14] In a moment, the academic had taken off her independent, advising-government hat and quietly slipped on her partisan, food-industry hat, in order to rubbish a rival. She had simply omitted to tell me she had changed hats in the middle of our conversation.

Because everyone in this world of hidden persuasion is a player with a concealed agenda, Donald Trump's description of government and the people who influence it as a 'swamp' was apt: knots and weeds tether those on the surface to something far bigger, lurking ominously at the bottom.

A decade before Trump stood for president promising to

drain this swamp, I interviewed Sir Michael Wilshaw, then head of a hugely successful academy school in Hackney, but soon to be promoted to become head of Britain's school inspectorate, Ofsted. I asked him what was the greatest hindrance to reforming education.

The problem, he said, with reforming anything in government was that it is 'like throwing a hand grenade into fog. The fog clears dramatically for a second and everyone congratulates themselves, only for the fog to descend again.' In Britain, it is a fog. In the US, a swamp. Neither can be eliminated on a whim when government itself is the obfuscating ecosystem. A system that hides but also protects itself when it comes under predatory attack.

THE ELITE SHOWDOWN: HARD HANDS *VS* SOFT HANDS

In *Jaws*, there is an early run-through of the Trump *vs* Zuckerberg showdown. The crew are about to assemble for the mission to kill the shark. The bad-tempered Captain Quinn, played by Robert Shaw, does not believe Police Chief Brody's shark expert friend, the 'college-educated' Hooper, has what it takes to catch a Great White. Quinn tests Hooper's seamanship skills by asking him to tie a sheepshank knot in front of him. Quinn is unimpressed. 'You've got city hands, Mr Hooper,' Quinn says, 'from counting money all your life.'

Trump painted himself as Quinn, the outsider and champion of working-class America. But he was no more working class or outsider than Hooper. The thing, Trump said during the election campaign, that he really hated about Silicon Valley billionaires was that they were hypocrites: saving the world with philanthropic solutions to global poverty, while offshoring American jobs as they saved it. Trump's friends in traditional industry had made their money with dirty hands, not soft, 'college-educated' Hooper ones.

Oil and steel billionaires sit on vast fortunes built from metal forged in molten fire and from black gold drilled from the ground. But these men are rarely self-made, they have inherited their empires, as Trump did. They do not have dirty hands, they are softer and more expensively educated than Hooper's or Trump's.

Yet because their money resides in the tangible world of making things the hard way, they have instant credibility and authenticity with self-made, heartland America, which genuinely does work hard for a living. These billionaires look like they are on the level – they can be trusted.

The West Coast tech aristocracy, ironically, is self-made, but is portrayed as a self-perpetuating 'elite'. Facebook's Sheryl Sandberg and Mark Zuckerberg, Apple's Tim Cook, and Jeff Bezos of Amazon tap softly away on keyboards and talk quietly about the positives of globalisation. Trump said in 2016 he did not trust them and neither, he surmised, would the US electorate.

It is not only these tech billionaires who are seen as untrustworthy, so too is their industry. They mine people, not coal. Trawling our confidential data and creating gossamer threads of networks, using algorithms to spy on us as we gaze impassively at glowing screens; an underpaid world in its downtime, scrolling Instagram and Facebook, mainlining Kim Kardashian as we ourselves are milked for every last detail of our lives.

The battle for the moral supremacy of one of these business elites over another is disingenuous and quaintly old-fashioned. The common dirty word with both is 'elite': no one wants to be associated with an 'elite'. Mark Zuckerberg wore a grey T-shirt and jeans and cycled to work, so he didn't look like was is in an elite, and Trump spat the word out like an expletive.

Once upon a time, elites were revered. They were trusted to the same degree they are supposedly distrusted today. A select few scientists, engineers, mathematicians, philosophers, clergy and business people understood what was best for the masses, and we the masses understood that they knew best for us.

The 'representative democracy' of Parliament is in itself a form of structural elitism: MPs make legislative decisions on behalf of those who elected them, rather than consulting this electorate on every decision as they would in a direct democracy. Capital punishment – a life for a life – has historically been a legislative decision the elite would never enact, but the public would. Because the elite governed on our behalf, it never happened. Brexit would not have happened if it had gone through the elite of Parliament first. But because the elite made the 'mistake' of putting it to the people, it did.

Elites have been conjured in times of crisis to fix the problem. In 1917, President Woodrow Wilson created a close-knit group of academic advisors called 'The Inquiry' to prepare him for the Versailles peace negotiations following the First World War. In 1933, President Roosevelt used a 'Brain Trust' of ten experts, including Columbia law professors Rexford Tugwell, Adolf Berle and Raymond Moley, to formulate the first 'New Deal'. This team broke up due to differences over strategy and the second New Deal was shaped by Benjamin Cohen, Tom Corcoran and Felix Frankfurter – an elite triumvirate from Harvard Law School.

In *The Revolt Against the Masses*,[15] Fred Siegel, a senior fellow at the Manhattan Institute, tied the rise of this belief in a new sharp-suited, post-war elite to the burgeoning expansion of the state. He described this new technocratic elite as a 'clerisy', a modern-day version of the clergy.

Siegel's book updated and broadened the scope of John Carey's classic attack on elitism, *The Intellectuals and the Masses*.[16] Carey accused the literary and intellectual titans of the early twentieth century – D.H. Lawrence, Virginia Woolf, Ezra Pound, H.G. Wells – as modernist elitists enthralled to a sense of narcissistic Nietzschian destiny, and a deep disgust for 'the masses', for whom eugenics or sterilisation was the only answer.

Siegel widened this attack on a ruling class of elitists to include the post-war expert, the manager, the technocrat, the academic and the self-appointed custodian of moral right, the media. *The*

Revolt Against the Masses came out a year before Donald Trump announced his candidacy for president, but set the groundwork for his particular attack on elitism, and specifically the West Coast Silicon Valley technocratic elite and the East Coast media elite of CNN, the *New York Times* and the *Washington Post*. Old Pronouncement Media *vs* New Post-Fact Echo Chamber Social Media, known for short as 'Twitter'.

This clerisy, Siegel said, operates under two delusions: first, they believe themselves independent-minded and objective, but in truth their fate is tied directly to the continuing growth of the state. They do not join these dots. Second, they see themselves as liberal and democratic in outlook. In reality, Siegel says, they despise the masses and the 'middle class', just as Virginia Woolf and D.H. Lawrence did. They are as narrow-minded as the people they secretly despise. The clerisy's true belief system is a cultural and intellectual superiority-complex over voters. A prejudice reinforced by voters continually wanting things the clerisy would never allow.

The prosaic truth is that the context determines how elites are judged at any moment in history. Sometimes we like and need them. Sometimes we don't. When things go economically well, we go along with elites, but when the wheels come off, we blame them. The surface noise becomes anti-elitism, but beneath the surface, the elites are regrouping, mouthing the language of anti-elitism to curry favour with the masses and mask their true elitist identity.

Team Trump and Team Zuckerberg – two elites that will always battle for power with different figureheads when Trump and Zuckerberg are dethroned – both talked the language of anti-elitism. This Business *vs* Business struggle is really a battle between two victors. The Silicon Valley elite and the new Washington elite of self-styled 'Leninist' outsiders clustered round Trump, who were intent on burning down the old house.

Because both sides came from business, neither side saw why anything should stand in their way. It was a zero-sum game, with only one winner left standing. Unless, this being business, they did a deal.

THE NATION-SHAPED COMPANY

Like Trump, Silicon Valley saw themselves as above and beyond government. In 2016, Apple refused to cooperate with the FBI when asked to unlock San Bernardino shooting suspect Syed Farook's phone.[17] Apple CEO Tim Cook said it was a civil liberties issue and Apple, not the government or the FBI, would decide what was morally right. 'This case is about much more than a single phone or investigation, so when we received the government's order, we knew we had to speak out.'[18]

In the past, companies would at least pretend to acquiesce to the demands of government. Not anymore. They are above it. And in the past, presidents would at least pretend to acquiesce to the demands of business. Not when you are a chairman president.

In his first weeks of power, Chairman President Trump of USA PLC harangued Ford, Boeing and Carrier for trying to relocate jobs. Any company moving jobs out of America would be slapped with a thirty-five-per-cent tariff.

Then Chairman President Trump tore up TTP/TTIP: the Transpacific and Transatlantic Trade Investment Partnerships brokered by Obama. TTP was the biggest proposed free-trade agreement in history, and the biggest deal since the creation of the World Trade Organisation. Its aim was to stitch Australia, Brunei, Canada, Chile, Japan, Malaysia, New Zealand, Peru, Singapore, Vietnam and Mexico into a partnership with the US, so creating a new axis of power centred on the Pacific. TTIP would be the European equivalent, creating another free-trade block with the US and the European Union.

Both were attempts to tool up and create bigger trade blocks in the face of bilateral trade agreements between China, India, Russia and the rest of the world. TTP took seven years to negotiate with the twelve largest economies on earth, together holding well over forty per cent of the world's GDP.

As the economist Joseph Stiglitz pointed out in 2015 as TTP/

TTIP brewed, 'trade agreements have always been sold on the grounds that they create jobs – and if that were true, workers should be among the loudest champions of these agreements. The reality . . . is otherwise, and the fact that our political leaders (not only Republicans, but Clinton and Obama as well) have tried to misrepresent these trade agreements in this way undermines confidence in them, and again reminds citizens of the extent to which our government reflects the interests of those at the top.'

The TTP/TTIP negotiations were conducted like an ISDS court – behind closed doors and away from the gaze of the billions of people whose lives would be changed by it. And it was opposed by both the Bernie Sanders left and the alt-right, Trump and Breitbart News. The left saw it as the completion of corporate capture: corporations could now sue governments, without realising this mechanism – the ISDS court – had already been in place for forty years.

The walls were going back up, protectionism was here. But could even this be believed? Trump had said everything from A to Z, and had stopped at all the letters in between. To this extent, he was like a politician. But politicians are weighed down with the baggage of conviction, which makes a change of mind 'hypocrisy'.

When President Trump changed his mind, it was business. And best to view it like that. When Trump's prospective ambassador to Europe, Ted Malloch, was asked what he thought of a bilateral agreement between Britain and the US post-Brexit and TTIP, he said it was best to view it as a business merger: one very successful company taking over a smaller, failing one. Business was the language by which you should now interpret everything. Trump could change policy on a whim, because he was not weighed down with the ideological baggage of conviction. It is business. A week may be a long time in politics, but in business it is an eternity. For Trump, every second was a new game with new rules.

The Trump camp did not plan on entering the devil's lair of elites any time soon: Davos, with its earnest debates about global warming, global inequality or global poverty. Davos – an annual forum for business leaders and heads of government – suddenly looked weirdly smug, dated and hubristic. Until next year, when it may suddenly become useful again in business terms.

And with Trump's victory, the 'social responsibility' agenda of the liberal axis was gone in a moment. Trump's team was 1982 bull-market old-school, intent on a new renaissance for American industry, even if the Chinese paid for it and built it. They were intent on rolling back globalised 'anti-American' concessions made by Obama and Bush, such as the Paris global-warming treaty and the post-2008 banking reforms. Unless Trump changed his mind.

In this respect, Trump was less a free-market president like Reagan than a capricious version of a depression-era interventionist like Hoover or Roosevelt, who also came from a business dynasty. Low interest rates to rebuild America. An infrastructure programme utilising the raw materials and labour of the nation. Trump believed it was all possible and said this not as a politician, but as a businessman.

In spite of their ideological differences, Zuckerberg, Apple's Tim Cook, and Trump shared the same approach to getting things their own way. And it is the approach of the limitlessly ambitious corporate leader. Go in hard, talk tough, and then make the concessions you were planning to make all along, coming away with the deal you were always expecting to get: that is the 'art' of the deal.

In 2017, we faced a new power dynamic on earth. The three most powerful economies explicitly run as corporations: Tsarist CEO Putin running an oil-and-gas conglomerate called 'Russia'; Trump high-fiving his way across the US like the larger-than-life CEO of an ailing car company like Chrysler; Xi Jinping, the quiet but confident spreadsheet-loving chair of the fastest-growing portfolio on the planet, China Unlimited.

Business has not taken over government, it has erased government. The struggle is now between two competing business visions of the future that old-style politicians did not have the energy or self-belief to compete with.

How did politicians rub themselves out? By eroding the confidence of the public by pulling the same old economic levers and nothing happening. Low interest rates simply meant we habituated to low interest rates with the promise of lower, potentially negative interest rates down the line. Politicians now pinned their hopes not to a manufacturing recovery, but more consumer spending, which meant more consumer debt.

No matter what levers they pulled, growth stayed resolutely at zero. When a business flatlines it is bankrupt, but you cannot foreclose on a nation. In this context, handing it over to be run as a business is not corporate capture, but the logical next step.

A country run as a business does not have to concern itself with the tropes of post-war liberal inclusiveness (tolerance, open borders, a welfare state, even taxation) only with its shareholders: the voters. China has the edge over its nation-shaped business rivals, because it does not even have an electorate of shareholders to worry about. It is a public limited company and the board run the show. When you run a country like a business, democracy simply gets in the way of efficient management.

In the twenty-first century, citizen shareholders first and foremost want their country to reassert its sense of nineteenth-century nationhood. The core brand. Trump conjured the bogeyman of globalised big business in his presidential campaign, but talked less about it in office. If global corporate power was the problem, patriotic business (not Silicon Valley's version) was the solution.

By appointing the CEOs of oil and steel companies to top White House jobs, the Chairman President tried to do away with the lobbying 'swamp' and even the need for the ISDS courts. If everyone is in the same room, the theory goes, you cut out every conceivable middle-man: lawyers, lobbyists and biddable politicians.

But paradoxically, this strategy relied for its success on a naïve belief in old-fashioned consensus in the room. As decisions begin failing to go the administration's way outside that room, as the legislative machine stops, and as the business world that failed to get an invite to the room starts its fightback, the closed room of trusted insiders starts to look smaller and smaller by the day.

Trump may have gone into the White House promising to drain the swamp, but when it refilled, he was little more than a helpless bystander watching it happen. Beyond America, a Chairman President who relied for his ability to make a deal on his uncompromising approach to business found himself in big school facing a cold, calculated psych-out with two other nation-shaped companies run by two peerlessly calculating CEOs. To win that mind game with Russia and China, you need not only friends in the Washington swamp, but some good old-fashioned political nous.

DAVOS: YOU'RE NEVER MORE THAN TEN FEET FROM A GIMP MASK

In May 1912, Thomas Mann visited his wife, Katia, at Dr Friedrich Jessen's *Waldsanatorium* in the mountain village of Davos, Switzerland. Nobody knew what was wrong with Katia. It was initially believed she had tuberculosis, but X-rays failed to find anything physically wrong. She was sent to the Wald Sanatorium to recuperate.

After visiting Katia, Mann decided to make the sanatorium in Davos the inspiration for the Berghof sanatorium in *The Magic Mountain*.[19] In Mann's novel, the consumptive bourgeois of Europe flocked to Davos to inhale its fresh Alpine air and cleanse themselves of sickness, alleviating symptoms for illnesses nobody knew the cause of nor had the cure for. As the book progressed, it became apparent that the idea of illness was itself the illness – drawing everyone sane and well to the sanatorium and into its psychosomatic clutches.

The Magic Mountain is set on the eve of the First World War and represents an allegory for a sclerotic European elite on the edge of extinction. It's not difficult to make a parallel and thus a cheap joke at the expense of the world's leaders and business elite that gather for the Davos World Economic Forum in the same village a century on, as I have just done.

Davos is its own sealed-off sanatorium, where this new self-questioning elite gather to cleanse themselves of the ills of the world for which they feel responsible. They sit in claustrophobic rooms debating global warming, global poverty and global inequality. Then they get back on Lear jets and fly home feeling a lot better about themselves and the future of the globe.

Rob Hersov is a South African mining mogul and one of the continent's most important power brokers between government and business, brokering deals with foreign investors and heads of state. I met up with Rob in London and asked him what he made of Davos. He smiled. 'Well, the thing I've noticed about Switzerland. Do you want me to tell you?' Please. 'You're never more than ten feet from a gimp mask.'

Rob recognises a sexual undertow to Davos: the fetishisation of power. The leaders of the world's mightiest economies mingle at warm 'coffee' with the leaders of the world's most virile companies, surrounded by an army of advisors and consultants – the groupies of power – aspiring to be close to this flame. It is a strange combination of self-congratulatory, self-reflecting importance and buttoned-up sexual tension.

Davos, like the Silicon Valley/Trump showdown, is really a gathering of winners. They are at Davos because they have made it, rule the planet, and this is the public display of that power. World leaders and CEOs mingle as equals, but they all know the real deal. Business is ascendant, CEOs are the alpha players and have relegated governments to the position of consultants on their business vision.

I asked Ken Rogoff, one of the world's leading economists, why he goes to Davos, expecting him to say that it matters.

'Because if you don't, then you stop being invited.' The real point of Davos is itself. To reflect its own reflection back upon itself, like those tiled walls of the Berghof sanatorium. And to have a space where business can debate with itself what it should do with this new global omnipotence.

THE NEW CAPITALIST STRUGGLE: THE BOSS *VS* THE SHAREHOLDERS

This omnipotence poses a dilemma if you are a CEO. Do you press home the advantage or use your new-found power for global good like a Marvel Avenger? Global corporations face the conundrum described by military strategist Sun Tzu in *The Art of War* in 500 BC when faced with a drowning enemy: help him out of the water or push him under till he is dead?

The most powerful business people on earth find themselves now playing God with the same conundrum: maximise profit or save the planet. Paul Polman is a quietly spoken Dutchman and to hear him talk, you would think he was a member of Occupy, not CEO of Unilever, one of the world's largest multinationals with annual global turnover of $50 billion.

'How long can we steal from the future?' he tells his audience. 'Our system is a great system, but it's not designed to function long-term. We could be the generation, in the next fifteen years, that solves the issue of poverty, that solves climate change.' Polman is a boss who even baulks at being called a boss. 'I always say I represent one of the biggest NGOs.'

Polman argues passionately that an obsession with profit is destroying sustainability and ultimately capitalism itself. Two seemingly contradictory impulses must coexist 'without compromise. Profit is not a purpose. It's an end product. I always want a deeper result. People assume that if you do something good, it must cost money. I don't know where they get that idea from.'[20]

Over at PepsiCo, another of the world's biggest corporations, accused of stoking obesity, CEO Indra Nooyi says, 'I believe we need to attack obesity. Let us be good industry that does one hundred per cent not grudgingly, but willingly.'

Polman and Nooyi are not bleeding-heart liberals from charity backgrounds parachuted in to greenwash their companies with some empty sound bites. For their entire working lives, they have climbed the corporate ladder. They are one-hundred-per-cent business people.

But they now see an unprecedented threat, not merely to the survival of the planet, but their bottom line. When Christine Lagarde of the International Monetary Fund talks about inequality, she says it is not simply iniquitous, it is the single greatest threat facing the long-term survival of capitalism.

Not so long ago, the capitalist struggle was simple: workers versus bosses. But with global labour-value plummeting steadily since the 1970s, thanks to the end of the long post-war boom, billions of workers across the globe were no longer protected from the scrapheap.

Corporations could suddenly go where they liked on earth, employing workers wherever favourable employment laws would dictate the lowest wage. Skilled workers, who had once had leverage thanks to their skills, were now expendable, too. The Marxist battle between capital and labour was over. The workers had lost.

But an unexpected new struggle in capitalism emerged. The battle within a company between the CEO and the investors and shareholders. On one side, progressive reformers like Polman and Nooyi and on the other, the people who put the money in, and want to see much more money coming out the other end.

When these two sides clash, it is not on a picket line with placards and fires made from piles of tyres. It is in giant anonymous conference rooms hired for the week in Las Vegas or Hong Kong, where shareholders and investors sit in silence sucking in their teeth as the CEO spouts on about 'social responsibility' and giving back to the planet.

To them, the progressive NGO-CEO is a profound threat to their return. They recognise the boss needs to make the right noises to the outside world, but not to endanger what Herman Abs called the natural right of a business to make a profit.

Polman has stated his position. 'I don't think our duty is to put shareholders first. I say the opposite.' He showed his reformist cards from the beginning by championing 'slow money': long-term investment in small sustainable businesses, rather than relentlessly chasing short-term profit. He has declared that one of his biggest successes at Unilever was ridding the company of its reliance on hedge funds, cutting them by half during his tenure as CEO.

Polman is clear where he stands with the paradigm shift from government to business, too. With corporate power over the destiny of the planet comes responsibility and to shirk that responsibility is immoral.

At Pepsi, one of Indra Nooyi's first decisions on taking over was to declare that she wanted the company to fight obesity, becoming 'post-sugar', in the same way that BP aims to go 'post-petroleum'. Nooyi started by hiring the World Health Organisation's Derek Yach and diversifying Pepsi's portfolio into a host of healthy brands such as Quaker Oats. She faced huge internal opposition.

Dr Marion Nestle, one of the world's leading nutritionists, made a study of the boardroom struggle within Pepsi following Nooyi's attempted health reforms of the company and found that Nooyi was effectively marginalised within her own company.

'Investors got very upset. In 2012 (they) got mad at Indra Nooyi for focusing on getting revenue from healthy products.' It put a fault line through the company and Nooyi was the axe. An accommodation was required: a deal between investors and the boss. 'Pepsi (now) wants to have it both ways,' Nestle says. 'To appear to promote healthier beverages while it fights public health measures to reduce soda intake.'[21] Nooyi was perceived by investors to be undermining the core brand: sugary drink, and now has to be mindful of seeming to protect it. It was a victory for the investors.

A struggle that once took place between workers and bosses now takes place between CEOs and investors in such hushed meetings. But it is a showdown every bit as fierce with far-reaching implications for all of us.

Who wins this internal battle – championing slow money versus chasing the fast buck – will determine the moral tenor of capitalism for years to come. In essence, it will determine whether business decides to save the earth, or squeeze every last dime of profit out of it before it dies in approximately sixty harvests' time.

The CEOs talk the talk of 'sustainability' – which will soon become the word 'survivability' – but there is a clock ticking, not only on the planet, but on how long they will be humoured by investors. While they feed the bottom line, progressive CEOs are safe. But when the economy constricts, the pressure on this bottom line becomes critical and the determination of the reforming CEO to maintain a defiant reforming course against investors is properly tested. How many of them are around after this is the real test.

In the early 1970s, parts of the US motor industry sought some tentative accommodation with the growing environmental movement, but found all momentum for change washed away by the global economic convulsion and downturn that followed the OPEC crisis. It was back to business and that meant making money first and worrying about the planet later.

Paul Polman strategically frames this dilemma not as a trade-off – an either/or – but as the most important deal Unilever will ever be part of. Get on board with sustainability and slow money now, rather than slavishly extracting profit every quarter, or the whole ship goes down with all hands, and that includes the shareholders and investors. For Polman, as for every progressive CEO, two letters stand in the way of the planet's route to survival: 'QR'.

THE NUMBER

QR is the central doctrine of post-1980s capitalism. If you are a shareholder, it is the only thing that matters. If you are a reforming CEO, it is the single greatest obstacle to meaningful reform. Both Nooyi and Polman have declared open war on QR, and seen a revolt from shareholders as a result.

Quarterly reporting began in the early 1980s, as Wall Street saw a way to speed up the cycle of profit. Instead of investors and shareholders getting an annual report on the company's profitability, it would now come every three months: every quarter.

This was not simply a change in accounting, the accelerator had been pressed down. As a result of QR, if a growing company failed to show the same rate of growth this quarter as in the previous quarter, then it was deemed to be slowing down. Thanks to QR, a successful company was now defined as failing.

On 17 August 1982, Henry Kaufman of Salomon Brothers wrote a note to clients. As you know, he said, five days ago the Dow Jones Industrial Average dropped to its 1980–82 recession low of 776.92. Almost the exact figure at which the Index closed in January 1964. Double-digit inflation is over, interest rates are about to hit an all-time low, the White House is removing the last regulations holding business down and slashing tax. The time is now for an explosion of free enterprise.[22]

Kaufman was firing a flare into the sky above Wall Street and lighting up the coming bull market: the biggest the world would ever see. Shareholders and investors, Kaufman said, could now put their foot to the floor when it came to demanding something unprecedented: a quarterly increase in profit. Then demand more the next quarter, and more again the quarter after that.

It was time to drive hard. The pedal to the metal would become the new mantra of Wall Street, and there was no reason not to demand the impossible each quarter, because the underlying economics were all there to deliver it. The biggest, longest bull market in history was about to begin and Kaufman's message was crystal clear: ride it into the ground.

CEOs who could handle this breakneck ride would become legendary. The CEO was transformed overnight from a glorified 1950s bank manager to a 'captain of industry', lauded on the cover of *Time* and *Fortune*. They became alchemists who could conjure perpetual profit, and QR was their Excalibur.

In *The Number: How the Drive for Quarterly Earnings Corrupted Wall Street and Corporate America*, Alex Berenson charts how QR took over Wall Street in the 1980s and early 1990s.[23] Berenson identifies QR as the key driver in changing the course of American capitalism: from long-term investment to short-term profit demanded by investors.

It was a simple but profound switch in priorities and the only way to maintain this relentless drive for greater profit was to cut the long-term plan. There was only one thing that mattered: the wall you were going to hit in three months' time. Everything else was irrelevant.

It was all dependent on timing. While the bull market built momentum, QR was an achievable hurdle, but when it began to slow, that three-month hurdle began to look like an increasingly high bar. And as the bull market turned slowly but inexorably into a bear market, then the reality of QR started to become apparent.

QR was a running machine no one could get off, and it was increasing in speed. You think you cannot cope now? See how much faster it will be in three months' time, and three months after that.

To survive, a new kind of boss was required. One who aligned with investors, not his or her colleagues in management, and saw the inertia of the company – the inability to run ever faster or jump ever higher – as the enemy. For this kind of CEO, it was not investors or the market who were the problem, it was the culture of the very company of which they were boss.

In the comedy film *Ruthless People*, Danny DeVito played a

caricature of this new hard-hearted 1980s boss. He slammed shareholders at the annual meeting for failing to understand the new dog-eat-dog world. Little old ladies and kind old colonels stared guiltily down at their shoes as DeVito laid down the law: kill the competition and extract the last drop of profit by any means necessary.

QR was the rationale for these new ruthless people, but the film itself was sentimental for a loyal kind of shareholder that had already disappeared. Hedge fund managers had bought out the little old lady investor and were switching portfolios as quickly as a card shark changes hands. Hedge fund managers were the human equivalent of QR – constantly moving on. No one had any loyalty to the company anymore, just loyalty to profit. Only the customer still bought the brand.

Huge established American household brands, which had traded successfully for decades, were now being run as vehicles for hedging and shorting on the projected profit of the company, not just in three months, but in three hours' time. The CEO and the board were now bystanders watching the price of their own company fluctuate on a flickering screen. QR was their *raison d'être*, everything else was background noise.

Two approaches to business began to calcify. CEOs like Unilever's Paul Polman who attacked QR, and companies who embraced it. Amazon, Twitter and Uber frequently fail to turn a profit, but keep investors fully informed of their long-term goals. For a company like Amazon that needs to innovate incessantly, QR is not about the relentless drive for a quarterly return but what's happening next: total data regarding what the company is up to gleaned from the quarterly report; and if shareholders have that information, they are willing to take risks over the long-term.

Amazon has invested in drone deliveries and stores staffed by robots, like their fully automated, human-free store in Seattle, because to them, disruption, risk and investment are the same thing. It is their business. For Unilever, built on huge, super-long future planning for a massive portfolio that takes in food, chemicals and household goods, QR makes no sense. For Amazon QR works, for Unilever it does not.

Quarterly Reporting was fifty years in the making. In 1934, at the height of the depression, companies were first required to file annual reports and disclose more information to investors. In 1955, this became semiannual, and in the late 1970s and early 1980s, quarterly.

With QR, the game changed. It was all about the curve and the curve needed to keep going up. This perpetual drive was primarily psychological: it was deliberately unobtainable in order to maintain a pressure that would never go away and could never be satisfied. It would never stop and that made investors happy. It was an insurance policy against stagnation and complacency.

Pro and anti-QR business now stands face to face, daggers drawn. In 2015, law firm Wachtell, Lipton, Rosen and Katz weighed into the battle, calling on the Exchange Commission to do away with QR. A joint report by City University, London and Duke University concluded that firms that increased QR necessarily reduced spending on long-term assets. It is a trade. One or the other. You cannot have both.

In 2016, on the election trail, Hillary Clinton said that 'the decline in investments for the most part reflects the effects of managerial myopia induced by increased reporting frequency.' She believed that slamming QR was a winner with both business and the electorate. 'CEOs and shareholders need to focus on the next decade rather than just the next day.'

But she lost, and Donald Trump won.

IF CARLSBERG RAN A COUNTRY, IT WOULD PROBABLY BE THE BEST COUNTRY ON EARTH

In 1983, Orson Welles voiced the first of Carlsberg Lager's 'Probably the Best' series of ads. 'In a brewery in Copenhagen,

Carlsberg's finest brewers endeavour to improve the taste of their lager. But given that Carlsberg is probably already the finest lager in the world, they have little hope of success.'

The 'Carlsberg . . . Probably the Best' ad campaign was rolled out to include all kinds of dream scenarios: if Carlsberg ran a bank, it would give free money to all its customers whenever they needed it; if Carlsberg ran a taxi service, the taxi would be there when you clicked your fingers. Uber before its time.

The underlying message of the Carlsberg ads was radical: it does not have to be this way. A parallel universe exists in which everything could be better if it was run by Carlsberg. Twenty years before the internet, these dream scenarios seemed simply that, but now we have credit on tap and Uber to deliver a cab at the tap of your phone, the Carlsberg fantasy is a reality.

In government, a similar fantasy was entertained and this time the dream was not that Carlsberg ran things, but John Lewis. Under the Blair and then Cameron governments, the 'John Lewis Model' of an inclusive, reputable business structure with employees as 'stakeholders' was revisited repeatedly as a path the public sector could follow, too.

Now the business fantasy for government is Google. Why, the argument goes, try to get Google to pay their taxes (and fail) when you could get them to run entire government departments like the school system or the NHS? At a tax reform event I spoke at in Geneva in 2016, the discussion among the corporations present was not how do we avoid tax by finding the best offshore arrangement, but what is our duty as nation-shaped companies: how do we save the bankrupt countries in which we do business? Why give them our tax when they misspend it and we could do a better job? Our inalienable right to make a profit, first laid down by Herman Abs, is already a done deal. The challenge now is the responsibility that has come with that power.

CHAPTER ELEVEN
NEWS: WHY THE
FACTS DISAPPEARED

SKIN CREAM AND GUN CONTROL

In April 2013, Professor Dan Kahan at Yale University decided to run an experiment. He asked a thousand people for their political views: were they Republican, Democrat or more extreme, and if so, how extreme? He then gave these same thousand people facts on two unrelated subjects: skin cream and gun control.

Kahan provided them with data on a new skin cream formulated to reduce skin irritation. Did the facts show the cream to work or not? He then asked the same people to go through the facts on gun control and tell him whether the data proved gun control would reduce crime.

Kahan was taken aback by what he discovered. When it came to the skin cream, a subject that had no underlying bias to it, the thousand participants were able to analyse the facts accurately and dispassionately, coming to an easily arrived consensus: yes, on balance the skin cream would work on a rash.

But when it came to gun control, the story was very different. People ignored the facts. Democrats shown data that gun crime was not as prevalent as they thought, did everything to resist the evidence. And Republicans shown that gun control would significantly reduce crime, did everything they could to avoid coming to a conclusion at odds with their pre-set view.[1]

'People,' Kahan concluded, 'interrogate the evidence and waterboard it until it tells them what they want to hear.'[2] The evidence on whether gun control actually reduces crime is not clear cut. It is messy. But no one wanted to hear that. They wanted to believe there was one answer, and that answer needed to be what they already believed.

The 'post-truth' debate that emerged in the presidential campaign of 2016 did not factor in Dan Kahan's experiment and his discovery that people are not interested in the truth to begin with.

The emergence of the 'post-truth' phenomenon was itself premised on a falsehood: that once upon a time, people listened to the facts and then rationally made up their mind who to vote for. This was never true. The extraordinary thing about 'post-truth' was not the promotion of lies to truth, but that we ever thought people listened to truth in the first place.

THE FIRST FAKE NEWS

When a politician stands for election, they need to tell you a lie: 'I want change.' They don't. They want to confirm your preju-dices, and the politician that gets closest to confirming those prejudices – or 'core values' – wins.

In 1979, Mrs Thatcher offered policies that were closer to the newly aligned values of Labour voters than the Labour party did. When Attlee won in 1945, Labour offered a position that was closer to the newly radical values of a post-war Britain demanding change.

Churchill had won the war, but his reward for losing touch was to be voted out of office. What we mistake for a radical government is actually a radical public that has realigned its values and a politician who merely sticks their finger in the air at the right moment and judges the new mood correctly.

When Karl Rove masterminded the surprise re-election of George W. Bush in 2004 – an administration mired by a war on the ground in Iraq and the looming threat of terrorism – no one believed he would be re-elected. So Rove went back to basics by 'feeding the base'.[3]

'Feeding the base' meant retrenching around the core fears of the Republican base, and it worked. In 2016, while Hillary Clinton sought to 'build bridges' and create rainbow coalitions, Trump was advised by Team Trump (Jared Kushner, Kellyanne Conway, Steve Bannon, and others) to 'feed the base', exactly as Rove had for George W. Bush. It worked for Bush, and it worked for Trump.[4]

Voters only entertain a 'vision' when it chimes with what they are already feeling. When JFK and Harold Wilson offered bright, new, shiny visions for America and Britain in the 1960s, it was because the economy was buoyant and this was what the voters wanted to hear. Fear was out and optimism was in. But generally, fear is in.

In 2001, years before fake news was diagnosed as a symptom of a 'post-truth' society, Professor Brendan Nyhan, of Dartmouth College, New Hampshire, decided to create fake news to see how easy it was to disseminate and affect public opinion with false information.[5]

Nyhan invented a story that Saddam Hussein was planning to seize weapons of mass destruction (WMDs) and give them to terrorists. He then published a retraction, making it clear there was no truth to his first article and no evidence of weapons of mass destruction in Iraq.

The results astonished Nyhan. People who wanted to believe there were WMDs not only resisted the truth that there weren't any, but became more convinced that there were WMDs when they heard that there weren't any. Nyhan called this 'the back-fire effect'.

Everything, he said, is processed through the prism of our existing prejudice. With new information, we are simply seeking to reinforce this existing prejudice and actively searching out information that does. Facts that run counter to this prejudice are 'waterboarded' until they fit.

Today, the 'echo chamber' of social media is a filtering system that simply makes this prejudice reinforcement a more instantaneous hit, but before Twitter and Facebook we had the echo chamber of newspapers; each with its own position, or ideological filter, to fit our existing prejudices.

Even when confronted with facts challenging our worldview, our worldview is reinforced anyway. 'You'll be sitting thinking "no" and actually thinking of arguments why that is not the case,' Nyhan says.[6] 'In developing these counter-arguments, people become more entrenched in their false beliefs.' We believe what we want to believe and shut out cognitively dissonant information. But we can be convinced of something new: that we are threatened.

FREUD, MAD MEN AND FEAR SELLING

The most potent way to connect with your electoral base is to connect with their fears, and years before Hillary Clinton and Donald Trump stood at the 2016 election podium conjuring fears about the election of the other, fear had already been sharpened as a tool for selling.

On Madison Avenue in the late 1950s, a tight-knit group of advertising geniuses – Bill Bernbach, George Lois and Jerry Della Felemina – were attempting to do something no one had done before: understand the primal, subconscious drives that can be used to persuade someone to buy something. They were in the business of bottling an intoxicating potion with which to beguile the public for the next century.

Consumer choice, like a political prejudice left, right or centre, is already set. All that is needed is to trigger the purchase. Bernbach, Lois and Felemina – the original 'Mad Men' – did not have neuroscience to pull this subconscious trigger, they had Freud.

Freud argued that all our rational decisions are motivated by subconscious desires. We seek either to free these desires or suppress them, but because liberating these desires is too dangerous for a society predicated on rules of what is and is not 'normal', we suppress them.

In the 1920s, thirty years before the Mad Men of Madison Avenue, Freud's nephew Edward Bernays invented public relations by enlisting Freud's theories of mass manipulation and the desire of the crowd to be manipulated. Wall Street banker Paul Mazur suggested that Freud could be used to reboot economic growth: 'We must shift America,' he said, 'from a needs to a desires culture.' Ernest Dichter used Freud to sexualize every mundane consumer purchase from eating chocolate to puffing on cigarettes.

By applying Freud to advertising, our sublimated desires could be exploited to sell us products that contorted these desires into the shape of something we wanted to buy: a pair of shoes; a car; or a perfume bottle. Just as we 'waterboard' facts until they tell us what we want to believe, the subconscious was to be straitjacketed into a thing that could be consumed.

Telling the consumer about the facts of a product – how fast a car goes, how many washes you will get from a detergent – is irrelevant. They don't want to know. They do not even know they don't want to know.

They seek a deeper release from buying, and no purchase is what it appears to be on the surface: a sports car is really a mid-life crisis; washing powder does not simply clean clothes, it scrubs away 'dirty' repressed desires behind the curtains of suburbia. Consumerism – these Mad Men said – was not simply shopping. It enabled sublimated fantasies to be satiated through a socially acceptable purchase.

But there was one advertising guru striking out on a very different path from the Mad Men. Rosser Reeves was one of Madison Avenue's most charismatic ad execs. A brilliant and original thinker, Reeves believed advertising should not make false claims for a product – the consumer would soon rumble this – but instead, hone in like a guided missile on its 'unique selling point' or USP, distilled into a single strapline such as M&M's 'melt in your mouth, not in your hand'.[7]

Reeves is famous for coining the term 'sex sells'. Except Reeves never said 'sex sells'. What he actually said was the complete opposite: 'Sex sells if you're selling sex.' The impulse that really drives a sale, Reeves said, is fear.

Reeves took the received wisdom on selling – that it fulfilled repressed desires – put it in a filing cabinet and pushed it off the top floor of Madison Avenue.

What consumers truly seek from their lives, he said, is happiness. And modern life, Reeves argued, had made us fearful. We fear failure, we fear rejection, our spouse leaving us, our boss demoting us. These fears are real, and in order to sell this fearful consumer a product, we must push these fear buttons to maximise anxiety and then – and this is the bit Reeves's business clients liked best – sell them the solution.

Reeves became the primary inspiration for Don Draper, the central character in the TV series *Mad Men*. In the first episode, he explains his philosophy to clients: 'Advertising is based on one thing: happiness. And you know what happiness is? Happiness is the smell of a new car. It's freedom from fear. It's a billboard on the side of the road that screams reassurance that whatever you're doing is OK. That you are OK.'[8]

Reeves did not care about the product – it was the manufacturer's job to make that as good as possible – he cared about the mind. By offering freedom from the fears of modern life, Reeves was providing a solution that would never stop us buying, or the manufacturer selling.

Today, we consume thousands of everyday products offering freedom from fear. They cover the supermarket aisle: breath fresheners and deodorants that take away the social stigma of smelling; anti-wrinkle creams that offer temporary respite from fear of ageing; surface sprays and wipes that play on our OCD fear of teeming germs.

The big fears are catered for, too: a luxury holiday for your children because you fear being an inadequate parent; 'peace of mind' life insurance to maintain a roof over their heads when you drop dead working too hard to pay for their holiday.

Rosser Reeves summed it all up in two words: 'fear selling'. The geniuses of Madison Avenue had turned facts into something new. Facts were simply putty in their hands to be moulded into whatever alternative reality or 'story' they wanted to tell. Facts were to be marshalled to a greater cause: the sale.

When Donald Trump offered up fear of Mexicans and the solution of a 'great, great wall' in 2016, it was pure Rosser Reeves. Fear is now a finely calibrated weapon of mass persuasion and to find out how brilliantly it is now being used, I arranged to meet the man who dragged fear selling into the post-9/11 world, and laid the foundations for the end of facts.

THE MAN WHO USED 9/11 TO SELL CARS

It is 7 a.m. and I am driving down a tortuous winding lane in Normandy looking for a castle. As my hire car drops with the road, I am plunged into soupy fog. My phone informs me a seventeenth-century Gothic chateau lies just ahead. I drive up the huge gravel driveway, lined with trees, and spot my host.

I am greeted by one of the strangest men I have ever met. Dr Clotaire Rapaille is in his seventies, with wild, back-combed white hair. He wears a red velvet suit with military medals on his lapel. A long, black silk scarf drapes dramatically behind him. White foundation is caked heavily on his face with a hint of lipstick and he is wearing sunglasses. Rapaille walks confidently out of the mist to shake my hand: a cross between Louis XIV and Michael Jackson.[9]

In the early 2000s, Rapaille took Rosser Reeves's idea of fear selling to a whole new scary level, paving the way for the 'post-truth' world. In his chateau, among suits of armour and huge family portraits of his ancestors, is a self-portrait: hands clamped on his head, crouched in a cave semi-naked, howling at the wind. It is hard to know what it means, but one thing's for sure: Rapaille knows fear and how to tap into it.

Rapaille's life divides into two halves. The first as a psychologist in hospitals across Northern France, diagnosing and working with autistic children. Rapaille was a successful and respected specialist in the field. Then, in 2000 as Dick Cheney and Tony Blair conjured the imagined 'fact' of weapons of mass destruction in Iraq, Rapaille glanced up at his TV one evening and saw a report on CNN that set fireworks off in his head.

Following the 9/11 attack on the Twin Towers, the report said, sales of Humvees were going through the roof with suburban car buyers. Ordinary Americans were buying a military vehicle designed to withstand a one-hundred-pound mortar-bomb attack in order to do their weekly shop at the supermarket.

What, Rapaille thought, would Freud have made of this? Humvee sales were exploding because the unconscious part of the American consumer's brain was responding to the primal fear of another terrorist attack. What Rapaille called the 'reptilian brain'.

Humvee had not marketed their vehicle at domestic consumers, people had just gone out there and started buying them. People themselves had identified the irrational fear they had and bought themselves the solution.

The events on 9/11 had turned what Rapaille calls the 'thermostat of anxiety' up to 1,000. In that moment, his life changed and a new course was set: as the world's leading advertising guru of fear selling, and heir to Rosser Reeves.

Rapaille's genius would be to upscale freedom from fear. We were not simply fearful of bad breath or neighbours not approving of our new car. We were now terrified of the phantasms of terrorism, paedophiles, refugees and global warming. These were new, expanding fears to be exploited to sell product and provide the consumer not with happiness, but security.

His first deal was with Chrysler. Rapaille met with the company's execs. He told them that suburban cars needed to start looking like Humvees to cash in on the post-9/11 climate of fear. What Chrysler needed was a new 4x4 that sold the same illusion of security as a Humvee, but at a quarter of the price: a high-up tank with bull bars and a steroid-enhanced chassis offering the appearance of safety in an unsafe world.

Rapaille was very clear about the uncompromising message the car should send out to other road users: 'I'm a weapon. Don't mess with me. If you want to bump me, I'm going to crush you and kill you.'

The Chrysler PT Cruiser was the result and it was an instant success. Ironically, like all SUVs it was more likely than a regular car to roll over in high winds. The very things that gave it the illusion of security – the high-up 'turret position' for the driver – made it potentially lethal.[10] The facts did not matter. The PT Cruiser looked safe and that is what drove sales.

Rapaille believes the new climate of fear drove the rise of a brand-new genre of defensive car: Sports Utility Vehicles or SUVs. In the early 2000s, the SUV went from zero to a fifth of all car sales in only three years. Every design detail reinforced the illusion of safety. Even the cup holders, Rapaille says, are not cup holders. 'They send a message of stability: put a cup here, I'm that stable.'

Rapaille was now an 'anthropologist of anxiety', selling his reptilian brain theory to the biggest companies on earth: everyone from tobacco giant Philip Morris to Kellogg's Corn Flakes. Fear selling was a blanket of safety that could be thrown over any product.

Nintendo carried out extensive research on the post-9/11 fears haunting the American family and spotted a huge gap in the games market.[11] Instead of designing a console for solitary teenagers to shoot up Iraqi insurgents in their bedroom, Nintendo set about designing a new console that would bring the family together around a cozy digital fireplace, playing bowling and Mario Cart together. They called it the Wii. The 'ii's nodded to the Asian market; the 'we' suggested togetherness.

Coca Cola followed suit, introducing a 'whiteboard of anxiety' into their brain-storming meetings with executives. At these meetings, they would list the top anxieties they believed the public were currently experiencing and how Coke could be marketed to provide a dozen swigs of respite.[12]

Whether these fears had a basis in reality, was not the point. What mattered was not the facts, but the emotional undertow for the public. Companies exploited clouds of nebulous anxieties thrown up by incessant news coverage of a collapsing planet: global warming; the implosion of the Middle East and subsequent migrant crisis; terrorism; pandemic; even the 'toxic home'.

Fear was a phenomenal tool for selling. We had never in history been safer in our homes, or less in danger of being killed by war or disease, but the perception of escalating fear was being ramped to a new plain of hysteria. The fact that you are more likely to be killed by your toaster than a terrorist attack was a fact that did not come into the equation.

Some products threatened to jump the shark. The Brickhouse Child Locator was an electronic tag you attach to your child. It was launched off the back of a spate of news reports about child abduction.

'Every parent's worst nightmare,' begins the advert. A mum is darting frantically around the playground searching for her missing son. This was anxiety at a heart-palpitating level. 'We enjoy the experience of the rollercoaster ride,' according to Rapaille, but was child abduction a step too far? Today the Brickhouse GPS Child Locator retails at $27.99 and is a massive commercial success.

In 1997, bird flu spread fear of a pandemic that would sweep the planet's airports. Bird flu was followed by dengue fever,

SARs and then in 2004, the re-emergence of the Great White Shark of pandemics, Ebola.

The fear was now visceral, and the soap industry was on hand to sell us the solution. We wanted something to annihilate germs and destroy the coming contagion: 'anti-bacterial' soap was invented to purge the fear. Soap went from a once-a-day luxury used in the bathroom soaking in a long bath, to a weapon used in a minute-by-minute battle with germs: in the kitchen with food; in the bathroom to protect children; and even with our pets.

The battle with germs was really a proxy battle with the contagions of the world we could not wipe clean with an anti-bacterial cloth – disease, pollution and the concocted phantasm of immigrants. All things beyond the control of the fearful consumer. But hygiene was a war we could win. Every domestic surface was identified in adverts as crawling with salmonella, *E. coli* and legions of microbes in need of manic spraying every fifteen seconds.

Anti-bacterial soap also tapped into a whole new market propelled into existence by pandemics: the OCD sufferer. Marketing that tapped into our worst fears about hygiene made anti-bacterial soap the obsessive-compulsive sufferer's new drug of choice.

Barry Shafe is a quiet man in a suit. In the early 2000s, he was head of product development at the world's largest soap manufacturer, Cussons, and the man behind Carex: the product that would launch anti-bacterial sprays on the world.

Exploiting the fears of the public, Barry says, was not even necessary. 'The background noise of pandemic fear was all that was needed to drive consumers to anti-bacterial soap.'[13] Why create scare stories in adverts when the news, filled with terrorist attacks and Ebola, does the advertising for you? Just like the Chrysler PT Land Cruiser, anti-bacterial sprays sold an illusion: security in a perilous world.

But this 'security' came at a real price. As we purged our domestic environment of germs, there was an accompanying rise in child asthma and eczema directly linked to this newly toxic home. The Environmental Protection Agency estimate that the average home is now two to five times more polluted than the air outside as a direct result of 'off-gassing' from household cleaners, air fresheners and strong anti-bacterial sprays.

In making our home germ-free, we had made it poisonous. But the facts of the toxic home created in decontaminating it were disregarded when placed beside the lurid fantasy of the 'dangers'. The fear was simply too intoxicating and trumped the facts. A frightening outside world filled with demons to be slain was a narrative we bought: no one wanted to hear the truth.

HOW NEWS KILLED THE FACTS

In 1986, three big networks owned American television: NBC, CBS and ABC. In a daring swoop, Wall Street corporate raiders bought the lot. NBC went to General Electric; CBS was bought by Lawrence Tisch's investment company Loew's; and Cap Cities, backed by Warren Buffet, bought ABC. The deals ranged from $2–3.5 billion, but the buyers saw it as a fire sale, scooping up hugely undervalued assets at a bargain price. It all happened within a matter of weeks.

Why? America had grown up with these networks. Each had an instantly recognisable 'ident' or logo, and news anchors such as Walter Cronkite whom the nation trusted. For this reason, they provided platforms from which to launch a revolution in commercial TV: new niche and satellite pay-for-view channels homing in on everything from movies and sports to kids and entertainment.

Goldman Sachs were asked by the Cap Cities/Warren Buffet consortium, who bought ABC, to carry out an in-depth analysis of the economics of the network (a study that became a template for the way all TV would be audited). Goldman quickly made a simple discovery: everything costs too much.

TV had 'the *Friends* problem'. Series one, Jennifer Aniston was getting $10,000 a show, but by series three, it was a million with a huge cut of the back-end. What was needed, Goldman

Sachs concluded, were repeatable formats; and news that runs as a continuous stream. And no Jennifer Aniston.

The following year, *Survivor*, the first reality TV format, was launched. It was TV exactly as Goldman Sachs said it should be: mass-produced, high-volume content with no expensive returnable stars, just disposable ones who could be replaced each season. If news was going to pay its way, it too needed to provide more screen time for less buck; and that meant 'rolling news'.

The star was no longer to be Walter Cronkite, but a kid who walks into his high school and kills his classmates with a gun. News had to up its game and get dramatic. It needed to become catastrophised if it was to stand out in a competitive marketplace.

The shift to catastrophised news was fast. In 1994, BBC satire *The Day Today* parodied this new bombastic way of presenting unfolding events with exploding graphics and breathless 'updates' of a story that had no urgent updates to report, but filled the need to put something on TV. Cataclysmic reporting built on half-truth or no-truth at all.

The escalation of rolling news, building to a crescendo of hysteria, was inherent in the format. The truth became merely a servant of the incessant update that required an escalation every fifteen minutes: a 'development'. This meant turning everything, no matter how comically mundane, into 'news'. In Channel 4's *Brass Eye*, Chris Morris played a stony-faced anchor delivering non-headlines as if reporting on the end of the world: 'Child's Face Used as Satellite Dish!' News was already a hyper-dramatic parody of itself.

BUDD DWYER – THE TEMPLATE FOR CATASTROPHISATION

In order to make this news loop of imminent invented catastrophe and shooting, robbery, assault, shooting, robbery, assault watchable, it needed to become dramatic.

We needed to know detail, and the detail needed to be gory. Just as reality TV heightened reality by faking and over-dramatising conflict between the contestants, so catastrophised news needed to go from reporting the facts in a balanced and measured way to hyping the story and becoming entertainment every bit as gripping as drama.

Yet there was an inevitable problem. More TV news needed more exciting things happening all the time to fill it. This created a moral dilemma for the people making it. How far can we push what we show? News got its first test on 22 January 1987.

The Republican treasurer of the Pennsylvania State Senate, Robert 'Budd' Dwyer, had just been convicted of receiving a bribe to secure a multi-million-dollar contract: an elaborate scam involving tax compensation for the wrongful penalisation of thousands of state employees.

Throughout the trial, Dwyer vigorously protested his innocence, even writing to Ronald Reagan pleading with him to intervene. But he was found guilty. Sentencing was scheduled for 23 July and Dwyer faced a potential fifty-five years behind bars.

The day before sentencing, Dwyer called a press conference. Five TV news outlets sent a crew. Dwyer handed out his resignation speech from a manila envelope. He thanked his constituents for their support and reiterated his innocence: 'Please tell my story on every radio and television station, and in every newspaper and magazine in the United States.'

He then took out another manila envelope from which he produced a loaded Smith & Wesson Model 27 revolver. The assembled press gasped and started screaming. Dwyer continued talking calmly, 'Please leave if you have a weak stomach or mind, since I don't want to cause physical or mental distress.' Two ushers tried to grab him, but Dwyer stepped back to avoid them, waving the gun. 'Don't, don't. This will hurt someone,' he warned them.

Dwyer then turned to the main news camera and looked

directly down the lens – known as 'looking down the barrel' – as if anchoring a news report about himself. 'Joanne, Rob, Dee Dee. I love you. Thank you for making my life so happy. Goodbye to you all. On the count of three . . .' But by the time he got to two, he had fired the gun into his mouth and blown away the top of his head.

Dwyer had timed his suicide to make the midday news. He knew what they wanted and did not disappoint. The channels were torn between the horrific graphic content and its dynamite potential to pull in viewers.

WPVI-TV in Philadelphia and WPXI-TV in Pittsburgh both showed the suicide. Channel 6 showed Dwyer pulling the trigger, but cut before the blood. Local Pennsylvania networks WCAU, KYW and KDKA froze the footage at the moment of the trigger-pull, but continued playing the audio of the gunshot and the horrified screams that followed. Action News broadcast the suicide from beginning to end. The *New York Times* questioned the morality of showing Dwyer's suicide, but it was a ratings winner.[14]

Dwyer had a co-defendant at the trial, another Republican governor called William Smith. In 2010, twenty-seven years after Dwyer killed himself, Smith admitted that he had lied under oath about Dwyer's involvement in the bribe in order to get a lighter sentence for himself.

Dwyer had been right all along about being framed. He was innocent and had killed himself because no one had investigated his claim. Smith received a one-year jail sentence for lying under oath in order to frame Dwyer and returned after six months to politics.

The news networks did not investigate Dwyer's claim that he had been framed, because they were too busy rehashing his suicide and finding new ways to cover it. Actually doing journalism and discovering the reason why he killed himself in the first place did not happen. The news cycle was turning too fast for that.[15]

Budd Dwyer's suicide was a test of the moral code of news in the new, highly competitive world. Dwyer had known what news wanted, what 'newsworthy' now meant, and used it to get coverage for his case.

Choosing between dignity for Dwyer and his family over graphic coverage of his suicide, the new channels went for the latter. Thanks to the sudden commercialisation of news, channels now demanded impact and the world obliged.

News will deliver the facts when we need them – during national disaster or crisis – but because of the underlying commercial imperative, the pressure to deliver a scoop, can also turn into a machine of misinformation when we least need it to be histrionic. In 2013, following the Boston Marathon bombing, CNN's John King was quick to identify the suspect as a 'dark-skinned male'.[16] Fox News's Megyn Kelly upped the ante by falsely confirming a suspect had been arrested. The *New York Post* published a picture of two men with rucksacks in the crowd, declaring them the 'Bag Men: Feds seek these two pictured at Boston Marathon' (they didn't, and it was not them).

News hasn't just been weighed down by commercial pressures, it has faced cuts. The result has been to slash investigative and new journalism, that seeks to look in unexpected places for a story, in favour of rehashing the familiar and becoming increasingly dependent on easy sources: press releases by pressure and consumer groups, the political circus of Westminster and Washington, the same old talking heads talking about the same old tried and trusted 'issues'. News became an echo chamber long before the term was coined.

Budd Dwyer's suicide had pre-empted live 'as it happens' and on-the-spot reporting, but as news became rolling news, and the commercial imperative combined with cuts to dedicated long-form investigation weighed down on new or accurate reporting, 'fake news' became inevitable.

SCIENCE BECOMES SCIENCE FICTION

T.S. Eliot once said that 'humankind cannot bear very much reality' and this was the lesson TV news learnt from Budd Dwyer. If a car bomb decapitates a child, we see a news report of that event deemed acceptable to Western audiences. It is a finely calibrated halfway house between what really happened and the 'acceptable', sanitised version, shots chosen deliberately in order to convey symbols of horror (a bloody shoe, a crying parent) without showing the graphic detail of the explosion: this is the trick of news reporting and constitutes 'truth'. The reported fact on what happened.

But news is not alone in needing to create a hybrid truth in order to walk a moral line, simultaneously catastrophising news stories, yet policing this inflation of claims. Science, too, has had to up the ante and the reason is that research needs coverage on news in order to maintain funding. If it is going to get coverage, it needs to be extreme, emphatic and wrong.

In 2013, Professor John Ioannidis at the Seventh Peer Review Congress in Chicago made a shocking revelation.[17] Most scientific studies are wildly inaccurate, and they are wrong because scientists are more interested in funding and furthering their career than scientific truth.[18]

Ioannidis illustrated his point with the *Boston Cookbook*. Of fifty randomly selected ingredients from recipes, forty had been linked with increasing or decreasing the risk of cancer. These cancer links had been reported and repeated in news and media reports thousands of times. Yet meta-analysis showed, Ioannidis said, that the scientific studies were 'correct' in almost no cases.[19]

Science by its nature needs to be measured and circumspect, yet this is the opposite of what news wants. If a news editor is given a choice of a story that blueberries have marginal health benefits versus 'blueberries cure cancer', or even better 'blueberries give you cancer', which will they run?

The public stopped believing claims for 'superfoods', and

'wonder drugs' or vitamins, when the claims changed every month, but what this process has done is to undermine confidence in science as a profession. It has turned science into fake science.

And when it comes to science around curing disease, it does not get any better. When genes were linked to specific diseases, Ioannidis said, analysis of hundreds of studies found a genuine provable link in only 1.1 per cent of cases.[20] When biomarkers of diseases were found in 127 prediction models, a high relative risk almost always turned out to have been exaggerated. Only a fifth of those 127 models even had further studies to validate them.

Ioannidis concluded that scientific bias is rampant, over-inflated claims are rife and the reason is simple: people need funding and to get funding for their work, they need to get noticed. As scientific 'research' has become a useful resource for the media to report dramatic 'developments' in science, both escalating health dangers and unrealistic solutions are reported as fact. In reality, they have been catastrophised, just as news has been.

Each week, waves of danger are reported approaching society like a tsunami, then washing over us and leaving society unscathed. Yet each wave is deemed more dangerous than the last: super-bugs, super-rats, super-bots, super-malware, super-fraud; super-summer smog and winter smog, everything from an approaching meteor about to destroy earth to an indestructible Japanese knotweed that will strangle your garden. These 'epidemics' are in reality a containable event catastrophised and upgraded into an imminent threat to humanity.

Science has become part of the fake news business, working with news to disregard the facts for the sake of a better story: 'killer coffee'; 'killer tea'; 'miracle coffee'; 'miracle tea'; 'harmful effects of cigarettes mitigated by drinking coffee and tea'.

But beneath these headlines is a power play. Behind every 'killer this' and 'miracle that' is scientific research funded by a specific commercial interest looking to lobby government, or shift a new product using the cloak of science. Research is covertly funded by either the food, health or drugs industry, each pushing a specific commercial product looking for a licence or to create a demand. Science does not work in a neutral zone of 'facts', any more than news does.

Sometimes this can be dangerous: in 1992, the contraceptive pill was suddenly declared to cause deep vein thrombosis. The following year, abortion figures rose unexpectedly, yet fears about thrombosis mysteriously vanished as quickly as they had first been made. The NHS put out advice that there was no increased risk with the progestogen-only contraceptive pill and only a 'slightly increased risk' with the combined oestrogen and progestogen pill. The victim was not the drugs company, or the media who reported the exaggerated claim, but those women who believed they were at risk.

THE ABERRATION OF 'TRUTH'

News and science did what they did for a reason, but it had an effect: the public simply stopped believing in the 'facts'. The Pew Research Centre is a non-partisan 'fact tank' based in Washington that has been monitoring levels of public trust in government and journalism for forty years.[21]

In 1958 – during Truman's administration – seventy-three per cent of Americans said they could trust government 'just about always or most of the time'. They trusted journalists, too. Trust in both professions remained high throughout the 1960s, reaching a high-water mark under President Johnson – when people felt safest – but in the 1970s, thanks to Vietnam and Watergate, trust in government plummeted spectacularly: thirty-six per cent in 1974; only twenty-five per cent by 1979.

Yet at the very moment trust in government collapsed, journalism came into its own. As a force for 'truth'.

In 1970, Seymour Hersh broke the story of the My Lai

massacre. In 1972, Bob Woodward and Carl Bernstein unearthed Watergate. The *Sunday Times* Insight team exposed scandal after scandal throughout the decade: from Thalidomide to the secret manufacture of nuclear weapons by Israel.

With trust in politicians crumbling, there was one place where the public felt it could reliably turn to tell the truth and keep politicians in check: the media. Belief in the power of this fourth estate grew in inverse proportion to plummeting respect for politicians.

In the 1970s, the public viewed journalists as knights in shining armour, bringing truth to the people: Watergate's Woodward and Bernstein were played by Robert Redford and Dustin Hoffman in *All the President's Men*. Journalism was a full-beam force for truth, unsullied by the weakness and venality perceived to have corrupted government.

But then there was a power shift. Proprietors who had sided with the outsider voice of journalists suddenly began wanting a slice of real power once more, which meant siding with politicians. They wanted to be insiders again.

In 1903, Lord Northcliffe, the first press baron of the twentieth century, saw the potential for power that his newspapers gave him: 'Every extension of the (voting) franchise renders more powerful the newspaper and less powerful the politician.'[22] By 1918, Northcliffe believed he had single-handedly won the First World War by using his power to remove Asquith and install Lloyd George as Prime Minister.[23]

In the 1930s and 1940s, Lords Rothermere and Beaverbrook used their power to interfere directly in affairs of state. Rothermere, owner of the *Daily Mail*, endorsed the British Union of Fascists and was openly sympathetic to Hitler whom he saw – as a substantial section of the British public did – a strong European leader surrounded by weak ones.[24]

Beaverbrook, who owned the *Daily Express*, the first newspaper to have a circulation of two million in the 1930s, joined forces with Rothermere to try and oust Prime Minister Stanley Baldwin. Effectively a *coup d'état*.

On 17 March 1931, at the Queens Hall in London, Baldwin said, 'Their newspapers are not newspapers in the ordinary acceptance of the term, they are engines of propaganda for their constantly changing policies, desires, personal wishes, personal likes and dislikes of two men. What the proprietorship of these papers is aiming at is power, but power without responsibility, the prerogative of the harlot throughout the ages.'[25]

The press barons of the early twentieth century had affected seismic change in politics. They were not simply players at the same table as politicians, they wanted to decide who would sit there.

The 1970s changed that. Journalism has skewed the power play by creating an aberration called 'truth'. Facts were no longer to be marshalled to garner political power for proprietors, but a force for revealing the lies of politicians to the public: diamonds in a mine to be discovered by investigative journalists and brought out into the light.

The proprietors went along with this version of events so long as it was good for business, but when it ceased to be, the press baron – now reborn as the media mogul – was to go back to the default setting of a big-time power player, influencing who sat at the table of power. And one mogul led the way.

THE FOX

In 1985, an Australian newspaper tycoon with an American passport, who had owned a bust of Lenin while a student in Britain, bought a tiny US news channel called WTDG.

Frank O'Donnell was a producer: 'For the first three years, he left us alone, partly because we were so successful. But one day, we received an order that we should cut away from our newscast and start airing a fawning tribute to Ronald Reagan that was airing at the Republican convention. We were stunned, because up until this point, we were allowed to do legitimate news. Suddenly we were ordered from the top to carry propaganda.'[26]

The staff of WTDG saw Rupert Murdoch as something new, but he wasn't. He had inherited his media empire and then built shrewdly upon it, just as Northcliffe, Beaverbrook, Rothermere and Cecil King had before him.

But Murdoch was shrewder and more ambitious than all of them. He had been a Leninist at university and his desire for revolution continued long after he stopped toying with student socialism.

O'Donnell believes that what he was witnessing first hand at WTDG with the top-down edict was the birth of 'post-truth', coming to fruition twenty years later. But this WTDG post-truth was merely a remarshalling of the facts as it had been under the old press barons: to influence and shape power.

In 1996, Fox News was launched with Roger Aisles at its head, an ex-strategist for Nixon, Reagan and Bush. 'We expect to do fair and balanced journalism,' he said: the watchwords for the channel. Within hours, memos were being sent round the building instructing journalists what could and could not be talked about. Abortion was, said Aisles, 'a trademark issue': Fox policy was pro-life. Race was another: it was a left-wing issue. AIDS, too. When the 9/11 inquiry began, one memo warned staff not to 'turn this into another Watergate'.[27]

Dissenting voices were booked for studio discussions merely to be shot down, or have their microphone cut in the middle of a discussion. This was not old-school 'balance', but balance was not the point. This was a full beam of polemic fired like a laser at Washington, and it worked. Fox journalist Bill O'Reilly told over sixty separate interviewees to 'shut up' and cut them off mid-sentence. Journalists schooled on Woodward and Bernstein were shocked.

Disgruntled staff said they were bullied into running stories that were either inaccurate or spun – like the Columbine shootings – to push the pro-gun lobby position. No one in control of Fox cared about these outdated criticisms. They were making the future of journalism, and soon everyone would understand.

Robert McChesney, professor of Journalism at the University of Illinois, who made a study of Fox News, said the network was the catalyst for 'post-truth' by creating the 'total elimination of journalism',[28] but Fox was really the elimination of journalism as 'truth' in order to make it once more a tool for political power.

Murdoch was not doing this to create a right-wing channel, or erase the news. He was doing it to become a power broker.

Murdoch, like the new breed of proprietor in the late 1970s and early 1980s – James Goldsmith, Robert Maxwell and Tiny Rowlands – wanted to influence government from within by replicating the conditions in which Rothermere and Beaverbrook had wielded empires, as sticks by which to cow politicians.

To become a player meant two things: taking an overt political stance and reining back on journalists digging into the misdemeanours of the people with whom you were seeking to get into bed, so undermining any bid to enter the inner sanctum. Or if you did find dirt, using it as leverage against them. It was a fork in the road: facts and journalism versus power. It was a choice, and the new proprietors chose power.

On 4 January 1981, the deal was done.

At a private lunch at her country residence of Chequers, Prime Minister Thatcher and Murdoch carved up the map of power as the lamb was carved before them. Thatcher needed a supportive press for her revolution, Murdoch wanted to buy the *Sunday Times*. They decided to do business.

The following day, the rules that applied to media monopolies suddenly changed. Murdoch was free to buy the *Sunday Times*, *The Times*, the *Sun* and the *News of the World*. He bought the satellite TV company BSB and renamed it Sky Television. In return, all were guaranteed to fire a concentrated beam of Thatcherism at every home in Britain.

In Wapping, Murdoch built a giant de-unionised fortress where he would roam the corridors like a ghost, saying little but watching everything. And adjusting any carpets he judged slightly askew.

The *Sunday Times* saw a power struggle with the champion of *Sunday Times* past, Harold Evans. Evans lost. In the US, where Murdoch's outsider credentials dovetailed with Reagan's, Murdoch bought Twentieth Century Fox, HarperCollins Publishers and the *Wall Street Journal*.

Murdoch was impossible to pin down – he was mercurial and all-powerful, his news and TV empire stretching over every continent. Over 100 TV channels, 175 newspapers, forty book imprints and one very big movie studio: Fox. Murdoch's combined media firepower reached a global audience of 4.7 billion people: three-quarters of the entire population of planet earth.

Politicians seeking power now sought his blessing. In 1995, Tony Blair flew to Hayman Island, off the coast of Australia, for a formal anointment. Murdoch did not want nor need to consult with Blair; he merely needed him to be on the end of a phone in ten minutes, should it be required. As Murdoch wryly said, 'I've never asked a politician to do anything in my life.' He did not need to.

In the early 2000s, Fox stepped up its game by promoting itself as the authentic voice of America against the new 'liberal elite' of Washington. Fox was no longer the outsider voice, but the mainstream voice. It was a genius sleight of hand: minorities and corporate interests, not the American people, had wheedled their way into the heart of government. Graphics wrapped the Fox logo in the American flag.

Blatant partisanship gave Fox an almost cool, outsider status in marked contrast to the staid news channels, regurgitating press releases and trotting along to Washington junkets. Their journalists were not fierce, right-wing firebrands like Fox's, but dull, bored men who talked to camera in a monotone drone, hamstrung by their version of balance and their version of the facts.

Fox was delivering news as edgy, echo-chambered entertainment and the reasons were nothing to do with Murdoch's real politics, which are those of any shrewd, opportunist businessman.

Owning an opinionated right-wing channel was merely good for business, and right for the times.

Fox began to redefine what the American right were about, coalescing first around the Tea Party, then Steve Bannon's Breitbart News and the alt-right. And the alt-right cleverly defined themselves in terms of what they were not.

They were not for gay marriage or the special pleading of minorities, they were not for gun control or abortion or immigration. They were not for elites or Washington or Islam. A negatively defined platform for a new political movement, but its calling card – what Rosser Reeves would have called its USP – was a refusal to believe in 'facts' as defined by traditional media.

There was a justifiable neurosis on the part of this so-called liberal 'elite' that the absolutist hegemony it had enjoyed for thirty years was over. But it was. We were back to the power play and 'truth' was merely a context.

Murdoch had not invented post-truth or erased the facts, he had taken advantage of the vacuum created. A disillusionment created by the incremental erosion of the credibility of news through its catastrophisation, and the accompanying inflated and schizophrenic claims of science. If people wanted extreme, he would give them extreme. It was a strange kind of honesty. In 2016, Fox News topped the ratings as the most watched cable news channel in America.

THE MYTH OF FACTS

In 1855, at the height of the Crimean War, Roger Fenton's photograph, 'The Valley of the Shadow of Death', published in *The Times*, poignantly captured the aftermath of British retreat in the face of the Russian army with a single image of an empty battlefield. There was only one problem. Fenton had constructed the entire scene, moving cannon balls artfully until he had the perfect image.

In 1945, on the beach of Iwo Jima, legendary war photographer Joe Rosenthal captured the most famous image of battle ever taken: the raising of the Stars and Stripes as American soldiers took the summit from the Japanese. It won him the Pulitzer Prize.

Both are a lie. The actual capture of Iwo Jima took place two days before Rosenthal even arrived. The real moment of victory was marked by a pathetically small flag raised on a makeshift flagpole and a sergeant named Louis Lowery recording it for posterity on a cheap camera. But the historic moment needed a fittingly heroic composition, so the army restaged it.

These falsified images dramatised a fact. A thing that actually happened. And the public believed it happened. In the 2014 blockbuster movie *Interstellar*, Matthew McConaughey's character marches into his son's school outraged that his son is being taught that the moon landings were faked.

But this is now the received wisdom for the majority of the population. Seventy-three per cent of the American public believe the moon landings were faked, fifty-two per cent of British adults believe the same. The younger you are, the more sceptical you will be. Seventy-eight per cent of eighteen-to-thirty-year-olds think the landings that Walter Cronkite solemnly reported as 'the greatest achievement in the history of mankind' were simply a couple of actors in a studio hamming it up in spacesuits and a sand pit.

Yet the moon landings are believable in the eyes of the public when placed next to news: ninety-four per cent of the US population believe all news reported by mainstream media is distorted or plain made up.

It is not balanced reporting that gets people's attention, but the high beam of a polemic that Fox pioneered. 'Facts' are marshalled into a compelling single argument, driven home by their selective use, pummelled into the intended target like bullets. The 9/11 conspiracy documentary *Loose Change*, arguing that the Twin Towers was a covert operation by the US government, is one of the most viewed documentaries on line ever made.[29] The fact that it has been widely discredited and debunked did not dampen its impact.

'Fake news' has been at the heart of the news as long as there has been news. Following the Spanish Civil War of 1936, George Orwell wrote:

> Early in life I had noticed no event is ever correctly reported in a newspaper. But in Spain, for the first time, I saw reports which did not bear any relation to the facts, not even the relationship that is implied in an ordinary lie. I saw great battles reported where there had been no fighting, and complete silence where hundreds of men had been killed. This kind of thing is frightening to me, because it often gives me the feeling that the very concept of objective truth is fading out of the world.

In April 2016, the world's mainstream media descended on the small Macedonian town of Veles. For some strange reason, Veles had been identified as the source of thousands of fake news stories on Facebook such as 'Michelle Obama is a Man' and 'Wikileaks Just Killed Hillary!'

Serious journalists from some of the world's best-respected broadsheet titles could not comprehend why such a thing could happen. They searched the town for meaning, interviewing sullen teenagers on street corners who might have been responsible. Even the Macedonian teenagers looked mildly embarrassed when asked by middle-aged reporters schooled on Watergate 'why they had done it'. Why do anything? They said. Boredom and money.

A twenty-two-year-old computer-science student from Veles tried to explain to the *Guardian*: 'I thought, what would interest Americans the most, and it was either this or American Football. Some of the news I write, and other parts I take from other web sites, I then translate them. I really don't know if what I translate is true or not, I am only doing this because of the Google ads.'

The Veles students were not trying to 'do' anything. They were not trying to help Trump to win. They were not alt-right or left, they were not satirists or YouTubers. They were merely entrepreneurial teenagers in a depressed Macedonian city who had done their research and identified a niche, and were now looking to do something wholly American: make money.

Fake news did not put Donald Trump in the White House, any more than Joe Rosenthal's faked capture of Iwo Jima changed the course of the Second World War. But the difference was that Trump's victory happened within a context in which very few people under twenty-five now believe the news is anything but propaganda, and President Trump tapped into that. Orwell lamented the 'fading out' of 'objective truth' and the subordination of facts to those making a naked play for power, but to those in power, power is the only fact that matters.

CHAPTER TWELVE
ROBOTS: THE HUMAN MACHINES

THE IMITATION GAME

'I propose to consider the question: can machines think?'

So opens Alan Turing's most famous paper written in 1950.[1] Turing had been integral to winning the Second World War by deciphering the Enigma Code of German U-boats. After the war, Turing used what he had learnt from code-breaking to take on what he considered to be the biggest challenge facing humanity.

To break the Enigma Code, Turing had used unimaginably complex sequences. These, thought Turing, now offered a glimpse into the future consciousness of machines. Could a computer develop to such a point that it could successfully mimic a human? 'Are there imaginable digital computers,' he wondered, 'which would do well in "the imitation game"?'[2]

Turing created a test: a human talks to a number of other humans behind a screen. But one of the humans is not human at all – it is a computer pretending to be human. If the questioner cannot tell which one is the computer, then the computer has successfully passed itself off as human. It has won the 'imitation game'.

Artificial intelligence, Turing said, would cease to be artificial, but real. And more importantly, humanity would have crossed the Rubicon to a world in which humans would ultimately be governed by robots. Turing surmised that computers would pass his test in 'about fifty years'.

It took sixty-two. In 2012, Vladimir Veselov at the University of Reading created a software program that successfully mimicked a thirteen-year-old Ukranian boy called 'Eugene Goostman'.[3] Veselov's reasons for this adopted persona were cunning. 'Our main idea was that Eugene can claim that he knows anything, but his age also makes it perfectly reasonable that he doesn't know everything.'

Computers trying to pass the Turing Test in the past had fallen at the first hurdle by failing to even understand the question asked by humans. But increasingly complex machines since 2010 have been able to adapt strategies to fool humans: they change the subject, ask questions of the judges and even simulate moods and typos in text exchanges: strategies to make themselves look more human. Their 'imitation' has become increasingly devious.

As a result, the bar for the Turing Test has been raised. For a computer to successfully pass today, it needs to fool at least one judge from a group of three human judges after a number of conversations lasting up to two hours.

This is a transcript of the conversation between Eugene and a human in 2012:

Judge: What music do you like?
Eugene: I like Eminem – because he doesn't have a thing to do with polite-correctness.
Judge: OMG i love Eminem, he's my favourite artist!
Eugene: I wonder what Eminem's nick mean. I associate it only with a word 'enema'. But he is a cool guy, I like his 'The Real Slim Shady'.
Judge: I know what his nick name means, his real name is Marshall Mathers. From the initials M&M phynetically (sic) sounding like Eminem.

Eugene: Eminem is a famous crapper. No, raper ... ripper ...
Yeah, I like his 'Stan' and 'The Real Slim Shady'.
Judge: I like 'Hailies song'.
Eugene: Interesting tastes. I like science fiction books, by the
way.

How anyone could seriously be fooled by Eugene is hard to
imagine. But Eugene, in spite of 'his' idiosyncratic answers,
successfully passed thirty-three per cent of such conversations.[4]
And in 'passing' the Turing Test, it became apparent that the
Turing Test might be missing the point about robots.

Robots are not about a bad simulation of humans; they are
about something new entirely. In 2017, I visited Uber's headquarters in San Francisco to meet one of their head designers,
Didier Hilhorst. On the face of it, Uber is a cab app. But it is not.
For Uber, providing an app that can merely order a cab is only
the beginning.

Uber has the potential, Didier says, to immerse itself fully in a
digital representation of the city. It is a form of 'augmented reality' – a hybrid of real life and a parallel representation on screen
in which the digital enmeshes itself in your day-to-day life, and
so becomes your life.

At the moment, Uber only provide cabs and food, with a little
car you can follow on screen *en route.* But the data Uber are
amassing allows the algorithms to begin predicting your needs
and suggesting them: would you like to go to a favourite restaurant, take your child to day care or to your girlfriend's place?
How about somewhere or something you have never done
before?

The next step is a sophisticated representation of you in a
virtual environment: a figure walking through the city. You in five
minutes' time. Do you want a coffee? It is ordered and ready in
the coffee shop as you approach. You see an avatar of yourself
approaching the coffee shop and the barista making it.

'In five years' time, will we still be using phones and apps to do these things? It's doubtful we'll still be using anything so clunky as having to take a device out of your pocket and tediously press screens. We already have contact lenses developed with screens projecting directly onto the eye allowing instantaneous decision-making. The job is to make the Uber experience as seamless as breathing. The potential for augmenting reality and making that our version of singularity is very exciting.'

This 'total Uber experience' will mean the avatar of you will be three steps ahead of the real you: shopping, buying tickets for the cinema, or dealing with problems such as a traffic jam before you have to, and using voice recognition or retina technology to do it. Whatever you do now on your phone will have been 'gamified' into the 'total Uber experience': no longer on your phone, but projected on the retina of your eye.

This is not Us Versus Robots, but a future enmeshed together in which the boundaries of where they end and we begin are blurred. Didier sees this robot future not as a Jetsons world of tin-can machines doing things for us, but digital technology and human life as a seamless whole: a singularity.

This augmented reality in our eye will be supplemented by in-body technology – blood-cleaning nano-computers; thermostatic control of heart rate, blood pressure and stress levels. This is not a world of giant striding machines, but microscopic tech hacks of human life.

Uber watched in 2014 and 2015 as Alexa and Siri were promoted by Amazon and Apple to provide mass-market automated assistants. A soothing voice that will book you a restaurant, turn on your lights at home, coach you through your morning workout, or play your favourite playlist.

But Didier and Uber are thinking beyond this to a world in which robot intelligence and human needs are utterly inseparable, and we ourselves have become the robot, with human parts.

So what happens when there is no singularity? I asked Didier what was the main problem with driverless cars. Uber already have trials of driverless fleets with paying passengers in San Francisco, Pittsburgh and Tempe, Arizona.

New technology in itself was not the problem, Didier explained, but when human error and new technology collided. In other words, the old human infrastructure of a higgledy-piggledy city clashing with the new technology of driverless cars inevitably creates a period of transitional mess.

For the technology to truly revolutionise our lives, it requires an entire reboot of the infrastructure: a clean slate from which to start again. The kind of thing that only happens after natural disaster or a war.

From this perspective, policy-making with the potential to create nuclear apocalypse can also be viewed from a tech perspective: it is a chance to not only get driverless cars on the road but to start society again from scratch. It reminded me of a *Yes, Prime Minister* sketch from the 1980s. The PM is shown round a brand-new hospital where everything works smoothly. Nurses walk calmly from ward to ward. Doctors consult with each other and nod in agreement. 'It all looks fantastic', the Prime Minister says. 'But where are the patients?' 'Oh, we don't want people getting in the way. They would ruin everything'.

I, FOR ONE, WELCOME OUR NEW COMPUTER OVERLORDS

As the thirteen-year-old 'Eugene Goostman' was being built in Reading, another computer was being prepared for a very different challenge, one with far more serious consequences for the human race.

In January 2011, Ken Jennings and Brad Rutter, two former champions of the US TV quiz show *Jeopardy!*, sat down before a TV audience of twenty million to face their toughest opponent yet: IBM computer Watson.[5]

In 1998, an IBM supercomputer called Deep Blue had

destroyed the world chess champion Garry Kasparov over six frantically fought matches. Deep Blue's emphatic victory was hailed as a kind of Turing Test being passed, but it was not. Chess is a game with distinct rules and finite (if multiple) options for any one move. It is merely a test of computing complexity, not AI.

In 2004, IBM executive Charles Lickel was in a steakhouse near Poughkeepsie eating dinner when he noticed something strange: the restaurant emptying. The diners were rushing out to the bar to watch the TV. On it was America's longest-running quiz show, *Jeopardy!* The diners were hooked on a phenomenon gripping America: the latest instalment of the amazing, seventy-four-game winning streak of Ken Jennings.[6]

In that moment, Lickel had an idea. Days later in a brain-storming session at IBM, in which executives were being asked to come up with IBM's next 'grand challenge', Lickel suggested they take on Ken Jennings in the ultimate *Jeopardy!* showdown. Man versus Robot.

That is the legend. In truth, a physicist at IBM called Dave Ferrucci, a fiercely smart New Jersey-born Italian American with a brain the size of an IBM computer, had been badgering his bosses for over a year to create a more demanding challenge. I met Dave in New York, where he is now working with the world's largest hedge fund, Bridgewater, to use artificial intelligence to hire and fire the staff handling $160 billion worth of assets. I assume he needs to get his new job right, just as he did with Watson playing *Jeopardy!*

'In terms of complexity, *Jeopardy!* was a huge step up from playing the world chess champion,' Dave says, 'which was merely a test of computing power.'

The randomness of *Jeopardy!*'s questions – from obscure 1980s pop culture to seventeenth-century philosophy – and phrased in a quirky, counter-intuitive and problematically human way – made it a far more difficult challenge for a computer. Compared to *Jeopardy!*, a game of chess was child's play,[7] because *Jeopardy!* was outside the computer's comfort zone.

IBM had no idea what they were up against. To begin with, Watson was uploaded with a Wikipedia's worth of information. But searching through this database using algorithms for an answer took Watson hours, not seconds.

'We initially made progress very quickly, but then it slowed and that was frustrating. We played an early game and it was terrible. Watson was destroyed and we just thought this was impossible.'

In 2009, five years after starting, IBM finally began testing Watson against former contestants of *Jeopardy!* as a dry run for the Jennings showdown.

Watson still had glitches. Responses could be unpredictable and wildly inaccurate. Questioned about the main characters in Dickens's novel *Oliver Twist*, Watson said 'The Pet Shop Boys'. Asked what 'no' is in German, Watson answered, 'What is fuck?' (The answer was 'What is *nein?*').[8]

Ferrucci realised that even when Watson could get the answer right, it would take hours to find it. Dave brought in an entirely new team of programmers simply to deal with the idea of what a question was to a computer, and another to deal with the speed at which this information could be processed.

'I was called in by the bosses at IBM and told, Get this right. This whole thing rests on – and they pointed their finger at me – you.'

Luckily for Dave and Watson's other programmers, the difference between machines and humans is that machines keep relentlessly improving. As humans learn more, the curve of improvement plateaus out. But with robots, it steepens dramatically: a lesson the contestants of *Jeopardy!* were about to learn the hard way.

In 2011, Watson was ready for its big day on TV. A large computer sat in the studio between two humans. Watson was 'about the size of a restaurant fridge'. But it was the most complex machine ever programmed.

A blue, convex robot eye stared out impassively and HAL-like from the middle of a blank screen as two humans fidgeted on their podiums. Watson was facing off with the all-time *Jeopardy!* champion, Ken Jennings, and another *Jeopardy!* super-brain, champion of champions, Brad Rutter.

Dave sat in the audience with the IBM bosses. He was so nervous, his fingernails dug into his legs. 'I knew we were going to win, though.' How come? 'We had worked so hard, we knew it. Watson was ready. It was going to be a walk-over.'

But it wasn't. Initially, the contest appeared pretty even. But then Watson suddenly kicked in. Dave breathed a sigh of relief. It began beating Jennings and Rutter to every answer faster; the same solemn unblinking eye staring out over the audience as it delivered correct answer after correct answer.

The glitches had gone. Jennings and Rutter looked at each other in bewilderment. Watson's supremacy over its human rivals was breathtaking. 'There were still times it could have gone the humans' way,' Dave says, 'because with *Jeopardy!* there's always a chance you can come back. And that came into my head. But I was the human rooting for the computer, it was strange, and all I was doing was demonstrating my irrational human fears.'

By the final question, these were the positions: Brad Rutter had amassed $21,600. Ken Jennings: $24,000. Watson had $77,147: over three times as much.

When the very last answer was given, 'Bram Stoker', and all three correctly answered the question – 'Who wrote *Dracula?*' – it didn't matter. Watson had crushed its rivals.

Watson's victory was greeted with stilted applause from the audience. Humans were applauding their own defeat. Ken Jennings smiled wryly and wrote a message on his answer card, which he showed to the millions of people watching at home: 'I, for one, welcome our new computer overlords.'

THEIR WEAK SPOT: MAKING A BED

On 5 April 2014, two of the world's foremost AI experts, Professors Erik Brynjolfsson and Andrew McAfee of MIT, held a meeting in New York with a hundred of the world's top programmers. The agenda: the implications of the Watson victory.[9]

Brynjolfsson and McAfee showed a graph with two lines of blue dots. One line marked the cognitive advancement of human *Jeopardy!* players; and the other showed the progress of Watson from the moment IBM began work in 2004 to the day Watson trounced Jennings and Rutter in 2011.

'Look at the dates,' Brynjolfsson said.

The human advance of dots went moderately upward. But Watson's advance of blue dots was astonishing: initially tentative; then moderate; then suddenly steep. But from 2008 on, the dots went up like a skyscraper. Watson had gone through the gears from terrible to genius in seven years, but its rate of learning in the last twelve months had accelerated at a speed never seen before.

What did this mean? It meant, Brynjolfsson and McAfee said, that once robots get to a baseline of learning, they can learn to do what we do very, very fast. They then move on, colonising what we cannot do fast as well.

In terms of the workplace, robots first conquer the manual stuff within their physical ambit, then they dry run for themselves managerial skills, which means they can oversee and manage what humans do. They become the boss, and do not need to be programmed to do this. They just do it.

'Think of the world of work,' Brynjolfsson said, 'as divided between "power systems" and "control systems".' The power systems are people, fork-lifts, planes and trucks. They move things. The control systems are plant managers, business plans and engineering diagrams: they decide where things move.

In the nineteenth century, the first industrial revolution

automated engines and factories and created a machine age that potentially threatened the entire usefulness of humans; our reason for existing. The power systems were disrupted and reshaped. But after a period of dislocation we adapted, taking over the control systems by becoming engineers and managers.

But this second machine age is very different. Now machines are not only reshaping the power systems, but taking over the control systems, too, and there is no possibility of humans fighting back.

Robots will take our jobs, but then they might choose not to do them. Yet because these first jobs will be gone, there will be no chance of us clawing them back. As Elizabeth Kolbert succinctly put it: 'Ken Jennings (the human *Jeopardy!* opponent of Watson) might be described as the first person to be made redundant by Watson.'[10]

In March 2017, thirty-four employees at the Fukoku Mutual Life Insurance in Tokyo became the next humans made redundant by Watson: the first employees anywhere in the world to be openly replaced by artificial intelligence.[11]

The Watson software had been bought by Fukoku to automate health insurance across the whole of Japan. The IBM computer that had won *Jeopardy!* would now be deciding who has an operation in a country of 127 million people.

Fukoku management calculate they will save 140 million yen (£1 million) a year in wages by cutting these thirty-four jobs. But by laying off 34,000 people in similarly well-paid, middle-management jobs, they could save a billion.

IBM say that Watson possesses 'cognitive technology that can think like a human enabling it to analyse and interpret all data, including unstructured text, images, audio and video.' Fukoku will use Watson to read tens of thousands of medical certificates, working out length of hospital stays and appropriate surgical procedures before calculating payouts. When humans did this job, they used their own judgment before making a decision. Fukoku say there is no need. The data will decide.

In south-western Japan, Henn-na Hotel is staffed entirely by robots. There is a multi-lingual dinosaur on reception and a hairless doll concierge with blinking Geisha eyes that answers any queries about breakfast. A robot trolley takes your bags to the room: face recognition is used as your key. A drone delivers room service. There is only one permanent human member of staff: Hideo Sawada, the owner.

Japanese hotels are expensive, but the Henn-na costs only 9,000 yen ($80 a night). The hotel is covered with security cameras and these are watched by a human from a security centre 200 miles away.

Yet when it comes to making your bed, there is a chink of light for humanity. The robots can't do it. No matter how hard Hideo Sawada tried, he could not get robot maids to successfully fold down and tuck under a sheet, pulling it tight to the degree that humans desire.

Beds, it turns out, are surprisingly complex in AI terms. They vary in size and shape; they are positioned differently in hotels, with surrounding furniture making access difficult. They require moving and repositioning. Making a bed is a multi-disciplined affair, it requires both delicate skills and spatial awareness as well as manual strength, and it stumps robots.

So the only other human staff at Henn-na Robot Hotel, apart from Mister Sawada, are the maids with the requisite and exclusively human skills of turning down a bed: skills the robots cannot master. Yet.

As well as hotels, robots are used extensively in care homes across Japan. Twenty per cent of the Japanese population are sixty-five or older: in the US, it is thirteen per cent (set to double by 2050); in Britain, the projections are similar. Merrill Lynch has projected a shortfall of a million careworkers in Japan by 2025. This care crisis has already hit Britain. But in Japan, the solution is Asimo: a 'carebot' built by Honda.

'Carebots' are a fraction of the cost of humans to employ and appear to offer a way out of the coming global care crisis, but carebots also raise unexpected legal questions.

Gurvinder Virk is a professor of robotics who has developed industry standards for human-robot interaction in the event of litigation due to an accident. If a robot drops or crushes a resident, who is responsible? It is not as straightforward as it seems.

Virk's robot litigation criteria is called ISO 13482 and it covers three types of robot: physical assistance robots, mobile servant robots and people carrier robots.[12]

These three models cover the basic needs of a care home resident: 'Resyone' is a robotic hybrid device that transforms from a bed to a wheelchair with no humanoid characteristics. This is because humans are used to being moved around by vehicles that do not look human.

'Robobear' is more overtly humanoid in appearance and is a lifter. The developers believe a semi-human-looking lifting device is comforting and reassuring to clients, as it feels nurturing, like a giant mechanical hand.

The Riken robot lab are working on a fully human-looking nurse, capable of complex bedside care combined with factory robot strength, for moving 'multiple persons'. Riken may well be able to make a bed, too.

Robots in Japan are already being used in every conceivable scenario: from care homes to hospitals, airports and hotels, to domestic kitchens and construction sites. Robot cats are used in care homes to keep the elderly company.

Robots are also being used to decommission the three reactors in Fukushima, which went into meltdown in 2011, the worst nuclear disaster since Chernobyl. Japan is fully embracing its robot destiny and this is because the Japanese government are spending nearly half their R&D budget on robots.

Companies across the world are also racing to produce the first fully functioning sex robot. The sex industry has always been quicker to take up new technology than other industries.

Pornography pioneered the switch from film to video tape in the 1980s, and streaming on the internet in the 2000s. Now four companies – Realbotix and BodAI in the US, Z-onedoll and Doll Sweet in China – are all looking to launch synthetic sex robots with AI that are 'fully responsive'.

By integrating the dolls with virtual reality and eventually adding warmth to the skin and genitalia through heat pads, these silicon companions could retail at close to $70–80,000.

But this karaoke version of a robot future – machines as dolls and servants, rather than our master – is based on a fast-evaporating assumption that humans will determine the relationship with robots and maintain the whip hand.

Alan Turing assumed that for a computer to pass the Turing Test, all it needed to do was to become more like a human. What he did not factor in was an alternative scenario: that we would become more like robots.

HOW WE BECAME THE ROBOTS

In 2013, the newly elected coalition government of David Cameron got an intimation of the next ten years. A research paper by Carl Frey and Michael Osborne at Oxford University gave a stark prediction of where Watson would shortly take the human race. By 2030, they said, half of all jobs could be automated.[13]

Pre-2013 crystal-ball gazing about automated work suddenly looked irrelevant. It was quickly becoming apparent that obsolescence meant anyone: doctors, lawyers, accountants, supermarket staff, cab drivers, care workers, journalists, even tech analysts assessing the future of robots. In May 2017, an AI algorithm developed by the Illinois Institute of Technology made high court judges obsolete, correctly predicting seventy-two per cent of high court verdicts (human judges could only predict sixty-six per cent).

MIT's Brynjolfsson and McAfee, working with colleagues

Daron Acemoglu and David Autor, put it like this: 'Imagine a matrix with two axes, manual versus cognitive and routine versus non-routine. Jobs can then be arranged into four boxes: manual routine, manual non-routine, and so on.[14] Jobs on an assembly line fall into the manual-routine box, jobs in home healthcare into the manual non-routine box. Keeping track of inventory is in the cognitive-routine box, dreaming up an ad campaign or writing a book is cognitive non-routine.'

The highest-paid jobs are clustered in the last box: managing a hedge fund, litigating a bankruptcy, creating a piece of art, are cognitive and non-routine. Manual, non-routine jobs tend to be the lowest paid: emptying bedpans, waiting on tables at a restaurant, cleaning hotel rooms. Factory floor and payroll or accounting jobs tend to fall in-between.

Of these four boxes – four boxes that categorise all human jobs – robots could potentially do three and a half.

Middle-class jobs are the easiest for robots to take over: clerical, administrative and any number-crunching such as accountancy. Robots struggle with making beds – as we know – and delivering a parcel in a city when no one is in, so these will remain human jobs a little bit longer.

But most jobs will be colonised, leaving only the odd doctor or supermarket supervisor to troubleshoot the occasional problem the robots cannot handle, as they already do in supermarkets when the checkout fails to scan a bunch of bananas and someone has to come over and punch in the code number.

AI expert Martin Ford says the big problem with this is not even the robots, but our complacency. We assume our job is safe because it is 'complex', when often it is not. We conflate the complexity of being human with the specificity of the job, which does not require human complexity.

As Ford puts it, 'A computer doesn't need to replicate the entire spectrum of your intellectual capability in order to displace you from your job: it only needs to do the specific things you are paid to do.'[15]

Governments quite simply freaked when they read the reports written by experts like Ford, Brynjolfsson and McAfee coming out of MIT and Oxford. President Obama was sufficiently panicked to commission a White House report: 'Artificial Intelligence, Automation and the Economy'.

'In recent years,' it concluded, 'machines have surpassed humans in the performance of certain tasks related to intelligence. It is expected that machines will continue (rapidly) to reach and exceed human performance on more and more tasks . . . aggressive policy action will be needed to help Americans who are disadvantaged by these changes.'[16]

Governments across the world began commissioning their own reports and all came to the same conclusion: we need to do something, but what? If machines make everyone redundant, how will we earn a living and what is everyone going to do all day? It was not just Turing who had prophesised this future. In the 1930s, Keynes painted the utopian and dystopian alternatives to automation – would we be enslaved, or lie in fields sunbathing all day long?

In 2016, the tech billionaires weighed in with their solutions. Elon Musk resurrected the idea of a 'universal living wage': an amount of money we are all paid to exist. Our job will be simply to be human and spend money in shops (something robots cannot yet do). By spending, we will keep consumerism alive and capitalism afloat, so the job is a serious one.

Bill Gates said we need to attack the wealth creation problem from the other end and tax robots on their labour. By charging companies on the savings made from cutting humans, a universal living wage could be funded and continue to pay for the state: roads, hospitals and armies.

Daron Acemoglu and Pascual Restrepo at MIT, two of the AI experts the US government had been reading assiduously, began to view this coexistence less as an inevitable, anxiety-inducing *fait accompli*, than an arms race to tool up and be smartest. A race humans need to win.[17]

THE ROBOT SWAP

At this fork in the road for humanity, a question arises: what is the best strategy for winning and what kind of human being do we create to win? A robot or a rule breaker?

Technology has already roboticised our lives: we monitor our productivity using health apps and wearable technology; chain ourselves to Instagram, Facebook and Twitter. We are incrementally replacing conversation with email, shutting down human interaction in public spaces by screen-blanking each other, and constantly seeking data-driven improvement: the creation of a machine-like optimal self. An automated self.

At the moment robots become more human, we are becoming more like robots. But in terms of survival in the workplace, is this good or bad? Should we continue automating our behaviour – out-roboting the robots – or punch out of the box and maximise our USP: our humanity?

In 2000, Tony Blair's government in the UK, already fearing children would become irrelevant in a brutal new workplace if they did not 'raise standards', embarked on 'academisation': the most radical reform of British schools since the war.

To its critics, academisation was the roboticisation of children. Education would no longer be open-ended learning and discovery, but passing tests relentlessly. Children's minds would be narrowed not opened; they would be ticking a box, instead of thinking outside it.

Tony Blair's chief educational advisor was Michael Barber. Under Barber's tutelage, Blair and then Gordon Brown embarked on the wholesale rebuilding of Britain's schools.

The programme was mammoth. Overnight, Victorian buildings and leaking 1960s comprehensives were ripped down, replaced by bright, shining, new, open-plan academies, created in 'partnership' with business: painted in primary Lego colours with giant IT rooms filled with computers donated by business and a central 'reception' staffed by someone wearing a headset.

Critics of academies called them soulless and a betrayal of education, selling off schools to business. Critics of the critics said this was middle-class elitism: what was wrong with children bettering their results and focusing on vocational training? What was so terrible about working-class kids getting a chance to go to university?

The very things that liberal parents and teacher unions hated about academies were the things its advocates loved. Academies prepared pupils for the workplace by building schools that looked like offices. Factories of productivity: good, said their supporters.

A decade into academies, the fear has shifted as the reality of automation begins to dawn. Have we done the wrong thing by turning children into robots at the very moment they need to optimise their human skills to survive?

Under the Blair government, Michael Barber was hailed a genius for his new vision for education. After leaving his government post, Barber went to work for management consultants McKinsey to advise them on what he had identified as the biggest, untapped cash cow of the digital revolution: worth $500 billion in the US alone, trillions globally. 'EdTech' or 'Educational Technology'.

THE MIRACLE OF THE HOLE IN THE WALL, NEW DELHI

EdTech is breathtaking in its scope. In a nutshell, it seeks to capture and monetise global education by turning every child on the planet from a school pupil into a personalised client of software.

Underpinning this momentous deal is an underlying proposition: teachers are over, and should be replaced by technology. Teaching, the argument goes, is an inherently unpredictable practice delivered by a human, with all the quirks and inconsistencies a human brings to the job.

Teachers do not promote a child's welfare, they hinder it by bringing their prejudices to bear – on a subject they like or dislike, and on an individual pupil they either favour or dislike. Computers are different: they do not have these prejudices. A child can excel by 'personalising' their own software teaching program to what they are interested in.

The inspiration for the EdTech revolution was an experiment carried out by educational guru and Ted talker, Professor Sugata Mitra of Newcastle University. In 1999, a computer appeared overnight in an empty ATM hole in New Delhi. No one knew how it got there. Street kids began to gather round and after a few minutes, they had figured out how to turn it on.

Within a day, these same kids – some of whom did not go to school and did not know how to read or write – were solving complex mathematical problems by asking the internet, which they had worked out for themselves how to use.

They could solve questions of moral philosophy and quantum physics, and they had worked out these answers with ease, because they had not been discouraged by a teacher; no one had told them that the questions were hard to solve.[18]

What the kids did not know was that they were part of an experiment. Mitra wanted to test how technology would be used by children in the absence of teachers. The results, he said, were mind-blowing.

Mitra said the absence of a teacher had freed the kids to learn fast themselves. When all the world's knowledge is available at a swipe, teachers are not merely redundant, he argued, they actively hinder the child's learning.

Word of Mitra's experiment spread like wildfire through Silicon Valley. This was music to their ears. Mitra argued that teaching and schools were themselves a colonial Western construct. The Indian school system had cemented inequality, designed originally to provide an army of obedient workers to service the British colonial machine.

Technology, however, offered the keys to freedom for the poor of the world. But Mitra had his critics. He wove, according to educationalist Neil Selwyn, 'a seductive story that masked insidious hyper-individualistic Silicon Valley thinking, at complete odds with genuine learning. Global standardisation under the smokescreen of freeing the child.'

By selling a utopian vision of barefoot children in awe at the wonderment of technology that they had discovered at a hole in the wall in New Delhi, Mitra – his critics argued – was cloaking the business interests of the tech giants, who wanted in on the EdTech cash cow.

The second sleight of hand was to sell the roboticisation of children as liberation from the shackles of teachers and schools. By getting rid of teachers, the tech giants could roll out software worth trillions and conquer the global education market.

Tony Blair's education guru, Michael Barber, had identified this key business target when he moved from government to working for McKinsey as their EdTech guru.

If children were to be turned into human robots, then the first thing you needed to do was claim they were being freed from teachers. To this end, Barber had been inspired not by Mitra, but two American academics from Stanford University, John Chubb and Terry Moe, authors of two books proposing a free-market revolution in education: *Politics, Markets and America's Schools*[19] and *Liberating Learning*.[20]

'The world,' Chubb and Moe said, 'is in the early stages of a historic transformation in how students learn, teachers teach, and schools and school systems are organised.'

Chubb and Moe said teachers are 'vested interests' that block change or progress by protecting their own jobs at the expense of the needs of children.

Moreover, the kind of person who goes into teaching often has an inherent bias against business and enterprise. They are invariably left-wing or openly socialist, they want to turn children against business, rather than admire financial success. Teachers bring these prejudices into the classroom and further disadvantage children by indoctrinating their pupils against success.

Schools need to be opened up to the market, and business should be brought into the heart of the curriculum, even finance the school system itself. An ideological transformation of the entire school culture is required.

Schools are not a 'job scheme for teachers', Chubb and Moe argued. They need to cut out the politicians and teachers who keep parents and business from running them properly together.

But it was how this revolution was to happen that was the most controversial part of Chubb and Moe's plan. Teachers should not be attacked through direct confrontation, but technology.

THE TECH TROJAN HORSE

I met Terry Moe at Stanford University in the huge, circular, wood-panelled room where presidents, philanthropists and now tech billionaires have come to address professors and alumni about their grand plans for the future for over two hundred years.

Terry was not what I expected: a wiry man with a sceptical twinkle in his eye. Terry told me excitedly how he was now working on a book about New Orleans after Hurricane Katrina.

Because the city's entire infrastructure was wiped out, the 'vested interests' of the teacher unions were washed away, too, allowing the education system to be built again from the ground up. The results, he said, had been 'remarkable'.

What was his problem with teachers?

'I'm painted as this neo-liberal market guy, I'm not. Teachers have a role to play, I'm not saying they don't, but the vested interest of teacher unions is not in the interest of children.'

Whether teachers like it or not, Terry said, the 'tech revolution is coming'. So what advice would he give to teachers facing redundancy? 'Understand what is happening. It's over. Accept that they need to work with the future happening now, rather than fight it.'

In *Liberating Learning*, Chubb and Moe had a cunning plan for how technology can be used to deal with teachers: it should 'seep' into the classroom, drip, drip – first through iPads, then rolling out personalised teaching to every single child, so gradually marginalising teachers in their own classroom. The more technology seeps in, the closer teachers come to obsolescence. Till one day, they are suddenly obsolete.

Chubb and Moe's *Liberating Learning* was described as 'an excellent book' by the then Minister of Education, Michael Gove.[21] Did Terry know he had been lauded by the British education secretary? 'No, I wasn't aware, but I am flattered.'

Their strategy for using technology as a Trojan Horse to break the unions could work not only in education, but across the public sector: in health, social care, in all forms of public service. The two authors were hailed on the New Right as neo-liberal prophets, although Moe is diffident about the association.

Chubb and Moe had created a template for a wholly privatised future through the Trojan Horse of technology. One that cleverly sidestepped difficult and unpopular political conflict with groups held in high esteem by the public: teachers, or doctors and nurses. Instead, by using technology, they could do the whole thing smoothly and silently.

I wanted to see what Terry Moe's school of the future might look like, so I visited the Flex Tech Lab in San Diego, one of the most advanced examples of so-called 'blended learning' using technology in the world.

The school was quite extraordinary. The principal, Sean, showed me round an open-plan class with about seventy pupils. They all work with laptops or desktop computers. There is only one teacher for the entire room, whom pupils merely consult if they have a problem.

Each pupil I met was pursuing their own interest, which had become their personalised learning plan: Stephanie, who was sixteen, wanted to be a marine biologist. Brendan was interested in astrophysics and was watching an advanced astronomy lecture online. He made notes on the side of the screen and stopped the lecture if he wanted to go back.

Sean, the executive principal, was evangelical about Flex Tech. But it was not the straightforward Terry Moe transplant. Sean said the school had undergone 'several iterations using technology. We began with a far more technology-based model and found it was too much, it didn't work. The teacher needed to come back in the classroom to guide learning and so now we have what we describe as "blended learning".'

I talked to the teacher, Steve. What is it like overseeing seventy pupils? 'Sometimes, it's a bit like being one of those checkout supervisors at a supermarket waiting for something to go wrong with a bar code. But for the children, it's a huge improvement. They are genuinely self-motivated and learn at their own speed, rather than having that dictated by a teacher at the front.'

How important is it that education is rooted in the job they will do when they leave? 'It's fundamental. It's everything. There is so much pressure and stress to do well at work. You don't have the luxury of screwing up at college and getting into student debt on the wrong course. You need to focus now. We have kids who stress and go too fast through the curriculum because they want to do well, and we actually have to slow them down. That's where the teacher comes in. It's not just about success, it's about being happy, too.'

Flex Tech has a waiting list of over a thousand pupils and is undoubtedly a very successful school. They are now talking to the designers of Google Maps to create a 'Google Maps for learning'.

But it is also in a prosperous part of San Diego – would it work in a deprived area of Detroit or Dagenham? Terry Moe says technology favours poorer pupils over wealthier ones, because they are less likely to be in a class setting dominated by more assertive, middle-class kids putting up their hand every five seconds.

Sean, the principal, also sees a paradox at the heart of their success at Flex Tech. 'We are using technology in a blended learning setting to create focus, where technology has defocused kids through phones and video games. We have never seen children more defocused and demotivated than now, and our job is to reverse that.' Technology to fight technology.

Sean thinks children are robots before, not after, they come into his classroom. They have already been trained up for repetitive work by the repetitive-task patterns of social media and gaming. He believes technology in the classroom can be used to deprogramme and focus kids: as a Trojan Horse for good, not bad.

THE MONEY

Whether EdTech will free children from becoming human robots, or turn every child from Riga to Rio into the perfect robot KFC employee, remains to be seen. What is not in question is the money to be made from this revolution.

In 2005, Michael Barber met New York mayor Michael Bloomberg and his education guru, Joel Klein. In effect, Klein was setting out to create a laboratory for educational experimentation using EdTech as the apparatus.

In the same year, Klein made the decisive move, putting out what researchers Tamasin Cave and Andy Rowell describe as a 'call to arms to corporate America. The business community needed to step up or America's position in the world was going to be significantly in peril.'

Klein's call was answered by a group of America's big-money philanthropists dubbed the Billionaire's Boys Club: Google's Eric Schmidt, Microsoft's Bill Gates, Facebook's Mark Zuckerberg, Apple's Steve Jobs, Time Warner's Rupert Murdoch, Eli Broad of Walmart and Michael Dell of Dell Computers.[22]

Klein's appeal to them was an appeal to the heart: school children are being failed by a crumbling school system, but technology can set children free. Education reform lobbyist Rick Berman said, 'We need to hit on fear and anger,' when talking to a gathering of wealthy philanthropists, 'and how you get the fear and anger is by reframing the problem.'

Berman was famous for his work attacking American unions and lobbying on behalf of the tobacco industry. Cave and Rowell have researched Berman's strategy. 'He told reformers that rather than intellectualise the education debate, they needed to trigger an emotional reaction in people.'

'Emotions will stay with people longer than concepts,' he said. So rather than a rational debate on the merits of their plans, reformers needed to motivate supporters by tapping into their fears for their children's future and provoking anger at those opposed to reform.'[23]

But Joel Klein and Michael Barber also appealed to something more fundamental to these billionaires: their wallets. EdTech will be worth $70 billion worldwide by 2020. The market for devices like tablets is set to be $32 billion. The online learning industry is looking to nearly double in size, worth $24 billion in the US alone.

And for governments, the appeal is a huge cut in the wage bill of teachers. If you have one teacher overseeing seventy to a hundred pupils, then you save billions overnight with a single swipe of the iPad.

This is not a gift horse, Klein told the tech billionaires, you want to be looking in the mouth. The global tech company that plants its flag in EdTech has the future of the human race in its hands; how it learns, can work more efficiently than a robot, and thus survive as a race.

Join the revolution, he said. But here is what's really in it for you. By 2020, EdTech will overtake MedTech as the biggest data gold rush on earth.

When Sugata Mitra first put his computer in a hole in the wall in New Delhi in 1998, he saw technology as a liberation from formal schooling. Schools had been used in India not to educate the poor, but to turn them into obedient workers for the Empire.

Yet EdTech had the potential to do exactly the same digitally: create the ultimate worker, tested and drilled on an iPad from four to sixteen years old, before going on to have the same at work with a day dictated by algorithms.

In 2015, Bill Gates's Microsoft bought Linkedin for $26 billion. Many financial analysts were stumped by the deal. It appeared to make no business sense. But the Linkedin deal is the key to EdTech.

LinkedIn has 433 million users: the biggest recruitment database on earth. Attaching this database to a child's pre-LinkedIn history means tracking from four to sixteen and beyond, determining employability from childhood to middle age.

By linking school 'career' and actual career and making them a continuum of monitoring, Microsoft have the potential to create the ultimate employment profile for a potential boss, tracking levels of conformity at any point in their lives.

At a job interview, the question becomes: 'Why did you go off the rails with your results when you were twelve, and again at work, when you were thirty-six?' You create the most unquestioning employees on the planet: people who will work from day one of their school careers like robots.

The EdTech race is on. Microsoft have created the 'school in a box'. Google want to be first to plant their flag in EdTech, too. The sales pitch for Chromebook is that it is 'the foundation for a one-hundred-per-cent web classroom'.

In 2010, Rupert Murdoch bought an education software company for $350 million. News Corporation's education division is called Amplify and its aim is to digitise the world's classrooms. 'We see a $500 billion sector in the US alone that is waiting desperately to be transformed by big breakthroughs,' said Murdoch. In 2015, Joel Klein left his job running the schools of New York to work for Murdoch.

THE CAR-WASH PARADOX

Teachers in academies have begun to notice an interesting shift. Children are able to pass tests and tick boxes spectacularly, but when it comes to interviews, they clam up. They are so used to conforming to rules, they do not know how to question them.

In this new world of robot children growing up to be robot employees, old-fashioned schools will still exist. Private ones will continue to teach Greek and Latin and play rugby on playing fields. These playing fields are symbolic. They send out a message: they broadcast ownership. We own education.

In these selective, elite schools, future politicians, and CEOs who will employ the human robots in warehouses and fast-food chains, will continue to have their minds broadened and be taught to question the question, just as Aristotle defined education two thousand years ago.

However, as Mitra discovered with his hole-in-the-wall computer in New Delhi and Flex Tech are discovering in San Diego, technology can do miraculous things as well as further enslave. Children have the whole of human history and knowledge at their fingertips on a phone and are creating their own path to the future, regardless of what educationalists or tech entrepreneurs have planned for them. Technological advance and the speed at which work is revolutionized are the unstoppable givens. The response of the human gatekeepers is to prepare for the storm.

As Sean at Flex Tech told me, 'The children you see in front of you will have ten, twenty, maybe fifty jobs in their lifetime. Who knows? What we are teaching them is not a lump of knowledge, but how to adapt and pick up new skills continuously. That is the only way they will survive.'

But for those who are not able to take command of their destiny, algorithms will tell them what to do. Robots will not replace them, they will be the boss.

Take a delivery driver. He or she makes forty or fifty deliveries in a day. Algorithms decide where they go next and if that last delivery was late. The algorithm can question why you turned left at that last junction, instead of right. You would have saved two minutes thirty-seven seconds if you had turned right.

In the future, ten such small errors a day and you will be ten deliveries down on your target. You will have cost yourself £40. Four days a week like that and you will not be able to pay your mortgage.

The first industrial revolution, after its initial technological disruption, created hundreds of millions of jobs. It did not lead to the end of work, it led to its total reinvention. Workers could organise and campaign for better wages by forming trade unions. Employers had no choice but to form a social contract with unions because workers held the cards. Their labour value was high.

This second industrial revolution – the robot revolution – is the same as the first one in one key respect. It will transform employment, and not in the obvious way.

Instead of ending human jobs, it could lead to full employment with the creation of billions of low-paid, routine-manual and non-routine manual jobs. The difference from the first industrial revolution is that this time, there is zero value to labour. Companies can pay what they want and we will be grateful for it.

This, in effect, is the robot swap. As robots become the boss, managing the logistics of our work, we become the robots working to their algorithmic program of efficiency.

We are seeing the beginning of this now, but have trouble computing this paradox of full employment on super-low income, because we still work with an economic paradigm of wage inflation and full-time employment created in the first half of the twentieth century. We cannot square the circle, but we will.

Seemingly contradictory economic trends happening in tandem will be the norm for the robot age: ever-rising employment with ever-lower wages. Precarious employment on casual terms for an amount we cannot live on, accurately reported as 'full employment'. This is the final irony of the robot age – it will deliver full human employment on ten per cent of the wages.

For this squared circle to function and not result in social unrest, it requires another piece of the equation to work: prices for basics like food and heating to stay at an historic low.

But they are not. They're beginning to rise. The robot swap only works when we can afford to live on what we earn. When prices rise, wages have to rise and that is when labour value rises once more. In Japan, Denmark, Sweden and Switzerland, governments have even toyed with negative interest rates, in order to keep inflation under control and prevent currency value going up.

In February 2017, David Freeman, a senior statistician at the ONS, explained how the squaring of the circle is working: 'The unemployment rate is now at its lowest in over a decade, but wage growth remains subdued by historical standards.'[24]

In the meantime, the robots are coming to oversee cheap labour from a fully employed workforce. Economist Paul Mason calls this paradox 'the economics of the car wash'.[25]

The machine car wash of the 1970s promised a sparkling robot clean for your Ford Capri. Big furry buds would roll all over your car, leaving it spotless and shining.

But since 2010, something unexpected has happened. Automated car washes have disappeared and been replaced by small gangs of humans frantically working over your car with sponges and cloths. Car washes are not showpiece machines working on ostentatious display as the centrepiece of a garage as they were in the 1970s. They now exist tucked away in cheap dead spaces: old disused car parks and derelict gas station forecourts. They pop up and disappear again in days.

The humans that replaced the machine can wash a car in half the time; they do a better job because they are terrified they will lose their job; and here is the key thing, they cost less.

The automated car wash broke down, needed servicing and

constant human attention. It was not the shiny future it promised, it became a cumbersome headache and stopped paying its way. And so, the automated car wash has become a model for how all work could go: humans replacing machines you pay nothing, who look after themselves, and need only the stick of unemployment to make them work harder.

This is the future of work. Watson in the control centre, an unblinking blue eye monitoring how many cars you and I are able to wash in an hour.

CHAPTER THIRTEEN
TECHNOLOGY: FIVE COMPANIES TO RULE US ALL

Imagine you turned on your computer and Google had gone. Next you turned on your iPhone. Black screen. Facebook, Twitter, Amazon and Microsoft had been wiped out, too.

It could not happen. Except that in 2007, it did: with the banks.

Overnight, the world was engulfed by the biggest financial crisis since 1929. No one predicted it, bar some bank insiders not powerful enough to be listened to, and some maverick financiers who foresaw the whole thing and shorted on it.[1]

The banks that were allowed to go under were not too big to fail, but the 'Big Five' tech giants are. When Lehman Brothers went bust, the banking system did not collapse. But the Big Five are so deeply enmeshed in the functioning of Planet Earth, they cannot be allowed to go under. They are not an addendum to the system; they are the system.

The key difference between the banks and the tech giants is this: when you have a heart attack, the blood can still be pumped artificially to the brain. But if the brain stops, you are dead. The banks pump the blood, but the Big Five tech giants are the brain.

This is how the brain breaks down in numbers: in just one year, 2016, Apple had revenue of $233 billion with profit of $53 billion, assets of $239 billion, and market cap of $586 billion. Alphabet (Google) did comparable numbers. Microsoft, Amazon and Facebook took the other chairs at the Big Five table in diminishing order of size. But their size is not what matters. The banks could be bailed out by government, but the tech giants are bigger than any one government. They built the world we live in and they own the keys.

Government could bail out the banks, because banks do only one real job: provide liquidity. When banks judder to a halt, governments pump money back into the system. For all the deliberate impenetrability of banking argot, what they actually do is remarkably straightforward: lend you money they themselves have borrowed.

What is a bank? 'Bank' is purely another word for other people's money and specifically, other people's debts.[2]

Before 2007, banks, like economists, operated behind a façade of competence, using the impenetrability of financial language successfully as a protective wall to keep people from asking too many questions. Like the modern-day use of Latin, its true purpose was to exclude. On Wall Street, the only really important calculations before the crash were to work out how long the charade could be kept going.

Once the myth of the competence of banks was blown by the crash, banks had to operate behind a different façade: independence. Since the bail-out, banks have been a nationalised industry held up by the grace of taxpayers' money, yet masquerading as independent. Banks are like petulant children in a playground. They think they are able to do everything themselves, but when something goes wrong, they call in the adults to sort it out.

The tech companies do not. They don't need anyone. This is because they do not simply operate above and beyond the scope of any one national government. They have manoeuvred themselves into a position where no one else can step in and do their job.

THE RHIZOME

The Big Five are not actually tech companies at all. Together, they form five interlocking parts of a hugely complex machine unlike any seen before.

No one controls this machine, because tech companies are the unwitting fulfilment of an idea formulated by the French philosophers Gilles Deleuze and Felix Guattari in their 1980 treatise, 'A Thousand Plateaus'.[3]

Deleuze and Guattari said the future destiny of capitalism lay not in its control by individuals with agency, but its mutation into a self-sustaining organism. In this new capitalism of a 'thousand plateaus', there was no hierarchical structure or bogeyman pulling the strings behind the scenes, only an impossibly complicated matrix of intersections; interwoven, overlapping and all-encompassing.

Deleuze and Guattari called this structure a 'rhizome': a term from botany to describe a vast root system growing fast and horizontally outwards in every direction.

Banks are not rhizomes, because they are finite entities with one overarching role, lending. But the Big Five tech companies have created the root system for trillions of transactions every millisecond of every day, between you, me and all the businesses on earth.

These transactions are not solely financial – we post oceans of information: videos, pictures, shares, vines, memes, likes and dislikes, we rate everything and transact advice, comment and pass opinion on nothing and everything. This sub-universe of data transactions, a continuous, fizzing digital world, is perpetually auctioned by algorithms, sifting the digital detritus for sellable data.

To be able to even conceptualise these digital auctions is like playing 3-D chess in space. As you stick a word in Google, an infinite hall of algorithmic mirrors opens up without beginning or end, reflecting forever to the data horizon.

For the moment, banks and tech companies have reached an

accommodation on data and payment systems – they work together – since accommodation is easier than a fight. But this relationship is lopsided, because the rhizome of tech companies is ever expanding, and potentially limitless. Long-term, banks need tech companies, but tech companies do not need banks, whom they will ultimately subsume into the rhizome.

SHAVING A MILLIONTH OF A SECOND = A BILLION DOLLARS

I am on the roof of a tower block in New Jersey looking back to Wall Street. A light flashes fifteen miles away through thunderous clouds, beaming from the top of One World Trade Center, the tallest building on Manhattan, built on the site of the Twin Towers.

You would think Wall Street was the nerve centre of global finance, but Wall Street cannot function without the infrastructure of the tech companies.

In 2010, the fibre-optic company Spread Networks built a data centre in an anonymous suburban part of New Jersey. The location – 1600 MacArthur Boulevard, Mahwah – was deliberate. The Spread Networks data centre for the New York Stock Exchange is a huge foreboding structure without windows on anonymous scrubland, protected by thousands of security cameras and electric fencing.

The data centre cost $300 million to build and provided a fibre-optic tunnel to Wall Street, allowing transactions to take place 0.7 of a millisecond faster between New York and Chicago. This infinitesimal increase in speed translated to billions more dollars transacted every second.

But it was not fast enough. A couple of years later and only a few miles away from Mahwah, on the top of the desolate tower block I am standing on, a laser technology company rented space on the rubbish-strewn roof to shave a further 4 milliseconds off a transaction. Huge white machines bristling with wires and antennae hum quietly; machines facing One World Trade Center communicating at light speed in code with machines facing Asia.

The block itself is poor project housing: the flats are damp; shouts and screams fill the corridors intermingled with the heavy smell of weed. But just above the heads of these residents, billions of dollars are being beamed every millisecond from Wall Street to the rest of the world. It is perhaps the most extreme convergence of incalculable wealth and poverty within a few metres of each other anywhere on the planet.

THE SAGRADA FAMÍLIA

In 1882, Antonio Gaudí began work on *La Sagrada Família* cathedral in Barcelona. Forty years into construction, Gaudí was asked when he thought his extraordinary creation – spiralling up above the Barcelona skyline and without a single straight line – might finally be finished. Never, Gaudí replied. It is alive and the very process of living is itself completion.

Like the Sagrada Família, the Big Five tech giants are in a perpetual state of becoming. Constantly striking out laterally by strategically acquiring companies that speak to the bigger plan, but make no sense to anyone else.

Google, Microsoft and Amazon plough profit relentlessly back into R&D and new acquisitions, because their eyes are on a distant prize only those within the top echelon are privy to. Bill Gates put this limitless ambition and necessity to mutate the plan in a simple aphorism: 'We overestimate what we can do in two years, and underestimate what we can do in ten.'[4]

The Big Five are the central roots of the rhizome from which everything we do flows. These companies are not only too big to fail, they are too big to define, because they are perpetually mutating and expanding what they do. Not one of the Big Five is focused now on what it was doing six months ago.

This leads to fevered speculation about what they are really up to and the inevitable conspiracy theories this creates.

In his 2013 novel *The Circle*, Dave Eggers makes a thinly veiled attack on a cult-like tech company, with its utopian rhetoric, sealed-off tech 'campus' and smiling, evangelical employees hiding a sinister plan for world domination.

The title of the book refers to the long-term goal of this imaginary tech giant: completion of 'The Circle'. Absolute control over every moment of our lives, and all under the perpetual gaze of an unblinking eye that sees and knows everything about us.[5]

Conspiracy theories package messy truth into a childishly simple plan executed by a handful of fiendish individuals in a room. But with *The Circle*, Dave Eggers described an all-controlling version of a fictional company that was an amalgam of the Big Five: a version that the Big Five tech giants could well argue is not so much a searing critique but actually undersells their ambition.

In 2015, Google became the least interesting subsidiary of Alphabet, a new umbrella company headed by Google's founders, Sergey Brin and Larry Page, and with a mind-boggling collection of new acquisitions.

Alphabet's aim is simple: to seek to improve the very nature of what it is to be human. What humans do, what humans are made of and how our brains function. This is not hyperbole, it is simply what they are about.

Alphabet's interests and acquisitions range from bio-tech (Life Sciences) to cracking longevity and eternal life (Calico); space; driverless cars; flying cars; the internet of things (smart everything); next-stage drone-delivery systems; using technology to leap-frog infrastructure gaps in the developing world; EdTech; pollution and global-warming solutions; nano-technology: in-body tech hacks, such as injectable nano-robots and microscopic DNA devices that fight leukaemia, or nano-gels that secrete insulin to tackle diabetes.

The founders believe that being seen as 'just' a company is

wide of the mark.[6] Alphabet are like an independent state hacking their way into the future.

Alphabet's acquisition of DeepMind marked their intention to begin decoding the very essence of intelligence: what it is, how it works, and how humans and machines will interact and communicate when intelligence has been cracked. What singularity will actually look and feel like.

Alphabet have honed this ambition to a single word: knowledge. Decoding it, and owning it. Dave Eggers's *Circle* conspiracy for a fictional tech giant did not do justice to the scope of ambition of a real one.

On 10 August 2015, CEO Larry Page explained what Google's metamorphosis into Alphabet meant. 'As Sergey (Brin) and I wrote in the original founders' letter eleven years ago: "Google is not a conventional company. We do not intend to become one." We did a lot of things that seemed crazy at the time. Crazy things (that) now have a billion users like Google Maps, YouTube, Chrome and Android.[7]

'We've long believed that over time companies tend to get comfortable doing the same thing, just making incremental changes. But in the technology industry, where revolutionary ideas drive the next big growth areas, you need to be a bit uncomfortable.'

Much was made of Alphabet's decision to drop the Google promise of twenty years ago: 'to do no evil'. But Alphabet are not evil, nor intend to do evil. They have their eyes fixed on a distant point that has nothing to do with the prosaic moral judgements of others. On a world entirely rebuilt from their insights. A world they will control.

THE FIRST GOOGLE

The grand tech ambitions of the Big Five began a long time ago. In 1997, I was in Seattle visiting the Microsoft campus. Microsoft had the same ambitions then that Google have today and were seeking to do something equally amazing: write a universal language for what we then called 'computers'.

In 1997, there was no mobile phone. No Facebook, Amazon or Google. Apple, run by outsider genius Steve Jobs, was considered a failing company stuck in the 1970s, resigned to cult status making expensive computers. Microsoft, not Apple, was king. On their 'campus' deep in the forest, they were writing the code to make a new world. They called this new world the 'digital world'.

Their CEO, Bill Gates, lived in a $60 million mansion on Puget Sound accessible by boat. Over the bay were the palatial homes of two other Seattle icons with growing brands: Kurt Cobain and Howard Shultz, the CEO of Starbucks. Gates was rarely there, but one detail about his house emerged that encapsulated the snobbery against him and the coming tech takeover of the world.

Gates's vast property – Xanadu 2.0, named in homage to Citizen Kane – with its sixty-foot swimming pool playing underwater music, 2,500 square-foot gym, artificial river stocked with salmon, and a beach with imported sand from Hawaii, also had state-of-the-art technology.[8]

Each bedroom and corridor was rumoured to be filled with 'plasma screens'. In 1997, this was an amazing and extravagant thing to own. They were said to line the long corridors like oil paintings.

Instead of having actual paintings, Gates would press a remote control and be able to access the world's greatest artworks via a blocky pixelated image on a screen. Gates could turn his house into the Louvre or MOMA in a moment, a blurry Mona Lisa staring out as he prepared his Granola breakfast.

A famous English novelist who lived in Seattle at the time and despised Gates asked him at a private party why he did not buy the original paintings. He had enough money. Plasma screens were such bad taste and surely anyone would rather have the real thing if they could?

Why? Gates replied. Those paintings are owned by the public.

They are not for sale, and everyone in the world should have access to them via a plasma screen.

A decade later, when Gates's friend and former colleague Steve Jobs transformed Apple with the iPhone, everyone was given the equivalent of a mobile plasma screen and could suddenly have access to the world's art galleries. Bill Gates was right and the novelist was wrong.

When I arrived at the Microsoft campus in 1997, landscaped to be low and unobtrusive in the forest near Redmond, it looked more like a Buddhist retreat than a tech company. Inside was a different story. Twenty-something coders lived on campus in a perpetual state of intense, frenzied industry. They would code for ten- to eighteen-hour stretches, drinking endless Coke and coffee, then crashing out to wake with their face in a stale pizza. They were Jesuitical in their belief in Microsoft.

These coders lived in small cells customised to look like student dorms with posters of obscure grunge bands and the obligatory Einstein or Jim Morrison. There were piles of take-away cartons and more pizza boxes, floppy discs for coding strewn across the floor, and somewhere beneath the detritus, their Microsoft pass on a chain.

Their boundless devotion and unstoppable obsession with coding the future, and doing it for the company, was clearly genuine. And naturally approved of and promoted by Microsoft, who created an entirely self-contained community on campus.

There was a supermarket, restaurants, gyms, a spiritual garden, date nights, Cuban dancing Thursday, and a cinema club showing French New Wave films. Very similar in fact to the fictional tech campus described in *The Circle* by Dave Eggers twenty years later.

Coders earnestly rushing around campus had a quiet air of world-historic determination about them, like slacker versions of code breakers at Bletchley Park. They knew they were impor-tant, making the future by inventing a new language that would soon be spoken all over the world: 'Windows' – the operating system to be spoken by every machine on earth.

One morning, I stopped a young coder in the canteen and asked him whether he felt like a 'Micro-serf' – the term coined by author Douglas Coupland to describe a slave coder at Microsoft.[9] Wasn't he a bit of a shmuck for giving away his Intellectual Property (IP) in exchange for a wage, rather than shares in the company? He seemed genuinely amazed by the question. 'I'm not a slave,' he said. 'I'm privileged to be here.'

I pointed out to him the strange rootless ambiance of the campus. Coding deep in a forest, you could be anywhere in the world: Kyoto, Adelaide or Finland. It does not even feel like America. 'That's true,' he said, musing, 'but I'm not an American. I'm a citizen of Microsoft.'

THE 'SOMEONE IN A GARAGE GUNNING FOR US' MYTH

Twenty years on, millenials see themselves as citizens of their belief system, rather than the nation they were born in. They have greater affinity with peers who share their moral outlook three continents away than with neighbours in close geographical proximity who hate immigrants or gays.

Microsoft understood back in the mid-1990s the importance of an employer tapping into this global belief system – this moral rather than geographical citizenship – and utilising this belief to make them believers in Microsoft. A complete alignment of employee and corporate morality which creates total devotion to the brand. This is why the 'citizens' of the Big Five tech giants, for whom Microsoft provided the template, are together creating an immense, aggressively expansionist eco-system. Because they have the hearts and minds of the foot soldiers to do it.

People who work for these companies, from the top to the bottom, believe one hundred per cent in the evangelical mission of their founders. Zen-like masters whose pronouncements are treated like pronouncements from Buddha. The employee's identity and self-esteem are umbilically tied to the success of the company and if they work for one and move on to another, they simply transfer their zeal: zealots trying a new religion.

Even we believe in the brands. They have so entrenched themselves in our lives, made themselves so indispensable, railing against them is like saying you are against sunlight or the ocean.

Tech analyst Farhad Manjoo believes that however powerful they are now, we have not seen anything yet. 'They have built several enormous technologies that are central to just about everything we do. In tech jargon, they own many of the world's most valuable platforms – the basic building blocks on which every other business depends. These platforms are inescapable; you may opt out of one or two of them, but together, they form a gilded mesh blanketing the entire economy.'[10]

In 2016, these five tech giants made up half of the world's top ten most valuable companies. Their wealth stems from their control of the inescapable digital infrastructure on which much of the rest of the economy depends – mobile phones, social networks, the web, the cloud, retail and logistics, and the data and computing power required for future breakthroughs.[11]

But this is where the tech ends and the rest of the world – the physical world – begins as an opportunity. Since 2012, they have begun to set their sights on the biggest industries outside tech: cars, healthcare, retail, transportation of goods, film, music entertainment, and taking over from the banks.[12]

The great myth of Silicon Valley is what Alphabet's Eric Schmidt calls 'someone in a garage, gunning for us'. Someone, somewhere, inventing a new idea that challenges the hegemony of the Big Five.[13]

The truth is that it won't happen, and Schmidt knows it. These companies were pioneers on the digital frontier and they own it for good. But now they are expanding onto everyone else's land and they will own that, too.

THE WOLF THAT TURNED INTO A DOG

You can understand the level of their ambition when you see how they are redefining what they do. Alphabet seek to own the DNA of knowledge itself and then apply this knowledge of knowledge to everything we do.

Amazon seek to reshape our world by transforming the nature of delivery and service, becoming every shop and every service using robots. In 2016, Amazon's founder, Jeff Bezos, trialled their first physical store in Seattle without humans, only robots, and no money passing hands.

Amazon Go is a 1,800 square-foot supermarket selling everything from food, drinks and groceries to clothes and books. You go in, scan an app as you enter, pick up what you want and walk out. No money is paid. Sensors throughout the store identify the items and charge them to your account.

But that's not even the clever bit. Thousands of cameras track your movements and by looking at these movements in the store, tracking you and your phone as you browse, Amazon are able to collect data not only on what you bought, but did not buy: what you considered or put back. It is a treasure-trove of data and these nudgeable 'live' decisions you will make next week, rather than 'dead' purchases you made today, are where data becomes gold.[14]

Beyond running robot supermarkets, Amazon seek to revolutionise all service delivery using drones: whether it be food, a book, or emergency triage at a traffic accident in India.

In this new world, Microsoft – the creator of Windows – are the central operating cortex. They built the rails on which ever faster, smoother and 'frictionless' services run. Microsoft are no longer a tech company: they are a linguistics provider who invented the global language of Windows that machines speak.

Apple no longer seeks to merely produce phones, tablets and laptops, it seeks to be the platform for all commerce.

Yet when Steve Jobs launched the iPhone, he did not even see the full extent of this potential for selling. It was code 'jail-breakers' hacking the iPhone as soon as it came out and customising it that turned Jobs on to third-party apps.

These jail-breakers developed a refined copy-and-paste system; and one in particular, Jay Freeman, the Godfather of jail-breaking, created Cydia – an app marketplace where phones could be jail-broken and freed up to use powerful software to customise outside the rigid control of Apple.

Apple could not believe it and needed to act fast. Within weeks, Apple decided to create the App Store to claw back control over the phone. It was the best thing Apple did from a business point of view, yet it was prompted not by the company's own programmers, but a bunch of hackers.

I arrange to meet Jay on a park bench in San Francisco. A tall man with shoulder-length hair, in a wide-brimmed hat and a leather coat, appears from behind the trees and strides purposefully over. Jay is sanguine about his achievement: that he inadvertently handed Apple a model for turning the iPhone into the world's most successful platform for selling.

'Sometimes I wish I hadn't done what I did, because if I hadn't, who knows what else Apple would have invented? On one level it opened things up, but also closed things down.' Did Apple ever offer you a job? 'They reached out to me, though I wasn't aware they were! I kind of turned them down, which you shouldn't do. Other hackers went to work for them: classic poacher turned gamekeeper.'

Off the back of Cydia, venture capitalist John Dooer lobbied Steve Jobs to make the App Store happen to neutralise the opposition. The loss of control in the wake of the iPhone's launch lasted just six weeks: the time it took Dooer to persuade Jobs. The App Store was launched and Apple was now a platform for third-party apps: a platform for selling, and with the potential to transform payment systems as well as ultimately replace banks.

The ability to absorb disruption into the rhizome is what marks the Big Five out as the root system from which everything else flows.

Facebook's ambitions are different. They seek to become the world's biggest vault of human data. As the largest data-bank on earth, holding intimate details on the lives of 1.8 billion people culled from photos, likes and dislikes, friend networks, and expressions of hopes, fears and expectations embedded in posts, Facebook will become the most powerful repository of human behaviour ever created.

Algorithms are the tool for making this happen and for the first time are ingratiating themselves properly with their quarry: human beings. How they do this is similar to how wolves became dogs.

Wolves were predatory animals that found it tough to get meat in winter, so ingratiated themselves and allowed themselves to be domesticated in order to guarantee food. We thought we were in charge, but the wolf was. Algorithms are the digital wolf.

We humans know this and resist the slide into algorithm dependency. In 2016, a paper called 'Algorithm Aversion' by University of Pennsylvania's Berkeley Dietvorst, Joseph Simmons and Cade Massey for the *Journal of Experimental Psychology* concluded that humans mistakenly continue to believe their judgment to be better than algorithms. We use this human bias to reinforce a fallacy of human superiority.

At this moment in history, the fallacy needs to be shored up for psychological reasons: humans are attempting to hold on to what makes them human at the very moment they see it slipping away forever.[15]

As an example of this human bias, the Penn University report cited the example of pilot error in plane crashes. The likelihood of a crash has been reduced dramatically by ground-proximity warning systems and autopilot. This is statistical proof that machines can outperform humans, but we humans do not want to know.

In everything from medical diagnosis to meteorology and finance, algorithms could at least match and usually surpass human analysis. Algorithms could more accurately predict the likelihood of a convict lapsing back into crime, or a start-up going bust.[16]

Yet in spite of this, humans are determined to think they are better. Google Maps only has to send you down a slower road once, or a playlist choose a depressing record when you are feeling OK, and we cite this anomaly as proof of the fallibility of algorithms.

The most glaring example is driverless cars. More than 30,000 people are killed each year in car crashes in the US. Ninety per cent are down to human error. The Harvard Business Review estimate that driverless cars could save up to 1.5 million lives in the US and up to 50 million globally over the next fifty years.

Yet in a March 2016 poll by the American Automobile Association, seventy-five per cent of American drivers said they don't care about the facts, they do not trust a driverless car.

In spite of this, we are slowly tipping from open distrust of algorithms to grudging trust and this is because algorithms are underscoring basic needs and tasks throughout the day: viewing suggestions, cheapest flights, most compatible dating partner. We are beginning to see the error of our ways and trusting the data. The wolf is turning itself into a dog.

ALL HAIL THE NEW GOD: 'DATA-ISM'

If we hand over life-changing decisions to algorithms, what will this mean? In 2013, Angelina Jolie took a genetic profiling test and discovered she carried a dangerous mutation of the BRCA1 gene. This gave her an eighty-seven-per-cent statistical likelihood of developing breast cancer. Though she was not ill, she made the rational decision to have a double mastectomy. This was preventive, data-driven decision-making. Any resistance to this would come from human bias, otherwise known as emotion.

In medicine, data can be used to determine a black-and-white decision. Emotion is extremely resistant to being overridden, but when overwhelming evidence that you might die is presented, it is. The trust we once put in doctors, we are now putting in numbers, and to such an unquestioning degree that historian Yuval Harare calls data a new secular religion: 'Data-ism'.

'Just as divine authority was legitimised by religious mythologies, and human authority was legitimised by humanist ideologies, so high-tech gurus and Silicon Valley prophets are creating a new universal narrative that legitimises the authority of algorithms and big data.

'This novel creed may be called Data-ism. In its extreme form, proponents of the Data-ist worldview perceive the entire universe as a flow of data, see organisms as little more than biochemical algorithms, and believe that humanity's cosmic vocation is to create an all-encompassing data-processing system, and then merge into it. We are already becoming tiny chips inside a giant system that nobody really understands.'[17]

Data-ism is a new God because data understands us better than we understand ourselves. It does not get clouded by human bias. 'We are now,' Harare says, 'at the confluence of two scientific tidal waves. On the one hand biologists are deciphering the mysteries of the human body and, in particular, of the brain and human feelings. At the same time, computer scientists are giving us unprecedented data-processing power. When you put the two together, you get external systems that can monitor and understand feelings better than we can.'[18]

Big Data systems already know us better than we know ourselves but now we are on the cusp of believing and acquiescing to it. When this happens, authority – not simply number-crunching – will shift from humans to algorithms. Once it was the Catholic Church and the KGB who knew everything about us and this was unquestioningly accepted. Now, that theocratic mantle is to be handed to the tech giants.

To see the Big Five as humanity's enemy seems perverse. Are these companies really as Orwellian as they sound? Take a look at Sergey Brin, Tim Cook or Mark Zuckerberg. They are not bad guys. They wear T-shirts from Gap, drive electric cars (if they drive at all – Zuckerberg cycles to work) and give extraordinary amounts of money to charity. They do not appear to want to control every aspect of our lives and turn us into cyborgs.

Their stated mission is to do the opposite of control us. They want to set us free from poverty, inequality, global warming and disease. What they have is power and the potential to bring about colossal change. Like Robert Dall, the man who invented securitisation on Wall Street, which led ultimately to subprime and the banking crash, they hold the key to nuclear fission. How they choose to use that colossal power is what we are waiting to see.

IF A SUPER-INTELLIGENT MACHINE DECIDED TO GET RID OF US, I THINK IT WOULD DO SO PRETTY EFFICIENTLY

In December 2014, three young Londoners flew to Los Angeles to do a deal. Demis Hassabis, Shane Legg and Mustafa Suleyman were the founders of DeepMind Technologies, a small AI company in East London. They were on their way cut a deal with Larry Page of Google.

No one on that flight knew it, but the three men sitting in row 43 were on their way to signing the most far-reaching deal in history.

DeepMind had come onto Google's radar within three years of starting. Unlike every other Artificial Intelligence start-up on earth, they did not concern themselves with the human/machine 'interface' – the functionality of machines and brains, and their interaction.

DeepMind was about something more fundamental. The root of intelligence. Not artificial or human intelligence. All intelligence. DeepMind had gone back to first principles: humans and robots are both merely outer shells driven by decodable intelligence. If you decode that intelligence, you understand how anything works, and you rule the world.

At Googleplex, Mountain View, California, the three young Londoners and Larry Page shook hands on the deal. Google paid $650 million for a company barely three years old. It was not only the most important deal in Google's history. It was the most important deal for humankind.

In creating the planet's most popular search engine, Google had built the most powerful machine on earth. But in buying DeepMind, Google has the potential to own intelligence. They could then put the brain inside the Google machine.

What does a brain inside the Google machine mean? The Google DeepMind deal opened the door to the creation of a new organism from what DeepMind call 'cognitive machine tissue'. Neither living nor dead, but cognisant. An entirely new species.

DeepMind's founder, Shane Legg, was remarkably upbeat and post-human about what this new species meant when interviewed in 2011.

'Eventually I think human extinction will probably occur, and technology will likely play a role in this.' Asked if he thought humans would suffer, he said, 'If by suffering you mean prolonged suffering, then I think this is quite unlikely. If a super-intelligent machine decided to get rid of us, I think it would do so pretty efficiently. I don't think we will deliberately design super-intelligent machines to maximize human suffering.'[19]

Elon Musk, a man not easily overawed by a dystopian future, was staggered. He called artificial intelligence 'more dangerous than nukes'. Stephen Hawking said it would 'end mankind'.

But Legg was simply being 'post-human' about the way events were going to pan out. Once intelligence is decoded and the brain is in the machine, why do humans have moral primacy over any other form: living or machine?

It was merely logical that once you connect cognitive machine tissue, an organism is created that can decide whether humans are needed or not.

For technology that would make us extinct, the Google DeepMind deal garnered remarkably little response from the rest of the human race. Stephen Hawking said an independent ethics committee was needed to scrutinise DeepMind's research, as it took us deeper into a brave new future. But it never happened.

The incredible thing is that no matter how terrifying the DeepMind deal appears, it does not stop there. A Pandora's Box has been opened that neither Google nor DeepMind can shut, nor control what happens next. And they were about to get a glimpse of what that meant.

THE ROBOT LANGUAGE HUMANS CAN'T UNDERSTAND

In September 2016, Google Brain – the AI research department of which DeepMind was now a subsidiary – turned on something called the Google Neural Machine Translation (GNMT).

GNMT is a program that allows machines to translate entire languages in the blink of an eye. It is first given an example of translation. It then scans entire sentences in the foreign language, gives the translation of that sentence, then extrapolates the whole language from these individual sentences.

After a month or so, researcher Mike Schuster at Google Brain began to notice something strange. Machines were blindly translating entire languages without being given the translation first. Schuster saw translations between Korean and Japanese, when Korean-to-Japanese examples had not even been shown to the system.[20]

Then the machines started going one step further. The system began making 'reasonable' translations of languages it had not even been taught to translate. Google Brain's AI machine was taught Portuguese to English and English to Spanish. It then began to translate from Portuguese directly to Spanish. 'To our knowledge, this is the first demonstration of true multilingual, zero-shot translation,' Schuster said, as perplexed as he was astounded.[21]

However, it was what happened next that really concerned the programmers. The machine began creating its own entirely new language.

'Visual interpretation of the results shows that these models learn a form of interlingua representation for the multilingual model between all involved language pairs,' Schuster said.

An 'interlingua' is a type of artificial language which is used to fulfil a specific purpose. In this case, the interlingua was being used by the machine to explain how unseen material could be translated.

'Using a three-dimensional representation of internal network data, we were able to take a peek into the system as it translated a set of sentences between all possible pairs of the Japanese, Korean, and English languages,' the research team wrote in a blog spot.[22]

The neural network was 'encoding something' about the semantics of a sentence, rather than comparing phrase-to-phrase translations. No one could quite work out what this 'something' was.

The system was inventing a language. An entirely new encrypted language only other machines had the capacity to learn. Humans would be shut out, because they did not have the computing power to decode it.

'We interpret this as a sign of existence of an interlingua in the network,' the team said. The machines had invented a machine language by working out the rules of what a language was and then creating their own. But they had taken it upon themselves to make an encrypted language for other machines, keeping humans out. The wolves that became dogs were becoming wolves again.

When I asked IBM Watson programmer Dave Ferrucci what he made of this new machine language, he expressed no emotion. 'It's scary, Dave. Don't you think?' 'It's an interlingua. It's there to solve a problem.' But it's a new language. 'Sure, yes. It's a new language. But are the machines ahead of the race with humans? Not yet.' Not yet.

The lesson from the GNMT experiment is clear. We think we can control this, but we cannot. Humans may have set this journey off, but machines will decide where it leads.

Alphabet, the umbrella company for Google, may have dropped 'Do No Evil' from their pledge, but humans will not be doing the evil, machines will. And it won't be evil, it will simply be the logical imperative of code.

THE TRADE-OFF

In 2016, DeepMind suddenly popped up back in London. *New Scientist* revealed what Google were up to next. They were secretly negotiating a deal with the Royal Free NHS Trust operating Barnet, Chase Farm and Royal Free Hospitals, and which holds the confidential data of 1.6 million patients.[23]

The deal would allow DeepMind to access millions of highly sensitive records without the consent of patients. Everything from data on acute care, accident and emergency to pathology, radiology, HIV and abortion stats.

Then in 2017, they showed their hand. Google announced the launch of Streams, an app that triggers mobile alerts when a patient's vital signs or blood results are flagged as abnormal. 'Ten thousand people a year are dying from acute kidney injury,' DeepMind's Mustafa Suleyman said. 'These are entirely preventable deaths. We can trigger an alert that allows nurses or doctors to take preventative action, like giving intravenous antibiotics when your kidneys are dehydrated, to prevent escalation to the ICU.'

Streams appears to be a remarkable piece of technology, but it is also a foot in the door. It will initially be used to spot people at risk of kidney problems, but is due to be expanded over the next five years. And the clue to understanding what it will do next comes in DeepMind's claims for it.

Suleyman sees Streams becoming key to the everyday running of the hospital. Not solely detecting acute conditions such as blood poisoning, but – and here's the key phrase – 'coordinating patient treatment'. Technology will sit at the beating heart of the hospital, algorithms not doctors potentially deciding what care you get, and Google holding the keys to the data.

Critics of the deal saw it as profoundly dangerous. Cambridge University's Julia Powles and Hal Hodson called the deal with the NHS 'inexcusable' and DeepMind's claims for Streams 'specious'.[24]

Google hit back quickly. An article appeared in technology magazine *Wired* claiming that Streams was "saving NHS nurses two hours a day.'[25] Suleyman then followed up by announcing DeepMind were developing a bitcoin-style tracking of patient data using blockchain technology to protect it.[26]

Google was beginning the fight to win the hearts and minds of a sceptical public and healthcare professionals. Trust us, they were saying. And this is the trade-off.

1.6 million patients data-mined (ten million if it is rolled out nationally) and what do you get in return? The cutting-edge technology you desperately need and the alleviation of pressure on the scarce time and meagre resources of frontline staff.

Technology enables a silent takeover of the health system, but DeepMind would say this is not a zero-sum game: you may all be patient zero, but you benefit. Using DeepMind, Google can steal a march on their Big Five competitors in the NHS and more lucratively, the biggest goldmine of the twenty-first century: global healthcare.

Hooking up with the World Health Organisation and the NGOs on the ground to roll out health systems across the developing world, the tech giants are the new shining knights in white convertible jeeps.

Once upon a time it was the Red Cross and Médecins Sans Frontières who did the triage in medical disasters, but with the funding crisis in British and American healthcare, the triage zone has widened exponentially and hence the potential market that can be captured when these health systems of the developed world collapse, too.

ONE RING TO RULE THEM ALL

In *Minority Report*, the 2002 movie adaptation of the Philip K. Dick novel, Tom Cruise plays a police officer in the LAPD 'Pre-Crime' unit. Using the premonitions of sentient mutants called 'pre-cogs', the police are able to predict when someone is going to commit a crime before it happens, swooping down from helicopters and arresting them on the street before they have committed a crime. Their 'crime' is that they merely thought about it.

Palantir, the CIA-backed start-up, is *Minority Report* come true.

Palantir are to data what McKinsey are to consultancy. All-powerful, yet no one knows they even exist. Palantir do not have an office, they have an SCIF on a back street in Palo Alto. SCIF stands for 'Sensitive Compartmentalised Information Facility'. Palantir say their building 'must be built to be resistant to attempts to access the information within. The network must be "airgapped" from the public internet to prevent information leakage.'[27]

Palantir's defence systems include advanced biometrics, and walls impenetrable to radio waves, phone signal or internet. Their data storage is block-chained: it cannot be accessed by merely sophisticated hacking, it requires digital pass codes held by dozens of independent parties, whose identities are themselves protected by block chain.[28]

What is Palantir protecting? A 'palantir' is a 'seeing stone' in J.R.R. Tolkien's *The Lord of the Rings*. A dark orb used by

Saruman to be able to see in darkness or blinding light. Palantir means 'one that sees from afar'. A mythical instrument of omnipotence.

In 2004, Peter Thiel created Palantir with ex-PayPal engineer Nathan Gettings, and Joe Lonsdale, Stephen Cohen and Alex Karp from Stanford University. Their intention was to create a company that took Big Data somewhere no one else dared to go.

In 2013, Alex Karp, Palantir's chief executive officer, announced that the company would not be pursuing an IPO, as going public would make 'running a company like ours very difficult'. This is why.

Palantir watch everything you do and predict what you will do next in order to stop it. They have a secret arm called Palantir Gotham. Their clients include the CIA, the FBI, the NSA, the CDC, the Marine Corps, the Air Force, Special Operations Command, West Point and the IRS. Up to fifty per cent of their business is with the public sector. In-Q-Tel, the CIA's venture arm, was an early investor.[29]

Palantir track everyone from potential terrorist suspects to corporate fraudsters (Bernie Madoff was imprisoned with the help of Palantir), child traffickers and 'subversives'. But it is all done using prediction.

In Iraq, the Pentagon used Palantir software to track patterns in roadside bomb deployment and worked out garage-door openers were being used as remote detonators by predicting it.[30]

Palantir allowed the Marines to upload DNA samples from remote locations and tap into information gathered from years of collecting fingerprints and DNA evidence: the results returned almost immediately.

Without Palantir, suspects would have already moved onto a different location by the time the field agents received the results. Using the most sophisticated data mining, Palantir can predict the future, seconds or years before it happens.

Samuel Reading, a former Marine who works in Afghanistan

for NEK Advanced Securities Group, a US, military contractor, says, 'It's the combination of every analytical tool you could ever dream of. You will know every single bad guy in your area.'[31]

Palantir are at the heart of the US government, but with their other arm, Palantir Metropolis, they provide the analytical tools for hedge funds, banks and financial services firms to out-smart each other.

Palantir do not just provide the Pentagon with a machine for global surveillance and the data-efficient fighting of war, they run Wall Street, too. Palantir is exactly what it says it is: a giant digital eye like Saruman's 'seeing stone' in *The Lord of the Rings*.

MINORITY REPORT FOR REAL

On the streets of Chicago and Los Angeles, Palantir are getting closest to Philip K. Dick's vision of the future, now. In the film, a premonition of an Orwellian thought-police state, crime rates drop to zero as the 'Pre-Crime' unit successfully imprisons thousands of individuals for merely thinking of committing a felony.

However, when Cruise's character begins to question the morality of what he is doing, his superiors detect a threat to the entire 'pre-crime' programme. In order to get rid of him, Cruise is framed for a murder by altering the data of his thought history. In the final showdown with his boss, it is explained to Cruise that sometimes the numbers need to lie for the greater good of society.

Minority Report is set in 2054, but Palantir are putting 'pre-crime' into operation now. The Los Angeles Police Department have used Palantir to predict who will commit a crime by swooping *Minority Report*-style on suspects. Palantir call their work with the LAPD 'improving situational awareness, and responding to crime in real time.'[32]

Military-grade surveillance technology has now migrated from Fallujah to the suburban neighbourhoods of LA, 'predictive policing' on illegal drivers and petty criminals through a redeployment of techniques and algorithms used by the US army dealing with insurgents in Iraq and with civilian casualty patterns.[33]

When America is described as a 'war zone' between police and young black males, it is rarely mentioned that tactics developed by the US military in a real war zone are actually being deployed. The use of Palantir predictive-policing software by the Chicago Police and LAPD has coincided with a sharp rise in fatal shootings of black male suspects. Is predictive policing as a counter-insurgency tactic a contributing factor in the epidemic of police shootings of unarmed black men in the last four years?

One could argue that sophisticated pre-crime algorithms are not necessary when being black and male is seen as reason enough for the police to swoop. What predictive policing has done is militarise American cities, creating a heightened culture of suspicion and fear in areas where tensions are highest and policing is already most difficult.

Professor Geoff Parker is an expert on data broking and says, 'The mere presence of police arriving in an area because of an algorithm creates tension.' Enough to ignite a powder keg and push a delicate policing situation over the edge.[34]

Ana Muniz is an activist and researcher who works with the Inglewood-based Youth Justice Coalition. 'Any time that a society's military and domestic police become more similar, the lines blur. The military is supposed to defend the territory from external enemies, that's not the mission of the police – they're not supposed to look at the population as an external enemy.'[35]

In 2010, the LAPD announced a partnership with Motorola Solutions to monitor the Jordan Downs public housing project with surveillance cameras. In 2013, they announced the deployment of live CCTV cameras with facial-recognition software in San Fernando Valley, reported to be programmed to ID suspects on a 'hot list'.[36]

Whitney Richards-Calathes, a doctoral student at the City

University of New York who researches predictive policing, warns that 'we have to be really critical about built-in assumptions made when data bases are created for "public safety", yet kids as young as nine and ten are being put in these data bases and automatically labelled gang members.'[37]

Data merely becomes a new way of reinforcing old prejudices. Critics of these analytics argue that from the moment a police officer with the pre-crime mindset that you are a criminal steps out of their patrol car to confront you, your fate has been sealed.

In 2013, TechCrunch obtained a leaked report on the use of Palantir by the LA and Chicago police departments. Sergeant Peter Jackson of the LA was quoted as saying, 'Detectives love the type of information (Palantir) provide. They can now do things that we could not do before.'[38]

Palantir are immensely secretive. They wield as much real-world power as Google, Facebook, Amazon, Microsoft and Apple, but unlike them, Palantir operate so far under the radar, they are special ops.

BREAKING THE MONOPOLY

Together the Big Five (plus the invisible sixth ring, Palantir, the all-seeing eye) compose a new superclass of corporate might. But post-Trump, Brexit and the resurgence of nationalist parties in Europe, they face a new threat: governments with a popular vote seeking to claw back national sovereignty from corporations.

The public mood on these companies is turning. They are no longer shiny new platforms delivering the future now, they are a twenty-year-old monopoly challenging the authority of government and even democracy.

On the 21st January 2016, EU commissioner Margrethe Vestager opened the door of her office in Brussels to Tim Cook, CEO of Apple. Cook was there to talk about Apple's tax arrangements in Europe. Witnesses reported hearing shouting coming from the office as Vestager pushed back on Cook's version of what Apple should or should not be paying in corporate tax.

Seven months later, Cook got Vestager's verdict. 'Apple's tax benefits in Ireland are illegal,' she announced to a packed press conference. Apple owed £11 billion plus interest. When Cook heard, back at Apple HQ in Cupertino, he was reported to have called the judgment 'political crap'.

The tech giants have started to look like the American dream gone sour. Apple perceived as tax dodgers and Amazon, once edgy tech-disrupters, as slayers of small local businesses on the high street. Apple appeased the Chinese government's demands to close down apps giving Chinese people access to the outside world, while simultaneously refusing the US government access to a suspected terrorist's iPhone.

In May 2017, when the world faced a cyber attack from Wannacry malware, made possible by exploiting software allegedly stolen by a hacking group called Shadow Brokers from the NSA, Microsoft's President and Chief Legal Officer Brad Smith blamed governments for stockpiling vulnerabilities and leaving the world open.

The tech giants are also battling amongst themselves. Uber's Travis Kalanick was hauled before Apple CEO Tim Cook for secretly tagging iPhones even after Uber's app had been deleted and the devices erased. A fraud detection manoeuvre that violated Apple's privacy guidelines.[39]

Julius Genachowski is the former chairman of the Federal Communications Commission and says, 'During the periods where incumbents are battling disrupters, in general the US has done a good job of encouraging disrupters.' Under Obama, he says, the Big Five were not a threat to government, they were the future, and various parts of the United States regulatory and legal infrastructure sought to protect and nurture them.

During Mr Genachowski's term at the FCC (and then again during the term of his successor, Tom Wheeler) the commission passed rules favouring so-called 'network neutrality', meaning companies could not favour some kinds of content online over others. A policy favoured by tech companies.

But as the disrupters grow into monsters the dynamic shifts. 'The next part of the arc,' Genachowski says, 'is that disrupters become very successful and in some ways turn into incumbents, and then you see two things: battles between incumbents and other incumbents, and a next generation of disrupters tackling incumbents.'

That is where we are now. The Big Five have become the incumbents and they are treated as such by governments, who look to both sides of the ledger – their benefits to society as well as their potential costs – when deciding how to police them.

But are the new players – Uber, Airbnb, Snapchat – any real threat? The battles for dominance in cloud services, artificial intelligence and data mining, as well as real-world dominance of driverless cars, drone deliveries and robot jobs – that is all between the original Big Five.

When Uber's Kalanick faced off against Tim Cook at Apple Headquarters in 2015, because Uber had pulled a fast one by camouflaging their app from Apple's engineers, it was a microcosm of the incumbent-versus-new-disrupter battle and there was only going to be one winner: Apple.[40]

The history of capitalism has been a war waged for and against monopolies. In 1890, the Sherman Anti-Trust Act created the famous 'Sherman Hammer' allowing the White House to smash companies seeking to create monopolies.

Tobacco, oil, steel and the banks have all been subject to antitrust legislation that tried to curtail monopolies working against the public interest. The Glass-Steagall Banking Act held in place for nearly sixty years preventing banks from becoming overly powerful and creating another Wall Street crash.

This was only possible because a baton passed quietly from legislature to legislature for over a century. A determination to maintain the authority of democracy. This was not an election pledge from a smooth-tongued politician seeking office by attacking big business, it was done quietly behind closed doors for the benefit of the public.

Tolkien had one ring to rule them all and tech giants have an uncompleted circle, buffering as they race to be the first to download humanity. When the tech companies are able to complete the circle, singularity will be upon us.

But there is no talk of breaking up the Big Five monopoly. They challenged the authority of government, and government – unlike the governments of the last century – capitulated. The Big Five know they cannot be tamed. They are remaking what it is to be human, and whether humans are even part of that story.

CHAPTER FOURTEEN
GLOBALISATION: HOW ASIA REWROTE THE RULES

TANK MAN

It is rare that one person whose name no one knew, and did nothing but stand still without a word passing his lips, changed everything.

But on 5 June 1989, as more than one million people gathered in Tiananmen Square in Beijing to demand democracy for China and tanks rolled in ominously to break up the crowds, one man dressed in a crumpled white shirt, with a carrier bag in each hand, stood calmly in front of a tank and refused to move.

The ensuing cat-and-mouse game between man and tank became emblematic of a change in direction for human history. The state was using military force to put down the individual, but this time the individual was more powerful. It was a turning point.

Each time the tank attempted to manoeuvre round the man, he shifted position. The process was repeated again and again. Other student protestors began to do the same, standing calmly and defiantly before other tanks. The army did not know how to respond. The crowd had not run away terrified. They had stood their ground. Whatever happened to them, however this panned out, they had won.

Three days later, the army did respond. Hundreds of protestors in Tiananmen Square were massacred, thousands more arrested, and the student protest crushed. But of all the people who had stood before the tanks, only one was photographed. 'Tank Man' became a blurred icon of dignified Gandhi-like resistance and Tiananmen Square became the catalyst for tipping China and the world onto a new axis.

Before Tiananmen Square, the Communist Party's reform programme for Chinese society had been controlled and top-down. The massacre turbocharged everything. It was now clear to Deng Xiaoping, chairman of the party, that even if a clamp-down in the immediate aftermath of the massacre quelled further protests temporarily, long-term, the game was up.

Tank Man had become symbolic for the rise of the individual. Intimidation with tanks would no longer cow a growing educated and aspirational middle class, emboldened in their demands for change. Only delivering greater economic prosperity would satisfy them – and if you delivered that, you cleverly dampened demands for democracy, the ever-looming spectre on the leadership's horizon.

Deng needed to deliver change, but without acceding to demands for democracy, and for that he needed a new plan: China would become the largest company on earth, with 1,387 million employees.

DENG XIAOPING

No one knows what happened to Tank Man. Some reports suggested he had been shot in the square, others that he had been arrested and executed fourteen days after the protest was crushed. Canadian journalist Jan Wong, who subsequently interviewed Communist Party officials, said they were never able to pin down his identity and believe he could still be alive on the mainland today.[1]

Tank Man and his fellow protestors had changed the balance of power in China, and hence the global power axis. Each time they moved to face a tank afresh, they underlined the quiet determination of thousands, and beyond the square, millions of Chinese people prepared to act without compromise.

The protestors of Tiananmen Square proved one thing above all to the Communist Party and the world outside: people were immeasurably more powerful than tanks. They could be halted temporarily, but the rise of the individual was inexorable.

The question for the ruling elite of the party was not how to crush this wave of people power for good, but how to harness a potentially destabilising force for change and turn it to their advantage.

For over a century, capitalism in America and Europe had boomed, crashed, and then reinvented itself by piggy-backing on the extraordinary ideas of unsung geniuses working deep beneath research buildings in sterile laboratories, or high up in the boardrooms of big companies.

These ideas had led to deals that would change the world: Tom Peters and Bob Waterman's '7S' model for work; Drazen Prelec's experiments with neural pain and cash; Robert Dall's discovery that you could 'securitise' Wall Street; Alfred Sloan inventing the perpetually upgradeable product and so transforming consumerism; Henry Gadsen's epiphany to reinvent the pharmaceutical industry by medicating modern life itself.

Communism now needed to reboot itself with a light-bulb moment of equal magnitude. In 1992, three years after Tiananmen Square, Deng Xiaoping, China's all-powerful leader, stepped up to the challenge. A moment that he had been waiting for his whole life.

Deng was quite simply the most brilliant leader of the twentieth century. But his brilliance stemmed not simply from his consummate ability to chart a course of reform for the most populous nation on earth, and to swim through the shark-infested waters of the upper echelons of the Communist Party with deft ease.

His true brilliance lay in setting a tripwire that would go off twenty years after his death. Because it is only now that Deng's plan is coming to fruition, reshaping the destiny of the twenty-first century by having reconfigured the paradigm of communism versus capitalism in the twentieth century.

Deng wanted to win the globalisation game by shifting the axis of world power decisively back to the East once more. Without him, China would not be the pivotal nation state on earth. And two decades after his death, the ideas that made it happen are falling into place.

Deng came from a well-to-do, land-owning family in Guang'an, in the Sichuan province, but travelled as a young man to Moscow and Paris – half a century later he told the Queen he was disappointed he could not see England from the top of the Eiffel Tower: the kind of conversational trap that Deng set for Western leaders.

When Deng returned to China in the 1920s, astutely he dropped any air of well-travelled cosmopolitanism in toeing the austere Maoist party line. But Deng kept what he had seen in the West in his pocket. He knew what capitalism had to offer people and how this could threaten the long-term survival of the Communist Party.

Deng rose quickly within the party hierarchy, playing an instrumental role in the Long March of 1934 where he gained Mao's trust. Short and pugnacious, with a habit of spitting frequently, Deng played the role of party disciplinarian to a tee, giving nothing away about his prosperous upbringing.

In 1949, Deng made his mark by playing a key role in the Communist defeat of Chiang Kai-shek's Nationalist government. His future at the top of the party was assured and Deng's credentials as a loyal servant of the proletariat were now beyond question; something that would later prove very useful.

In 1956, everything changed. The new Soviet premier Nikita Khrushchev launched a profound attack on the Stalinist principles of Soviet communism. Khrushchev had questioned God and it rocked the Soviet Communist Party to its foundations.

Mao Zedong feared an equivalent attack on the cult of Maoism in China. In the West, consumerism had begun to deliver on the promises of capitalism – freedom and fridges – and it was only a matter of time before this 'propaganda' polluted the Chinese proletariat. Mao believed communism needed to go back to first principles and crush reform.

It was in this moment that everything hinged: stick or twist for Deng, who saw a chink of light and an opportunity to open up. He made his move. Far from creating collective wealth, he said, the 'collectivisation' of farms – a central plank of both Stalinism and Maoism – had impoverished millions.[2]

Mao's 'Great Leap Forward' had industrialised China rapidly, but also created famine on an unprecedented scale. Deng took it upon himself to order the reversal of collectivisation and the return of farms to the ownership of smallholding peasants. To individuals. When Mao heard of Deng's plan, he quipped, 'Which emperor authorised that?'[3]

Like Khrushchev, Deng had questioned God. It was a direct challenge to Mao's authority and Mao sensed a rival building a power base. Deng had committed heresy and at its heart was the elevation of the individual and markets.

IT DOESN'T MATTER IF A CAT IS BLACK OR WHITE, SO LONG AS IT CATCHES MICE

Deng had set himself on a collision course with Mao. In July 1962, Deng addressed the Communist Youth League and made a gnomic statement that would travel with him to his grave. Sixteen words that set out his theory of *Realpolitik* and would determine the future course of Communist China.

'It doesn't matter,' he told the young Maoist zealots, 'if a cat is black or white, so long as it catches mice.'

It was classic Communist Party Confucianism pitched perfectly at two audiences. What did it mean? To the Maoist faithful, it was interpreted as 'the ends justifying the means'. If the goal was communism, then we must achieve that goal by any means necessary.

However, to the reformers, it meant the complete opposite. To them, this was like Bob Dylan suddenly picking up an electric guitar. Maoist dogma, he was saying, was a blind path. China must be open – as it was 2,000 years ago – to learning from the West, even if that meant adopting elements of market economics. Communism must be able to mutate and evolve on its own terms. Above all, to be ruthlessly pragmatic.

Communist China, Deng said, could choose whether to disregard or subsume these new ideas, but the important thing was to be adaptable. The cat could be any colour, but it was the end goal that mattered, not dogma. Only by winning did the cat catch the mouse.

Deng could not have chosen a worse moment to renounce Maoism, which is why it was so important that it appeared to be not a disavowal of Maoism, but its endorsement.

In May 1966, Mao eviscerated any chance of Deng's market-reform plans by exploding the Cultural Revolution on the heads of 1.6 billion people; the most brutal obliteration of Western 'influence' on Chinese society in living memory. A total war, not only on Mao's political enemies, but on the very concept of ideas and anyone other than Mao daring to have them.

Red Guards armed with sticks rounded up teachers, academics, doctors and dentists, who were beaten or executed for harbouring 'bourgeois' Western values. Books were destroyed, as were reading glasses – another bourgeois implement for spreading the 'false consciousness' of education. Thousands were arrested and families torn apart as Maoist students denounced and informed on their 'counter-revolutionary' parents.

Meanwhile, counter-revolutionary students at universities in cities were forcibly removed to the country to work on the land in order to reindoctrinate them with Maoist first principles.[4]

The Communist Party was purged of reformers, and this meant Deng Xiaoping. By the early 1970s, the Cultural

Revolution had done its work. The entire administrative and managerial architecture of China – the veins and arteries of the body politic – had been destroyed. There was simply no one left qualified to do a job beyond tilling a field. The country was in ruins.

THE FIRST TIANANMEN SQUARE

On 4 April 1976, thousands of protestors gathered in Tiananmen Square demanding a reversal of the disastrous consequences of the Cultural Revolution.

As Mao grew increasingly ill, the Maoist clique of the 'Gang of Four' took control. Hardliners Jiang Qing, Zhang Chunqiao, Yao Wenyuan and Wang Hongwen, sought collectively to prevent a return for Deng and the reformers.

Yet nearly two million protestors came to Tiananmen Square in support of Deng and his recently deceased reformist ally Zhou Enlai. The Gang of Four called the campaign 'counter-revolutionary'.

Like the second Tiananmen Square protests of 1989, the demonstrators were ruthlessly crushed by force. But only months later, following Mao's death and the arrest of the Gang of Four, the reformer Deng began to outmanoeuvre Mao's weak, anointed successor Hua Guofeng in what became a classic boardroom coup, taking power for himself in 1978.

Deng was now the boss: the leader of the most powerful nation on earth in waiting. And the seeming contradiction of a communist leader in thrall to market economics was no contradiction at all.

Deng Xiaoping believed in the 'socialist market economy' – business and Marxism coexisting in one nation – as deeply as Mao believed in Maoism. The principle that outlined Hong Kong's independence from Britain in 1997 could have been written for Deng's China as a whole: 'one country, two systems'.

Thirteen years after the suppression of the first Tiananmen Square uprising, here was another. In 1989 Deng found himself again on an inspection visit to a rural region of the South, just as he had been in 1961. This time he had only two words to say: '*kai fang*'. It was time once again to 'open up'.

MADE IN CHINA

Playing with my Hot Wheels car set as a kid, I was struck by something odd. To a child growing up in the late 1970s and early 1980s, Hot Wheels was the epitome of cool American culture. The cars spoke of Evel Knievel jumping gorges on his stars-and-stripes rocket bike; the go-fast flames on the Mustangs and Dodge muscle cars were pure *Dukes of Hazzard*. Yet if you turned the car over, it was stamped not with 'Made in the USA', but with a puzzling moniker: 'Made in China'.

So how did China become the world's workshop?

The reason is simple, as Harvard economist Joseph Nye explains: 'If we looked at the world in 1800, you'd find that more than half of the world's people lived in Asia and they made more than half the world's product. Now fast forward to 1900: half the world's people – more than half – still live in Asia, but now they're making only a fifth of the world's product.

'What happened? The Industrial Revolution, which meant that all of a sudden, Europe and America became the dominant centre of the world. What we're going to see in the twenty-first century is Asia returning to being more than half the world's population and making more than half of the world's product.[5]

Deng did something in the late 1970s and early 1980s that reverberated in the 2016 US election: he remade China from an inward-looking, rigidly socialist backwater into the workshop of the world, carving the heart out of the Western manufacturing base.

It was not only Hot Wheels that got made in China. The cheap consumer goods that fuelled the spending boom of the West had 'Made in China' – or Korea or Japan or Singapore – stamped on them, too.

Tiny metal toy cars became big real cars as Asia began to dominate the world's car market. Japanese tech innovation enabled a spectacular volte-face on electrical goods, turning a reputation for cheap, shoddy radios and TVs in the 1970s into reliable, affordable excellence a decade later.

Toyota, Nissan and Sony became General Motors and Chrysler. Asia drove hard at the West and planted a flag at the heart of manufacturing, turning the West's own Great Leap Forward – the Industrial Revolution – to rust.

Two centuries ago, Napoleon warned: 'Let China sleep, for when the dragon awakes, she will shake the world.' It was not simply China that reawakened to show the world what it could do, it was the whole of Asia.

China's economy is today bigger than India's, Russia's and Brazil's put together. Growing at six per cent a year (compared to India's seven per cent) China will still create the equivalent of two new Indias by 2020. China has a middle class of 100 million people and in spite of extraordinary pollution levels created by rapid industrialisation – as bad as the industrial heartland of nineteenth-century England – life expectancy is seventy-six, higher than the world average or in any developing country.[6]

Yet it is China's impact on the world economy that is truly breathtaking. Less than ten per cent of the world's population is fully industrialised. As China industrialises further, it could treble that global figure, sucking in and industrialising a further twenty per cent of the planet's population by igniting growth in Asia, Latin America, Africa and even reinvigorating the industrial West. Protectionist guru Peter Navarro's fear that the West will inevitably suffer 'death by China' could well turn out to be the opposite, 'rescue by China'.[7]

China's continuing growth will stimulate colossal demand for raw materials, energy, imports and capital flow. This reboots everyone else. Their win is not necessarily at everyone else's expense. But their economic implosion would be.[8]

China is the largest market for seventy countries and the largest trading partner for 120, more than half the population of the world.

China imports the equivalent of £1 trillion worth of goods and over the next five years, will import $8 trillion of goods. It will be a bigger net importer than the European Union by 2020. As the chairman of Goldman Sachs, Jim O'Neill, puts it succinctly: 'China is the biggest example of growth and poverty reduction in history.'[9]

And as China and Asia begin to come into their own once more, the West retreats to the comfort blanket of protectionism, like hiding under a desk before a nuclear war.

The only leverage the US now holds over China is how much money it owes China. Like a bigger Goldman Sachs or Citibank, the US is now a superpower that is 'too big to fail'.

This astronomical US debt perversely gives the US a new form of power. In 2016, then-Presidential-nominee Trump said: 'We owe them money . . . this gives us tremendous power.' In February 2017, that debt to China was estimated at $1.059 trillion.

HOW CHINA CHANGED THE RULES BY STICKING TO THE OLD ONES

Post-match analysis of football or a baseball game often does the winner a disservice by focusing on the failure of the losers, rather than the skill of the winners.

This chapter is about the winners: the creation of a base for winning, and the numbers that brought that win home. China and Asia quite simply had more: more people, more resources, and a phenomenally larger market. But they also had a game plan that involved taking advantage of the poor game plan of their opponents.

In 2016, Goodyear Tyres closed the gates of their UK factory in Bushbury Lane, Wolverhampton for the last time.[10] For eighty-nine years, workers had built tyres for the US rubber conglomerate founded in 1898. In 2008, Goodyear was ranked sixteenth in the *Forbes* annual listings of companies with the best reputation as an employer in the world.

Cyril Barrett, one of the union representatives at the Wolverhampton plant said, 'It's a really sad time as the work-force is really like a family. We've seen generations grow up with the company. It's a time of great emotion. In times gone by, Goodyear was a great company and that's what makes it even sadder.'[11]

The jobs were going to Mexico. On a noticeboard in the factory, employees were told that anyone interested in a job could move to Mexico, where Goodyear would be happy to re-employ them. The staff response was to wear Mexican hats on their last day.

This is globalisation. But globalisation does not really exist. What actually exists are the market and wages and the rules that apply to both. Turkish economist Dani Rodrik at Harvard believes that China's victory in the globalisation game has simply been an ability to bend these rules to suit their game plan.

In the 1990s, Rodrik says, globalisation became 'hyperglobal-isation' and this was 'not about creating healthy economies, but removing all barriers to trade, so we confused ends with means.'[12]

Rodrik believes, 'An intellectual framework became estab-lished in the 1990s by the World Bank and the WTO (World Trade Organisation), whereby globalisation was seen as the way countries would grow. That narrative failed to see that countries that did well under globalisation did so on their own terms. They maintained strong infrastructure and investment in combination with taking advantage of globalisation. So we only got half the story.'[13]

Whilst the West played the game of globalisation one way, China played it another, interpreting the rules differently. 'When you look at how China achieved this feat,' says Rodrik, 'it violated nearly every rule of post-1990 globalisation. It controlled capital flows, subsidised industries, it required investors to use local content, violated trade agreements, violated property rights. It maintained wide state ownership, largely to protect employment. (China) benefited from all the other countries following the rules of hyperglobalisation.'[14]

China cunningly followed the old rules as everyone else followed new ones for 'hyperglobalisation', created in the aftermath of the collapse of the rules first established for capitalism after the war.

In leafy New Hampshire on 1 July 1944, a deal was struck by the most powerful post-war economies on earth – the forty-four allied nations – at the United Nations Monetary and Financial Conference at Mount Washington Hotel, overlooking the sleepy town of Bretton Woods.

The aim of the Bretton Woods Agreement was simple: creating the rules for post-war capitalism. National currencies would be tied to a fixed exchange, pegged to gold and the US dollar, and a bank of last resort called the IMF would provide nations with bridging loans on imbalances of payment.

The message of Bretton Woods was as important as the mechanisms: rules and institutions would govern the flow of global finance. The idea of Bretton Woods was to allow regulated free trade across the globe within firm parameters. Nations were locked into a system that both policed their behaviour and enabled them to trade equitably.

On 15 August 1971, the world changed. Bretton Woods collapsed and new rules came into operation – the rules for 'hyperglobalisation'. President Nixon unilaterally terminated convertibility of the US dollar to gold. Exchange rates were now floating and the keys to capitalism were handed over from men with clipboards in Geneva, circumscribing what nations could and could not do, to Wall Street traders with calculators looking to see how they could use this new, rule-free world to make money by speculating on currency exchange.

Yanis Varoufakis, the economist and former Greek Minister of Finance, is clear why Bretton Woods collapsed. 'Bretton Woods worked till the US stopped running trade surpluses. After 1971, the system simply couldn't continue because the US lost its surpluses. Then America started recycling everyone else's surpluses. It was operating like a vacuum cleaner, sucking in the net surplus wealth and net profits into Wall Street to close the loop.'[15] The implication is that the same thing could happen in the future with China.

Bretton Woods was key to rebuilding the world. It allowed US trade surpluses to be recycled by countries with trade deficits. This allowed the US to send money and continue sending money to rebuild Germany, Japan and Korea.[16] Paul Mason believes that we have made an error in demonising 'globalisation', because we have defined it incorrectly, conflating 'the interconnectedness of the world with the failures of neo-liberalism'.

The end of Bretton Woods ushered in this thing we now call 'globalisation', which turned out in reality to be a handy catch-all for one game played by two sets of rules. Jim Kim of the World Bank sums it up neatly: 'Globalisation worked marvellously for Korea, China, and for most of East Asia, but not in Iowa or Wolverhampton – who voted Brexit and Trump.'

POLITICAL NATIONALISM BAD, ECONOMIC PATRIOTISM GOOD

In 2015, as anti-globalisation placards began to be stencilled and held up at rallies for Trump, Brexit and on anti-TTIP marches in Britain, America and Europe, something else was going on hidden in the business pages.

More than half of British companies were declared as having foreign shareholders. In 2014, fifty-four per cent of the value of the UK stock market was officially declared as 'owned outside the UK'. In 1998, it was thirty-eight per cent.[17]

In the US, foreign ownership has increased steadily over twenty years. The biggest American companies are now owned by the Chinese and their appetite is growing across a bewilderingly varied array of industries.

In 2013, processed-meat conglomerate Smithfield Foods was bought by Shuanghui International for $7.1 billion. Professor Minxin Pei at Claremont McKenna College called the deal 'a masterstroke to expand its ability to supply a fast-growing market with premium-brand pork at higher prices . . . Shuanghai might (also) use Smithfield as a channel to sell its products in the US.'

In just one year – 2016 – Chinese investors bought the following:

- Starwood Hotels, incorporating the W Hotel chain, bought by Anbang Insurance in a deal worth $14.3 billion.
- Ingram Micro, a tech company and number sixty-two on the Fortune 500 companies, bought by Tianjin Tianhai Investment for $6.3 billion.
- General Electric Appliances, selling toasters and dishwashers, was bought by Qingdao Haier for $5.4 billion.
- Combine harvester manufacturer Terex Corp went to Zoomlion for $5.4 billion.
- Motorola Mobility got scooped up by Lenovo for $3.1 billion.[18]

My old friend Wang at Dalian Wanda bought film company Legendary Entertainment Group, who made *Jurassic Park* and *Pacific Rim*, for $3.5 billion (to go with AMC, America's largest cinema chain, which Wang bought in 2012 for $2.6 billion). So now we know where he spent that $7 billion loose change.

And this only skims the surface of what was bought by Chinese investors in the States in a single year. When one begins to understand who really owns what in any country, talk of a trade war starts to sound a little imbecilic. Trade war with whom? With yourself?

When Bretton Woods collapsed, there was no going back to the old world. Even Yanis Varoufakis, a self-proclaimed 'leftist', is realistic about the options. 'What we don't need is what we did between the mid-1970s and 2008, which is to stabilise global capitalism through an expanding trade deficit by the US. Allowing Wall Street bankers to financialise, creating torrents of speculation on the stream of capital flows. We need a new Bretton Woods: a new managed capitalism just like we had between 1944 and 1970.'[19]

It is simply not going to happen. 'Of course, this is a new paradigm,' Varoufakis says, 'we're not going to have fixed exchange rates, or a dominant power like the US, so we better learn how to cooperate at the political level in order to create economic equilibrium that is capable of averting the rise of nationalism.'

Yet we do have a dominant power – China – and we do have the rise of nationalism. And to understand how China won the globalisation game, you need to understand the difference between the West's idea of patriotism, and China's.

In the West, we have a disconnect: a head and a body politic moving in different directions. The head says jobs need to be repatriated, foreigners need to be sent home, elites should be punished, trade tariffs should go up and global corporations should be made to pay their way. The head votes accordingly.

The body meanwhile is floating merrily off in the opposite direction: corporations can do what they like and should be wooed by the lowest tax-break incentives, the globalised market should determine wages and where jobs go. In short, we should not put the kind of fetters on business that the head demands.

The West could sustain a head/body disconnect while cheap goods (the positive of globalisation) were offset by the loss of jobs and diminishing wages (the downside). But not anymore.

The patriotic head and the globalised body working in schizo-phrenic tandem have not made for great coordinated economic policy.

Now go to China. When two million steel workers were laid off, this is what they did. Retrained them as entrepreneurs running start-ups. A policy decision was made to boost income in the aftermath of their redundancy rather than cut it, and maintain rising wages as well as improve the condition of migrant workers.

The slogan for this mammoth programme was telling of China's approach to reinvestment in the workforce and thus the economy as a whole: 'Do not leave a single individual behind.'[20]

Economist Yasheng Huang sees China's authoritarianism and lack of democracy as the very reason for this relentless focus. One reason why the head and body work so efficiently in tandem. Because the head has no chance to express its opinions.

But Jim Kim of the World Bank compares this coordinated policy with what happened in the West. 'When NAFTA (the North American Free Trade Agreement) and the great trade agreements were made, there was a plan to retrain people with programmes as jobs were lost. But with cuts, these programmes never happened. Silicon Valley complains there's not enough skilled people for jobs, whilst in Iowa there are people who need jobs but don't have the right skills because they weren't retrained.'

In Asia, even victory is no excuse for complacency. 'In China and South Korea, there's a paranoia about being ready for the next wave. They've perfected the semi-conductor business, of going faster and faster, but now they're going "what's next?" and a paranoia amongst parents about preparing children for what happens next. That didn't happen in Iowa.'[21]

This is head and body working in tandem. As Yasheng Huang says, there may be no democracy, but this is a state dedicated to 'semi-conductor' levels of ever-increasing speed and productivity, further turbocharged by an awareness that constant retraining and adaptability are needed to stay ahead in the globalisation game.

20,000 ELON MUSKS

GWC is a Sino-Japanese tech company with ambitions that make the Silicon Valley tech giants look modest. With offices in Beijing, Tokyo and in Mountain View, California, where Google are based, GWC are scaling up tech entrepreneurship to industrial grade with the aim of producing 20,000 Elon Musks.[22]

In 2013, GWC hosted a pitching session in Beijing for budding mobile executives, developers, investors and entrepreneurs at their annual Global Mobile Internet Conference (GMIC). Their aim was fulfilled: 20,000 budding Elon Musks turned up and began frantically pitching ideas.[23]

The 'G-Summit' is a global competition to find innovations they will back with $1 million. In 2016, winners from Bangalore, Sao Paulo and Taipei were given the green light to develop ideas with multi-platform potential across the planet.

Silicon Valley is alert to the threat. 'The Valley needs to think more globally,' says Facebook's VP Vaughan Smith. 'With its focus on Asia, GMIC is among the few tech conferences that's focused on important trends happening outside the US.'

In 2015, Apple's CEO Tim Cook signed up to a social media site: Weibo, China's answer to Twitter. This was not because Apple's boss wanted to post cuddly pictures of pandas. Both Twitter and Facebook are banned in China and by creating an official presence on China's biggest social network site, millions of Chinese now had access to Apple through the portal of Cook's verified account.

Apple are one of the few tech giants with their feet under the door in China and this is not least because the Chinese have little need for the others. Chinese companies no longer ape Silicon Valley but lead the way, and China does not really need to open the door to Google, Facebook, Uber or Amazon. They have their own versions, steaming ahead of their progenitors.

Baidu is China's Google, providing the same breadth of service from maps and cloud storage to payment systems, food delivery, healthcare ventures, driverless cars and research into AI, while Alibaba is China's online payment platform, the largest e-commerce company on Planet Earth.

Ten Cent is China's Facebook, with WeChat – a clever combination of WhatsApp, Facebook, Apple Pay and Google News – hoovering up over 700 million subscribers.

JD.com is China's Amazon but, as Jason Hiner of tech innovation website ZDnet points out, 'It's actually racing ahead of Amazon.' JD.com have addressed Chinese consumer concern about mass-produced fake goods by authenticating deliveries of global brands and are now offering same-day deliveries to 600 million customers (next-day delivery to the whole of China), working on drones to remote areas.

Didi is China's Uber, with $1 billion investment from Apple. Unlike Uber in the West, Didi have a 'Didi Bus', a driver service that will pick you and your car up if you have had too much to drink. Didi are using big data and machine learning to attempt to solve China's huge traffic congestion and pollution problems in cities by moving cars off the streets at peak hours.[24]

These companies – like the Silicon Valley Big Five – see no territorial limits on their ambition. Huawei and Xiaomi provide mobile devices and are looking to break into the Samsung and Apple market. Xiaomi hired Google's Android chief Hugo Barra to realise their ambitions, not just in Asia but across the globe.

These companies, like GWC with their 20,000 Elon Musks drive, are not looking for one breakthrough idea, they are looking for 20,000. And this industrial scale of entrepreneurialism is down to a cultural preset to think big. Asia does not think big as a grandstanding pose, but because of a fundamental philosophical predisposition.

THE RICE FIELD AND THE HUNTER

In 1999, psychologists Kaiping Peng of Berkeley and Richard Nisbett of the University of Michigan ran a fascinating experiment into the difference between Western and Eastern ways of approaching a problem.[25]

They gave Chinese and American college students a range of scenarios describing conflicts between people and asked for advice on how best to resolve them.

Seventy-two per cent of the Chinese students gave compromise-orientated responses, taking into account the arguments on both sides. Seventy-four per cent of American students found fault on one side or the other, and then sided accordingly.[26]

The Peng–Nisbett 'contradiction' experiment tested a two-thousand-year-old philosophical schism. Western conceptions of the truth are based on the principle of *principium tertii exclusi* – 'the law of the excluded middle' as defined by Aristotle in *Ethics*: 'There cannot be an intermediate between contradictories. But of one subject we must either affirm or deny any one predicate.'[27]

A Western answer to a problem is derived by two people debating. One is exclusively right and the other is exclusively wrong, and the exclusively right 'answer' prevails.

The Chinese, by contrast, follow the 'doctrine of the mean'. In a debate, both parties will be partly right and partly wrong in their argument. The truth will lie somewhere in the middle.[28]

Confucian scholars Li-Jun Ji, Albert Lee and Tieyuan Guo argue that the 'doctrine of the mean' comes directly from Confucius and is thus widely considered the highest ideal of Confucianism.

'Chinese are encouraged to argue for both sides in a debate or to assign equal responsibilities in a dispute. This presents an interesting contrast with the law of the excluded middle in Western philosophies, according to which one ought to eliminate ambiguity or inconsistency by selecting one and only one of the conflicting ideas. Unlike the Chinese tradition, it assumes no merit in the middle ground.'[29]

The middle ground does not mean wishy-washy consensus, but a pooling of knowledge and a preset for the communal good. Psychologist Richard Nisbett ascribes this fundamental difference of approach to landscape.[30]

'The ecology of China, consisting as it does primarily of relatively fertile plains, low mountains and navigable rivers, favoured agriculture and made centralised control of society relatively easy. Agricultural peoples need to get along with one another. This is particularly true for rice farming, characteristic of southern China and Japan, which requires people to cultivate the land in concert with one another.'

The rice field became not merely a place for collaboration, but a metaphor for the nation: people are like grains of rice, both supremely significant and insignificant. Their significance is their contribution to the harvest, their insignificance is the pointlessness of the individual and individual ego.

By contrast, Western individualism grew out of personal struggle. On the barren terrain of the Greek Islands two thousand years before the birth of Christ, survival depended on a solitary hunter outwitting the hunted animal.

When this translated to the Greek *polis* of Plato and Aristotle, the cut and thrust of the hunt became the cut and thrust of debate: the dialectic. The basis for Western philosophy and a cult of the individual that set us down a route of enlightenment, individualism, property and democratic 'rights' for the next two millennia. For better or for worse.

THE EMOJI MING VASE

These profound philosophical differences count. Conservative political philosopher Michael Oakshott makes a profound distinction between two ways a society can be run: one is 'teleocratic' and the other 'nomocratic'.[31]

Teleocratic societies have a declared goal: a higher end. The Enlightenment was teleocratic; it believed greater knowledge would continuously improve society. Communism is teleocratic; it seeks a classless nirvana. Technocracy is teleocratic; it believes in continuing improvement of the human condition through technological advance.

Some teleocratic utopias like communism have an end goal after which history stops. Others seek advance as an end in itself. Progress as a road without destination.

Nomocratic societies, Oakshott said, are very different. They are bound by rules and tradition, by history and precedent. They have attained if not perfection, a state of lived, empirical best practice. Oakshott believed conservatism had achieved this in Britain. The rule of law and parliamentary democracy had together delivered unprecedented stability for two hundred years.

When Harold Macmillan resigned as Prime Minister in 1963, he is rumoured to have been asked what his greatest achievement in office had been. 'Fucking up as little as possible' was his glorious and apocryphal reply. That is nomocratic politics.

In China, the nomocratic philosophy is embodied in the Ming vase. An artefact embodying perfection that can only be ruined. In 1450, it symbolised China's pre-eminence as the world's most powerful dynastic state.

As Professor Craig Clunas of Oxford and Jessica Harrison-Hall of the British Museum say in their catalogue to the 2014 ceramic exhibition *Ming: 50 Years That Changed China (1400–1450)*: '(Dynastic China) had greater land area, bigger cities (and more big cities), bigger armies, bigger ships, bigger palaces, bigger bells, more literate people, and more religious professionals.'

'Ming' was not a family title, but an adjective meaning 'bright', 'luminous' or 'shining'. It was adopted by Zhu Yuanzhang, the founder of the Ming dynasty at the turn of the fifteenth century as a description of what dynastic China would bring to the world.

The Ming vase was an unimprovable piece of pottery, its perfection dictated by rules going back centuries as to how it would be produced. The vase carried complex messages in its decoration – a meaning understood only by those who understood the rules for reading it. The Ming vase delivered coded messages for those playing power politics in the court of the emperor. When looking at a Ming vase in 1450, you saw a complex system of messages, some subversive, some humorous, others revelatory. Today you look at a Ming vase and see a weeping willow and some pretty blue birds flying over a bridge.

In 1998, a software designer called Shigetaka Kurita was working for Japanese mobile operator NTT DoCoMo, who were in the process of creating a platform with which to access the internet from a handheld device.

They needed something to distinguish their 'i mode' messaging system from everyone else's, and Kurita believed he had the answer. Kurita was obsessed with weather forecasts. A cloud symbol is instantaneously understood by everyone, yet it is actually shorthand for an immensely complex meteorological process unfolding over hours.

The point was not the simplicity of the image, but the fact we accept it as a shorthand for something we know to be far more complex. We do not care that at three o'clock it will be slightly cloudier than at two o'clock, we simply want to know it will be cloudy.

The detail does not matter. It is too much information. We want a shorthand code for the day's overall weather that is easily deliverable.

Kurita then became fascinated by the way manga cartoons had taken stock symbols and used them to express emotions. We might not be interested that a cloud gets darker or lighter throughout the day, but if we are reading a graphic novel, we are interested in the nuance of a character's emotional state and development. The nuance is relevant.

How could a character simultaneously feeling anger, desire and euphoria, have these contradictory, conflicting emotions described by a single icon – a version of the cloud?

Manga cartoons had unwittingly invented the emoji. They distilled the essence of the human condition into a single graphic icon just as the Ming vase conveyed complex messages in a glazed brushstroke, or the curve of a swallow's tail, five centuries before.

The very first emojis created by Kurita were 172 12-pixel by 12-pixel images based on Japan's *kaomoji* – 'face letter' – culture. They look very different from the ones we use today – a version of a smile, a version of sad, annoyed and surprised.

But they are unmistakably emojis, and they derive not simply from a light-bulb moment by Kurita in 1998, but from a deeply, profoundly held Eastern mindset: that any degree of complexity of human life can be distilled and simplified into a language, a set of icons, decipherable to all if everyone understands and follow the rules.

When an unidentified man stood before a tank in Tiananmen Square in 1989, he was breaking the rules in a way immediately identifiable to a Western TV audience of billions. What appeared to be the end of communism was in fact the birth of a new China, built on foundations laid five centuries before.

CHAPTER FIFTEEN
NOW: THE NEW WORLD

CAMDEN: THE END OF THE EARTH AND THE BEGINNING OF TOMORROW

Camden in New Jersey is the most violent city in America. Avenues of once-prosperous housing are boarded and chained up with the same municipal stamp on the door telling drug dealers this is a 'monitored property'. Gardens are piled high with broken twentieth-century goods: refrigerators, TVs, sewing machines, tyres. I have to swerve my car to avoid a sofa sitting proudly in the middle of the road. Buicks and Cadillacs, once driven by businessmen, now stand tyre-less on bricks in alleyways with makeshift curtains across the windscreen. A place to doss for the night.

Camden's once-great factories producing machine goods and textiles lie derelict, needles and wraps for drugs strewn on the floor. Prostitutes stand bored on street corners, dealers cruise in huge blacked-out Escalades, men high on crack ride children's bikes, cavorting wildly across the road screaming and shouting.

Camden is like a post-apocalyptic movie, and yet it is also one of the most optimistic and life-enhancing places I have ever visited in America. Because Camden is not solely the most violent city in America, it is also the city with one of the fastest growing numbers of start-up companies. On the surface, Camden looks over, but behind this facade, it is alive.

Paul is a big Texan with a broad smile and an infectious laugh. He moved thousands of miles from the deep South to Camden because he saw it not as a catastrophe, but as an opportunity on the map. Paul had plans to start a handmade printing press and identified Camden as the ideal spot.

He took over a disused car body repair shop. Paul now employs thirty local people with plans to expand into the derelict back-yard due to a two-year backlog of orders.

Joe is one of the locals Paul employs. A giant of a man – liter-ally twice my size – Joe turns out sixty or seventy T-shirts a day for everyone from local pizzerias and colleges to record labels, skate-wear shops and boutique fashion brands, with orders coming from across the world. 'People like the handmade qual-ity, people even come in to see how we do it. We've spotted a gap in the market and it's booming.'

Joe grew up in Camden in the 1970s and 1980s and remem-bers it as a thriving and prosperous town to which people aspired to move. 'People would come to the waterfront on Sunday after-noons and dress up and promenade. This was a place people dreamt about moving to!' he says, laughing.

A huge shipyard and countless factories, including Campbell's Soup, provided employment for tens of thousands. Then, Paul says, two things happened: 'globalisation and the bridge'. Of course, companies took advantage of the new globalised labour market and relocated to cheaper territories in South America and the Far East. But the killer, Paul says, was the bridge across the Delaware River to Philadelphia.

Overnight, those promenading customers using local cafés, restaurants and hotels were gone. Philadelphia offered bigger department stores and suddenly provided manufacturing with a cheaper, faster route to market. Philadelphia could undercut Camden and suddenly Camden's ability to trade with the world was chopped off at the knees.

It is the story of twenty-first-century America. Once indestructible brands holding up the economies of entire cities from
Camden to Portland and New Orleans collapsed overnight. The
huge bales of copper wiring and tungsten steel that stood in
factories waiting to be turned into gleaming finished goods for
foreign markets were exchanged for tumbleweed, blowing across
empty factory floors.

This is the America that logically voted Trump – a nation that
increasingly looks like a nation on its way out and reminds me of
another time and another place.

In the late 1980s, I travelled to both the US and to communist
Eastern Europe for the first time. America seemed impossibly
exciting in those days: the bright shining future pulling itself out
of recession.

In Poland and the Soviet Union, by contrast, you could sense
it was over. The lights were on half power at night, casting a
sickly, yellow glow over the cities. The people were demoralised.
Even the police did not bother to check anyone's papers. They
knew the game was up.

Now the US is starting to feel like those communist countries
once did: a crumbling infrastructure, a sense of disillusionment
with the political 'elite', and streets populated by the homeless
and mentally ill, whom no one can afford to look after. Trump
promised to make America great again, but in Camden, there
are people on the ground already doing it for themselves.

In America's most violent city, there is a miracle going on.
Camden's very destitution has been seized on by hundreds of
entrepreneurs who have flocked there to start businesses. Down
the road from Paul's printing press is a tech start-up, a shoe
business and a whisky distillery run by two twenty-three-year-
olds from New York. They have orders from across the world
and part of their brand is that they are proud to come from
Camden.

In 2013, Paymon Rouhanifard, a one-time financial analyst
on Wall Street, was appointed to turn around Camden's schools.

In 2016, they returned a surprising upswing in results. Poverty, he says, underscores everything they try to achieve, but the schools are now in turnaround and, most importantly, kids are turning up in the morning.

Joe, who works for Paul at the printing press, says that if he was not working there he would 'one hundred per cent' be selling drugs, and after a couple of years of that 'probably dead'.

'A kid can earn two hundred bucks a day on the street and what could I earn on minimum wage – fifty? Sixty? What are you going to choose when that legitimately earned money can't feed a family? Those kids selling drugs are putting their lives at risk, but they're smart. They know how to turn cocaine into crack. That makes them chemists. They need to put those skills to something legal. They're also the sharpest business people on this street because they've survived and grown their business. That skill needs to be channelled properly.'

Beneath the crumbling city is a real community. The kind of community that has disappeared from once-destitute areas that have become revitalised and then gentrified thanks to outliers like Paul.

In Brooklyn, in East Berlin and in East London, the life that was breathed back by artists and young alternative businesses, seizing an opportunity to work somewhere cheap, was snuffed out once a tipping point was crossed from 'actually dangerous' to 'fashionably edgy'. It happens time and time again.

Serious money arrives with its tinted-glass cars and gentrified gates, and the shutters on a genuinely connected community come down. This is not inverted snobbery, it is purely the way it is. Camden does not yet have the luxury of turning away the well-to-do who want to live somewhere edgy. They still have community, because the community needs to work to survive for now.

People call out to each other across the street to ask how they are; young and old neighbours who have known each other for decades look out for each other, and protect their community from petty crime such as burglary as best they can. In spite of the crime, they get on with it. The place feels alive and loved, not killed by new money.

The new entrepreneurs in Camden sense the value of what they are joining. They do not see themselves on a mercy mission, but proud of what Camden is.

As Paul explains, 'We feel like we are re-inhabiting what lost empire has deserted. I could come here and start any business. It's not what I do that even matters, it's the place we are investing it. I think the people who have come here – sure they have come here because of cheap rents, but the difference is they see what the place has – its incredible vibrancy and community – and they want to stay and be part of it.'

Camden's new business outliers reminded me of what Tom Peters, the man who remade the workplace with his vision of self-determined work back in the late 1970s, told me when we met in Boston. 'Whoever you are, however safe you think your job is, and well-insulated your future looks, forget it. It's over.'

Reading this, you might think Camden has little to do with your town or your job – but you would be wrong. Camden is not an interesting, picaresque diversion into underclass America, it is a warning to everyone. This is what the world is fast becoming. Everywhere.

The old certainties – the mental factory you travel to every day in your mind – is about to shut down. The town, suburb or village you live in might not end up looking like Camden, but the same economic principles apply. Prepare yourself for change and get the right mindset to deal with it.

Walking down the battered streets of Camden, New Jersey, is no different from walking down the High Street in Camden, London. It is no different from the street markets in Nairobi, the sprawling food stalls in Sao Paulo or Bogota, or impromptu markets that spring up anywhere in the world where there is a dusty road and people to sell to. Each delivers the same epiphany of hope and energy.

I mentioned this to Tom Peters and he exploded with enthusiasm. 'Yes! Precisely! Exactly!'

To me, I said to Tom, if you walk down any street anywhere in the world, what do you see? You see people who have had an idea. They have taken that stupid, crazy notion to run a shop selling coffee, old furniture, umbrellas, psychotherapy, carrots or dry cleaning, and turned it into a reality.

After a year, two years, five years, that business has either gone under or thrived. The people have either made a go of it or they have moved on to another stupid, crazy idea that has either thrived or gone bust.

To look at a high street is to see human endeavour and capitalism at its purest. The high street is a rolling conveyor belt of human beings forever striving, each with their own individual epiphany made real through business. And the busker is the ultimate exemplar of this spirit: without shame, selling their talent by putting it out there.

No matter what governments or corporations or tech companies attempt to do to control or monetise the human condition, this is the one thing that remains beyond the ambit of their control: the primal, human engine of the mind, pumping out ideas. We as humans cannot help it: we see an opportunity and go for it.

THE RETURNABLE ROCKET

On 30 March 2017, I was standing in Peter Thiel's office in San Francisco when something happened. Elon Musk's SpaceX, looking to land the first rocket on Mars, and in which Thiel and his partner Jack Selby have invested 'significantly', flashed up on the news.

After five years of relentless testing and retesting, the SpaceX Falcon 9's rocket had taken off hours earlier from Cape Canaveral in Florida and successfully launched a communications satellite into orbit, before touching back down on a drone ship floating in the Atlantic Ocean.

It was an extraordinary moment and made me think that these tech billionaires may look like humble guys in T-shirts, but they are in the mould of the great, eccentric, visionary business leaders of the past: Howard Hughes with his flying boat and William Randolph Hearst with his castle fall of tigers and giraffes.

Musk appeared immediately on the company's live stream: '(This) means you can fly an orbital-class booster, which is the most expensive part of the rocket. This is going to be, ultimately, a huge revolution in spaceflight.'

Jack Selby smiled and chuckled to himself. I asked him what was so funny. 'That's not why this is so important. Of course, yes. A returnable rocket, colonisation of space eventually and saving Earth, sure.' But? 'But the reason this is important is because of what space is really a platform for.'

Which is? 'How do you get the internet on your phone?' I turn on my phone. 'And how does it get to your phone?' Via a satellite signal, so what's your point? 'Exactly. And how quickly does that happen?' It depends where I am. 'Precisely.'

The returnable rocket Elon Musk landed on a postage stamp in the middle of the Atlantic Ocean is going to change the world, but the most immediate way is also the least immediately apparent.

By owning space, you own the platform for beaming the internet directly back to Earth without the time lag. Internet access currently depends on satellites, but the 'latency' – the time it takes receiving a request and responding – limits everything.

It is not only impractical for the ocean of real-time applications: everything from online gaming to live streaming and teleconferencing, such as Skype or Face Time, it puts the brakes on the realisation of the 'Internet of Things'. The inter-connectedness of everything we do and use.

For five years, Musk had been in a race with Greg Wyle, founder of OneWeb, backed by Richard Branson's Virgin Galactic. But Musk was backed by another player: Google.

High-speed satellite internet connection changes everything. Speed will no longer be measured by an evolution of G's – from 4G to 5G to 6G – with success defined by incrementally less buffering time. It will mean you will be able to stream anything immediately. Boom. Like that.

Google have invested in SpaceX, but Google will no longer call the shots on the internet. Elon Musk will. Oh, and his friend Jack Selby, smiling in the corner. They will not simply be the new Verizon or Comcast, they will control internet access to Mars and the Moon when SpaceX's returnable rockets ferry people back and forth from Earth, having colonised them, too.

In the immediate future, the returnable rocket changes life on Earth for one very simple reason. It will allow low-orbit satellites, approximately 100 miles above the planet, to do the job satellites currently do with a fraction of the lag. In 2015, *Wired* calculated the increased internet speed from low-orbit satellites and estimated they would cut a 500-millisecond lag to 20 milliseconds: the same speed of delivery as a fibre-optic, home internet connection now. No wonder Jack Selby kicked back in his chair that day and slicked back his hair.

THE GIANT LEAP-FROG

The immediate beneficiary will not necessarily be Wall Street, but places like Camden. Instantaneous internet connection from space suddenly eradicates the need for terrestrial infrastructure: so where that infrastructure has collapsed, or was never there to begin with, there will no longer be a problem.

Time and time again, tech entrepreneurs have told me that the greatest hindrance to their coming revolution is the outdated twentieth-century infrastructure they have to deal with. If all this was gone, they say, we could have singularity and the Internet of Things in a heartbeat.

Decrepit roads and run-down transport networks, crumbling buildings and public amenities, pre-internet laws and regulations governing how things should be moved in the internet age, how people should be employed in the internet age, how the internet itself should operate in the internet age. These laws and rules, they say, were invented for a different industrial revolution.

Look at the world waiting to have the go button pressed: drone deliveries, driverless cars, flying cars, global climate recalibration, space habitation, pre-fab 3-D printed houses; fake clouds and orbiting solar panels to save the Earth.

Then there is the stuff on the ground and in the body: MedTech and gene editing, EdTech and the school in a box, the robot/human interface, work surveillance, bio-policing of the body, vertical farming, predictive policing and pre-crime arrests, iPhone technology now possible on a contact lens.

Not to mention Elon Musk's other pet project: the 'hyper loop' – a frictionless pod levitating at 800 miles per hour inside a giant metal tube – a 'cross between Concorde, a rail gun and an air-hockey table' – taking you from London to Edinburgh or LA to San Francisco in thirty minutes. These are the myriad facets of singularity waiting for the lawyers to catch up.

This revolution, they say, is being held up by vested interests tied into protecting an outdated infrastructure from being dismantled. Politicians and bureaucrats holding on to what little legislative and bureaucratic power they still have left.

But once the internet is beamed from space, physical and legal obstacles on Earth to these transformations melt away. And places like Camden could be in poll position to take advantage fastest.

This is the twenty-first-century twist of fate. The cities that built a deep, complex infrastructure for the first industrial revolution and then extracted further power and resources for themselves in the late twentieth century by allowing places like Camden to fall prey to globalisation, are now going to get their comeuppance.

Once London and Paris and Nairobi and Shanghai and New York could suck the life from the hinterland around them, but there was a price to pay: they saddled themselves with an unwieldy infrastructure. They believed themselves indispensable and all-powerful. But then the twenty-first century happened.

The tech revolution and the internet from space offers a new paradigm. The very places where the infrastructure was either wiped out or never happened – rural Malawi, rural Wales, the rust belt of the American Midwest, the Australian outback – suddenly have the advantage. In one technological jump, they can leap-frog the twentieth-century mega-cities held back by cumbersome twentieth-century infrastructure and complacent twentieth-century thinking.

One word will enable a company, an individual, a city, to survive this coming revolution: adaptability. The obstacles preventing adaptation are not simply physical, but mental. The enemy is not robots or the tech companies, immigrants or the Chinese, it is complacency and the sense that you either do not need to change because you are safe from change, or cannot change because you don't know how.

To anyone saddled by this thinking, Camden is not the past, it is the future, and with a lesson for all of us.

WE ARE ALL BUSKERS NOW

As night fell on a street corner, a busker played a smashed guitar fixed up with gaffer tape, banging the splintered wood with a lollipop to create his own rhythm section.

Buskers were once outsiders. We would walk past and try to work out their story. Were they a genius musician who never got the breaks? A loser with nothing better to do than beg for money? Was this a lifestyle choice: to stay outside society's rules by deciding they would do their own thing?

Suddenly society stopped having rules. Jobs were no longer for life. Savings could disappear in a blink. The whole economy could go belly up in an instant if banks bet the wrong way. Hard work and diligence were not enough. The busker stopped looking like an outsider and started to look like an entrepreneur.

We all need to be buskers now. Using what talent and guile we have to forge a life. The world the busker looks out on is not a bleak, post-industrial landscape of disappointment, but a prairie of continuous hope onto which he walks out each day and gives it a go.

That busker in Camden is my role model. Here is a man in the most violent city in America prepared to stand on a street corner as night falls, tune his guitar and begin to go to work.

NOTES ON SOURCES

1. CASH: WHO IS KILLING IT AND WHY

1 UK Payment Methods 2016 report, Payments Council, 20 May 2016: www.paymentsuk.org.uk/industry-information/annual-statistical-publications.
2 'Brother, can you spare a contactless payment? Homeless go hi-tech', IBTimes, 1 March 2017.
3 Bill Maurer, *How Would You Like to Pay? How Technology Is Changing the Future of Money*, Duke University Press, 2015.
4 eCorner.stanford.edu, 21 January 2004. Thiel and Levchin discuss their first meeting
5 Ibid.
6 Drazen's interview with MIT magazine *Spectrum*, Winter 1999. I interviewed Drazen for my 2014 BBC series *The Men Who Made Us Spend* (episode 3) in which he tells the story of the experiment in full.
7 Ashlee Vance, *Elon Musk: Tesla, Space X and the Quest for a Fantastic Future*, Ecco, 2015.
8 MIT *Spectrum*, Winter 1999.
9 'Credit Card Debt: Average US Household Owes $16,000', *Time* magazine, 20 December 2016.
10 For a full account of how debt window-dresses the figures on growth, see interview with Matt Whittaker, Resolution Foundation in my series *The Super-Rich and Us*, BBC, 2015.
11 eBay media centre, 8 September 2014.
12 Interview with Benjamin Barber in *The Men Who Made Us Spend* (episode 3), BBC, 2014.
13 'Customer Data: Designing for Transparency and Trust', *Harvard Business Review*, May 2015.
14 Steve Jobs introduces the App Store – iPhone Software Roadmap Event, 2008.
15 'Banks Did It Apple's Way in Payments by Mobile', *New York Times*, 11 September 2014.
16 Bill Maurer, *How Would You Like to Pay?*

17 Kenneth Rogoff, *The Curse of Cash*, Princeton Press, 2016.
18 'How Big Is the Black Market?' Freakanomics.com, 25 June 2012.
19 'Drug Money Saved Banks in Global Crisis, Claims UN Advisor', *Guardian*, 12 December 2009.
20 'The Defence Advanced Research Projects Agency (DARPA) awards $1.8 million contract to research block chain for military security', *Quartz* magazine.

2. RISK: HOW CHAOS CAME TO WALL STREET

1 There are many accounts of Bouazizi's death, but the most detailed are in 'The Real Mohamed Bouazizi', *Foreign Policy*, 16 December 2011, which pieced events together one year on, and 'How A Man Setting Fire To Himself Sparked An Uprising in Tunisia', *Guardian*, 28 December 2010, for a report in the immediate aftermath.
2 'The Tragic Life of a Street Vendor', Al Jazeera, 20 January 2011. Yasmine Ryan's investigation discovered that Hamdi was subsequently dismissed.
3 This specific quote has been widely repeated in reports of Bouazizi's death. In the myth-making of the Arab Spring that followed his suicide, Bouazizi was alleged to have also threatened the officials with setting himself alight.
4 Professor Jane Harrigan, *The Political Economy of Arab Food Sovereignty*, Palgrave Macmillan, 2014.
5 'Not A Game: Speculation Versus Food Security', Oxfam report on financialised food markets, 3 October 2011.
6 *Fat Land* by Greg Critser, Houghton Mifflin, 2004, on the back story of the power wielded by the farming lobby and corn producers in 1970s American politics.
7 Professor Jane Harrigan's inaugural lecture at SOAS, 28 April 2011: 'Did Food Prices Plant the Seeds of the Arab Spring?' puts the rise in wheat prices in the wider context of the fragile food system of North Africa.
8 Professor Rami Zurayk, 'Use Your Loaf: Why Food Prices Were Crucial in the Arab Spring', *Guardian*, 16 July 2011.
9 Ibid.
10 Interview with Robert Dall in *The Super-Rich and Us*, BBC, 2015.
11 Ibid.
12 *Der Speigel*, 8 February 2010; 'Greek Debt Crisis: How Goldman Sachs Helped Greece to Mask Its True Debt', *Independent*, 10 July 2010, on the plan to sue Goldman Sachs for massaging Greece's accounts; and BBC News, 20 February 2012, with an account on the history.
13 Michael Sandel, *What Money Can't Buy: The Moral Limits of Markets*, US Macmillan, 2012, for the context of viaticals and the 'deaths futures' market.
14 'Physician pleads guilty in massive securities fraud', *Orlando Sentinel*, 28 December 2006.
15 US District Court notes: Southern District of Florida. Case no. 04-60573–CIV–Moreno/Simonton.

16 'The subprime mortgage is back. It's 2008 all over again': Tyler Durden article for Zerohedge.com, 15 June 2016.

17 Ibid.

18 'Chinese Shadow Banking', *Financial Times*, 29 April 2016.

19 'China: The power behind the $700 billion bailout', *Wall Street Journal*, 10 December 2008.

20 William Pesek, Barrons.com, 6 July 2016.

21 *Financial Times*, 29 April 2016.

22 George Monbiot, *Guardian*, 25 March 2015.

23 Ibid.

24 'Why Trading Water Futures Could Be in Our Future', CNBC, 2 July 2014.

25 Ibid.

26 'California drought spurs protest over "unconscionable" bottled water business', *Guardian*, 19 April 2015.

27 'Forest Service: Expired Nestlé Water Permit a Priority', *Desert Sun*, 11 April 2015.

28 'A 280,000% mark up for water. A look inside the bottled water industry', Zerohedge.com, 29 July 2013.

29 'California water prices set to rise next year: Finch', Reuters, 18 August 2015.

30 CNBC, 2 July 2014.

31 'The Anthropocene Epoch: scientists declare dawn of human-influenced age', *Guardian*, 29 August 2016.

32 Ibid.

33 Ibid.

3. TAX: WHY EVERYWHERE WANTS TO BE THE CAYMAN ISLANDS

1 'Panama Papers: 11.5 million files from Panama-based law firm shed light on murky offshore money and transactions', CBC News, 4 April 2016.

2 *Britain's Trillion Pound Island – Inside Cayman*, BBC, 2015.

3 Richard Stott, *Daily Mirror* archive.

4 For a full account of Rossminster: Nigel Tutt, *The Tax Raiders: The Rossminster Affair*, Financial Training Publications, 1985.

5 'Taxman', George Harrison, © 1966, 1967 Northern Songs Ltd.

6 *The Super-Rich and Us*, BBC, 2014: Ex-tax inspector Richard Brooks gives a detailed account of Rossminster's business practices.

7 Jan Fichtner, *The Anatomy of the Cayman Islands Offshore Financial Center: Anglo-America, Japan, and the Role of Hedge Funds*, Amsterdam Institute for Social Science Research, University of Amsterdam, 2016.

8 Nicholas Shaxson, *Treasure Islands: Tax Havens and the Men Who Stole the World*, Bodley Head, 2011, gives a full account of George Bolton and the key role of the eurodollar in the offshore story.

9 Ibid.

10 *The Super-Rich and Us*, BBC, 2014: my interview with Arthur Laffer.

11 Ibid., interview with Richard Brooks.

12 Richard Brooks, *The Great Tax Robbery*, Oneworld, 2014: A full account of

Brooks's investigation into the tax system.

13 Jan Fichtner, *Anatomy of Offshore*, University of Amsterdam, 2016.

14 Ibid.

15 Financialsecrecyindex.com, Review, 2015.

16 *Britain's Trillion Pound Island – Inside Cayman*, BBC, 2015.

17 Jan Fichtner, *Anatomy of Offshore*, University of Amsterdam, 2016.

18 *Britain's Trillion Pound Island – Inside Cayman*, BBC, 2015.

4. WEALTH: INEQUALITY AS A BUSINESS OPPORTUNITY

1 Melanie Kramers, 'Eight people own same wealth as half the world', Oxfam pre-Davos report, 16 January 2017.

2 'Never Mind the Gap: Why We Shouldn't Worry About Inequality', Institute of Economic Affairs, 23 May 2016.

3 Arnold Schwarzenegger, 'I Don't Give a Damn' (about climate change deniers), Fortune.com, 8 December 2015.

4 'Revisiting Plutonomy: The Rich Getting Richer', Citigroup Equity Strategy, 5 March 2006.

5 Thomas Piketty interviewed in *The Super-Rich and Us*, BBC, 2015.

6 'Mothers campaign group to leave Newham flats', BBC News, 2 October 2014.

7 Robin Wales of Newham Council subsequently apologised: 'I apologise to the Focus E15 families but this is a London housing crisis', *Guardian*, 6 October 2014.

8 Friedrich Engels, *The Condition of the Working Class in England*, published by Otto Wigand, 1845.

9 Mike Davis, *Planet of Slums*, Verso, 2006.

10 ONS statistics quoted in *The Super-Rich and Us*, BBC, 2015.

11 Ibid.

12 Ibid.

13 Robert Frank, *Richistan: A Journey Through the American Wealth Boom and the Lives of the New Rich*, Crown, 2007, gives a detailed description of this sealed-off world.

14 NASA's Goddard Space Center and the US National Science Foundation modelling inequality research project, March 2014.

15 'Monitoring Poverty and Social Exclusion', Joseph Rowntree Foundation and New Policy Institute, 2015.

16 Richard Baldwin, *The Great Convergence*, Harvard Press, November 2016.

17 David Graeber interviewed in *The Super-Rich and Us*, BBC, 2015.

18 Simon Jenkins, 'We should cash-bomb the people not banks', *Guardian*, 26 November 2014.

19 David Graeber, *Debt: The First 5000 Years*, Melville House Publishing, 2013. For the historical context to the ideas outlined by Graeber in *The Super Rich and Us*, BBC, 2015.

20 Thomas Piketty in *The Super-Rich and Us*, BBC, 2015.

21 Zoe Williams, 'Housing: are we reaching a tipping point?', *Guardian*, 29 March

2015.

22 Nick Hanuer interviewed in *The Super-Rich and Us*, BBC, 2015.

23 The DCDC Global Strategic Trends Programme 2007–2036, 23 January 2007.

24 *Weekend World*, LWT, 12 p.m., 6 January 1980. A transcript of the whole programme can be found on the Margaret Thatcher Foundation website.

25 Nick Hanuer, op. cit.

26 For a full account of trickle-down and the Laffer Curve from a Keynesian perspective: Ha-Joon Chang, *Twenty-Three Things They Don't Tell You About Capitalism*, Penguin, 2010.

27 DCDC Report, 23 January 2007.

28 Edmund Burke's letter to Charles Fox, 8 October 1777.

5. FOOD: OWNING FAT AND THIN

Notes taken from: Jacques Peretti, 'Fat profits: how the food industry cashed in on obesity', *Guardian*, 7 August 2013; Jacques Peretti, 'Why our food is making us fat', *Guardian*, 11 June 2012.

1 Newarke Houses Museum: http://www.leicester.gov.uk/your-council-services/lc/leicester-city-museums/museums/newarkehouses/.

2 Daniel Lambert: http://www.bbc.co.uk/leicester/content/articles/2009/06/23/daniel_lambert_feature.shtml.

3 Obesity rates: http://www.telegraph.co.uk/health/healthnews/7307756/obesity-rates-20-per-cent-higher-now-than-in-the-1960s.html.

4 Greg Critser, *Fat Land: How Americans Became the Fattest People in the World*, Houghton Mifflin Harcourt, 2003.

5 John Yudkin, *Pure, White and Deadly*, Viking, 1986.

6 Professor Philip James: http://www.iaso.org/about-iaso/iasomanagement/experts/wptjames/.

7 Redux: http://en.wikipedia.org/wiki/fenfluramine/phentermine.

6. DRUGS: THE MEDICATION OF MODERN LIFE

1 Centers For Disease Control and Prevention (CDC), Therapeutic drug use US overview, 19 January 2017.

2 'The Hispanic Paradox', *Lancet*, 16 May 2015.

3 For a full account of Gadsen's interview and its ramifications: Ray Moynihan and Alan Cassels, *Selling Sickness: How the World's Biggest Pharmaceutical Companies Are Turning Us All into Patients*, Douglas & McIntyre, 2006.

4 *Daily Telegraph*, 16 December 2016.

5 Ray Moynihan and Alan Cassels, *Selling Sickness*, op. cit.

6 R.D. Laing, *The Divided Self: An Existential Study in Sanity and Madness*,

Harmondsworth Penguin, 1960.

7 Philip K. Dick, *A Scanner Darkly*, Granada, 1978.

8 Howard Markel, 'Patents, Profits and the American People: The Bayh-Dole Act of 1980', *New England Journal of Medicine*, 29 August 2013.

9 John Abramson, *Overdosed America: The Broken Promise of American Medicine*, HarperCollins, 2004.

10 Ibid.

11 Peter Rost, *The Whistle Blower: Confessions of A Healthcare Hitman*, Soft Skull Press, 2006.

12 Vince Parry, 'The Art of Branding a Condition', *Medical Marketing & Media*, Vol. 38, Issue 5, May 2003.

13 'Why your workplace wellness program isn't working', *Business Journal*, 13 May 2014.

14 '80% of American adults don't get recommended exercise', CBS News, 3 May 2013.

15 'Quantified self: self-knowledge through numbers': quantifiedself.com.

16 'Could brain altering nootropic drugs make you smarter?' ABC 7, 16 November 2016.

17 'Facebook blocks Admiral from using profiles to price car insurance', *Daily Telegraph*, 2 November 2016.

18 US Health Insurance Cover – CDC FastStats: www.cdc.gov.

19 Vince Parry, 'The Art of Branding a Condition', op. cit.

20 David Healy, *Let Them Eat Prozac: The Unhealthy Relationship Between the Pharmaceutical Industry and Depression*, NYU Press, 2006.

21 Data and Statistics: ADHD – CDC FastStats: www.cdc.gov.

22 David Rosenhan, On Being Sane in Insane Places', *Science*, 19 January 1973.

23 Robert Spitzer obituary, *New York Times*, 26 December 2015.

24 Allen Frances, *Saving Normal: An Insider's Revolt Against Out-of-Control Psychiatric Diagnosis, DSM 5, Big Pharma, and the Medicalization of Ordinary Life*, William Morrow, 2014.

25 Ibid.

26 Moynihan, Cooke, Doust, Bero, Hill, Glasziou, 'Expanding Disease Definitions in Guidelines and Expert Panel Ties to Industry: A Cross-sectional Study of Common Conditions in the US', *PLOS Medicine*, 7 February 2013.

27 Erin White, 'Behind the Boomer Coalition: A Heart Message from Pfizer', *Wall Street Journal*, 10 March 2004.

28 Howard Wolinsky, 'Disease Mongering and Drug Marketing', EMBO report: www.ncbi.nlm.nih.gov.

29 Barbara Ehrenreich, *Smile or Die: How Positive Thinking Fooled America and the World*, Granta, 2010.

7. WORK: FROM WHAT WE DO TO WHO WE ARE

1 Dr Nerina Ramlakhan, 'Tech-free bedroom for a peaceful sleep', Silentnight/ Ofcom 2014, 5 March 2015.

2 'Cellphones can damage romantic relationships, lead to depression', Baylor Study, 29 September 2015.
3 Dr Nerina Ramlakhan, op. cit.
4 Daniel Nelson, ed., *A Mental Revolution: Scientific Management Since Taylor*, Ohio State University Press, 1992.
5 Matthew Stewart, *The Management Myth: Why the Experts Keep Getting It Wrong*, W.W. Norton & Company, 2009.
6 Frederick Winslow Taylor, *The Principles of Scientific Management*, Harper and Brothers, 1911.
7 'Guru: Frederick Winslow Taylor', *The Economist*, 6 February 2009.
8 Joseph Raynus, *Improving Business Process Performance*, Auerbach Publications, 2011.
9 Richard Sennett, *The Culture of the New Capitalism*, Yale University Press, 2007, is a superb overview of the development of the ideas underpinning corporate belief systems.
10 John Hayes, *The Theory and Practice of Change Management*, Palgrave MacMillan, 2014.
11 Tom Peters and Robert Waterman, *In Search of Excellence: Lessons from America's Best Run Companies*, Warner, 1984.
12 'Join the cult and give up any free time in your life', former recruitment coordinator for Airbnb in Dublin, Glassdoor App.
13 'The Impact of EU Enlargement on Migration Flows', Home Office Online Report, 3 March 2003.
14 Tom Peters, 'Tom Peters's True Confessions', *Fast Company*, 30 November 2001.
15 My interview with John Bennett in *Who's Spending Britain's Billions?*, BBC2, October 2016.
16 Rachael Orr, 'How to Close Great Britain's Great Divide: The Business of Tackling Inequality', Oxfam, September 2016.
17 'Uber CEO caught on video arguing with driver about fares', Bloomberg, March 2017.
18 Marc Levinson, *The Box: How the Shipping Container Made the World Smaller and the World Economy Bigger*, Princeton University Press, 2008, tells the story in forensic detail.
19 My interview with Steve Howard in *The Men Who Made Us Spend*, Ep. 1, BBC2, September 2014.

8. UPGRADE: ENGINEERING DISSATISFACTION

1 I visited Livermore fire station in 2014. For the full history, their website is 'Home of the World's Longest Burning Light Bulb': www.centennialbulb.org.
2 Cosima Dannoritzer's 2010 documentary *The Light Bulb Conspiracy* examines the evidence for planned obsolescence extensively, interviewing key protagonists.
3 'Does the UK have a problem with old sofas?' BBC News, 11 December 2015.
4 'Death of the Seven Year Itch: average relationship is now just 2 years 9 months', *Daily Mail*, 4 February 2014.

5 *The Light Bulb Conspiracy*, op. cit.

6 *The Men Who Made Us Spend*, Ep. 1, BBC2, September 2014.

7 Ibid.

8 'Smart Africa: smartphones pave way for huge opportunities', *Financial Times*, 26 January 2016.

9 Ibid.

10 Glenn Adamson, *Industrial Strength Design: How Brook Stevens Shaped Your World*, MIT Press, 2003.

11 Alfred P. Sloan Jr, *My Years with General Motors*, Bantam Doubleday Dell, originally published 1964, reprinted 1998.

12 *The Men Who Made Us Spend*, op. cit.

13 Ibid., Ep. 3.

14 Steve Jobs – iPhone Introduction, 9 January 2007, YouTube.com.

15 'Bottled air started as a joke. Now China can't get enough', Mashable, 12 May 2016.

16 Ibid.

17 Ibid.

18 Ian Sample, 'Body upgrades may be nearing reality, but only for the rich', *Guardian*, 5 September 2014.

9. POWER: THE FIRM WHO KNOW EVERYTHING

1 James Ledbetter, *Unwarranted Influence: Dwight D. Eisenhower and the Military-Industrial Complex*, Yale University Press, 2011, explains Eisenhower's speech in the context of an escalating Cold War.

2 James Ledbetter, 'What Ike Got Right', *New York Times*, 13 December 2010.

3 Ronald C. White, *American Ulysses*, Random House, 2016, is an exhaustive biography of the president including his early military career.

4 Barry Popik, 'Origin, Myth of the 'Lobbyist', RedState, 31 January 2010,' delves into the first historical references for the term.

5 'Powell Memorandum: Attack on American Free Enterprise System', Washington and Lee University School of Law: https://law2.wlu.edu/powellarchives/.

6 Confidential Memorandum, 'Attack on American Free Enterprise', 23 August 1971. To: Mr Eugene B. Sydnor, Chairman Education Committee, US Chamber of Commerce. From: Lewis F. Powell, PBS Supreme Court Primary Sources.

7 Lee Drutman, *The Business of America is Lobbying: How Corporations Became Politicized and Politics Became More Corporate (Studies in Postwar American Political Development)*, OUP USA, 2015.

8 Jane Mayer, *Dark Money: The Hidden History of the Billionaires Behind the Rise of the Radical Right*, Knopf Doubleday, 2016.

9 F.A. Hayek, *The Road to Serfdom*, Routledge, 1944.

10 Adam Smith, *The Wealth of Nations*, Penguin Classics, first published 1776.

11 *Come and See*, directed by Elen Klimov, Mosfilm/Belarusfilm, Soviet Union, 1985.

12 *The Business of America is Lobbying*, op. cit.
13 Malcolm Moore, 'Ancient Chinese "cheat sheets" discovered', *Daily Telegraph*, 15 July 2009.
14 Duff McDonald, *The Firm: The Story of McKinsey and its Secret Influence on American Business*, Simon & Schuster, 2014.
15 Ibid.
16 'War for Talent', the McKinsey survey: https://Invosights.wordpress.com.
17 *The Super-Rich and Us*, Ep. 2, BBC2, 2015.
18 'McKinsey's close relationship with Enron raises question of consultancy's liability', *Wall Street Journal*, 17 January 2002.
19 Ben Chu, 'McKinsey: How does it always get away with it?', *Independent*, 7 February 2014.
20 Ibid.
21 George Monbiot, 'The great free market experiment is more like a corporate welfare scheme', *Guardian*, 4 September 2007.
22 Ibid.
23 Allyson M. Pollock, *NHS plc: The Privatisation of Our Healthcare*, Verso, 2005.
24 Ibid.
25 *Who's Spending Britain's Billions?*, BBC2, 2016.
26 Ibid.
27 Ibid.
28 Harriet Agnew, Miles Johnson and Patrick Jenkins, 'Inside McKinsey's private hedge fund', *Financial Times*, 6 June 2016.
29 Ibid.
30 *Who's Spending Britain's Billions?*, op. cit.
31 Walter Kiechel, *The Lords of Strategy: The Secret Intellectual History of the New Corporate World*, Harvard Business School Press, 2010.
32 Josh Marshall, http://talkingpointsmemo.com, 11 April 2006.

10. BUSINESS: WHY CORPORATIONS TOOK OVER

1 For an excellent account of Abs and his early career: Harold James, *The Nazi Dictatorship and the Deutsche Bank*, Cambridge University Press, 2004.
2 Ibid.
3 Claire Provost and Matt Kennard, 'The obscure legal system that lets corporations sue countries', *Guardian*, 10 June 2015.
4 Antonio Parra, *The History Of ICSID*, OUP Oxford, 2012.
5 Provost and Kennard, 'The obscure legal system', op. cit.
6 'Investor-State Dispute Settlement: The Arbitration Game', *The Economist*, 11 October 2014.
7 'The obscure legal system', op. cit.
8 Ibid.
9 Ibid.
10 Kathleen Chaykowski, 'Mark Zuckerberg's Manifesto is Facebook's State of the Union', *Forbes*, 16 February 2017.
11 *Who's Spending Britain's Billions?*, BBC2, October 2016.

12 Tamasin Cave and Andy Rowell, *A Quiet Word: Lobbying, Crony Capitalism and Broken Politics in Britain*, Bodley Head, 2014.

13 Tamasin Cave and Andy Rowell, 'The truth about lobbying: ten ways big business controls government', *Guardian*, 12 March 2014.

14 Business Insider report on Oxfam infographic, 'These ten companies control everything you buy', 28 September 2016.

15 Fred Siegel, *The Revolt Against the Masses: How Liberalism Has Undermined the Middle Class*, Encounter Books, 2014.

16 John Carey, *The Intellectuals and the Masses: Pride and Prejudice Among the Literary Intelligentsia, 1880–1939*, Faber & Faber, 1992.

17 'FBI breaks into San Bernardino gunman's iPhone without Apple's help, ending case', Fox News, 29 March 2016.

18 'Tim Cook says Apple's refusal to unlock iPhone for FBI is a "Civil Liberties" Issue', *Guardian*, 22 February 2016.

19 Thomas Mann, *The Magic Mountain*, Secker & Warburg, 1945.

20 'Unilever boss Paul Polman slams capitalist obsession with profit', *Daily Telegraph*, 28 January 2015.

21 Marion Nestle, 'Pepsi to reduce sugar in its drinks? Really?', FoodPolitics.com, 18 October 2016.

22 Alex Berenson, *The Number: How the Drive for Quarterly Earnings Corrupted Wall Street and Corporate America*, Random House, 2004.

23 Jason Trennert, 'Remembering the Reagan Bull Market', *Wall Street Journal*, 13 August 2009: www.jasontrennert.com.

11. NEWS: WHY THE FACTS DISAPPEARED

1 Dan M. Kahan, Ellen Peters, Erica Cantrell Dawson and Paul Slovic, 'Motivated Numeracy and Enlightened Self-Government', Yale Law School, Cultural Cognition Project Working Paper No. 116, 8 September 2013.

2 'The New World: Nothing but the Truth', BBC Radio 4, 2 January 2017.

3 'Four more years attributed to Rove's strategy', *Washington Post*, 7 November 2004.

4 'How Jared Kushner won Trump the White House', *Forbes*, 22 November 2016.

5 Brendan Nyhan et al., 'When Corrections Fail: The Persistence of Political Misrepresentations', Dartmouth.edu, cited in: Brendan Nyhan and Jason Riefler, 'Misinformation and Fact-Checking', Media Policy Initiative Research Paper, New America Foundation, February 2012.

6 'The New World: Nothing but the Truth', op. cit.

7 Rosser Reeves, *Reality in Advertising*, Widener Classics, originally published in 1961.

8 'Smoke Gets in Your Eyes', written by Matthew Weiner, *Mad Men*, season 1, episode 1, 2007.

9 *The Men Who Made Us Spend*, Ep. 2, BBC2, September 2014.

10 Ibid.

11 Ibid.

12 Ibid.

13 Ibid.

14 'Pictures raise news issue', *New York Times*, 23 January 1987.
15 *Honest Man: The Life of R. Budd Dwyer*, directed by James Dirschberger, Eighty Four Films, 2010.
16 Catherine Taibi, 'Biggest media screw-ups of 2013', Huffington Post, 23 January 2014.
17 John Ioannidis, 'Why most published research findings are false', PLoS Med 2 (8) e124.doi: 10. 137/journal.pmed 0020124, 30 August 2005.
18 Richard Smith, 'Time for science to be about truth rather than careers', *BMJ*, 9 September 2013.
19 Ibid.
20 Ibid.
21 'Beyond Distrust: How Americans View Their Government: 1958–2015', Pew Research Centre, 23 November 2015.
22 James Curran and Jean Seaton, *Power Without Responsibility*, Routledge, 2003.
23 David McKie, 'Rupert Murdoch is not the first press baron with a thirst for power', *Guardian*, 14 July 2011.
24 Ibid.
25 Peter Jackson and Tom de Castella, 'Clash of the Press Titans', BBC News, 14 July 2011.
26 *Outfoxed: Rupert Murdoch's War on Journalism*, directed by Robert Greenwald, MoveOn.org/Ryko Distribution, 2004.
27 Ibid.
28 Ibid.
29 *Loose Change 9/11: An American Coup*, directed by Dylan Avery, distributed by Microcinema International, 2005.

12. ROBOTS: THE HUMAN MACHINES

1 Alan Turing, 'Computer Machinery and Intelligence', University of Manchester, 1950, and Jack Copeland, *The Essential Turing: The Ideas That Gave Birth to the Computer Age*, Oxford University Press, 2004.
2 Ibid.
3 'Computer AI passes Turing Test in "world first"', BBC News, 9 June 2014.
4 'Eugene the Turing Test-beating "human computer" in his own words', *Guardian*, 9 June 2014.
5 John Markoff, 'Computer wins on *Jeopardy!* Trivial, it's not, *New York Times*, 16 February 2011.
6 Stephen Baker, *Final Jeopardy: Man vs. Machine and the Quest to Know Everything*, Houghton Miffin, 2011.
7 Ibid.
8 Elizabeth Kolbert, 'Our Automated Future', *New Yorker*, 19 December 2016.
9 Ibid.
10 Ibid.
11 'Japanese insurance firm replaces 34 staff with AI', BBC News, 5 January 2017.
12 'Safe human robot interaction with industrial and service robots', Eurobotics Forum, 6 March 2012.
13 Carl Benedikt Frey and Michael A. Osborne, 'The future of employment: How

susceptible are jobs to computerisation?', Oxford Martin School, University of Oxford, 17 September 2013.

14 'Our Automated Future', op. cit.

15 Martin Ford, *The Rise of The Robots: Technology and the Threat of Mass Unemployment*, Oneworld Publications, 2016.

16 'Artificial Intelligence, Automation and the Economy', Executive Office of the President of the United States, Washington DC 20502, 20 December 2016.

17 Daron Acemoglu and Pascual Restrepo, 'The Race Between Machine and Man: Implications of Technology for Growth, Factor Shares and Employment', MIT, 2016.

18 Sugata Mitra, 'The Hole in the Wall Project and the Power of Self-Organized Learning', Edutopia, 3 February 2012.

19 John Chubb and Terry Moe, *Politics, Markets and America's Schools*, Perseus, 1990.

20 John Chubb and Terry Moe, *Liberating Learning: Technology, Politics and the Future of American Education*, Jossey-Bass, 2009.

21 Tamasin Cave and Andy Rowell, *A Quiet Word: Lobbying, Crony Capitalism and Broken Politics in Britain*, Bodley Head, 2014.

22 Ibid.

23 Ibid.

24 'UK wage growth outpaces inflation', BBC News, 15 February 2017.

25 Paul Mason, 'Our problem isn't robots, it's the low-wage car-wash economy', *Guardian*, 12 December 2016.

13. TECHNOLOGY: FIVE COMPANIES TO RULE US ALL

1 Michael Lewis, *The Big Short: Inside The Doomsday Machine*, Penguin, 2011.

2 David Graeber, *Debt: The First 5000 Years*, Melville House Publishing, 2013.

3 Gilles Deleuze and Felix Guattari, 'A Thousand Plateaus: Capitalism and Schizophrenia', Les Editions de Minuit, 1980; University of Minnesota, 1987; Bloomsbury Academic, 2013.

4 Bill Gates, *The Road Ahead*, Viking, 1995.

5 Dave Eggers, *The Circle*, Penguin, 2014.

6 Dominic Rushe and Sam Thielman, 'Inside Alphabet: why Google rebranded itself and what happens next', *Guardian*, 11 August 2015.

7 Larry Page, 'Larry's Alphabet Letter: G is for Google', Google Founder's Letter, 2015, abc.xyz.

8 Sean Keeley and Sarah Anne Lloyd, '25 Facts About Bill Gates's Medina Mansion', Seattle.curbed.com, 16 February 2017.

9 Douglas Coupland, *Micro-serfs*, Harper Collins, 1995.

10 Farhad Manjoo, 'Tech's frightful five will dominate digital life for foreseeable future', *New York Times*, 20 January 2016.

11 Ibid.

12 Ibid.

13 Ibid.

14 Natt Garun, 'Amazon just launched a cashier-free convenience store', The Verge, 5 December 2016.

15 Berkeley Dietvorst, Joseph Simmons and Cade Massey, 'Algorithm aversion: people erroneously avoid algorithms after seeing them err', publicly accessible Penn dissertation, University of Pennsylvania, 2016.

16 Ibid.

17 Yuval Noah Harare, *Homo Deus: A Brief History of Tomorrow*, Harvill Secker, 2016.

18 Ibid.

19 'Shane Legg Q and A on Risks of AI', Less Wrong Community Blog, 2011.

20 Mike Schuster, 'Zero-Shot translation with Google's multilingual neural machine', http://research.googleblog.com, 22 November 2016.

21 Ibid.

22 Ibid.

23 Hal Hodson, 'Revealed: Google AI has access to huge haul of NHS patient data', *New Scientist*, 29 April 2016.

24 Julia Powles and Hal Hodson, 'Google Deepmind and healthcare in an age of algorithms', *Health and Technology*, 16 March 2017.

25 Matt Burgess, 'DeepMind's Streams app is reportedly saving NHS nurses two hours a day', *Wired*, 27 February 2017.

26 Alex Hern, 'Google's DeepMind plans bitcoin-style health record tracking for hospitals', *Guardian*, 9 March 2017.

27 'The CIA-backed start up that's taking over Palo Alto', CNBC, 12 January 2016.

28 Ibid.

29 Ibid.

30 Matt Burns, 'Leaked Palantir doc reveals uses, specific functions and key clients', TechCrunch, 11 January 2015.

31 Ibid.

32 'Responding to crime in real time at the LAPD', https://www.palantir.com.

33 Darwin Bond-Graham and Ali Winston, 'Forget the NSA, the LAPD spies on millions of innocent folks', *LA Weekly*, 27 February 2014.

34 TechCrunch, op. cit.

35 *LA Weekly*, op. cit.

36 Ibid.

37 Ibid.

38 TechCrunch, op. cit.

39 Mike Isaac, 'Uber's CEO plays with fire', *New York Times*, 23 April 2017.

40 Ibid.

14. GLOBALISATION: HOW ASIA REWROTE THE RULES

1 Jan Wong, *Red China Blues: My Long March from Mao to Now*, Doubleday Canada, 1997.

2 'Visions of China: Reformer with an Iron Fist', CNN, 2001.

3 Ibid.

4 Frank Dikotter, *The Cultural Revolution: A People's History: 1962–76*, Bloomsbury, 2016.

5 Joseph Nye, 'Global Power Shifts', Ted talk, October 2010.

6 Jim O'Neill, 'The New World: Fixing Globalisation', BBC Radio 4, 6 January 2017.

7 Peter Navarro, *Death by China: Confronting the Dragon – A Global Call to Action*, Pearson FT Press, 2011.

8 Yi Wen, 'China's Rapid Rise: From Backward Agrarian Society to Industrial Powerhouse in Just 35 Years', Federal Reserve Bank of St Louis, April 2016.

9 Jim O'Neill, 'The New World', op. cit.

10 'Wolverhampton Goodyear factory work to stop by Christmas', BBC News, 30 November 2016.

11 'Goodyear Closure: Wolverhampton factory shuts gates for last time after 89 years', *Express & Star*, 20 December 2016.

12 'The New World', op. cit.

13 Dani Rodrik interviewed for 'The New World', 6 January 2017. For more on the roots of globalisation: Dani Rodrik, *The Globalization Paradox*, Oxford University Press, 2012.

14 Ibid.

15 'The New World', op. cit.

16 Paul Mason, *PostCapitalism: A Guide to our Future*, Allen Lane, 2015.

17 'Ownership of UK Quoted Shares: 2014', ONS, 2 September 2015.

18 Stephen Gandel, 'The biggest American companies now owned by the Chinese', *Fortune*, 25 March 2016.

19 'The New World', op. cit.

20 Ibid.

21 Ibid.

22 GWC, 'Mission & History', en.gwc.net.

23 Ibid.

24 Jason Hiner, 'Chinese companies that will shape the future of the Tech industry: My week in Beijing', ZDnet.com, 22 May 2016.

25 Kaiping Peng and Richard E. Nisbett, 'Culture, dialectics and reasoning about contradiction', *American Psychologist*, September 1999.

26 Drake Baer, 'The fascinating cultural reasons why Westerners and East Asians have polar opposite understandings of truth', Business Insider, 21 May 2015.

27 Aristotle, *Ethics*, OUP Oxford, World Classics, 2009.

28 Business Insider, 21 May 2015, op. cit.

29 Michael Harris Bond (ed.), *The Oxford Handbook of Chinese Psychology*, OUP, 2015.

30 Richard E. Nisbett, *The Geography of Thought: How Asians and Westerners Think Differently and Why*, Free Press, 2004.

31 Michael Oakeshott, *On Human Conduct*, OUP, 1975.

ACKNOWLEDGEMENTS

I want to thank everyone who took the time and effort to be interviewed. Robert, Kate and everyone at UA. Rupert for getting it in an instant and helping shape the book so deftly. Rebecca, Cameron, Ben and everyone at Hodder. Barry for checking every word. Nicola at Keystone Law, Nick and co at Harper US. Jonathan at Curtis Brown NY. Everyone I worked with on the films for the BBC that are based on the book, including Fatima, Tom Mac, Fiona, Mike, Charlotte, Janis, Kim, Patrick, Adam, Don, Martin, Gian and Clive. Everyone at Pulse: Will, Stu, Ed, Tom, Annabel, Izzy, Emma, Claire, Marissa and Tomas. Everyone who shot, researched and edited the series: Johan, Andy, Ariel, Adam, Jay, Brendan, Tim, Petra, David, Alex and the legion of other dedicated professionals who had to put up with me. Everyone at the *Guardian* and the *Observer*, including Malik, Tim, Nicole and my old friend Ian. Melanie and Rachel at Oxfam, Liz and everyone at the OU. Jo, Gudren, Holly and everyone I worked with at Fresh One. Roy who pushed me to do it in the first place, David G and Helen, Lucy for all the advice and support, Vic for pointing and repointing me in the right direction. Tamasin at Spinwatch. Gerard, Janet, Fenton, John D, PT Pete, Ronnie, John, Neil, Guy, Sean and Dave. Bernadette. Everyone who worked with me on the Channel 4 films. Hannah who was there from start to finish. Alina, Peter, and my brother Andreas for their love and encouragement to write from ten years old.

INDEX